PSYCHOANALYTIC GEO

Psychoanalytic Geographies

Edited by

PAUL KINGSBURY
Simon Fraser University, Canada

STEVE PILE
Open University, United Kingdom

ASHGATE

Published by
Ashgate Publishing Limited
Wey Court East
Union Road
Farnham
Surrey, GU9 7PT
England

Ashgate Publishing Company
110 Cherry Street
Suite 3-1
Burlington, VT 05401-3818
USA

www.ashgate.com

British Library Cataloguing in Publication Data
A catalogue record for this book is available from the British Library.

The Library of Congress has cataloged the printed edition as follows:
Kingsbury, Paul (Paul Thomas)
 Psychoanalytic geographies / by Paul Kingsbury and Steve Pile.
   pages cm.
 Includes bibliographical references and index.
  ISBN 978-1-4094-5760-2 (hardback)—ISBN 978-1-4094-5761-9 (pbk.)—ISBN 978-1-4094-5762-6 (ebook)—ISBN 978-1-4724-0721-4 (epub) 1. Geographical perception. 2. Geography—Psychological aspects. 3. Human geography. 4. Psychoanalysis and culture. I. Title.
 G71.5.K55 2014
 910'.019—dc23

2013043987

ISBN 9781409457602 (hbk)
ISBN 9781409457619 (pbk)
ISBN 9781409457626 (ebk – PDF)
ISBN 9781472407214 (ebk – ePUB)

Printed in the United Kingdom by Henry Ling Limited,
at the Dorset Press, Dorchester, DT1 1HD

Contents

PART II: PSYCHIC LIFE AND ITS SPACES

PART III: THE TECHNOLOGIES OF BECOMING A SUBJECT

PART IV: SOCIAL LIFE AND ITS DISCONTENTS

List of Figures

Notes on Contributors

Virginia L. Blum is Professor of English at the University of Kentucky and a research candidate at the Cincinnati Psychoanalytic Institute. Author of two monographs, *Hide and Seek: The Child between Psychoanalysis and Fiction* (1995) and *Flesh Wounds: The Culture of Cosmetic Surgery* (2003), she specializes in psychoanalytic theory, theories of the body, star culture, and intimacy.

Liz Bondi contributes to professional education in counselling and psychotherapy and to interdisciplinary research training at the University of Edinburgh, UK. She has published on feminist, emotional and psychoanalytic geographies. She is a founding editor of *Emotion, Space and Society*. Her current research focuses on the interconnections between religion, spirituality and psychotherapy in Scotland and on psychoanalytic approaches to autoethnography.

Felicity Callard is Senior Lecturer in Social Science for Medical Humanities at Durham University, UK. She has broad research interests in the history and present of psychiatry, psychoanalysis and cognitive neuroscience. She is incoming co-editor of *History of the Human Sciences*, and is currently researching historical geographies of clinical and experimental investigations of anxiety.

Laura Cameron is Associate Professor in the Department of Geography at Queen's University in Kingston, Ontario. She heads the Transnational Ecologies subcluster of NiCHE (Network in Canadian History and Environment). Her published work addresses cultures of nature, art and science. Currently she is completing *Freud in Cambridge* with John Forrester.

Sheila L. Cavanagh is Associate Professor at York University in Toronto, Canada. Her scholarship is in the area of queer theory, gender and psychoanalysis. Cavanagh co-edited *Skin, Culture and Psychoanalysis* (2013), and wrote *Queering Bathrooms: Gender, Sexuality and the Hygienic Imagination* (2010) and *Sexing the Teacher: School Sex Scandals and Queer Pedagogies* (2007). She is currently writing a book on queer theory and Lacanian psychoanalysis.

Joyce Davidson is Associate Professor of Geography at Queen's University, Canada. She is author of *Phobic Geographies: The Phenomenology and Spatiality of Identity* (Ashgate, 2003) and a founding editor of *Emotion, Space and Society*. Co-edited collections include *Emotional Geographies* (2005) and *Worlds of Autism: Across the Spectrum of Neurological Difference* (2013).

Jessica De La Ossa is a PhD Candidate in the School of Geography and Development at the University of Arizona. With funding from the National Science Foundation and Dartmouth College, her current research explores the affective and emotional dimensions of citizenship along the US–Mexico border.

John Forrester is Professor of History and Philosophy of the Sciences, University of Cambridge, author of *Language and the Origins of Psychoanalysis* (1980), *The Seductions of Psychoanalysis* (1990), (with Lisa Appignanesi) *Freud's Women* (1992) and *Dispatches from the Freud Wars* (1997). He is interested in reasoning in cases in science, medicine and law. He is the editor of *Psychoanalysis and History*.

Stephen Healy is Senior Research Fellow in the Institute of Culture and Society at the University of Western Sydney. He is a geographer and founding member of the Community Economies Collective. Psychoanalytic and Marxian theory inform his approach to community-based research. He is a co-author of *Take Back the Economy: An Ethical for Transforming Our Communities* (2013), with Jenny Cameron and J.K. Gibson-Graham.

Paul Kingsbury is Associate Professor in the Department of Geography at Simon Fraser University. His research uses the social theories of Jacques Lacan and Friedrich Nietzsche to explore cultural geographies of power and aesthetics. He is the author of numerous journal articles and the co-editor (with Gavin J. Andrews and Robin Kearns) of *Soundscapes of Wellbeing in Popular Music* (2014).

Cheryl McGeachan teaches Geography in the School of Geographical and Earth Sciences at the University of Glasgow, UK. She has published on issues concerning the historical and cultural geographies of mental ill-health and asylum spaces. She is currently working on projects relating to Scottish art therapy, transcultural psychiatry and British psychoanalyst Marion Milner.

Nazanin Naraghi is a PhD candidate and filmmaker in the Department of Geography at Simon Fraser University. Her research is concerned with the Iranian diaspora, aesthetics, geopolitics and nationalism. She is especially interested in psychoanalytic theory, the emergence of a "new" Lacanian film theory, and the future of the image.

Heidi J. Nast is Professor of International Studies at DePaul University, USA. Her work examines the political economy of fertility and reproduction in relation to critical theories of ontologies of sexuality, race and gender. She has published widely across disciplines. Her most recent work, *Petifilia* (forthcoming, University of Georgia Press), examines how the commodification of the pet body became intertwined with racial projects of empire-building and industrial and finance capitalism.

Hester Parr is Reader in the School of Geographical and Earth Sciences at Glasgow University. Her research explores social and cultural geographies of mental health, emotional lives and, more recently, missing people. She is the author of numerous journal articles and a monograph entitled *Mental Health and Social Space* (2008).

Steve Pile teaches Geography in the Faculty of Social Sciences at the Open University, UK. He has published on issues concerning place and the politics of identity. He is the author of *Real Cities* (2005) and *The Body and The City* (1996). He is currently working on early Freudian psychoanalysis and geographies of the body.

Jared Powell is a PhD candidate in the School of Geography and Development at the University of Arizona. His dissertation historicizes recurrent calls for "education reform" in the post-Second World War US by analyzing the geopolitical, economic and psychosocial rhetoric deployed in the dynamic and many-sided struggle over public school governance.

Jesse Proudfoot teaches urban geography at the University of Toronto Scarborough. His PhD research draws on Lacanian psychoanalysis and ethnographic fieldwork to understand drug use and drug policy in a gentrifying neighborhood in Vancouver, BC, Canada. His SSHRC postdoctoral research at DePaul University in Chicago, IL, US, examines drug treatment and race in the US inner city, as well as methodological questions about psychoanalytic ethnography.

Karen Rodríguez serves as an Academic Dean at the School for International Training (SIT) and as an affiliated faculty member in the Interdisciplinary Postgraduate Program in the Arts at the Universidad de Guanajuato, México. Drawing from psychoanalysis and cultural studies, her research explores how the self encounters others and makes ongoing sense of difference. She is the author of *Small City on a Big Couch* (2012).

Anna J. Secor is Professor of Geography at the University of Kentucky. Her research focuses on theories of space, politics and subjectivity. Recently she has developed ideas of topology in geography by engaging the work of Lacan, Deleuze and Agamben. Her research on Islam, State and society in Turkey has been funded by the National Science Foundation.

Ian G.R. Shaw is Lecturer in the School of Geographical and Earth Sciences at the University of Glasgow. He is a political geographer interested in geopolitics and philosophy. He is currently researching the social, territorial and existential impacts of drone warfare, for his forthcoming book *The Predator Empire* with the University of Minnesota Press.

Maureen Sioh teaches in the Department of Geography at DePaul University in Chicago. She trained as a hydrologist and worked in East Asia and with First Nations communities in Canada on erosion and pollution. Since then, she has published on nature and postcolonial territorialization and is currently working on anxiety and financial decision-making in emerging economies.

Melissa Stepney is Lecturer in Human Geography in the Department of Geography at the University of Worcester. She has research interests in gender identity, consumption and health. Her recent publications have explored the practices and meanings associated with drunkenness, and the development of online research methods in health.

Elizabeth R. Straughan is currently Postdoctoral Research Associate at the University of Glasgow, UK. Her research unravels the volatile nature of the body through attendance to the skin as well as the material and metaphorical dynamics of touch. She has published in international journals such as *Social & Cultural Geography*, *Emotion, Space and Society*, and *Geography Compass*.

Deborah Thien is Associate Professor of Geography at California State University, Long Beach, USA. Her published work examines issues of gender and emotion, including women's emotional well-being in rural and remote places, and men's mental health in recovering from post-traumatic stress disorder. She is currently working on a book that develops a feminist geography of post-traumatic stress disorder.

Mary E. Thomas is Associate Professor in the Department of Women's, Gender and Sexuality Studies at the Ohio State University, US. Her book, *Multicultural Girlhood: Racism, Sexuality and the Conflicted Spaces of American Education*, was published by Temple University Press in 2011. She is currently researching peer relationships in a juvenile detention facility for young women.

Preface

Paul Kingsbury and Steve Pile

When in Rome ...

> Now, let us make the fantastic assumption that Rome is not a place where people live, but a psychical entity with a similarly long, rich past, in which nothing that ever took shape has passed away, and in which all previous phases of development exist beside the most recent (Freud 1930 [2002]: 8).

In *Civilization and Its Discontents*, Sigmund Freud famously uses Rome as an analogy for memory. Because Rome's past and present exist side-by-side amidst its ancient ruins and recent renovations, it is significant for Freud that Rome is dubbed the "Eternal City": a city that could last forever, both as an idea and as a physical presence, much like memory. Freud makes it clear, however, that psychical memory is better than Rome at preserving its past. Freud (1930 [2002]: 8–9) continues:

> For Rome this would mean that on the Palentine Hill the imperial palaces and the Septizonium of Septimus Severus still rose to their original height, that the castle of San Angelo still bore on its battlements the fine statues that adorned it until the Gothic siege. ... And where the Coliseo now stands we could admire the vanished Domus Aurea of Nero; on the Piazza of the Pantheon we should find not only the Pantheon, bequeathed by Hadrian, but the original structure of M. Agrippa; indeed, occupying the same ground would be the church of Maria sopra Minerva and the ancient temple over which it is built. And the observer would perhaps need only to shift his gaze or his position in order to see the one or the other.

Sadly, Freud says, the analogy cannot be taken further. Furthermore, he confesses that the result of his fantasy is absurd: surely, it is ridiculous to think that the Domus Aurea of Nero can exist in the same space as the Coliseo?

> If we wish to represent a historical sequence in spatial terms, we can only do so
> by juxtaposition in space, for the same space cannot accommodate two different
> things [...] Even the most peaceful urban development entails the demolition and
> replacement of buildings, and so for this reason no city can properly be compared
> with a psychical organism (1930 [2002]: 9).

Despite Freud's misgivings, the analogy endures. So, we are delighted to include, in this book, a series of images from Sharon Kivland's recent series "The Unconscious is a City" (first exhibited in January 2013 at the Domobaal Gallery, London). For us, the images not only extend and elaborate upon Freud's Rome analogy; they also demonstrate how wrong he was to suggest that the same space could not accommodate two different contents. Rather, Freud should have pursued the implications of his remark that the observer can see different contents in the same space by a shift in gaze or position. Indeed, "shifting" itself becomes a useful metaphor for thinking about not only unconscious processes, but also the unfolding spaces for the psychoanalytically inspired geographer.

This book contains eight images taken from Kivland's series. These have been selected to convey the mess and jumble of the psyche with the ruins of the past abutting things in the present and the future; the coexistence of different elements within the same space; a visual metaphor not only for psychic processes, but also for the embodiment of those processes, as well as their intersection with everyday socio-symbolic life; and also, to illustrate Freud's examples of how the form of the city, both its physical and social characteristics, shifts and changes, sometimes radically, sometimes not. In addition to these "postcards" of Rome, which are analogies for unconscious processes, adorning the book's back cover is Kivland's version (on another postcard) of the map found in Freud's "Rat Man" case study (1909 [2002]). All of these images, then, are postcards of Rome, sent by Sharon to us. They are simultaneously postcards of the city and the unconscious.

To create her postcards, Kivland simply took some 1950s postcards of Rome that she had lying around and painted over the top of them. She also reversed the highlights and shadows in the images by painting over them in white, for the darker areas, and black, for the lighter areas. Out of simplicity, however, a wide range of effects can be made and discerned.

The first way of seeing Kivland's postcards is for what they present to us. On the surface, the images look like paintings. The brushstrokes are clear and the images appear almost monochromatic. Indeed, there is a sharp contrast between light and dark, which seems to be created by a chiaroscuro technique.

Yet, as we linger on the images, a background begins to emerge from behind the chiaroscuro of the scene. A sepia image seeps through, suggesting another scene. Patches of white and black, rather than a chiaroscuro, now appear to be a mask behind which further details of the scene are partially hidden; buildings, landscape features and people exist like a mirage in the scene. Not there, and yet also there. We have in these images, then, not two, but three scenes: Kivland's painting, the underlying original postcard and the interaction between these "layers." To "see" these scenes does not, in fact, require the observer to shift physical position, but rather to shift their attention between the visible, barely invisible and imaged scenes in the postcards. As Freud would have it, shifting our attention—to space, to its juxtapositions, to its layers—changes the scene and its meaning.

There is more. Kivland has ultimately ruined the original postcard by painting over it, rendering the original scene irretrievable. It cannot be recovered or restored. The original is gone. Indeed, on a recent trip to Rome, we visited various antique shops to see if it was still possible to buy old 1950s postcards. We found none. Indeed, contemporary postcards of Rome seem preoccupied with fewer locations than Kivland's collection. Sure, postcards of the Coliseo and the Pantheon are still common, but you will struggle to find a postcard of the Villa Pamphili, the Piazza del Popolo or even the Fontana del Mosé. So, much of the "postcard world" of the mid-twentieth century Rome has now, in various ways, itself receded into the past. This is not the only kind of disappearance the postcards evoke.

Where in Rome ...

Since the 1950s, Rome has and has not changed. Visiting the locations where these pictures were taken enables us to see something else in the postcards. To begin with, there is a persistence and resilience of place. For some of the postcards, it is possible to stand where the photographer stood, all those years ago, and reproduce, almost exactly, the original image. Little, if anything, seems to have changed. For other postcards, what is difficult to recreate is the exact perspective: the original photographer was able to attain vantage points that can no longer be easily accessed, or at all. For a few postcards, the scene no longer exists as such for two reasons: first, trees and shrubs have grown in ways that obscure the scene; second, less frequently, features in the postcard have vanished. Rome may be the Eternal City, but this does not mean its physical and social forms are static, and it does not mean its perspectives are fixed.

On the cover of the book, we see a scene of the Foro Romano. The photographer has a high vantage point, looking over the Tempio di Castore e Polluce (the three columns in the foreground) towards the Il Vittoriano monument (in the top left of the image). Kivland's rendering of the postcard gives the scene the kind of chaotic jumble that we think evokes the potpourri of the psyche. Yet, out of this chaos and jumble, the city can perhaps suggest elements of psychoanalytic space. Fancifully, we might see the Il Vittoriano as a Superego, looking down on the Foro Romano, dominating it, not with rules and laws, but with a peculiar affect. But let us not make the mistake of thinking that this is the only form of Superego in the postcard: we can see churches, too, and we can even glimpse parts of government offices. If the Superego is best thought of as an affectual structure, then we should be clear that this is more than one thing: guilt, shame, obedience, duty, obligation and the like, take many forms. Behind the Tempio di Castore e Polluce is the Ego of the modern city, negotiating the past of the Foro Romano and the demands of the Il Vittoriano. This is where the people live, but they do not do so without the Foro Romano or Il Vittoriano and their representatives. Yet, just as the Superego takes place in more than one form, so does the Id: the unconscious site of tumultuous libidinal forces. Rome, the idea of Rome, is built upon the ancient city, which now lies in ruins—but there is much still to be seen in the ruins.

Figure P.1   The Foro Romano as seen from the Capitoline Hill
Source: Steve Pile.

The Foro Romano is, as commonly seen in contemporary postcards, often seen from a vantage point on the Capitoline Hill. The Capitoline Hill itself shows very little evidence of its ancient past, as it is now almost entirely covered by medieval and renaissance palaces, with a piazza designed by Michelangelo. It is easy to image Freud strolling around, admiring Michelangelo's vision, whilst at the same time wondering what happened to the city beneath. From this perspective, the unconscious of the city has more than one content and, importantly, more than one kind of unconscious process. There are evidently the ruins of temples; columns stand for a certain timelessness of desires and fears. There are also other kinds of buildings, especially, of course, the Coliseo, the circus of life and death. Yet the Foro Romano is also an ordinary place, with markets and cramped streets. It was (and remains) cosmopolitan, with many different "things" bumping along together. And it remains, somehow, ordinary; convertible into postcards and miniatures. If the Foro Romano stands for the Id, then this is not a fixed and pre-given Id, nor an ideal of mythic proportions, but one that emerges out of its ordinary social life. What emerges from the Id, from this perspective, is less a structure or a thing than a response to all the ruins of desires and fears that are present to us.

Kivland's postcards, then, evoke not only the shifting spaces of the city, but also the shifting perspectives of the observer—in this case, the shifting perspectives of the psychoanalytically informed urban observer. Not only do her images evoke the very ways in which the same space—the postcard, the city—can have more than one content, we can also witness how the psyche and psychical processes are more than one thing, even when we consider such seemingly singular entities as "the unconscious" or "the Superego." The problem, as Freud rightly observed, is not how to see space as a container of a single content, but how to grasp its forever changing forms, as well as the ruins of previous forms with which we all live. This book, we trust, is testament to this problem: not as an obstacle, but as an opportunity to shift perspectives, to see new spaces, to reveal new contents and to open up new lines of inquiry.

Creatio ex Seattle

Psychoanalytic Geographies began as four paper sessions (organized by us) that were convened in Seattle during the 2011 Association of American Geographers' Annual Meeting. The purpose was simple: to gather together those who were working with psychoanalysis in geography and related fields, to map out the breadth and depth of psychoanalytic geographies, and to foster new and developing work in psychoanalytic geography. Consisting of 20 papers, the presenters explored the session title themes of "trajectories," "positions," "technologies" and "engagements" of psychoanalytic geographies. In particular, we'd like to thank Laura Cameron, Sheila Cavanagh, Stephen Healy, Hilda Fernandez, Cheryl McGeachan, Nazanin Naraghi, Heidi Nast, Jessica De La Ossa, Jared Powell, Jesse Proudfoot, Karen Rodríguez, Anna Secor, Ian Shaw, Wendy Shaw, Nick Schuermans, Maureen Sioh, Jason Starnes, Melissa Stepney, Elizabeth Straughan, Deborah Thien and Sara Westin for their thought-provoking papers and their vital role in making the conference session such a success. Given the quality of the papers and the richness of the subsequent dialogues, it was an easy decision to pursue some kind of publication project. Subsequently, this book collection has evolved, beyond the conference session, to include people whose work is central to the "psychoanalytic project" in geography. So, thanks to all the authors, too, for their hard work and, at times, their patience!

Clearly, a special mention must go to Sharon Kivland: we started, cap in hand, hoping for one image, *gratis*. We ended up making our cap larger and larger as she showed us more of her postcards. Sharon has astonished us with her generosity of spirit. Our pursuit of this project has been supported by many people, but we'd like to thank especially Carolyn Court, John Ng and Brenda Sharp. Thanks also to the teams that play either side of Stanley Park for enabling us to put the pressures of editing in proper perspective. Finally, we would like to thank Katy Crossan at Ashgate for her enthusiasm for this project as well as the (anonymous) reviewers for their critical insights. We also wish to thank the Department of Geography at Indiana University, the OpenSpace Research Centre at The Open University and the Department of Geography at Simon Fraser University for providing us with time, space and a little money.

This book is for Grace and Ben.

Introduction

The Unconscious, Transference, Drives, Repetition and Other Things Tied to Geography

Paul Kingsbury and Steve Pile

Mapping the Psychoanalytic Psyche

Gone are the days when it was controversial, or simply befuddling, to declare an interest in both psychoanalysis and geography. Perhaps this change has to do with geographers' enduring engagements with psychoanalytic thought: a conversation that can be traced back to the 1930s and even earlier (see Cameron and Forrester, this book; also Matless 1995). Exchanges between geography and psychoanalysis, moreover, have not been one-sided. For its part, psychoanalytic thought, in its inception, has consistently drawn on geographical ideas to explicate its own concepts and practices.

One of the earliest instances of "geography" in Sigmund Freud's writings is in a love letter written to his fiancée Martha Bernays in 1885. Freud, then 29 years old and an ambitious neurologist specializing in nervous disorders, has traveled to Pitié-Salpêtrière Hospital in Paris. Although he only has funds to visit for five months, Freud is excited at the prospect of boosting his career through his association with the most famous neurologist of the time, Jean-Martin Charcot. But, Freud laments, "There are things that are tied to geography, and because of the distance between Paris and Hamburg I cannot take you in my arms and kiss you as I would like to" (Freud 1885 [1960]: 182). Clearly, Freud is, as lovers do, complaining about the physical distance that separates them: their limbs and lips—their bodies—are divided by geography. Perhaps the most striking feature of this sentence is how Freud also suggests that more is "tied to geography" than the separation of lovers by the distance between cities. Covertly, Freud seems to propose that psyches are also tied to geography, that desires can be thwarted by geography and that geography intervenes in even the most intimate human relationships. While the remainder of Freud's letter is silent about these "things," the following five decades of his writings are downright thunderous.

Freud's works are filled with spatial thinking, geographical imaginings and worldly descriptions about landmarks, cities, regions, nation-states, planet earth and even the "astronomical geography" (Freud 1883 [1960]: 77) of the human being. Early in his publishing career, Freud (1900 [1976]) called his first model of the psyche "topographical," in which he divided the mind into three systems: the unconscious (Ucs), preconscious (Pcs) and conscious (Cs). When Freud supplemented his topographical model of the psyche with a "structural" model—involving the "agencies" of the Id ("Es"), the Ego ("Ich") and the Superego ("Über-Ich")—he retained a spatial understanding of their relations (Freud 1933 [2003]: 72–9). Thus, for Freud, a personality was divided into "three realms, regions, provinces," yet importantly, he warned, these should not be "pictured [with] sharp frontiers like the artificial ones drawn in political geography," but rather as a "country with a landscape of varying configurations—hill country, plains, and chains of lakes—, and with a mixed population: it is inhabited by Germans, Magyars and Slovaks, who carry on different activities" (Freud 1933 [2003]: 73).

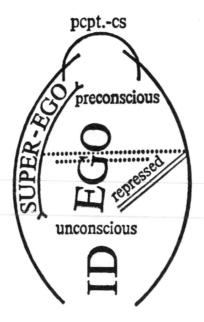

Figure I.1   Freud's 1933 map of the psyche

Here, the map of the psyche is less a political geography, with clearly marked territories, than a jumble of ill-defined terrains and inter-mingled peoples. His psyche is spatially patterned, yet also marked by the ultimately indeterminate nature of its landscape boundaries along with the internal mobility of its different "populations." We can see this mapped out in Freud's (1933 [2003]: 72) accompanying diagram (Figure I.1).

Freud's map of the psyche is not characterized by the distinct and unaligned "nations" of the unconscious, preconscious and conscious. It is evidently differentiated and inexact, indeterminate and enigmatic. There are no clear borders between the "nations," say, of the Ego and Id. A forest of dots traverses the Ego. Meanwhile, even his topographical and structural models seem oddly located: there is the Superego off to the left, while pcpt.–cs (perception–conscious) floats outside the psyche and the Id seems to be unbounded at its base. The psyche, in this view, is more of a topological landscape, in which some "things" are closer to others (or further away), yet somehow all capable of being in contact with one another. Is it fanciful to think of this landscape as a physical geography, with forests (that run through the Ego, making passage between its unconscious and preconscious elements difficult), mountain ranges (between Ego and Superego) and streams (such as the canalized river of the repressed)?

Ever the natural scientist, elsewhere Freud explicitly deploys an analogy drawn from the physical landscape to convey his understanding of the paths and flows of sexual drive-forces (or libido):

> In neurotics the sexual constitution, which also contains the expression of heredity, works alongside the accidental influences of life, which disturb the development of normal sexuality. Water that encounters an obstacle in one river-bed is driven back into older courses previously destined to be abandoned (1905a [2006]: 40; see also p. 68).

If the body provides a rudimentary physical terrain—perhaps involving both the Id and inherited bodily predispositions (arguably explaining why the 1933 diagram is "open" at its base)—then through this landscape flows drive-forces, much like water running through a valley. Furthermore, the model is developmental. Freud understands that the landscape has changed over time and that the course of the river has been modified, probably by repression, but certainly by upbringing, mainly family life and social conventions. Alongside such geographical metaphors, Freud also develops a more abstract spatial language of "paths," "networks," "direction" and the like.

Spatial thinking thus informs Freud's writings on the "associative paths" and "networks" of dreams that localize and locate meanings (Freud 1900 [1976]), as in: the "symbolic sexual geography" of a dream, where a dense forest symbolizes (female) pubic hair (Freud 1905a [2006]: 87); unconscious thoughts "stretched out" over embodied hysterical symptoms "like garlands of flowers draped over metal wire" (Feud 1905a [2006]: 72); the "suffering in three directions" from the "decay" of the body, the "merciless forces" of "the "external world," and from "our relations to other men [*sic*]" (Freud 1930 [2002]: 77); and the infantile "*fort/da*" (gone/here) struggle to master rather than mourn the loss of a mother (Freud 1920 [2003]). Freud (1909 [2002]) even sketched a map that depicted the itinerary of one of his patients to help guide readers through the impossible maze of obsessional neurosis. Sharon Kivland's sketch of the sketch map adorns the back of this book's cover.

Finally, one of Freud's (1933 [2003]: 80) most celebrated and contested aphorisms about the goal of psychoanalysis—"where Id was, shall Ego go" (our translation) [*Wo Es war, soll Ich werden*]—implies that the Ego should occupy the territory of the Id, yet it also draws upon a sense that the Id is mobile and fugitive, requiring the Ego to constantly follow it. Thus, the Ego must not only explore the landscape of the Id, it must also protect itself against the Id's drive-forces. Often ignored by commentators, Freud reinforces the spatial duality of psychoanalytic practice by way of an analogy to landscape engineering: "It is a work of culture—not unlike the draining of the Zuider Zee" (ibid.).

Beyond Freud's oeuvre, every psychoanalytic approach keenly engages, in one way or another, with things that are tied to geography. Prominent psychoanalytic concepts include, for example, Jacques Lacan's (1986 [1992]) "topology of subjectivity" that explores how psychical life takes place; Melanie Klein's (1975 [1988]) "introjection" and "projection" locates the interactions between the "outer world" and "inner life" (see Stepney, this book); R.D. Laing's "worlding" of the unconscious (see McGeachan, this book); Julia Kristeva's (1982) "abjection" helps explain how phobias result from uncertain boundaries (Sibley 1995); Donald Winnicott's (1971 [1991]) "potential space" designates a therapeutically playful intermediary site between people and things; while Didier Anzieu (1985) theorizes the "psychic envelope" of skin and, evocatively, Christopher Bollas (1987) refers to the ways that objects cast "shadows" upon the psyche.

And there is more besides. In highlighting the spatial thinking that is so apparent in psychoanalytic writing, we suggest more than a reading of psychoanalysis that simply underlines words in psychoanalytic texts that have a spatial undercurrent and more than psychoanalysis being a rich, and barely tapped, resource for geographers. We are, rather, hinting that psychoanalysts—even while their aims differ radically from those of (almost all) geographers—have necessarily had to become "good enough" geographers to make sense of their patients' worlds. That is, they have had to recognize that their patients' suffering has its origins fully in the external world, even while their patients' suffering is expressed through the topological twisting of their worlds, both psychic and corporeal, both internal and external (Kingsbury 2007; Blum and Secor 2010; Pile 2014; see also Blum and Secor, this book). In some ways, this makes psychoanalytic models of worlding more sophisticated than geographical models of space that rely on geometrical maps where space itself does not fold or stretch. Hence Lacan's assertion that the "unconscious is outside" is best represented not by images of dark caves and shadowy archetypes but by *and in* the midst of the world's bustling cityscapes such as "Baltimore in the early morning" with its "heavy traffic" and flashing "neon sign[s]" (Lacan 1970: 189). Psychoanalysis affirms a radical incorporation and openness toward the extraordinary diversity that is life and the world (see Davidson and Parr, this book; Rodriguez, this book).

Geographers have not been slow to recognize this. More than simply a model of the personal psyche, psychoanalysis has offered geographers a way to understand the unconscious on the outside; the worlds' unconscious worlds. Following the foundational work of Jacquie Burgess and David Sibley in the late 1980s, an identifiable sub field of psychoanalytic geography has emerged (Philo and Parr 2003) and we trust this book is evidence of the vibrancy, diversity and increasing maturity of this subfield. From a position of marginality, psychoanalysis is now amongst the many useful and illuminating theoretical and methodological resources in geography capable of exploring phenomena ranging, for example, from post-Apartheid landscapes (Hook 2005a, 2005b; or, see Gelder and Jacobs 1998) to the politics of the Anthropocene (Robbins and Moore 2012; see also Healy, this book).

Like historical materialism and Marxism, psychoanalysis both emphasizes how modes of living are inescapably historical and social, and also strives—through its practice—to ameliorate the conditions of people's lives. Alongside feminist theories, psychoanalysis brings to the fore questions about people's gendered/sexed relations, enactments, embodiments, conflicts and expectations (see Cavanagh, this book). Methodologically, psychoanalytic geographers have fostered critical research techniques by drawing comparison with the psychoanalytic method of "evenly-suspended attention" (Freud 1912

[1958]: 111). That is, an attendance to the emotions and affects contained in, or represented by, words and symptoms, the networks of meanings associated with words and actions, the partiality and situatedness of knowledge, and the dynamic blurring of the boundaries between the researcher and the researched, and, crucially, the analyst's critical reflexivity (see for example Rose 1997, Bondi 2003, 2014; see also Bondi, this book; Callard, this book). With poststructuralist theories, psychoanalysis posits that much of the world and people's lives take place through the dynamisms, fixations and uncertainties of language. With non-representational theories, psychoanalysis focuses on how non-conscious affect and embodied material forces are situated within complex sets of inter-subjective and non-human relations. With postcolonial geography, psychoanalysis recognizes the ways in which the psyche can be "colonized" by imagined geographies of superiority and of the racial and migrant body (see also Nast, this book; Naraghi, this book). This does not exhaust the list of approaches that have drawn inspiration from psychoanalytic ideas and methods, yet, it also has to be noted that psychoanalysis has been viewed with some ambivalence (even by those using psychoanalytic concepts), and oftentimes a degree of suspicion and hostility. Nonetheless, renewed interest in emotions and affect across the breadth of critical human geography—and the social sciences as a whole—has produced a stronger sense of fellow traveling amongst these diverse (and too often competing) traditions and approaches.

What we find remarkable is the sheer breadth, depth and maturity of psychoanalytically inspired approaches to geography. Over the last 20 or so years, to use psychoanalysis in geography, unlike psychoanalytic research in cultural studies, literary theory and the humanities more generally, required both an apology and a restatement of basic principles. Numerous geographers now feel confident enough to embrace psychoanalytic approaches in ways that are unfettered by a sense of marginality or a fear of crude caricatures or deliberately contrary interpretations (often based on widely held misunderstandings of the place and role of sexuality in Freud's thought). *Psychoanalytic Geographies* gathers this "confident moment" in psychoanalytic geographies, its enthusiasm and its promise, as well as its diversity and unfolding opportunities for further development. It assembles a wide range of authors who elaborate a variety of psychoanalytic approaches that affirm geographical imaginations and a commitment toward spatial thinking. The book's aim, then, is two-fold: first, to present to readers as wide a set of options for taking psychoanalysis forward in their own work as possible; and, second, to demonstrate the breadth, depth and promise of cutting edge work in psychoanalytic geographies. Obviously, it is not only geographers that can think psychoanalytically and geographically. *Psychoanalytic Geographies* draws on inter-disciplinary approaches with many of its chapters written by scholars affiliated with departments other than geography.

Our goal in the remainder of the Introduction is not to survey the histories, axioms or limitations and controversies surrounding psychoanalysis and psychoanalytic geographies. Such a task has been done before (Pile 1996; Philo and Parr 2003; Kingsbury 2004, 2009a, 2009b; see also Davidson and Parr, this book). And we feel no compulsion to repeat. Rather, we wish to introduce a spatialized understanding of psychoanalysis through a discussion of four fundamental concepts (following Lacan 1973 [1981]) namely: the unconscious, transference, drives and repetition. In part, we find Lacan's identification of these particular concepts intriguing because he maps out the kind of double architecture with which psychoanalysis is littered: two agencies (the unconscious and the drives) and two actions (transference and repetition). In psychoanalytic thought, we find, "things" are never less than doubled, split, mirrored, paradoxical, contradictory and reversible into opposites. In addition, operating with Lacan's choice of concepts also reflects our (and the discipline's) orientation toward Freudian–Lacanian approaches. Thus, the concepts are useful because they not only already play important roles in the various psychoanalytic approaches in the chapters that follow, but they also provide the architecture for much existing psychoanalytic geography.

It is important to realize that psychoanalytic ideas, such as the unconscious and the drives, neither emerged out of psychoanalytic theorizing, nor as fully-fledged concepts. They are produced over a long time out of a protracted and often painful and unsuccessful interaction between Freud and his patients. For this reason, we will focus in our discussions of the unconscious and transference not on Freud's conceptual writing but on a particular case study: "Dora" (1905a [2006]). A gleeful Freud intended the case study to be a supplement, and therapeutic proof, of the validity of his interpretation of dreams (1900 [1976]). Yet, as the first truly psychoanalytic case history, Dora is troublesome. To be sure, not only is Freud's account itself troublesome, Dora herself makes trouble for Freud. Ultimately, what is of interest to us is that notions of the unconscious and transference emerge out of the thoroughly unsatisfactory relationship between a patient and her doctor. A far from gleeful Freud has to admit, ultimately, what he does not know.

For us, psychoanalysis does not rest on fundamental concepts like a roof on the pillars of a temple. Instead, the pillars of psychoanalysis emerge out of the unstable ground of ordinary human suffering; like Rome, psychoanalysis lives in its ruins.

The Unconscious: The Case of Dora, Between Coughing and Talking

We have argued that psychoanalysis has its origins, not in a pre-existing conceptual framework or a pre-determined model of human psychical development, but in the external world. This is as true of Freud's patients' symptoms as the psychoanalytic concepts and techniques that have emerged over the last 130 years or so. Let us be clear, psychoanalysis emerges as a therapy in response to some extremely puzzling medical problems that had already baffled medicine for well over 150 years before Freud. As we said, in 1885 Freud is in Paris with Charcot. What Freud witnesses is astonishing (see Figure I.2).

Figure I.2   *A Clinical Lesson by Doctor Charcot* (1887), by Pierre-André Brouillet. Photograph by Steve Pile

Source: Musée d'Histoire de la Médecine, Paris.

What we see in this painting is Professor Charcot proving, to a fascinated and baffled audience, that the origins of some nervous disorders, such as hysteria, do not lie in the body but solely in the mind. He is demonstrating that a patient's symptoms could be turned on and off, literally, by the gentle touch of a hand. Put another way, what clinicians were (and still are) faced with was a wide variety of physical symptoms that appeared to have no foundation in physical problems, despite a prolonged search for explanatory physical abnormalities in autopsies of dead patients (with particular emphasis on the search for lesions in the brain, which was Freud's own purpose as a budding neurologist). You will spot the instruments that lie on table by the standing central figure, Charcot. These consisted of probes and electrical stimulation devices. Using these, Charcot demonstrated that his patients' symptoms were not simply faked or simulated. Paralyzed limbs really were paralyzed, beyond the conscious control of the patients. Yet, using hypnosis, Charcot could make the paralysis completely disappear (and reappear). Here was proof of the power of the mind to dominate the body not consciously, but *unconsciously*. Returning to Vienna, brimming with enthusiasm and confidence, Freud sets about developing a cure for hysteria using hypnosis.

In collaboration with Joseph Breuer, Freud imposed therapeutic regimes consisting of daily massages, rest and relaxation, restricted diets and hypnotic sessions on their hysterics. Despite the mixed results, Breuer and Freud presented case studies that indicate a confidence in hypnosis as the cornerstone technique for a complete cure for hysteria (Breuer and Freud 1895 [2004]). Indeed, it is Breuer's patient, "Anna O." who coins the expression "talking cure" so often (yet misleadingly) associated with psychoanalysis. Freud, however, remains doubtful of the success of hypnosis. For example, the curative effects appear to wear off after, at best, a few months. Within a year, some of his patients were back in therapy, with different doctors (notably "Emmy von N."). Embarking on a radical and punishing period of self-analysis in the wake of the death of his father in 1896, Freud becomes increasingly confident of the benefits of approaching his patients' symptoms through an entirely different technique: dream analysis. Indeed, it is in 1896, some eleven years after his encounter with Charcot's hysterics, that Freud begins to call his therapy psychoanalysis. Two years later, in 1898, a father brings his 16-year-old daughter to Freud. She is suffering from a variety of symptoms, which appear not to have physical origins. In his case history (published years later in 1905), Freud will call her Dora, who we now know to be Ida Bauer (Mahony 1996).

In October 1900, Freud began treating Dora (who turned 18 on 1 November 1899). As it happens, Dora lived on the same street (at Bergasse 32) as Freud, so he had already witnessed her coughing and hoarseness in the summer of 1897. Yet, she had also suffered from a feverish condition in the winter of that year, which was initially (wrongly) diagnosed as appendicitis. Dora, according to her parents, was suffering from mood swings and character changes. As Freud puts it:

> she was clearly no longer happy either with herself or with her family, she was unfriendly towards her father and could no longer bear the company of her mother, who constantly tried to involve her in the housework. She tried to avoid contact with anyone; in so far as the fatigue and lack of concentration of which she complained allowed, she kept herself busy by attending public lectures, and devoted herself seriously to her studies (Freud 1905a [2006]: 17).

Freud presents Dora as an intelligent woman, who is curiously beset by contradictory motivations. Typical teenager, you might think. Except, what really shocks Dora's parents is the suicide note they discover. While they do not think that Dora is seriously intending to kill herself, they are nonetheless horrified. On top of this, she is suffering from fits of unconsciousness and also amnesia. For Freud, Dora is an "ordinary" case, exhibiting common hysterical symptoms, such as shortness of breath (*dyspnea*), a nervous cough (*tussis nervosa*), loss of voice (*aphonia*), along with migraines, mood swings, hysterical irascibility and a weariness of life (*tedium vitae*) that is "probably not to be taken seriously" (1905a [2006]: 18). We can almost hear Freud yawn, but what piques his interest is the possibility of using Dora as an addendum to his *The Interpretation of Dreams* (1900 [1976]). She is to be the proof of his dream pudding. Dora, however, is not going to play along.

Volumes have been written on the Dora case study (see, for example, Bernheimer and Kahane 1985, Decker 1991, Lakoff and Coyne 1991, Mahony 1996; or, for a creative intervention, see Kivland 1999), but our purpose here is to illuminate the emergence of Freud's concept of the unconscious in the course of his analysis of Dora. It will take a further 15 years, after Dora, for Freud to formulate his concept of the unconscious (1915a [2005]), but in this case study we can already glimpse its key features—importantly, as a response to the experiences and symptoms that Dora suffers. Though Freud's own account turns upon the analysis of two dreams, we will use the incident by the lake as the focal point of our analysis. This incident gives us a stronger grip on the "outsideness" or externality of the unconscious. More than this, it also shows that, while Freud is increasingly focused on what we might call the repressed unconscious (and it is mostly this form of the unconscious that is identified with psychoanalytic thought), there is more than one kind of unconscious in play (see Pile, this book).

So, what happened by the lake? And what might this have to do with Dora's coughing and breathing problems? When Dora was 16 years old, she went on holiday with her father. After a few days, Dora's father intended to return to Vienna. The plan was for Dora was to spend several weeks with Herr and Frau K. (pseudonyms for Hans and Peppina Zelenka).

> But when her father prepared to set off, the girl suddenly announced very resolutely that she was going with him, and she had done just that. It was only some days later that she gave an explanation for her curious behaviour, asking her mother to inform her father that while they were walking to the lake to take a boat trip, Herr K. had been so bold as to make a declaration of love to her (Freud 1905a [2006]: 19).

Herr K. and Papa respond somewhat predictably. Herr K. denies that he had done anything that would even have permitted Dora such an interpretation of his behavior. For his part, Papa declares that he believes the whole incident to be a fantasy. Indeed, Frau K. is blamed for the fantasy: she had talked too deeply and intimately with Dora about "sexual matters," and even allowed her to read Paolo Mantegazza's *Physiology of Love* (published in 1896), which, according to Papa and Herr K., had clearly inflamed Dora's erotic imagination. Consequently, when Dora demands that her Papa severs his links to both Herr and Frau K., he steadfastly refuses to do so. In particular, he defends his relationship to Frau K., which he says is "an honest friendship" which can do nothing to hurt Dora (1905a [2006]: 19). Frau K., he protests, is suffering very badly from her nerves and he is her sole support. Indeed, as he "gets nothing" from his wife (Dora's mother), his friendship with Frau K. is also a comfort to him.

The picture presented to Freud, then, is of two entirely innocent men; Papa and Herr K. could have done no harm to Dora (they say). Dora, it seems, is a victim of an overly sexualized imagination, caused by the overly intense and intimate nature of her relationship with Frau K. Freud is instantly suspicious; there must be, he surmises, more to the story. Indeed, there is. Freud solicits from Dora an earlier experience with Herr K.

> Dora told me of an earlier experience with Herr K., which was even more apt
> to act as a sexual trauma. She was fourteen years old at the time. Herr K. had
> arranged with Dora and his wife that the ladies should come to his shop in the
> main square of B. [Merano, northern Italy] to watch a religious ceremony from
> the building. But he persuaded his wife to stay at home, dismissed his assistant
> and was on his own when the girl entered the shop. As the time of the procession
> approached he asked the girl to wait for him by the door which opened on to the
> staircase leading to the upper floor, as he lowered the awning. He then came back,
> and instead of walking through the open door, he suddenly pulled the girl to
> him and pressed a kiss upon her lips ... But at that moment Dora felt a violent
> revulsion, pulled away and dashed past him to the stairs and from there to the
> front door. After this, contact with Herr K. none the less continued; neither of
> them ever mentioned this little scene, and Dora claims to have kept it secret even
> at confession at the spa. After that, incidentally, she avoided any opportunity to
> be alone with Herr K. (Freud 1905a [2006]: 21).

Freud's response is, at first sight, alarmingly sexist: instead of understanding
Dora's reaction as a perfectly normal response to an unwanted and forced
sexual advance, Freud wonders why she is repulsed and runs away. Later, in
the case study, a far more complex picture of the erotic relationships in Dora's
world comes into view. The problem, for Dora, is that she is secretly in love
with Herr K. Part of her motivation, then, in wishing Papa to break off his
affair with Frau K. is so that Herr K. and Frau K. can divorce. Yet, she is also
"in love" with Frau K., and does not want to simply replace her in Herr K.'s
life. Indeed, she actually wants Papa to return home, and wants nothing to do
with Herr K.

   It is not that Dora is confused by all of this; her problem is that she is too
aware of it and this forces her to repress her feelings and thoughts and, to this
end, she places one idea *in front of* another idea. Thus, her symptoms of coughing
and difficulty in breathing, which started at the time of the lake incident, refer
back to her repulsion of the kiss. Furthermore, the coughing is also connected
to Dora's witnessing of how her Papa was treated when he was ill with a severe
cough. This is no "innocent" illness, in Dora's mind, as she assumes that it is
connected with her Papa's syphilis (which he contracted prior to his marriage
to Dora's mother). Worse, Dora assumes that her Papa's syphilis has been passed
on to her (1905a [2006]: 65). In the analysis, then, Freud is constantly trying to
follow the twists and turns in Dora's sexual, erotic and emotional relationships,
many of which are "hidden" by secrecy or "forgotten" through repression.

Alongside the twists and turns of Dora's sexual worlds (involving her own emerging sexuality, Papa, her mother, a governess, Herr K. and Frau K.), Freud (1905a [2006]: 30) notes various ways in which unconscious processes work to hide or repress the impossible demands of these worlds as Dora experiences them. One unconscious process concerns "contiguity" and "the temporal proximity of ideas." According to this, ideas are associated with one another through some kind of closeness. Thus, through her cough, Dora demonstrates not only her distress at her Papa's illness, but also her love of Herr K., as her attacks coincided with times when Herr K. was absent on business (Freud 1905a: 30). Another feature of contiguity is the "closeness" between the repressed idea and the physical symptom; love for Papa and love for Herr K. manifests itself as a cough because there is a direct link between Papa and Herr K. And the symptom: syphilitic illness and the repulsive kiss. There are further contiguities between Papa and Herr K., not just through Frau K., but also through Dora herself. Dora refuses, angrily, to be "the gift" that Papa gives Herr K. to buy his acquiescence over the affair with Frau K. The cough is, as with all symptoms, *over-determined*, that is, determined by more than one idea. Freud writes: "a symptom has more than one meaning, and serves to represent several unconscious trains of thought" (Freud 1905a [2006]: 36). Indeed, it is this multiplicity of thoughts—and their movement along chains of association—that generates enough "force" to create a symptom. So, another key aspect of unconscious processes is the way that thoughts move and interact, dynamically, with one another.

Furthermore, it is this coexistence of contradictory ideas that creates the kind of intensity that requires repression. Thus, if two ideas coexist excessively intensely—*I want Papa to love me more than Frau K.* and *Papa's sexuality frightens and disgusts me*—this itself can cause repression, such that both ideas become unconscious. These contradictory unconscious thoughts, because of the intense affects associated with them, gain enough force to create symptoms and their dynamism. Thus, the symptom can readily take on new meanings, whilst at the same time jettisoning others. The same thoughts can, on the other hand, create new symptoms. To exemplify this, Freud reaches for a geographical metaphor: a dammed river. Like a river, an idea can be blocked, dammed up by repression, but it can always find new channels, albeit preferring ones already gouged out. Indeed, the unconscious is highly conservative, allowing not only for the preservation of thoughts from different times of life, but also for contradictory thoughts and ideas (*I love Herr K.; Herr K. disgusts me*) to exist side-by-side without conflict (Freud 1905a [2006]: 43). It is the conservative aspect of unconscious processes that can manifest itself as a compulsion to repeat. This compulsion to repeat is, of course, one of therapy's greatest challenges, hence Lacan's identification of it as a fundamental concept (1973 [1981]), and why we will discuss repetition in depth below.

A significant feature of unconscious processes is the conversion of an idea into its opposite. Freud uses the metaphor of a pair of *astatic needles* (yet another spatial metaphor) to describe how conscious and unconscious thoughts can run in exactly the opposite direction yet be driven by the same force and point along the same line as one another (Freud 1905a [2006]: 43). The significance of unconscious processes, that can contain contradictory ideas and reverse ideas into their opposites, is difficult to underestimate. For, these can manifest themselves in very ordinary symptoms such as confusion, ambivalence, internal conflict and aggressiveness—as with Dora's mood swings and apparent changes in character. Let us be clear, these mood swings are consistent in Dora's internal world, the problems arise from their interaction with her external worlds. It is not just that her parents do not understand her, or that social conventions have forced her to hide or repress aspects of her sexuality (such as her masturbation and, allegedly, her lesbianism), it is that she is struggling to handle the all-too-real sexual experiences and desires that she encounters in the world. Her consistent response is, simply, to deny that she knows what is going on because knowing what is going on is too traumatic to acknowledge openly (Freud 1905a [2006]: 46).

The unconscious, then, is not a place, as if it were a tightly sealed container inside the mind where we "bottle-up" all the painful stuff; nor is it a set of contents, as if the bottle only held repressed sexual desires associated with the father. The unconscious is not a locked box where Oedipus wrecks. Significantly, the Oedipus myth is mentioned only once in the Dora case study, in passing; indeed, Freud is clear that the myth most closely associated with this case study is that of Medea (Freud 1905a [2006]: 44 and 48). Rather, the unconscious is best associated with *processes* such as "the contiguity of ideas," reversal into opposites, repression, over-determination, trains of thought, chains of association, timelessness, contradictoriness and conservatism. In this sense, the unconscious is how thoughts and ideas are placed at a distance from consciousness or blocked from becoming conscious; even as the dam prevents the Zuider Zee from being swamped, it does not stop the seas from moving, nor having its own forces and dynamics, nor does it seal the oceans in a bottle.

We have indicated that the unconscious is "outside," like the seas that surround the Zuider Zee. We should not stretch the metaphor too far.

The unconscious is also communicative. Earlier, we suggested that the "talking cure" is a misleading metaphor for psychoanalysis. In the next section, we would like to explain why, this time by reading the unconscious communication between Dora and Freud *spatially*. Significantly, it is this that causes Dora to break off her analysis with Freud—and that causes Freud to fail to appreciate exactly what was going on in the analysis. Indeed, it is for this reason that transference takes an increasingly central role in psychoanalysis in contrast to a form of "cure" that relies upon the patient bringing unconscious material to light merely by talking.

Transference: A Part to Play

Somewhat troublingly, throughout his case history, Freud seems very far from being gentle or deft in his handling of Dora's sexual experiences and traumas (see also Kivland 1999). For example, Freud admits to playing tricks on Dora to solicit "hidden" material, as when he places matches on his desk (Freud 1905a [2006]: 62). Similarly, Freud jumps to seemingly unfounded or fanciful conclusions, as when he connects Dora's intimacy with Frau K. to a repressed "lesbian" desire for Frau K. (ibid.: 47). There appears to be a rush to judgment on Freud's part, in his eagerness to prove both his theory that hysteria has its origins in sexual trauma and also the therapeutic importance of his dream analysis. Perhaps it is for this reason that Dora abruptly ends her analysis? Freud wonders:

> Could I have kept the girl in treatment if I had found a part for myself to play, if I had exaggerated the importance of her presence for myself, and shown her a keen interest, which, in spite of the attention caused by my position as a doctor, would have resembled a substitute for the kindness she longed for? I don't know (1905a [2006]: 95).

If Freud had found a part for himself to play? Later in the case history, Freud begins to suspect the exact opposite: that, in fact, he already had a part to play, that he had become, for Dora, a man much like other men, a man much like her Papa and Herr K. "But I ignored the first warning," Freud bemoans,

> telling myself that we had plenty of time, since no other signs of transference were apparent, and since the material for the analysis was not yet exhausted. So transference took me by surprise, and because of whatever unknown factor it was

that made me remind her of Herr K., she avenged herself on me, as she wanted
to avenge herself on Herr K., and left me, just as she believed herself deceived
and abandoned by him. In that way she was acting out a significant part of her
memories instead of reproducing them in the cure (1905a [2006]: 106).

So far, the psychoanalysis of Dora has involved Freud, basically, conducting
two kinds of investigation. On the one hand, he has examined Dora's sexual
experiences and traumas, from her earliest childhood memories up to her
relationships with Papa and her mother, with Herr and Frau K. with forensic
detail and gynecological objectivity. On the other hand, Freud has utilized his
theory of dreams to explore Dora's conscious and unconscious worlds of meaning
and affect. Significantly, this does not involve a "talking cure," but rather acts
of *translation* (Freud 1905a [2006]: 38). Freud has to translate unconscious
meanings into conscious ones. As with any translation between any language
and any other, this translation is fraught with difficulties. It is made no easier
by the fact that the unconscious is only like a language in a few respects, and its
contents are less like a dictionary of definitions, than a jumble of dynamically
interacting memories, ideas, images, affects and so on.

Freud has deployed his understanding of unconscious processes to attempt
to map what might be going on for Dora *unconsciously*. But this only describes
Dora's *repressed unconscious*: a tempestuous sea of affects that she attempts to
keep from swamping her. There is another unconscious in Freud's model:
a *communicative unconscious*—and this is doing something else entirely. It is this
communicative unconscious that forces Freud to think through the dynamics of
transference, which, he admits, he not only missed or ignored, but he also did
not fully appreciate its force nor its use therapeutically (if at all). Freud's failure
is (at least) two-fold: not only did he not take account of the transference of
affects between them, albeit unconsciously communicated, he also let his own
presumptions about Dora get in the way of the analysis.

As we have said, Freud's interpretations in this case study appear to side,
very strongly, with the assumptions of a patriarchal culture and not with its
discontents. A young teenage girl who is trapped by an older man, who then
forces a kiss upon her, Freud says, *ought* to have responded as if this was
"an occasion for sexual excitement" (1905a [2006]: 21). He asserts that women
are prone to a more intense jealousy than men (ibid.: 50) and he imagines Dora
"felt not only the kiss on her lips but also the pushing of the erect member against
her body" (ibid.: 22), without giving any reason for thinking that this ought to
have been the case. He imposes interpretations upon Dora, as when he tells her

there is "no doubt" that her coughing was designed "to turn her father away from Frau K." (ibid.: 32). He asserts that the coughing represents "a situation of sexual gratification *per se*" (ibid.: 37), and so is directly associated with oral sex. Yet, when Dora says "no" or "I *knew* you'd say that" to his interpretation, Freud responds by taking this as proof that his interpretations are correct (ibid.: 46 and 60). He shares knowledge of what Frau K. allowed Dora to read with Dora, so that she was clear that the adults were communicating about the most intimate aspects of her life behind her back (ibid.: 49) and Freud even puts words in Dora's mouth when he seeks to translate an unconscious thought into a conscious form, thus: "Since all men are so appalling, I would prefer not to marry. This is my revenge" (ibid.: 107).

Indeed, the outcome of the analysis seems to have proved to Dora that "all men were like Papa" (Freud 1905a [2006]: 71), including Freud. Too late, Freud recognizes that, somehow, he has become embroiled in Dora's internal worlds. For her, Freud is just another of the "so appalling" men. So Dora's abrupt breaking off of analysis comes as a total surprise to Freud, yet he belatedly comes to realize that it makes perfect sense for Dora. She avenges herself upon him, just as she sought to avenge herself on Papa and Herr K. So, in this regard, transference refers to the way that Dora came to see Freud as if he were Papa, Herr K. and, indeed appallingly (for Dora and Freud), "all men." This explains why Freud wonders how therapy would have proceeded if he had either resisted Dora's transference, or indeed played into it—by becoming even more like Papa and Herr K. Either way, Dora has taught Freud that transference is an inescapable aspect of, and consequently fundamental to, psychoanalytic therapy:

> If one goes into the theory of analytical technique, one comes to the understanding that the transference is something that it necessarily requires. In practical terms, at least, one becomes convinced that one cannot by any means avoid it (Freud 1905a [2006]: 104).

Sure, Freud says, it is easily possible to learn the method of dream analysis and to translate the dream's unconscious thoughts and memories into conscious interpretations (Freud 1905a [2006]: 104). But transference makes the process of psychoanalytic interpretation fraught with uncertainty. It is not just that the patient begins to treat the doctor as if they were a pre-existing character in their psychodrama, as when Dora appears to treat Freud *as if* he were Papa or Herr K. (Freud 1905a [2006]: 105). The real problem is that the doctor himself is also treating the patient "as if" they were a character in their own psychodrama. Perhaps this is why Freud imagines an erect member? Has he fallen in love with his "intelligent" patient with "agreeable facial features" (Freud 1905a [2006]: 17)? As Freud admits, transference effectively reduces the analyst's work to guesswork (Freud 1905a [2006]: 104). This is, perhaps, psychoanalysis's saving grace; it is necessarily humble and uncertain in the face not only of the patient's symptoms, but also of the process of analysis itself. It is Freud's failure to fully appreciate the dynamics of transference that causes the analysis to break down. Yet, alongside dream analysis, it is Freud's deepening understanding of transference—of unconscious communication—that allows him to develop a new form of therapy: psychoanalysis.

Three facets of the puzzle of transference stalk psychoanalysis. First, it is not clear what unconscious thoughts the patient is transferring onto the therapist. Second, the same is true of the therapist: no matter how critically reflexive they are, unconscious thoughts remain illusively unconscious. Third, the projection of unconscious ideas is not like a cinema with an opaque screen in the middle, with two different films, the patient's and the analyst's, being cast onto each side of the screen. The screen is translucent, such that the unconscious thoughts of the patient and analyst communicate, that is, people's unconscious thoughts can be received unconsciously and those thoughts can be worked upon unconsciously—a model best demonstrated in Freud's later discussions of telepathy (Freud 1921 [1953]; see also Campbell and Pile 2010). These processes are not, Freud insists, unique to the clinical setting, nor are they an insurmountable obstacle, but rather therapy's greatest asset.

> Psychoanalytic cure does not create the transference, it only reveals it, as it does other phenomena hidden in mental life [...] The transference, destined to be the greatest obstacle to psychoanalysis, becomes its most powerful aid if one succeeds in guessing it correctly on each occasion and translating it to the patient (1905a [2006]: 105).

If one succeeds in guessing it and can translate it. A big "if" and a bigger "and." As Freud admits:

> I did not succeed in mastering the transference in time; the readiness with which Dora put part of the pathogenic material at my disposal meant that I neglected to pay attention to the first signs of the transference, which she prepared with another part of the same material, a part that remained known to me (1905a [2006]: 106).

It is not that Freud misses either the way that Dora compares him to her Papa or the resemblance between how she warns herself about the bad intentions of Herr K. and how she cautions herself against Freud (1905a [2006]: 105–6). It is, rather, that Freud neglects to use these intuitions in the course of the therapy. Dora is troublesome: she refuses Freud many times over and, ultimately, despite Freud's claim that the therapy had partial success, the case history does not work as convincing proof either of dream analysis or of psychoanalysis. However, through the intensity of the transference, what Dora has given psychoanalysis cannot be underestimated, not because she is somehow a "special case," but because she demonstrates what is *ordinarily* going on.

Both Dora and Freud must be careful when grasping at an understanding of unconscious thoughts, for it is never clear whose thoughts they are, nor why they take the form they do, nor even how forms and affects are entangled. Yet, this does not mean that they cannot be presented and re-presented. And it certainly does not mean that they cannot be interpreted and worked through. What psychoanalysis presents is a dynamic landscape of the psyche, which can be appreciated in various ways, but not fully known. Again, we might drain the Zuider Zee, but this does not mean that volatile seas do not press upon it. Psychoanalysis offers ways for patients to construct dams—new dams—against painful and traumatizing experiences and affects, but it does not do so without guesswork, supposition, intuition and the like, despite appearances to the contrary. The certainties of interpretation maybe a destination, but they are not the starting point, nor the journey. As Freud says, psychoanalysis is a bit like trying to describe the world from a moving railway carriage. This is no less true of psychoanalysis' other two fundamental concepts: the drives and repetition.

The Drives: Between Biology and Culture

Although Freud never settled on a definitive concept of the drive (*Trieb*), much of his drive theory, which includes several dozen related compound words (hence the common practice of using the plural form "drives"), explores the twists and turns of the following premise: "the initial cause of the libidinal economy resides in the erotic energy of the human body itself; but this energy is always-already channeled through non-natural mediums, namely vicissitudes organized by images and ideas" (Johnston 2005: 261; see also Sioh, this book). The drives, then, are what Freud frequently calls a "borderland" or "frontier" concept insofar as it does not belong exclusively to the body or the mind. Rather, the drives are the result of the dynamic interrelations of these two terms: it "is a border, which is never fully crossed; something is left behind the lines [e.g. the nucleus of the dream or the kernel of the unconscious] and operates in an insistent way from behind these lines" (Verhaeghe 2001: 56).

Freud variously defined the drives as an organic "stimulus," psychical "representative," and more intriguingly something that "exerts pressure" across an "epistemo-somatic gap" (Verhaeghe 2001: 94). The drives, which are frequently mistaken for the waxing and waning of innate biological instincts that secure survival or fleeting psychological wishes that seek well-being, exert a menacing and constant pressure on the psychoanalytic subject. It is a fundamental concept because it is central to how psychoanalysis tackles age-old riddles concerning the dualisms of the mind and body, sex and gender, society and nature, as well as human sexuality, more generally. Below, we focus on the conceptual history of the drives in Freud's writings and then turn to examine its reception in post-Freudian psychoanalytic approaches, social theories and contemporary human geography.

At the beginning of twentieth century, the German word *Trieb*, which in post-Enlightenment scholarship was regularly associated with the regeneration of organic substances via the two main drives of hunger and reproduction, was central to turbulent scientific debates in Austria and Germany about the differences between animal and human sexuality. These debates concerned the following questions: is there such a thing as a natural-born criminal? How many drives are there? What is the origin and location of the drives? What are the drives anyway? Freud contributed to these debates through professional and personal correspondences with psychiatrists, neurologists and historians.

Although "*Trieb*" first appeared Freud's earlier works including *The Project for a Scientific Psychology* (1895 [1966]), *The Interpretation of Dreams* (1900 [1976]) and other texts and lectures during this period, the drives do not become a fundamental psychoanalytic concept until the first edition (there were six in Freud's lifetime) of the *Three Essays on the Theory of Sexuality* (1905b [2006]). In this path-breaking and subversive work, which includes essays entitled "Sexual Aberrations," "Infantile Sexuality" and "Transformations of Puberty," Freud developed the concept of the drives to investigate human sexuality through a panoply of issues including the libido or sexual drives, bi-, homo-, and hetero-sexuality, perversions, fantasy, embodiment, self-eroticism, gender, sadism and masochism, scopophilia and exhibitionism and, quite controversially, the ability of the "polymorphously perverse" human infant to derive sexual pleasure from their innate physical constitution.

In the *Three Essays*, Freud formally departed from his "seduction theory," that is, the hypothesis that hysteria and neuroses were primarily caused by the failed repression of memories of sexual abuse in childhood. By contrast, Freud now asserted that human sexuality was central to the etiology of neuroses. According to Freud, sexuality is characterized not by distinct, unified and polar orientations such as heterosexuality versus homosexuality, perversion versus normality, child versus adult sexuality, but by profound continuity, variability and partiality across and within these domains. Specifically, Freud argued that sexuality was composed of "partial" drives (oral, anal, phallic and genital) that took place as a disjointed "montage" and therefore resisted a smooth mapping onto the genitals (another reason for using "drives" rather than "drive"). Tim Dean claims that Freud's "partializing of the drive discredits not only the viability of sexual complementarity, but also the possibility of subjective harmony" (2003: 247).

From the outset, psychoanalysis suggests that human sexuality is a question of dis-orientation rather than orientation because it is characterized by a fraught relationship between procreation and pleasure, as well as the radical variability of "love-objects." Freud not only believed that "the sexual drive is probably at first independent of its object, and in all likelihood its origins do not lie in its object's attractions" (1905b [2006]: 126–7), but also that there was no such thing as a pre-determined "natural" love-object because "all human beings are capable of making a homosexual object-choice and have in fact made one in their unconscious" (1915c [2006]: 145). Thus, for Freud, human sexuality lacks a "natural" object and the ostensible perversions of masturbation, fetishism and same sex desire are not only normal, but also constitutive of the human subject.

A decade later, in the essay *Drives and their Fates* (usually translated as *Instincts and their Vicissitudes*), Freud famously located the drives, which had now become more central to his metapsychology,

> on the borderline between the mental and the physical—the psychic representative of stimuli flowing into the psyche from inside the body, or the degree of work-load imposed on the psyche as a result of its relation to the body (1915b [2005]: 16).

In this essay, Freud elaborated further on the partiality of the drives. He defined a drive as a "delegate" that represents the constant physiological energy emanating from a part or "source" (*Quelle*) of the body which results in psychical labor that varies in its degree of tension or "pressure" (*Drang*). The "aim" (*Ziel*) of the drives, in keeping with the pleasure principle, is satisfaction, that is, relief from tension or excessive somatic excitation that can be achieved through the drives' "object" (*Objekt*)—a highly mutable entity that is extraneous to the drive's action such as a bodily organ, another person, or an everyday object. Crucially, the drives always fail in their representative mission of translating the demands of the mind and the body because "a drive can never become an object of consciousness, only the idea representing it" (Freud 1905b [2006]: 59). This is no small matter because it means that the drive "in itself, independent of any externally determined trauma, has a potentially traumatizing effect, to which the psyche has to come up with an answer, that is, with a psychological elaboration" (Verhaeghe 2001: 56). Given the partial nature of the drives, Freud emphasizes the contingencies of these elaborations, that is, the unpredictable structural transformations and outcomes of various psychical translations that include repression, sublimation, "reversal into the opposite" and "turning back on the self" (Freud 1915b [2005]: 20).

While Freud hoped the essay would put to rest his questions about sadomasochism in the *Three Essays*, it elicited another round of questions: how to account for the prevalence in his clinical observations of masochism, hostility and negative transference? In order to solve these riddles, Freud made two important theoretical modifications. First, in the pivotal essay *On the Introduction of Narcissism* (1914a [2003]), Freud declared that the original opposition between the Ego drive and sexual drives was no longer tenable because the Ego drive is itself sexual and the sexual drives are in service of the Ego. Second, the psychoanalytic subject (according to the homeostatic pleasure principle) was no longer concerned with the acquisition of pleasure, with the discharging of tension, but rather with the avoidance of unpleasure that paradoxically yielded an even more alluring pleasure: an uncanny painful pleasure that Lacan would call "jouissance" (Kingsbury 2008; see also Shaw, Powell and De La Ossa, this book; Proudfoot and Kingsbury, this book).

Dissatisfied by the monism of the drives, Freud embarked on another round of revisions in the 1920 essay, *Beyond the Pleasure Principle*. Having also been shocked by the severity of the social implications and effects of the First World War, Freud returned to a dualistic theory of the drive in terms of the death drive and the life drives. The former is arguably Freud's most controversial concept, which he defined as "*a powerful tendency inherent in every living organism to restore a prior state* ... a kind of organic elasticity, or, if we prefer, as a manifestation of inertia in organic life" (1920 [2003]: 76). The latter referred to the tendency of the living entities to pursue unification, coupling and the merger into larger scale entities. It is important to note that the death and life drives not only overlap, they are also relative: "the death drive is actually a life drive depending on how one looks at it, and vice versa, the life drive implies the death of something else" (Verhaeghe 2001: 93).

In *The Ego and the Id* (1923 [2003]), Freud made his final major revisions to the drives wherein he situated the life and death drives in the Id. In this "structural" model, the Ego is charged with defending against the incursions of the Id's drives through "defenses" that include holding off, delay and altering. In this final model, the drives become subsumed by the mental structures of the Id, Ego and Superego.

Psychoanalysts' subsequent interpretations of the drives in *The Ego and the Id* are numerous, contested and significant because they are frequently central to the attempts to define the goals of psychoanalysis. The development of "Ego Psychology" during the 1930s onwards through the works of Anna Freud, Heinz Hartmann, Ernst Kris, Erik Erikson and others, aims to strengthen the Ego's defenses in order to better regulate the Id's tumultuous libidinal forces so that people can adapt to their social realities. Lacan rallied against the normative ramifications of this paradigm, which soon dominated the International Psychoanalysis Association (IPA), by asserting the imaginary status of the Ego, as well as the centrality and radicality of Freud's theories of the unconscious and the drives, especially the death drive. For Lacan, "every drive is virtually a death drive" (1966 [2006]: 719). Similarly, Melanie Klein, who influenced the works of Donald Winnicott and other psychoanalysts associated with the Object Relations school, rejected the conformity of Ego Psychology by asserting the Ego's vulnerability and secondary status to the drives in terms of guilt, aggression and persecutory and depressive anxiety that comprised the Oedipal fantasy life of children younger than three years old (Klein 1975 [1988]).

Earlier, we stated that the drives are central to how psychoanalysis answers the age-old dualistic mind and body problem. The answers are perplexing and troubling for two main reasons. First, the lived spaces of the drives—that is, their near endless capacity for plasticity, partiality and multiplicity—repeatedly agitate the Ego's imaginary capacity for securing a sense of totality and coherence rendering "the human body so anarchic and fragmented that it makes surrealist anatomy appear positively classical" (Dean 2008: 132). Because psychoanalysis locates the drives in a space that separates rather than blurs biological imperatives and social demands, the psychoanalytic subject never quite feels at home in her own skin and is frequently buffeted by the discontentment in civilization (Freud 1930 [2002]). Second, while objects such as food and water can satiate the instincts of hunger and thirst, the drives derive satisfaction by encircling or missing their object. Thus, the drives are associated with activities that are excessive, repetitive and potentially destructive because the drives have "no goal, but only an aim, this is because its object is no longer a means of attaining satisfaction, it is an end in itself; it is directly satisfying" (Copjec 2002: 38).

Like the unconscious, the drives have been the target of numerous trenchant critiques that allege Freud falls foul of deterministic and reductive biologism, materialism and pansexualism. Jung, for example, tartly asserted that the generalizing "nomenclature" of Freud's drive theory would "lead us to classify the cathedral of Cologne as mineralogy because it is built of stones" (Freud 1916 [1991]: 130). Yet Freud averred that the drives are multifarious and dynamic entities, chiding Carl Jung (and Alfred Adler) for picking "out a few cultural overtones from the symphony of life" and failing "to hear the mighty and powerful melody of the [drives]" (1914b [1957]: 62).

Receptions of the drives in the humanities and social sciences usually fall into two camps: either siding with Jung's accusation of Freud's pansexualism or siding with Freud's insistence on the plurality of the drives. In the former, many critics understandably throw out the concept entirely because they follow James Strachey—the general editor of the canonical yet "willfully turgid and often obfuscatory" *Standard Edition* (Reddick 2003: xxxiii)—in mistranslating the drives as "instincts," a word with strong ahistorical, biological and deterministic overtones. Unfortunately, this maneuver is still common in geography (see for example Aitken and Herman 1997: 71; Thrift 2004: 25). The latter camp consists of close readings of the drives and therefore more nuanced critiques that often result in productive theoretical conversations and innovations in psychoanalytic and critical social theory, more generally. Such critiques correctly assert that the drives endow humans with creative capacities, as well as a sexual life that is not and cannot be entirely determined by either biology or culture because the drives are inherently partial, plastic, conflicted and multiple.

Ever since Herbert Marcuse's *Eros and Civilization* (1955 [1974]), the drives have played an important role in Freudian-Marxist social theories of the dogged persistence of socio-economic injustice. For Adrian Johnston, the drives mean "the human individual isn't entirely enslaved to tyranny of the pragmatic utilitarian economy of well-being, to a happiness thrust forward by the twin authorities of the pleasure and reality principles" (2008: 185).

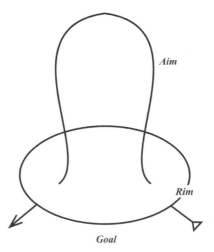

Figure I.3   Lacan's map of the drives (1964)

In the past two decades, Lacanian theories of the drives have spawned numerous cultural and political studies across the humanities and social sciences. Notably, Slavoj Žižek has drawn on a Lacanian understanding of the drives to explore ideology (1989), political ontology (1999) and global capitalism (2011), amongst other things. For Lacan, the drives generate jouissance—an alluring painful pleasure—by following its "goal" of encircling and continually missing a non-empirical, that is, uncanny object: the *objet petit a*. For Lacan, much of the drives' return journeys (the "aim") take place around the "rims" or orifices of the body: see Figure I.3.

Also drawing on Lacan, Tim Dean and Christopher Lane (2001: 5) have asserted that "defining the drive as unnatural, as operating *contra naturem* [*sic*], Freud effectively 'queers' all sexuality" in ways that can provide useful, anti-normative insights into queer sexualities, sexual politics, AIDS and safe sex education (Dean 2000). In the field of aesthetics, Joan Copjec has drawn on the drives, especially in terms of the creative "solder[ing] together" of "construction and discovery, thinking and being, as well as drive and object" (Copjec 2002: 39) to examine ethics and sublimation in a wide range of artistic works including Cindy Sherman's *Untitled Film Stills* (1977–1980) photographs, Kara Walker's paper cut-out artworks (1994–1997) and Pier Paolo Pasolini's film *Salò* (1975). Finally, Adrian Johnston's *Time Driven: Metapsychology and the Splitting of the Drive* is a useful conceptual exploration of the drives in terms of seven theses that include: "drives are internally differentiated mechanisms," "all drives, in their very structure, are split drives," "the constitutive antagonism within drives is temporal in nature" and "drives are inherently incapable of obtaining their own aims" (Johnston 2005: xxix–xxiii).

Repetition: Dying to Go Beyond Pleasure

According to Jean Laplanche and Jean-Bertrand Pontalis (1973: 78), "[i]t is quite obvious that psycho-analysis was confronted from the very beginning by repetition *phenomena.*" In the early writings of Freud, such phenomena took place in analysis as clinical transference—"the love [that] consists of new editions of old traits and that ... repeats infantile reactions" (Freud 1915d [1958]: 168)—as well as the everyday world of the repetition of memories, dreams, symptoms, hysterical attacks and acting out. Repetition is typically aligned with the "compulsion to repeat" or "repetition compulsion." This concept first gained prominence in Freud's essay "Remembering, Repeating and Working Through" (1914c [2003]) that addressed how a proper handling of transference was central to converting the patient's compulsion to repeat into an impulse to remember in terms of an "intermediate realm between sickness and a healthy life by means of which [through transference] the transition from one to the other is accomplished" (Freud 1914c [2003]: 40–41). Such a transition concerned the arduous overcoming or "working-through of the resistances" (Freud 1914c [2003]: 37) that enabled the patient to recall significant memories and discover the repressed drive impulses. Only through cooperation, Freud affirms, can the analyst and patient manage the intense drive impulses "that sustain the resistance; and it is only by directly experiencing it in this way that the patient becomes truly convinced of its existence and power" (1914c [2003]: 155).

Repetition eventually becomes a fundamental psychoanalytic concept in *Beyond the Pleasure Principle* (1920 [2003]). In this essay, repetition takes place according to the logic of the death drive, which Freud argues is "independent of" and "more elementary" than the pleasure principle (1920 [2003]: 23). In subsequent works, Freud sought to extend the repetition compulsion in terms of the "power of the compulsion to repeat" qua "*the resistance of the unconscious*" (Freud 1926 [1954]: 159–60) and social "order" that "enables people to make the best use of space and time, while sparing their mental forces" (Freud 1930 [2002]: 30). Given the controversies surrounding Freud's notion of the death drive, interpretations of repetition in post-Freudian approaches are numerous and contested. Laplanche and Pontalis note that the debates about repetition revolve around two interrelated questions: "First, what is the tendency towards repetition a function of? ... Secondly, does the compulsion to repeat really cast doubt on the dominance of the pleasure principle, as Freud contended?" (1973: 80). Answers to these questions either focus on the death drive or turn to Freud's final structural model of the Id, Ego and Superego (see Figure I.1) and its relation to trauma.

Notable responses include Klein's, who argued that "in an early stage of development the Ego" is unable "to deal sufficiently with guilt and anxiety" which results in "the need ... to repeat certain actions obsessionally" in order to overcome a "depressive position," that is, a normal phase of development often coinciding with the distress of weaning (1940: 132). Edward Bibring (1943), meanwhile, highlighted the Id's "repetitive" tendencies that created trauma and the Ego's attempts to return to a pre-traumatic state through its "restorative" tendencies. Subsequently, Hans Loewald (1971) focused on the interplay between "passive, reproductive repetition" wherein a person unconsciously acts out painful childhood memories and "re-creative repetition" wherein a person consciously aims to master (rather than eliminate) the elements of a destructive past via dissolution and reconstruction.

In the remainder of this section, we focus on repetition and its relationship to pleasure and the death drive. This brings into sharp relief a theoretical kernel that distinguishes psychoanalysis from the other paradigmatic approaches to society, subjectivity and space that comprise much of human geography: that is, the "problem" of understanding the distance, or its lack, between "subjects" and their "objects."

One of Freud's most well-known concrete illustrations of the relationship between repetition and pleasure is his account of the *fort/da* (gone/here) game. Watching his 18-month-old grandson, Ernst, throwing small objects into the corners of a room and under a bed, including a wooden spool with some string tied around it, Freud wrote:

> he beamed with an expression of interest and gratification, and uttered a loud, long-drawn out "o-o-o-" sound, which in unanimous opinion of both his mother and myself as observer was not simply an exclamation but stood for *fort* ("gone"). I eventually realized this was a game, and that the child was using all his toys for the sole purpose of playing "gone" with them. Then one day I made an observation that confirmed my interpretation. The child had a

wooden reel with some string tied around it ... keeping hold of the string, he skillfully threw the reel over the edge of his curtained cot so that it disappeared inside, all the while making his expressive "o-o-o" sound, then used the string to pull the reel out of the cot again, but this time greeting its reappearance with a joyful *Da!* ("Here!"). That, then, was the entire game—disappearing and coming back—only the first act of which one normally got to see; and this first act was tirelessly repeated on its own, even though the pleasure undoubtedly attached to the second (Freud 1920 [2003]: 53).

There is also a less celebrated vignette in a footnote to the above passage where Freud described his Grandson's reinvention of the game, this time using a mirror:

One day when the child's mother had been absent for many hours, she was greeted on her return with the announcement "Bebi o-o-o-o!," which at first remained incomprehensible. It soon turned out, however, that while on his own for this long period of time the child had found a way of making himself disappear. He had discovered his reflection in the full-length mirror reaching almost to the floor, and had then crouched down so that his reflection was "gone" (Freud 1920 [2003]: 248).

According to Copjec (1994: 43), each game exemplifies how "the rediscovery of something already familiar, is pleasurable because it economizes energy." From a Lacanian perspective, she notes that in the *fort/da* game, when the child "throws the cotton reel, he throws that part of himself that is lost with his entry into language. The child thus situates himself in the field of language; he chooses *sense* rather than the being that sense continually fails to secure.

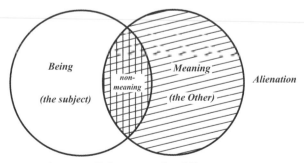

Figure I.4   Lacan's map of alienation (1964)

He thus becomes a subject of desire, lacking-in-being" (Copjec 1994: 182). In the mirror version of the game, the infant "takes up the position of the cotton reel, he situates himself in the field of being; he chooses being, jouissance, rather than sense" (ibid.). According to Lacan (1977), the human subject emerges through the process of "alienation" and is situated in a shadowy place of "non-meaning" that results from a forced choice between being and meaning (see Figure I.4).

The two games involve two different forms of repetition: the former repetition is propelled by desire and the latter is propelled by the drives. For Luce Irigaray (1985 [1993]), the *fort/da* game is a decidedly gendered account because it is authored by a male and describes a male infant's development. Furthermore, Irigaray (1985 [1993]: 98) contends that a female's game of repetition would eschew the male's mastery of instrumentalization, distanciation and dichotomization that comprise the "gone"/"here" of throwing the reel in favor of a "dance" that repeatedly "reproduces around ... her an energetic circular movement that protects her from abandonment, attack, depression, loss of self". For Jacques Laplanche (1999: 139), the *fort/da* game illustrates how the signifier of the absent mother or father becomes repeatedly "implanted," that is, "fixed, as onto a surface, in the psychophysiological 'skin' of a subject in which the unconscious agency is not yet differentiated" (on skin, see Straughan, this book).

The *fort/da* game is not only useful because it demonstrates varying theorizations of repetition; it also elicited one of Freud's most notable considerations of the dynamic mutuality of repetition and pain. Further in the text, Freud observes:

> The going away of the mother cannot possibly have been pleasant for the child, nor even a matter of indifference. How then does this repetition of this painful experience fit in with the pleasure principle? It may perhaps be said in reply that her departure had to be enacted as a necessary preliminary to her joyful return, and that it was in the latter that lay the true purpose of the game (1920 [2003]: 53–4).

Significantly, Freud speculates that the game does not merely provide a way for the boy to cope with his absent mother; the reenactment of the mother's departure actually increases the joy that will be obtained from her eventual return. More radically, the game's painful reenactment of the separation from his mother yields an exquisite joy. For Freud (1920 [2003]: 16), this joy bore "witness to the operations of tendencies beyond the pleasure principle, that is to say, tendencies which might be of earlier origin and independent of this." Later on, Freud aligns these tendencies with the death drive.

An enormous amount of time and effort has been devoted to interpreting and reinterpreting (over and over again!) the concept of the death drive. Rather than seeing repetition as the ineluctable fate of the death drive, however, Copjec emphasizes the relationship between the death drive, the biological body and symbolic life:

> Freud, far from contrasting repetition with life, interprets repetition as the invariable characteristic of the drives that fuel life. The being of the drives, he claims *is* the compulsion to repeat. The aim of life is not evolution but regression, or in its most seemingly contradictory form, the aim of life is death ... Freud's text [*Beyond the Pleasure Principle*] is incomprehensible if one confounds instinct with drive, or—in a distinction made by Lacan, who finds it latent in Freud's work—if one confounds the first and second death. The first is the real death of the biological body, after which there is usually another, the second, exemplified by the various rituals of mourning that take place in the symbolic. It is with this second death that we are concerned with when we speak of the Freudian concept of the death drive (Copjec 1994: 46).

Far from opposing the pleasure principle as a "will to die" or "death wish," repetition compulsion and the death drive extend the pleasure principle because they are "inevitable corollaries of *symbolic* life" (Copjec 1994: 46) insofar as they are consequences of signifying networks that comprise language, rules, customs, codes and other textual entities through which human geography and history are repeatedly inscribed (see also Butler 1990: 145).

Crucially, the relation between repetition and symbolic life "is ruled by the death drive" (Copjec 1994: 39). More pointedly, Žižek (1997: 89) asserts that the death drive is "the symbolic order itself, the structure which, as a parasite, colonizes the living entity." The symbolic machinations of repetition and the death drive take place as the disruptive and potentially lethal adversary to what Freud in *Civilization and Its Discontents* (1930 [2002]) dubbed "Eros": the tendency for human beings to join together into larger entities such as families, communities and nations. How so? Because our bodies, thoughts, imaginations and speech are not pre-given, they are inscribed through and cut up by unstable, incomplete and often unkind social bonds of language that repeatedly produce

> always something more, something indeterminate ... One cannot argue that the subject is constructed by language and then overlook the essential fact

of language's duplicity, that is, the fact that whatever it says can be denied. This duplicity ensures that the subject will *not* come into being as language's determinate meaning. An incitement to discourse is not an incitement to being. What is aroused is the desire for nonbeing, for an *in*determinate something that is perceived as *extra* discursive (Copjec 1994: 54–6).

The arousing pursuit of "something" beyond language helps us understand why Ernst gleefully lobs the cotton reel time and time again. From this perspective, the desire for "nonbeing" helps explain why so many people in different parts of the world repeatedly refuse to follow their individual and collective interests. That is to say, paradoxically, the paltry pleasure that can be garnered from securing material gains and a peaceful existence is hardly a match for the fiercely thrilling yet bitterly strained enjoyment or jouissance (as Lacan has it) that charges modes of life beyond the pleasure principle wherein they are justified by aggression, strife and conflict. Such a thesis has informed numerous psychoanalytic interpretations of the ubiquitous repetitions of racism (Lane 1998), violence (Žižek 2008) and murder (Bond 2009).

Towards *Psychoanalytic Geographies*

Psychoanalytic understandings of the unconscious, transference, the drives and repetition are not only enhancing traditional geographical concerns with space, place, landscape and the environment, they are also transforming key areas of geographical research itself (Philo and Parr 2003; Kingsbury 2009a, 2009b; Thomas 2010). The incorporation of psychoanalytic thought into an engagement with geography's core concerns is underway—as the collection of essays in this book amply demonstrates. As you will discover, this book clearly illustrates the sheer variety of ways that psychoanalytic concepts and styles of thought are used to open up new questions, new objects of study and new forms of understanding: an understanding that is both psychoanalytic and geographical. Such a catholic attitude has arguably emerged not only because of the relative openness toward new paradigms that characterizes contemporary geographical research, but also because of geographers' willingness to tarry with psychoanalysis' seemingly tricky, perhaps off-putting, yet rewarding concepts such as the unconscious, transference, drives and repetition. Echoing Freud (1905a [2006]: 101), the psychoanalytic geographer can "work with unconscious ideas, trains of thought and impulses as though, as objects of psychological study, they were just as good and as certain as conscious phenomena," allowing them to move between worlds of thought, discourse, experience, imagination, affect and action, more fluidly than many other approaches to human geography.

During the last decade or so, by attending to the unconscious—"that interiorized place of embodied-spatialized desire and fear that is repressed and glossed over through imaginary-symbolic devices" (Nast 2000: 223)—geographers have explored how unspoken and forbidden desires inform racist and colonial landscapes (Nast 2000; Hook 2005a, 2005b; Pile 2011), urban life (Pile 2005), the feelings of others (Bondi 2003) and the geographies of phobia (Davidson 2003). By considering transference—"[the] reenactment of intense infantile emotions, demands, experiences and identifications in the analytic session by projecting them onto the analyst" (Kingsbury 2009a: 482)—geographers have reappraised subjective experiences in fieldwork (Bondi 2003; Thien 2005; Thomas 2007; Pile 2010). By acknowledging the drive—"[which] tends toward dissolution and repetition as opposed to novelty and bonding" (Proudfoot 2010: 511)—geographers have questioned geography's dominant models of political subjectivity (Callard 2003). By recognizing repetition—"the iteration of activities that aim for something beyond mere pleasure" (Kingsbury 2010: 529)—geographers have investigated the recurring human and nonhuman fear of animals (Pile 2014) and the commodity-form's enduring allures and injustices that conduct tourism activities in the Global South (Kingsbury 2011).

And yet, despite all of the above work, the possibilities of psychoanalytic geographies still eclipse its accomplishments. The assertion that psychoanalysis has transformed key terrains in human geographical research is arguably an overstatement because of the relatively small numbers of geographers who align themselves with psychoanalytic research. Furthermore, there are important thinkers in psychoanalysis such as Helene Deutsche, Erik Erikson, Anna Freud, Sandor Ferenczi, Carl Jung, Melanie Klein and Jacques Laplanche (though see Thomas, this book), whose works have been relatively neglected by geographers (Philo and Parr 2003). The list grows even longer when considering contemporary psychoanalytic writers such as Jessica Benjamin, Christopher Bollas, Adam Phillips and Thomas Ogden. Consequently, up to now, psychoanalytic geographers have been spread somewhat thinly, such that even the works of central figures such as Freud and Lacan remain relatively untapped. Yet, in this book, we can begin to see the emergence of new styles of psychoanalytic geographies and new engagements with previously marginal figures, as we move towards broader and profounder *Psychoanalytic Geographies*. And, as these engagements unfold, we will see even more possibilities for future work that weaves together psychoanalysis and geography.

While the days of asking whether psychoanalysis and geography have anything in common are fading, today's psychoanalytic geographies beam with questions about its current ideas, about what it has to say and where it might be going. *Psychoanalytic Geographies*, not only provides some answers, it also keeps these questions in play.

References

Aitken, S. and Herman, T. 1997. Gender, power and crib geography: transitional spaces and potential places. *Gender, Place & Culture: A Journal of Feminist Geography*, 4(1), 63–88.

Anzieu, D. 1985 [1989]. *The Skin Ego*. New Haven: Yale University Press.

Bernheimer, C. and Kahane, C. (eds) 1990. *In Dora's Case: Freud–Hysteria–Feminism*. 2nd Edition. New York: Columbia University Press.

Bibring, E. 1943. The concept of the repetition compulsion. *Psychoanalytic Quarterly*, 12(4), 486–519.

Blum, V. and Secor, A. 2010. Psychotopologies: closing the circuit between psychic and material space. *Environment and Planning D: Society and Space*, 29(6), 1030–47.

Bollas, C. 1987. *Shadow of the Object: Psychoanalysis and the Unthought Unknown*. New York: Columbia University Press.

Bond, H. 2009. *Lacan at the Scene*. Cambridge, MA: The MIT Press.

Bondi, L. 2003. Empathy and identification: conceptual resources for feminist fieldwork. *ACME: An International E-Journal for Critical Geographies*, 2(1), 64–76.

Bondi, L. 2014. Understanding feelings: engaging with unconscious communication and embodied knowledge. *Emotion, Space and Society*, 10(1), 44–54.

Breuer, J. and Freud, S. 1895 [2004]. *Studies in Hysteria*. Harmondsworth: Penguin.

Butler, J. 1990. *Gender Trouble: Feminism and the Subversion of Identity*. London: Routledge.

Callard, F. 2003. The taming of psychoanalysis in geography. *Social and Cultural Geography*, 4(3), 295–312.

Campbell, J. and Pile, S. 2010. Telepathy and its vicissitudes: Freud, thought transference and the hidden lives of the (repressed and non-repressed) unconscious. *Subjectivity*, 3(4), 403–25.

Copjec, J. 1994. *Read My Desire: Lacan Against the Historicists*. Cambridge, MA: The MIT Press.

Copjec, J. 2002. *Imagine There's No Woman: Ethics and Sublimation*. Cambridge, MA: The MIT Press.

Davidson, J. 2003. *Phobic Geographies: The Phenomenology and Spatiality of Identity*. Aldershot: Ashgate.

Dean, T. 2000. *Beyond Sexuality*. Chicago: University of Chicago Press.

Dean, T. 2003. Lacan and queer theory, in *The Cambridge Companion to Lacan*, edited by Jean-Michel Rabaté. Cambridge: Cambridge University Press, 238–52.

Dean, T. 2008. An impossible embrace: queerness, futurity, and the death drive, in *A Time for the Humanities: Futurity and the Limits of Autonomy*, edited by James J. Bono, Tim Dean and Ewa Plonowska Ziarek. New York: Fordham University Press, 122–40.

Dean, T. and Lane, C. 2001. Homosexuality and psychoanalysis: an introduction, in *Homosexuality and Psychoanalysis*, edited by Tim Dean and Christopher Lane. Chicago: University of Chicago Press, 3–42.

Decker, H. 1991. *Freud, Dora, and Vienna 1900*. New York: The Free Press.

Freud, S. 1883 [1960]. Letter to Martha Bernays, 16 December 1883. *Letters of Sigmund Freud*, edited by Ernst L. Freud. New York: Basic Books, 77–80.

Freud, S. 1885 [1960]. Letter to Martha Bernays, 19 November 1885. *Letters of Sigmund Freud*, edited by Ernst L. Freud. New York: Basic Books, 182–3.

Freud, S. 1895 [1966]. Project for a scientific psychology, in *The Standard Edition of the Complete Psychological Works of Sigmund Freud. Volume 1: Pre-Psycho-Analytic Publications and Unpublished Drafts*, edited by James Strachey. London: The Hogarth Press, 295–397.

Freud, S. 1900 [1976]. *The Interpretation of Dreams*. Harmondsworth: Penguin.

Freud, S. 1905a [2006]. Fragment of an analysis of hysteria (Dora). *The Psychology of Love*. Harmondsworth: Penguin, 1–110.

Freud, S. 1905b [2006]. Three essays on sexual theory. *The Psychology of Love*. Harmondsworth: Penguin, 111–220.

Freud, S. 1909 [2002]. Some remarks on a case of obsessive-compulsive neurosis [The "Ratman"]. *The "Wolfman" and Other Cases*. Harmondsworth: Penguin, 123–202.

Freud, S. 1912 [1958]. Recommendations to physicians practicing psychoanalysis, in *The Standard Edition of the Complete Psychological Works of Sigmund Freud. Volume 12: Case History of Schreber, Papers on Technique and Other Works, 1911–1913*, edited by James Strachey. London: The Hogarth Press, 111–20.

Freud, S. 1914a [2003]. On the introduction of narcissism. *Beyond the Pleasure Principle and Other Writings*. Harmondsworth: Penguin, 3–30.

Freud, S. 1914b [1957]. On the history of the psycho-analytic movement, in *The Standard Edition of the Complete Psychological Works of Sigmund Freud. Volume 14: On the History of the Psycho-Analytic Movement, Papers on Metapsychology and Other Works*, edited by James Strachey. London: The Hogarth Press, 3–66.

Freud, S. 1914c [2003]. Remembering, repeating, and working through. *Beyond the Pleasure Principle and Other Writings*. Harmondsworth: Penguin, 33–42.

Freud, S. 1915a [2005]. The unconscious. *The Unconscious*. Harmondsworth: Penguin, 47–86.

Freud, S. 1915b [2005]. Drives and their fates. *The Unconscious*. Harmondsworth: Penguin, 13–31.

Freud, S. 1915c [2006]. Three essays on sexual theory. *The Psychology of Love*. Harmondsworth: Penguin, 111–220.

Freud, S. 1915d [1958]. Observations on transference love, in *The Standard Edition of the Complete Psychological Works of Sigmund Freud. Volume 12: 1911–1913, Case History of Schreber, Papers on Technique and Other Works*, edited by James Strachey. London: The Hogarth Press 159–71.

Freud, S. 1920 [2003]. Beyond the pleasure principle. *Beyond the Pleasure Principle and Other Writings*. Harmondsworth: Penguin, 45–102.

Freud, S. 1921 [1953]. Psychoanalysis and telepathy, in *Psychoanalysis and the Occult*, edited by George Devereux. London: Souvenir Press, 56–68.

Freud, S. 1923 [2003]. The ego and the id. *Beyond the Pleasure Principle and Other Writings*. Harmondsworth: Penguin, 105–49.

Freud, S. 1926 [1954]. Inhibitions, symptoms and anxiety, in *The Standard Edition of the Complete Psychological Works of Sigmund Freud. Volume 20: An Autobiographical Study, Inhibitions, Symptoms and Anxiety, Lay Analysis and Other Works 1925–1926*, edited by J. Strachey. London: The Hogarth Press, 75–174.

Freud, S. 1930 [2002]. *Civilization and its Discontents*. Harmondsworth: Penguin, 1–82.

Freud, S. 1933 [2003]. Introductory lectures on psychoanalysis: new series. *An Outline of Psychoanalysis*. Harmondsworth: Penguin, 3–172.

Gelder, K. and Jacobs, J.M. 1998. *Uncanny Australia: Sacredness and Identity in a Postcolonial Nation*. Melbourne: Melbourne University Press.

Hook, D. 2005a. Monumental space and the uncanny. *Geoforum*, 36(6), 688–704.

Hook, D. 2005b. The racial stereotype, colonial discourse, fetishism, racism. *The Psychoanalytic Review*, 92(5), 701–34.

Irigaray, L. 1985 [1993]. Gesture in psychoanalysis. *Sexes and Genealogies*. New York: Columbia University Press, 89–104.

Johnston, A. 2005. *Time Driven: Metapsychology and the Splitting of the Drive*. Evanston, IL: Northwestern University Press.

Johnston, A. 2008. *Žižek's Ontology*. Evanston, IL: Northwestern University Press.

Jung, C.G. 1916 [1991]. *The Psychology of the Unconscious: A Study of the Transformations and Symbolisms of the Libido*. New York: Moffat, Yard and Co.

Kingsbury, P. 2004. Psychoanalytic approaches, in *A Companion to Cultural Geography*, edited by James S. Duncan, Nuala C. Johnson and Richard H. Schein. Oxford: Blackwell, 108–20.

Kingsbury, P. 2007. The extimacy of space. *Social & Cultural Geography*, 8(2), 235–58.

Kingsbury, P. 2008. Did somebody say jouissance? On Slavoj Žižek, consumption, and nationalism. *Emotion, Space and Society*, 1(1), 48–55.

Kingsbury, P. 2009a. Psychoanalysis, in *International Encyclopedia of Human Geography, Volume 8*, edited by Rob Kitchin and Nigel Thrift. Oxford: Elsevier, 480–86.

Kingsbury, P. 2009b. Psychoanalytic theory/psychoanalytic geographies, in *International Encyclopedia of Human Geography, Volume 8*, edited by Rob Kitchin and Nigel Thrift. Oxford: Elsevier, 487–94.

Kingsbury, P. 2010. Locating the melody of the drives. *The Professional Geographer*, 62(4), 519–33.

Kingsbury, P. 2011. Sociospatial sublimation: the human resources of love in Sandals Resorts International, Jamaica. *Annals of the Association of American Geographers*, 101(3), 650–69.

Kivland, D. 1999. *A Case of Hysteria*. London: Book Works.

Klein, M. 1940. Mourning and its relation to manic-depressive states. *International Journal of Psycho-Analysis*, 21, 125–53.

Klein, M. 1975 [1988]. *Envy and Gratitude, and Other Works: 1946–1963*. London: Virago.

Kristeva, J. 1982. *Powers of Horror: An Essay on Abjection*. New York: Columbia University Press.

Lacan, J. 1966 [2006]. Position of the unconscious: remarks made at the 1960 Bonneval colloquium rewritten in 1964. *Écrits*. New York: Norton, 703–21.

Lacan, J. 1970. Of structure as an inmixing of an otherness prerequisite to any subject whatever, in *The Structuralist Controversy: The Languages of Criticism and the Sciences of Man*, edited by Richard Macksey and Eugenio Donato. Baltimore: Johns Hopkins University Press, 186–200.

Lacan, J. 1973 [1977]. *The Four Fundamental Concepts of Psychoanalysis*. New York: Norton.

Lacan, J. 1986 [1992]. *The Ethics of Psychoanalysis*. New York: Norton.

Lakoff, R. and Coyne, J. 1993. *Father Knows Best: The Use and Abuse of Therapy in Freud's Case of Dora*. New York: Teachers College Press.

Lane, C. 1998. *The Psychoanalysis of Race*. New York: Columbia University Press.

Laplanche, J. 1999. *Essays on Otherness*. Routledge: New York.

Mahony, P. 1996. *Freud's Dora: A Psychoanalytic, Historical and Textual Study*. New Haven: Yale University Press.

Marcuse, H. 1955 [1974]. *Eros and Civilization: A Philosophical Inquiry into Freud*. Boston: Beacon Press.

Matless, D. 1995. The art of right living: landscape and citizenship, 1918–39, in *Mapping the Subject: Geographies of Cultural Transformation*, edited by Steve Pile and Nigel Thrift. London: Routledge, 93–122.

Nast, H. 2000. Mapping the "unconscious": racism and the Oedipal family. *Annals of the Association of American Geographers*, 90(2), 215–55.

Philo, C. and Parr, H. 2003. Introducing psychoanalytic geographies. *Social & Cultural Geography*, 4(3), 283–94.

Pile, S. 1996. *The Body and the City: Psychoanalysis, Space and Subjectivity*. London: Routledge.

Pile, S. 2005. *Real Cities: Modernity, Space and the Phantasmagoria of City Life*. London: Sage.

Pile, S. 2010. Intimate distance: the unconscious dimensions of the rapport between researcher and researched. *The Professional Geographer*, 62(4), 483–95.

Pile, S. 2011. Skin, race and space: the clash of bodily schemas in Frantz Fanon's *Black Skins, White Masks* and Nella Larsen's *Passing*. *Cultural Geographies*, 18(1), 25–41.

Pile, S. 2014. Beastly minds: A topological twist in the rethinking of the human in nonhuman geographies using two of Freud's case studies, Emmy von N. and the Wolfman. *Transactions of the Institute of British Geographers*, 39(2), 224–36.

Proudfoot, J. 2010. Interviewing enjoyment, or the limits of discourse. *The Professional Geographer*, 62(4), 507–18.

Reddick, J. 2003. Translator's preface. *Beyond the Pleasure Principle and Other Writings*. Harmondsworth: Penguin, xxxi–xxxvi.

Robbins, P. and Moore, S. 2012. Ecological anxiety disorder: diagnosing the politics of the Anthropocene. *Cultural Geographies*, 20(1), 3–19.

Rose, G. 1997. Situating knowledges: positionality, reflexivities and other tactics. *Progress in Human Geography*, 21(3), 305–20.

Sibley, D. 1995. *Geographies of Exclusion: Society and Difference in the West*. London: Routledge.

Thien, D. 2005. Intimate distances: considering questions of "us," in *Emotional Geographies*, edited by Joyce Davidson, Liz Bondi and Mick Smith. Aldershot: Ashgate, 191–204.

Thomas, M.E. 2007. The implications of psychoanalysis for qualitative methodology: the case of interviews and narrative data analysis. *The Professional Geographer*, 59(4), 537–46.

Thomas, M.E. 2010. Introduction. *The Professional Geographer*, 62(4), 478–82.

Thrift, N. 2004. Intensities of feeling: towards a spatial politics of affect. *Geografiska Annaler, Series B*, 86(1), 57–78.

Verhaeghe, P. 2001. *Beyond Gender: From Subject to Drive*. New York: The Other Press.

Winnicott, D.W. 1971 [1991]. *Playing and Reality*. London: Routledge.

Žižek, S. 1989. *The Sublime Object of Ideology*. New York: Verso.

Žižek, S. 1997. *The Plague of Fantasies*. New York: Verso.

Žižek, S. 1999. *The Ticklish Subject: The Absent Centre of Political Ontology*. New York: Verso.

Žižek, S. 2008. *Violence*. New York: Picador.

Žižek, S. 2011. *Living in the End Times*. New York: Verso.

PART I
Histories and Practices

Chapter 1

Freud in the Field: Psychoanalysis, Fieldwork and Geographical Imaginations in Interwar Cambridge

Laura Cameron and John Forrester

A great wave of enthusiasm for psychoanalysis had struck the University of Cambridge. Arthur George Tansley, having resigned from the Cambridge Botany School in 1923 to study with Freud in Vienna, was one of the chief fomenters. This was a productive moment for psychoanalytic applications in numerous fields and key insights in economics, psychology, English, and anthropology can be traced to Freudian inspiration (Forrester and Cameron forthcoming). Can we say the same for the discipline of geography in its Cambridge context? On the face of it, the answer seems a pretty safe "no." After "generally lamentable beginnings" with the first lecturer Henry Guillemard resigning when pressed to actually lecture (Stoddart 1989: 25), the early teaching focus was physical geography. Founding figures of Cambridge geography like Antarctic scientist Frank Debenham and historical geographer H.C. Darby (the first PhD in 1931) exhibited little interest in psychoanalysis.

And yet, one of the first people to introduce psychoanalysis to Cambridge students was Tansley who taught plant geography in the Natural Sciences Tripos *and* in the Geographical Tripos during the height of psychoanalytic fervor. The father of Tansley's psychoanalytic colleague, James Strachey, was Sir Richard Strachey who had been integral, as President of the Royal Geographical Society, in the establishment of the first lectureship in geography at Cambridge in 1888 (Stoddart 1989: 24). Such details are just beginnings to the story. Drawing from a larger study, *Freud in Cambridge*, this chapter considers the reception of psychoanalysis amongst Cambridge staff and students in the years before and after the Great War, and argues that geographical methods and concepts taken for granted by contemporary researchers such as "participant observation" and the "ecosystem" have, if not direct links to psychoanalysis (and Cambridge geography), collateral descent.

Besides unearthing some new kin for present day psychoanalytical geographers, this chapter diverges from a standard history of psychoanalysis in at least two important ways. First, in departing from the historiography of British psychoanalysis centering on London and the institution-building work of Ernest Jones, our story involves a non-standard cast of characters, including non-professional psychoanalysts. Secondly, in locating psychoanalytic interest in a key center of the natural sciences we defamiliarize the present understanding that psychoanalysis belongs within the realm of culture, a tool of the human geographer only. Our story is a jolting reminder of a time when psychoanalysis was also recognized as a science, when it was a marker of scientific modernity to be psychoanalyzed and when a dream, as a matter of course, had the serious potential to change an academic's life.

Cambridge Before and After the First World War

Geography made its disciplinary debut at the University of Cambridge in 1888. With funds from the Royal Geographical Society (RGS), the university appointed a lecturer in geography. In order to illustrate what that lecturer, once selected, should be teaching, the new RGS President, Sir Richard Strachey, delivered four public lectures on "Principles of Geography," dealing mainly with "external nature" and drawing on his considerable knowledge of physical geography and the history of geography. However, he also referred to nature's influence on the development of "man's emotional, intellectual, and moral faculties" (Strachey 1888: 290).

> A knowledge of the relations that subsist among living beings, which is a direct result of geographical discovery, shows us man's true place in nature; our intercourse with other races of men in other countries teaches those lessons needed to overthrow the narrow prejudices of class, colour, and opinion, which bred in isolated societies, and nourished with the pride that springs from ignorance, have too often led to crimes the more lamentable because perpetrated by men capable of the most exalted virtue.

Figure 1.1 Some members of the Torres Strait Expedition: Haddon (seated) with (l–r) Rivers, Seligman, Ray, and Wilkin. Mabuiag, 1898

Source: Reproduced by permission of the University of Cambridge Museum of Archaeology and Anthropology (N.23035.ACH2).

Although physical geography was strongly emphasized, geography teaching early on included the subject of anthropogeography (the scientific study of human geographical distribution and relationship to environment) taught for two decades by Alfred Cort Haddon, himself a member of the Royal Geographical Society from 1897 (RGS 1921).

Famously, Haddon (see Figure 1.1) led the 1898 Cambridge Anthropological Expedition to the Torres Straits. The event was formative for Cambridge *and* British anthropology, involving the development of field methods, with Haddon at this time introducing to anthropology the standard geographical survey term "field-work" (Herle and Rouse 1998: 17; in geographical usage, see, for instance, Pringle 1893: 139). His companions included W.H.R. Rivers, a Cambridge psychologist who would find his interests diverted to anthropology through the experience, and C.S. Myers, a former student of

Rivers's who would later share Rivers's interest in Freudian psychoanalysis. Another was Charles Seligman, member of the RGS from 1906, whose subsequent fieldwork would also involve studies of dreams and the unconscious. Funded mainly by the university with smaller donations from the RGS and other societies (Herle and Rouse 1998: 58), Haddon envisaged the expedition as a "multidisciplinary project encompassing anthropology in its broadest sense" (ibid.: 3) and, once safely returned, Haddon provided the RGS with a public demonstration of film, phonograph recordings and lantern slides from the expedition (ibid.: 129) and would seek from its members continued support for further investigations in Melanesia (Haddon 1906). For Rivers, the Cambridge Torres Straits Expedition had initially been a project in comparative psychology, yet his intensive methods led him to address and resolve problems in anthropology and geography. The soberly qualified psychological findings were most straightforwardly interpreted as demonstrating little if any difference between the perceptual capacities of white Europeans and Torres Strait Islanders. These probably did form the starting-point for the anti-racism or non-racism, particularly of Rivers and Myers, and thus demonstrated a clear-cut estrangement from the evolutionist assumptions of Victorian anthropology (Richards 1998: 136–57, 1997).

Teaching virtually ceased during the war of 1914–18 as Cambridge became a site for regiments to be drilled and housed, and libraries were transformed into hospitals. Rivers turned immediately from ethnography to the treatment of the war neuroses, most famously those of officers at the Craiglockhart Hospital. In parallel with this activity, Rivers had been seized with scientific enthusiasm for Freud's theory of dreams, his interest intensifying markedly as he worked on his own dreams (Forrester 2006: 65–85). Following the armistice, Rivers gave 19 lectures at Cambridge on "Instinct and the Unconscious," published as a book of the same name in 1920. He also lectured on dreams; after his sudden death in June 1922, this lecture series was published by his literary executor Elliot Smith as *Conflict and Dream* (1923). Although in both books Rivers revealed himself in new and unprecedented ways, *Conflict and Dream* was especially revealing of Rivers's internal world, since he followed Freud's example in both spirit and letter in using principally his own dreams (with settings and associations from Cambridge furnishing significant aspects of the dream material) to examine critically Freud's theory of dreams. As emboldened students like Harry Godwin "tried our hand at dream analysis and collected our own instances of the 'Psychopathology of everyday life'" (1985: 30), Cambridge dreaming Freudian-style was in full swing.

Field Imaginations

The Making of Participant Observation

W.H.R. Rivers's premature death in 1922 inflicted considerable distress on his students and friends. Rivers had lectured alongside geographers in Indian Civil Service Studies, but his specific contribution to the discipline of geography had much to do with his innovations in "intensive" field methodology. Haddon had been involved in "the intensive study of limited areas" (Herle and Rouse 1998: 15–16) before the 1898 expedition, but credit for the full development of participant observation is often ascribed to a transmission of thought and practice from Rivers to Bronislaw Malinowski.

Participant observation, in which the ethnologist herself becomes a research tool and has explicit interaction and involvement with those people being studied, figures prominently in human geography textbooks on method (for example, Clifford and Valentine 2003; Flowerdew and Martin 2005), yet, as to its origins, most geographers likely would suggest it is an example of recent interdisciplinary borrowing from anthropology. Furthermore, such texts do not link psychoanalysis to the history of fieldwork (though Ian Cook provides a suggestive passage in which he recommends recording dreams in a diary; Flowerdew and Martin 2005: 180). Indeed, if at all, Freud or psychoanalysis explicitly comes up in such methods textbooks only in relation to feminist and textual analysis. In this section, we highlight not only participant observation's psychoanalytical connections, but also its more geographical associations through the work of Rivers.

There are two mythicized founding dates for social anthropology in Britain: the Torres Straits Expedition of 1898 and the publication in 1922 of both Malinowski's *Argonauts of the Western Pacific* and Radcliffe-Brown's *The Andaman Islanders*. The second of these dates also marks the aforementioned death of the leading anthropologist of the period 1898–1922: W.H.R. Rivers, whose career began with the Torres Straits Expedition. Another way of putting this is to claim that what was started in 1898—the intensive fieldwork approach to understanding "primitive" cultures—came to fruition with the publication of two monographs by practitioners who had learned the lessons of the Torres Straits program and put them into practice in the 1910s, and were thus as a consequence able to produce perfectly formed exemplars of intensive fieldwork and the understanding based upon it.

This account places all the emphasis upon method: that ideal of the lone researcher going out, immersing in one very specific native culture, becoming a "participant observer" (a mid-1920s term) and reporting back. Part of the eventual prestige of social anthropology would come to rest on the sheer arduousness of the labor involved and hardships undergone in this process and upon the fact that no other researchers were involved or had ever been there; the new fieldwork ideal was strangely solitary and naïvely empiricist in its conception of professional expertise. Yet there was an accompanying *conceptual* transformation in the period 1898–1922: where the center of gravity of anthropology had been evolutionism and religion, the new social anthropology was non-evolutionist (because synchronic structural-functionalist) and preoccupied with social structure and order. The key area for understanding social structure became "kinship," investigated using the "genealogical method," what Stocking calls the "the major methodological innovation associated with the Cambridge School" (1995: 112), developed in Rivers's work with the Todas, the Solomon Islands, Melanesia, and Polynesia during the first decade of the twentieth century. A new ideal was promoted in the section Rivers wrote for the Royal Anthropological Institute's updated 1912 edition of *Notes and Queries* (Urry 1972: 45–57) contrasting "survey work" with what was now required—"intensive work":

> A typical piece of intensive work is one in which the worker lives for a year or more among a community of perhaps four or five hundred people and studies every detail of their life and culture; in which he comes to know every member of the community personally; in which he is not content with generalized information, but studies every feature of life and custom in concrete detail and by means of the vernacular language (Rivers 1913: 7).

In these *Notes*, Rivers set out a "concrete" field methodology, giving license to the "model of the lone field ethnographer, 'immersing' himself in 'the natives'' way of life" (Buzard 2005: 9); Malinowski would bring these *Notes* to Papua New Guinea where he would conduct ethnographical fieldwork from 1915–18, receiving in addition detailed instructions from Seligman on how to "observe those facts relevant to Psycho-Analysis" (Malinowski unpublished) as well as "a short account of dreams" (Stocking 1986: 31). Alongside Rivers, Haddon and Myers, the chief contributor to the 1912 edition of *Notes and Queries* was the scholar of ancient geography, James Linton Myres, life member of the RGS since 1896. Following a section in which Myers and Haddon discussed the recording of emotions ("a snap-shot camera will be found invaluable", Freire-Marreco and Myres 1912: 181) and gestures, *Notes and Queries* reprinted the RGS official scheme for the transcription of place-names (1912: 186–92). Myres provided instructions regarding geographical topics such as "path-finding," "landmarks," and "modes of travel" (98–101). At the same time as Rivers was preparing his "General Account of Method" for *Notes and Queries*, which suggested that native terms should be used whenever possible, he was also involved with Myres, Haddon, and Sydney Ray (the language specialist member of the 1898 expedition) in discussions with the RGS on the geographical nomenclature for the Melanesian Islands (Thurn et al. 1912: 464–8). Rivers's formal presentation to the RGS in March 1911, illustrated with several specially prepared maps, was published in *The Geographical Journal* in May 1912 (Rivers 1912: 458–64). His critical examination of naming practice argued for the use of native names for practical and political reasons but stressed also the confusions that can result. Intense fieldwork in one area requires attention to geographical specificity as sometimes, for instance, a name for a local district might be the same name for the island as a whole. He appealed to the RGS, most sensibly in collaboration with Royal Anthropological Institute, to take action.

> The modern movement in ethnology attempts to portray native institutions by giving concrete accounts of things as they are from the native point of view ... Such a concrete method will come more and more into use in the future, but such concreteness can result in nothing but confusion unless native names, including those of places, are used in accurate and well-defined senses (459–60).

Though he mapped out the terrain of participant observation, Rivers never fully entered on it himself. Always aware of issues of objectivity and the interests of the observer, he stood on the verge of recognizing that the observer's implication in the scene of inquiry was constitutive of the field of the human sciences. In the field of psychotherapy, he hoped to escape from Freud's recognition that in both dreams and the neuroses, there was no avoiding the implication of the subject's own desires and the observer's relationship with his patients—indeed, this implication was being turned around by Freud into the foundation stone of the theory and therapy of the "transference neuroses." As Buzard (2005: 9–10) astutely notes,

> [A]uthority derives from the demonstration not so much of some finally achieved "insideness" in the alien state, but rather from the demonstration of an *outsider's insideness*. Anthropology's Participant Observer, whose aim was a "simulated membership" or "membership without commitment to membership" in the visited culture, went on to become perhaps the most recognizable (and institutionally embedded) avatar of this distinctively modern variety of heroism and prestige.

With Rivers's sudden death, the program of rapprochement between psychoanalysis and anthropology that he had begun was unexpectedly transformed by his replacement as the intellectual leader of British anthropology by Bronislaw Malinowski who, despite his manifest and self-declared great debt to Freud, would later be recalled more for his *rejection* rather than incorporation of psychoanalysis on behalf of the discipline he did so much to professionalize. Both Rivers and Malinowski repeatedly acknowledged the "genius" of Freud; both Rivers and Malinowski mounted fierce critiques, based on their ethnographic expertise, of key features of psychoanalysis. Their contemporaries, for their own reasons, heard only the criticisms, not the admiration. Malinowski's field diary from the Trobriand Islands (1915–18), published only in 1967, was no mere record of events but what he called "[a] location of the mainsprings of my life" (1967: 104, quoted in Stocking 1986: 23); it revealed his innermost feelings—fears, anger, love, sexual anxieties, and his dreams—and is best read as an "account of the central psychological drama of Malinowski's life—an extended crisis of identity in which certain Freudian undertones were obvious to Malinowski himself" (Stocking 1986: 23). For Malinowski, following the ghost of Rivers, the novel method of participant observation required the observer to pass through the phases of participation and return, the going out and the coming back, capable of rendering that transmutation of his very being which he had undergone not only into objective data but also into a body of theory. The imperial side of the project was not new and nor was it given up by the new practitioners. What Malinowski added was a Freudian obverse, a requirement that the interior and the exterior be mapped onto each other.

Roots of the Ecosystem

The scene is Vienna, March 1922. Fifty-one-year-old A.G. Tansley, FRS, following an increasingly well-trodden trail between Cambridge and Freud's couch, begins analysis. Reporting to a colleague in London, Freud describes him as "a nice type of the English scientist. It might be a gain to win him over to our science at the loss of botany" (Paskauskas 1993: 468).

Freud, the founder of psychoanalysis; Tansley, the founder of British ecology—about to undertake several months of psychoanalytic dialogue. Although undoubtedly it was Tansley's dreams and unconscious they were exploring, Tansley recalled that theirs was a relationship of equals (Cameron and Forrester 1999: 64–100). With words like "dynamic" and "complex" being key terms for each of these new sciences, we might well wonder how Freudian ideas might have overlapped, interlocked with Tansley's ecology.

Would Tansley's creation of the concept of the "ecosystem" in 1935 have any connection with psychoanalysis? The answers may be neither direct nor linear but the questions become more promising as we approach the couch and begin to trace Tansley's life geography.

Tansley first came to Cambridge as an undergraduate in the early 1890s. He recalled that, besides advancing his knowledge of botany, zoology, geology, and physiology, he took part in the "usual interminable discussions on the universe—on philosophy, psychology, religion, politics, and sex" (Cameron 1999: 6). At Cambridge, even before the First World War, Tansley had been sparking interest in psychoanalysis amongst botany students such as Margot Hume and E.P. Farrow by mentioning Freud in his lectures. Farrow, whose own dream led to pioneering studies of rabbit attack on Breckland, would correspond with Freud and publish a book on self-analysis (Cameron and Forrester 2000). In the post-war Geographical Tripos, teaching alongside Tansley, was geophysicist Harold Jeffreys, Tansley's colleague in an informal psychoanalytical seminar that would meet in Cambridge in 1925 (ibid.). A month after Rivers's death, Tansley played an important role in the Symposium on the Relations of Complex and Sentiment for the 1922 Meeting of the British Psychological Society. In contrast to the position papers of Rivers and Alexander Shand (whose language of "sentiments" was the homegrown English competitor with the vocabulary of "complexes"), Tansley argued that "complex" was a key connecting term for normal and abnormal psychology and should not be excluded from the former field.

Like Rivers, Tansley's intense interest in Freud began with a nocturnal epiphany. Somewhere in London during the First World War, Tansley dreamt that he was standing in a clearing, holding a rifle, surrounded by "savages" (Cameron and Forrester 1999: 65). It was, as he would later make very clear, one of the major turning points in his life. From the self-interpretation of this dream came his interest in psychoanalysis and the desire to write the 1920 *The New Psychology and its Relation to Life*, a bestseller reprinted 10 times in four years (see Figure 1.2). Swamped with requests for advice he felt he had little authority to give, the dream journey took a radical turn in 1923 with his resignation from his Cambridge job to undertake further study with Freud in Vienna. During this time of upheaval, however, Tansley and his young colleague Harry Godwin continued experiments at the Cambridgeshire National Trust reserve, Wicken Fen. Their work perhaps affords us a glimpse of one of professional ecology's resonant field sites (Cameron 2013) at a time when dream analysis and vegetational analysis might work hand in hand.

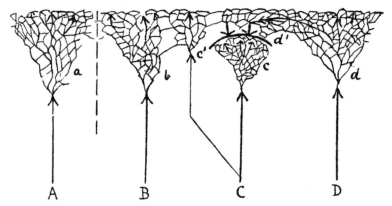

FIG. 8.—RELATIONS OF DIFFERENT COMPLEXES TO ONE ANOTHER AND TO THE
ACTIVATING INSTINCTS (SECTIONAL VIEW).   A, instinct activating complex
a which is segregated in a compartment of the mind, but in which the
mental processes and outlets are normal. B, instinct activating complex *b*
which has normal connexions with the rest of the mind.   C, instinct
activating two complexes, *c* and *c'* : *c* is repressed by *d'*, a branch of *d*,
giving rise to conflict along the curved line representing a "shell" of
repression : the energy of C, having no escape through *c*, finds a partial
outlet through the weak substituted complex *c'*.   D, instinct activating
complex *d*, a branch of which, *d'*, uses part of the energy derived from D
to repress the complex *c*.

Figure 1.2   Tansley's relations of different complexes (1920)
Source: Tansley 1920: 51.

At Wicken Fen, Godwin and Tansley were investigating vegetational succession:
the idea (developed in part by the American, F.E. Clements) that natural
vegetation, when left to itself, progresses from "pioneer communities" such as
fen, to "climax communities," such as oakwoods. In this model, mature normal
vegetation existed in isolation from humans, but Tansley was not willing to
apply this notion to his beloved English countryside, a landscape which was
largely, in his new coinage, "anthropogenic" (1923: 50–51; meaning produced
by man). Instead, after setting aside plots (the first in 1923, see Figure 1.3), they
identified deflected successions due to human cutting activity, "plagioseres," that
deviated from the normal course of vegetational succession. The "plagioclimax"
with its characteristic species could re-enter normality when cutting ceased. But
at Wicken Fen, and elsewhere in the British Empire, appropriate management
for Tansley did not entail ending human intervention; the new ecological
experts aimed to locate and control the deflecting factors which produced the
vegetational types that they judged to be desirable (Cameron 1999: 13–15, 18).

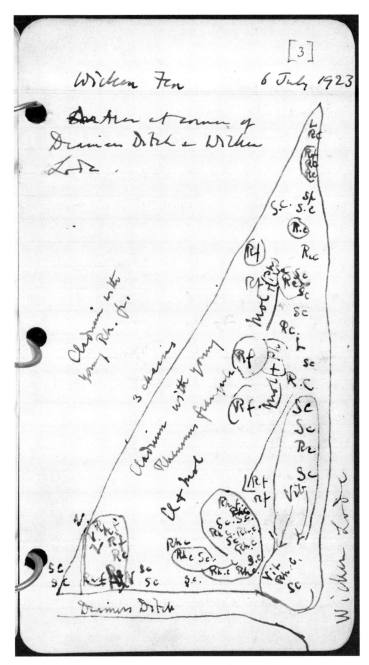

Figure 1.3   Sketch of "Godwin Triangle" by Tansley (1923)

Source: Cambridge University Library: M.S. Tansley: B.38: f.3r.

In 1927, Tansley returned to what Godwin referred to as the "mother subject" of ecology, accepting a Chair in Botany at Oxford. But he was still preoccupied with psychology. Introducing a paper for the Magdalen Philosophy Club in 1932 with the admission that he didn't know if he was "regarded primarily as a biologist or as a psychologist by my fellow members of this club" (Tansley 2002: 614), Tansley proceeded to outline his scheme for approaching the gap between psychology and biology. Here Tansley's concept of mind is an "interwoven plexus of moving material ... a more or less ordered system or rather a system of systems ... acting and reacting" (2002: 619–20), its ontology bearing intriguing resemblances to the concept of "ecosystem" he would describe three years later in a paper entitled "The use and abuse of vegetational concepts and terms." Echoing Freud, Tansley had argued in 1920 that all life, including mental life, was dominated by the need to discharge energy, aiming towards an equilibrium state. Like the mind, an ecosystem aims at equilibrium: its components, both organic and inorganic, maintain the system through their interaction. In his understanding of "positions of equilibrium," Tansley was modern (and Freudian) in stressing how rarely, if ever, the stable state was achieved: "on the contrary they contain many elements of instability and are very vulnerable to apparently small changes in the factor-complex" (Tansley 1939: vi).

The master factor—for maintenance and disturbance of nature—was man. "Regarded as an exceptionally powerful biotic factor which increasingly upsets the equilibrium of preexisting ecosystems and eventually destroys them, at the same time forming new ones of a very different nature, human activity find its proper place in ecology" (Tansley 1935: 303). Wicken Fen, for instance, contained abnormal successions created by man, but in the study of ecology—as in Freudian analysis—one could study the disturbed to study mechanisms at work in the normal: "anthropogenic ecosystems differ from those developed independently of man. But the essential formative processes of the vegetation are the same, however the factors initiating them are directed" (ibid.: 304). Fieldwork here entwined with dreamwork. In his obituary for Freud written for the Royal Society, Tansley wrote: "The great importance of Freud's work on dreams lies in the fact that in it he was able to demonstrate for the first time the principles and mechanisms he had discovered in neurotic minds at work also in a perfectly normal activity of the healthy mind. This led the way to psychological constructions of universal validity" (Tansley 1939–41: 260).

An enthusiastic review of Tansley's *Practical Plant Ecology* in *The Geographical Journal* declared that "the essentials of plant ecology are a necessary part of geographical study" (B. 1924: 259). A dynamic relationship existed between formative concepts in ecology and psychoanalysis, extending to the new role of the ecologist as the expert who might work to stabilize vulnerable systems. The countryside was "unbalanced" (Tansley 1939: 142) and required special care. If the components of life were inside the ecosystem, so were the seeds of its own destruction.

Conclusion

Reading these accounts of Freudian fieldworkers, a key difference between them and Freud becomes glaringly apparent. While Tansley and particularly Rivers roamed in the style of European adventurers, taking full advantage of the opportunities supplied by British imperial hegemony, truly putting a girdle round about the earth, Freud was comparatively less mobile, voluntarily chained to his medical practice, his family, and his consulting room. The Freudian adventure is a "*voyage autour de ma chambre*." Yet in an important sense, Rivers and Tansley can also be seen as attempting to apply Freudian insights to their respective fields, in both disciplinary and physical senses, i.e. Wicken Fen as a suggestive "field." As Naylor, quoting De Bont, notes: place "plays a role in orienting the scientist towards a particular type of research and to a particular use of the spaces at his disposal," such that they "can be led in various directions depending on the 'ecologies' in which they work" (Naylor 2005: 3). Haddon's 1898 expedition had enormous and lasting resonance, its methodological innovations identified with the "Cambridge School" rippling beyond British anthropology—even, perhaps most remarkably, into a local nursery school. Geoffrey Pyke, co-founder of the Malting House School (1924–9), a Cambridge enterprise based on psychoanalytic principles, maintained that the children should be free to "discover the human world as an anthropologist discovers Torres Islanders [*sic*]" (Pyke 1925: unpublished).

Acknowledgements

We thank Michael Young for making unpublished material by Bronislaw Malinowski available to us. The "Roots of the Ecosystem" section reworks and updates material published in Laura's essay, "Ecosystems" (2004).

References

B., R.N.R. 1924. Reviewed work(s): practical plant ecology by A.G. Tansley. *The Geographical Journal*, 63(3), 259.

Buzard, J. 2005. *Disorienting Fiction: The Autoethnographic Work of Nineteenth-Century British Novels*. Princeton, New Jersey: Princeton University Press.

Cameron, L. 1999. Histories of disturbance. *Radical History Review*, 74, 2–24.

Cameron, L. 2004. Ecosystems, in *Patterned Ground: Entanglements of Nature and Culture*, edited by Stephan Harrison, Steve Pile and Nigel Thrift. London: Reaktion Press, 55–7.

Cameron, L. 2013. Resources of hope: Wicken Fen stories of anthropogenic nature. *Cambridge Anthropology*, 31(1), 105–18.

Cameron, L. and Forrester, J. 1999. A nice type of the English scientist: Tansley and Freud. *History Workshop Journal*, 48, 64–100.

Cameron, L. and Forrester, J. 2000. Tansley's psychoanalytic network: an episode out of the early history of psychoanalysis in England. *Psychoanalysis and History*, 2(2), 189–256.

Clifford, N. and Valentine, G. (eds) 2003. *Key Methods in Geography*. London: Sage.

Flowerdew, R. and Martin, D. (eds) 2005. *Methods in Human Geography: A Guide for Students Doing a Research Project*. Second Edition. Harlow, UK: Pearson.

Forrester, J. 2006. Remembering and forgetting Freud in early twentieth century dreams. *Science in Context*, 19(1), 65–85.

Forrester, J. and Cameron, L. forthcoming. *Freud in Cambridge*. Cambridge: Cambridge University Press.

Freire-Marreco, B. and Myres, J.L. (eds) 1912. *Notes and Queries on Anthropology*. Fourth Edition. Edited for the British Association for the Advancement of Science. London: The Royal Anthropological Institute.

Godwin, H. 1985. *Cambridge and Clare*. Cambridge: Cambridge University Press.

Haddon, A.C. 1906. A plea for the investigation of biological and anthropological distributions in melanesia. *The Geographical Journal*, 28(2), 155–63.

Herle, A. and Rouse, S. (eds) 1998. *Cambridge and the Torres Strait. Centenary Essays on the 1898 Anthropological Expedition*. Cambridge: Cambridge University Press.

Malinowski, B. 1924. "A savage myth of incest: some results of psycho-analytical theory applied in anthropological Fieldwork," unpublished section omitted from Malinowski, B. 1924. Psychoanalysis and anthropology. *Psyche*, 4, 293–332. TS of 6 pages. Malinowski Papers, Yale University Library, New Haven, II/153.

Malinowski, B. 1967. *A Diary in the Strict Sense of the Word*. New York: Harcourt, Brace & World.

Naylor, S. 2005. Introduction: historical geographies of science—places, contexts, cartographies. *British Society for the History of Science*, 38(1), 1–12.

Pringle, J.T. 1893. With the railway survey to Victoria Nyanza. *The Geographical Journal*, 2(2), 112–39.

Pyke, G. circa 1925. Draft lectures for the British Psychoanalytical Society, Pyke Papers, unpublished.

Richards, G. 1998. Getting a result: the expedition's psychological research 1898–1913, in *Cambridge and the Torres Strait*, edited by A. Herle and S. Rouse. Cambridge: Cambridge University Press, 136–57.

Richards, G. 1997. *Race, Racism and Psychology: Towards a Reflexive History*. London: Routledge.

Rivers, W.H.R. 1912. Island-names in Melanesia. *The Geographical Journal*, 39(5), 458–64.

Rivers, W.H.R. 1913. Anthropological research outside America. *Reports on the Present Condition and Future Needs of the Science of Anthropology*. Washington: Carnegie Inst. [Publication No. 200].

Royal Geographical Society, London. A list of the honorary members of the Royal Geographical Society CORRECTED TO 30th SEPTEMBER, 1921. Available at: http://www.archive.org/stream/listofhonoraryme00royauoft/listofhonoraryme00royauoft_djvu.txt [accessed: 28 February 2013].

Stocking, G.W. 1986. Anthropology and the science of the irrational: Malinowski's encounter with Freudian psychoanalysis, in *Malinowski, Rivers, Benedict and Others. Essays on Culture and Personality. History of Anthropology 4*, edited by G.W. Stocking. Madison, WI: University of Wisconsin Press, 13–49.

Stocking, G.W. 1995. *After Tylor: British Social Anthropology, 1888–1951*. Madison, WI: University of Wisconsin Press.

Stoddart, D.R. 1989. A hundred years of geography at Cambridge. *The Geographical Journal*, 155(1), 24–32.

Strachey, R. 1888. Lectures on geography, delivered before the University of Cambridge, 1888. Lecture IV, *Proceedings of the Royal Geographical Society and Monthly Record of Geography*, New Monthly Series, 10(5), 275–93.

Tansley, A.G. 1920. *The New Psychology and Its Relation to Life*. London: Allen and Unwin.

Tansley, A.G. 1923. *Practical Plant Ecology. A Guide for Beginners in Field Study of Plant Communities*. London: Allen and Unwin.

Tansley, A.G. 1935. The use and abuse of vegetational concepts and terms. *Ecology*, 16, 284–307.

Tansley, A.G. 1939. *The British Islands and their Vegetation*. Cambridge, UK: Cambridge University Press.

Tansley, A.G. 1939–41. Sigmund Freud (1856–1939). *Obituary Notices of Fellows of the Royal Society*, 3, 247–75.

Tansley, A.G. 2002. The temporal genetic series as a means of approach to philosophy. Originally written in 1932. *Ecosystems*, 5(7), 614–24.

Thurn, E.I., Corney, B.G., Haddon, A.C., Ray, S., Drew, Mr., Myres, J.L. and Rivers, W.H.R. 1912. Island-names in Melanesia: discussion. *The Geographical Journal*, 39(5), 464–8.

Urry, J. 1972. "Notes and queries on anthropology" and the development of field methods in British anthropology, 1870–1920. *Proceedings of the Royal Anthropological Institute of Great Britain and Ireland*, no. 1972, 45–57.

Chapter 2

On Freud's Geographies

Liz Bondi

Introduction

During the first quarter of the twentieth century psychoanalysis was taken up enthusiastically in the United States of America, the United Kingdom and many other parts of Europe. Sigmund Freud's (1926e/2002) essay, 'The Question of Lay Analysis' is widely cited as an important 'state of the art' account of his theory and practice of psychoanalysis in the 1920s, and is still frequently recommended as an introduction to his thinking. However, as a postscript published in 1927 explained, Freud's reason for writing the essay was not to provide an accessible introduction to his ideas, but to contribute to the defence of his 'non-medical colleague Dr Th.[eodor] Reik' against 'a charge of fraudulent medical practice' (Freud 1927a/2002: 163). In mounting this defence, Freud (1926e/2002: 155) argued that psychoanalysis should not be 'swallowed up by medicine and then be stored away in the psychiatry textbooks' and that people other than medical doctors should be able to train and practice as psychoanalysts. Although 'four-fifths of the people that I acknowledge as my students are doctors' (Freud 1926e/2002: 138), Freud was determined to defend the rights of others to train and practise as well, noting that 'lay people who are practising analysis today are not just anybody, but educated people, PhDs, teachers and individual women with a great deal of experience of life and outstanding personalities' (Freud 1926e/2002: 152). Given restrictions on women's entry to the medical profession in the early twentieth century, Freud's advocacy of lay analysis was especially important in making psychoanalysis accessible to female practitioners.

Freud suggested that medical training 'is more or less the opposite' of the kind of preparation required for practising psychoanalysis, which requires a shift 'from scientific medicine to the practical art of healing' (Freud 1926e/2002: 139). Although a 'curriculum for the analyst has yet to be created' (Freud 1927a/2002: 164), he argued that psychoanalysis should be understood as an intrinsically multidisciplinary field, preparation for which required the study of 'subjects that are far removed from medicine, and with which doctors would never come into contact: cultural history, mythology, the psychology of religion and literary studies' (Freud 1926e/2002: 154). The centrality he accorded to the psychological expression and meaning of myths, creative arts and historical events underlay his view that psychoanalysis 'cannot do without the collaboration of people trained in the humanities' (Freud 1927a/2002: 169).

As well as arguing for collaboration between psychoanalysis and non-medical academic disciplines, Freud argued for collaboration between psychoanalysis and other fields of practice. For example, he suggested that psychoanalysts and educationalists might work together in support of child development, and speculated about the possibility of investing 'money into training in analysis the social workers [...] and making them into an auxiliary force to combat cultural neuroses' (Freud 1926e/2002: 157). He insisted that psychoanalytic theory must be firmly grounded in practice, emphasizing the 'mutual dependence in psychoanalysis between healing and researching', and arguing that psychoanalytic practice is essential to the development of theory through which 'we deepen our dawning insight into human mental life' (Freud 1927a/2002: 168).

In promoting his vision of a multidisciplinary approach to psychoanalytic education and practice, Freud (1926e/2002, 1927a/2002) made no direct reference to geography as an academic discipline or field of study. Since then, compared to several other disciplines, the interface between psychoanalysis and geography has remained relatively neglected, notwithstanding this book. However, in 'The Question of Lay Analysis', Freud very clearly referenced geographic concerns in two different ways. On the one hand, his argument for lay analysis was articulated with specific reference to geographical variations in the circumstances in which psychoanalysts practised, and on the other hand, he drew attention to the value of spatial concepts to psychoanalytic theory. In this chapter I discuss both of these features of his account and use them to elaborate geographical engagements with psychoanalysis as both a body of theory and a set of practices. On the theme of geographical variations, I show how Freud assumed that psychoanalysis could develop into a universally invariant theory and practice unaffected by local circumstances. Aligning my analysis with objections to this kind of universalism, I illustrate how psychoanalysis has been shaped by the contexts in which it has developed, generating a dynamic pattern of spatial variations in the conditions in which it is practised, as well as different theoretical strands or schools that originated in particular places. Turning to the theme of spatial concepts, I endorse this aspect of Freud's geographies and illustrate how spatial thinking continues to pervade psychoanalytic thinking and practice. Indeed I argue that its reliance on spatial concepts has generated a language shared across a wide range of different post-Freudian theoretical positions. In this context I suggest that, in a variety of ways, psychoanalytic thinking appeals to and explores the construction of, and interplay between, 'interior' and 'exterior' worlds.

On Geographical Variations in Psychoanalytic Theory and Practice

How Place Matters

Freud's defence of lay analysis drew attention to differences between Austria, where, in the mid-1920s (and in common with France), the right to treat the sick was legally restricted to medical doctors, and both Germany and America where 'a sick person can elect to be treated in anyway and by anybody he likes' (Freud 1926e/2002: 95). While the original essay was prompted by the charge brought by the Viennese authorities against Dr Reik, the 1927 postscript closes with reference to the very different context of psychoanalysis in America, from where 'the most vehement rejection of lay analysis' emanated (Freud 1927a/2002: 169). Referring to this American context, Freud (1927a/2002: 169) acknowledged, 'lay analysts are responsible for a good deal of mischief and abuse of analysis, and are thereby harming patients as well as the reputation of analysis'.

Freud was clearly well aware that the conditions in which psychoanalysis was developing varied from place to place because of such factors as differences in legal frameworks and existing health-care practices. He expressed sympathy with American colleagues in relation to the specific problems they faced, but argued that their rejection of lay analysis was misguided:

> It is understandable that in their outrage they want to distance themselves from these pests [those causing 'mischief and abuse of analysis'] and to exclude lay people from participating in analysis at all. But this state of affairs is sufficient in itself to reduce the significance of their statements. For the question of lay analysis must not be decided by practical considerations alone and local conditions in America cannot by themselves be decisive for all of us (Freud 1927a/2002: 169–170).

Thus, Freud insisted that the *principle* of who should be eligible to train as an analyst should be considered and settled separately from and without reference to any 'practical' or 'local' circumstances. In so doing he sought to provide foundations for the new profession of psychoanalysis unaffected by the specificities of time and place. Put another way, while Freud recognized that geographical variations impacted on the practice of psychoanalysis in the 1920s, his vision and aspiration was that such local anomalies could be transcended, and that psychoanalysis would in the end become a profession operating in the same way everywhere in the world.

Freud's account deploys a commonplace understanding of the difference that place makes, namely as a more or less idiosyncratic local context from which universal and implicitly placeless ideas and practices need to be abstracted. Furthermore, the idea that progress might expunge significant aspects of local variability is a widespread trope of twentieth-century thought (Harvey 1989). It is closely linked to the aspirations of scientific theories and practices of many kinds, in which fundamental principles are formulated without reference to context. Universalism of this kind has been subject to criticism from a range of perspectives. For example, Donna Haraway (1988) has argued that knowledge is necessarily 'situated', in the sense of arising from a particular perspective or location, and therefore as bearing the impress of its originating context. In another register, Bent Flyvbjerg (2001) has argued that a key characteristic of the social sciences is that they address concerns that lose their meaning if abstracted from real, context-specific examples. Focusing more specifically on spatial variations, Doreen Massey (2005) argues that, far from being contingent anomalies, they are constitutive of an enormous range of phenomena.

In what follows I echo these criticisms of universalism. With reference to the legal parameters of psychoanalytic practice and traditions of psychoanalytic theory, I show how, in the decades since Freud's defence of lay analysis, psychoanalysis has continued to be characterized by geographical variations. I argue that these variations are far from being contingent anomalies but are better understood as intrinsic to psychoanalysis.

Geographical Variations in the Legal Parameters of Psychoanalytic Practice

The legal parameters within which psychoanalysts practice have become more rather than less geographically variable in the decades since Freud's original intervention on the question of lay analysis. During his lifetime, positions on the question of lay analysis hardened: while in Europe psychoanalytic training remained open to those without medical qualifications, in the USA psychoanalysis was effectively captured by the medical profession, and by the mid-1930s had become institutionalized as a psychiatric specialism accessible only to qualified medical doctors. This situation created a rift within the international community of psychoanalysis, which was resolved only when, in the 1980s, the American Psychoanalytic Society finally opened training routes for those other than medical doctors (Wallerstein 1998).

The legal framing of psychoanalytic practice has been further complicated by the proliferation of forms of psychotherapy inspired or informed by psychoanalysis. These have generated a plethora of titles, which are subject to different forms of, and requirements for, licensing and regulation in different places. For example, the relatively new title of 'counsellor/counselor' is subject to different licensing arrangements in different states of the USA and provinces of Canada.

In the UK, psychoanalysts, psychotherapists and counsellors remain unregulated, meaning that there is no legal restriction on the use of these titles. However, since 2009, titles including the term 'psychologist' have acquired legal protection in the UK. The discrepancy between the position of, say, a psychoanalyst and a psychologist has arisen as an outcome of a round of discussions about regulation initiated in 2001 when the then (Labour) UK government announced its intention to regulate all of what it called the 'psychological therapies'. After much debate, the route for regulation was specified as the Health Professions Council, which had been created in 2001 as a successor body to the Council for Professions Allied to Medicine (and which has recently been renamed the Health and Care Professions Council). Bodies representing psychoanalysts, psychotherapists and counsellors were united in their opposition to regulation via a body so strongly influenced by medicine, but the main body representing psychologists accepted the proposal. In these circumstances, the regulation of psychologists proceeded while that for psychoanalysts, psychotherapists and counsellors was delayed while, without any shift in government policy, further discussions took place. Then, in 2010, a general election ushered in a new Coalition government and the plan to extend regulation by the Health Professions Council to apply to psychoanalysts and others was abandoned.

This recent British story, and the national and sub-national variations in licensing arrangements in North America, illustrates how laws and regulations are always geographically framed (even when they are international in scope). The British story also shows how laws and regulations covering practices including psychoanalysis are often influenced by highly contingent local circumstances, such as the electoral fortunes of parties, which themselves often make policy commitments in response to quite specific pressures. At the same time, what happens in one place influences what happens elsewhere. Freud (1926e/2002: 143) recognized this himself, suggesting that, if it became impossible for non-medical analysts to practice in Austria, 'they will probably emigrate to Germany' with consequences for the newly formed training institutes in Vienna and Berlin. In relation to the British struggle over regulation, opponents of the proposals for the regulation of psychoanalysts by the Health Professions Council drew on experiences in other countries to make their case (Parker and Revelli, 2008) and no doubt others elsewhere will draw on the British experience to inform future debates and developments.

Geographies of Psychoanalytic Theory

Accounts of the works of major psychoanalytic thinkers often draw attention to the impact of their particular life stories on their thought, pointing, for example, to connections between the multiple tragedies of Melanie Klein's life and her emphasis on destructive psychic forces (Grosskurth 1986), and between Ronald Laing's highly controlling mother and his concept of the schizophrenic family (Burston 1996). It is a small step from this to consider the cultural shaping of psychoanalysis, for example the influence of anti-semitism on Freud's work (Gay 1989). Of course, such cultural influences are themselves intrinsically geographical.

Prior to the First World War, psychoanalysis was attracting international interest and was travelling well beyond its original central European origins. In the 1930s, the geography of psychoanalysis was massively impacted by the rise of Nazism and the outbreak of the Second World War, which decimated psychoanalysis in Austria, Hungary and Germany, and dispersed refugee psychoanalysts from central Europe around the world. Political ideologies, cultural conditions and the meeting of people from different backgrounds in particular places determined not only whether psychoanalysis could be practised at all, but also how it developed as a body of theory and practice (Roazen 2001). For example, in the UK, after Freud's death and during the Second World War, the future of British psychoanalysis was deeply influenced by the Controversial Discussions, in which two immigrant Jewish women, Anna Freud and Melanie Klein, led impassioned debate about their respective claims to be the true inheritors of Sigmund Freud's psychoanalytic theory (King and Steiner 1991). In war-torn London, their conflict was moderated by women and men from the majority Christian culture, including Sylvia Payne, D.W. Winnicott and James Strachey, who argued for, and eventually achieved, a compromise in which three training divisions (Kleinian, Freudian and Independent) secured recognition and arrangements for co-existence within the British Psychoanalytic Society.

Language has also been an important influence on the evolution of psychoanalysis. Translation between languages has been of critical importance but is never a neutral, transparent process. For many decades *The Standard Edition* has been the most widely used English-language version of Freud's original, German-language papers. However, some of the choices made by James Strachey in his capacity as chief editor and primary translator of Freud's works have generated ongoing debate and discussion. For example, Alan Bance, who translated 'The Question of Lay Analysis', for a new English-language translation edited by Adam Phillips, has contributed to criticism of Strachey's use of 'Ego' and 'Id', insisting instead that Freud's own choice of colloquial terms 'obliged [him] to use the terms "I" and "It"' (Freud 2002: 158n3). The challenges of translation between languages have themselves prompted debates about psychoanalytic concepts. In this context, the dominance of English has led to relatively few psychoanalytic papers written in other languages being translated into English, depriving the English-language literature of a potential source of enrichment.

Since Freud's death, different 'schools' of psychoanalysis have developed, broadly aligned with national states or geographical regions, including the British school of object relations, the North American school of self-psychology, the French Lacanian school and the Latin American school of analytic field theory. These schools have not remained bound by national boundaries but have themselves travelled, shaped by and shaping cultural and political circumstances they encountered and in which they became embedded. Philip Cushman (1996) has explored one highly influential example by tracing the interplay between American psychotherapy and American consumerism. On his account, the self-psychology of Heinz Kohut, who had arrived in the USA from Austria in 1940, and the object relations theory of the British psychoanalyst D.W. Winnicott, both foregrounded a theorization of the self as an internal world 'peopled' by internal objects. Cushman's key point concerns how, in the American context, the spaces between these internal objects became crucial, such that the self came to be understood in terms of lacks, gaps and emptiness. For Cushman, the idea of the self as an empty vessel or landscape to be populated in some way fitted perfectly with the logic of consumerism in which ceaseless acquisition promised but forever failed to fill these internal voids.

The local shaping of psychoanalytic theory has also been explored in relation to a number of other geographical contexts. For example, Gavin Miller (2008) has argued that classic Scottish contributions to psychoanalytic theory – including the work of Ian Suttie, Ronald Fairbairn, Hugh Crichton-Miller, Ronald Laing and John Sutherland – bear the impress of a distinctively Scottish philosophical and theological tradition. Miller emphasized the importance of communion or fellowship within Scottish religious, cultural and intellectual life, which he has traced through the writings of Scottish psychoanalysts and their transfer to other places. Developing this theme, David Fergusson (2012) has pointed to connections between the work of the Scottish philosopher John Macmurray and the Scottish psychoanalysts Ian Suttie and Ronald Fairbairn, especially in their emphasis on personal relationships. He has shown how Macmurray applied ideas inflected by the psychoanalytic writings of Suttie and Fairbairn to relationships between professional experts and their patients, clients or pupils, and how Suttie and Fairbairn in their respective contributions to what became the British object relations tradition in psychoanalysis drew on a distinctly Scottish strand of thinking, which has been described as 'personal relations theory' (Clarke 2006).

Spatial Thinking In and Beyond Freud's Exposition of Psychoanalysis

Freud's Spatial Metaphors

In 'The Question of Lay Analysis', Freud drew attention to the importance of a spatial perspective for psychoanalytic theory and it is to this aspect of his geographies that I now turn. He appealed to 'the spatial relationship of "in front" and "behind", "superficial" and "profound"' (Freud 1926e/2002: 105) to describe what he called 'the structure of the mental apparatus we have formed during our analytical studies' (Freud 1926e/2002: 104). Where it might have passed unnoticed, he chose to emphasize his reliance on spatial thinking:

> let us imagine that the I [Ego] is the outer layer of the mental apparatus, the It [Id], modified by the influence of the external world (by reality). You can see from this how seriously we in psychoanalysis take spatial concepts. The I for us really is the surface, the It the deeper layer – as seen from outside naturally (Freud 1926e/2002: 106).

Thus, although Freud viewed differences between places as local idiosyncrasies that detracted from the rational development of psychoanalysis, he found abstract ideas about space essential to his theory, and he acknowledged that the position of the knower matters; what is on the surface and what lies deep inside depends upon one's position.

Freud (1901b/2002) conceptualized the unconscious as timeless; the unconscious cannot forget and 'knows no time limit'. Unconscious material persists, liable to return regardless of the passage of time, for example in the unremitting immediacy of traumatic flashbacks, and the reappearance, sometimes in new forms, of apparently long-forgotten symptoms. In Freud's formulation, the unconscious does not conform to the rules of Euclidean space any more than it does time. But the language of space offers what George Lakoff and Mark Johnson (1980) have called orientational metaphors, which they link to our bodily experience of negotiating our physical environments. Freud understood mental life to be biologically grounded and conveyed a strong sense of the centrality of embodied existence to the unconscious. Thus, resonating with Lakoff and Johnson's (1980) account of 'metaphors we live by', Freud's use of spatial metaphors in 'The Question of Lay Analysis' and elsewhere, reflected his understanding of the embodied materiality of mental life.

A Common Spatial Language?

A feature of psychoanalytic theory from Freud onwards is that it offers a way of thinking about how what originates outside our minds, including other people (or parts of them), the cultures into which we are born, and the material entities that surround us, gets inside, and how what is inside gets outside. Psychoanalysis understands the boundary between interior and exterior to be unstable, porous and mutable. Boundaries, and the distinction between inside and outside, are intrinsically spatial ideas. Not surprisingly, therefore, post-Freudian psychoanalytic writers have followed his example in using richly spatial language. For example, within Anglophone psychoanalysis, much of Winnicott's development of psychoanalytic theory focussed on the dynamic relationship between infant and primary carer (which he assumed would be the infant's mother) for which he utilized spatial concepts. These included his idea of the 'facilitative environment', which situates the needs of a person (archetypically the infant) in relation to a surrounding landscape of provision, the qualities of which support or undermine the person's development and flourishing (Winnicott 1965). He also introduced the idea of a third area, neither inside nor outside but between, for which he used the term 'potential space' and which he described as zone in which illusions can be allowed, enabling the infant to begin to gain a sense of active engagement with its environment (Winnicott 1971). Another influential example is Wilfred Bion's (1963) concept of containment, which gives spatial form to the dynamic relationship between container (archetypically the mother's mind) and contained (archetypically the infant's unconscious experience). Arguably the whole edifice of object relations theory relies heavily on spatial concepts, portraying unconscious life as figures or objects in a landscape (Cushman, 1996). The Spanish-language tradition of Argentinian psychoanalysis developed different spatial concepts. In a paper first published in Spanish 1962 but not available in English until 2008, Willy and Madeleine Baranger (2008) described the analytic situation as a temporal and spatial structure, and drew on the metaphor of the 'field' to explore the unconscious and conscious dynamics that ensue.

This reliance on, and development of, spatial concepts by classic psychoanalytic writers, continues into numerous contemporary contributions, of which I outline two. To begin with a recent discussion of depression, mourning and melancholia, informed by both Lacanian and object relations theory, Darian Leader (2008) has described the work of mourning in terms of four motifs or elements, each of which is intrinsically spatial. The first concerns 'the introduction of a frame to mark out a symbolic, artificial space' (Leader 2008: 168), which enables the losses that haunts us to be represented and thereby contained or demarcated. The second arises from what Leader describes as the need to lay our dead to rest symbolically, and which requires some kind of spatial separation to be made between the living and the dead, such as burial in a demarcated space. The third motif is about separating 'the images of those things that matter to us from the *place* that they occupy' (Leader 2008: 131, original emphasis). In the language of object relations, mourning requires 'the mourner to be able to differentiate, at an unconscious level, between the object and the place of the object' (Leader 2008: 131). In other words, in mourning, we separate our image of the lost person from the place they occupied in our unconscious life. The final motif in Leader's account involves the converse process in which, in mourning we 'giv[e] up the image of who we were' (Leader 2008: 168) for the person we have lost, which requires us to separate our continuing sense of who we are from the image of our place in the life of our lost loved one.

I turn next to a recent reading by Thomas Ogden (2007) of a paper by Howard Searles, much of whose writing gathers together clinical illustrations of a particular theme (Searles 1965). For Ogden (2007: 353), Searles is unrivalled 'in his ability to capture in words his observations concerning his emotional response to what is occurring in the analytic relationship'. Consequently Searles has been influential in elaborating and developing how clinicians understand and make use of the dynamics of transference and counter-transference in psychoanalytic work. He explored in depth how these dynamics can be re-enacted in relationships between clinicians and their clinical supervisors (Searles 1965) making him a potentially important psychoanalytic theorist of the transmission of affect.

Ogden's account draws on several of Searles's clinical illustrations including a session in which an elderly patient brought a letter from her daughter, from whom she had not heard for several years. The patient gave the letter to Searles to read, a request that made him uncomfortable. Noticing his own emotional experience, and in the process of responding to her request, he was able to connect his feelings with those of his patient. Having noticed his reluctance to read the letter because he wasn't the person to whom it was addressed, he said 'but I wonder if *you* feel that *you*, likewise, are not the person to whom the letter is addressed' (Searles 1990: 214–15, original emphasis). His speculation acknowledged that his patient felt herself to be a different person from the woman her daughter imagined her to be. In Ogden's (2007: 362–3) reading:

> On the basis of this feeling/thought, Searles did something with the situation that, for me, is astounding: he turned [his] experience 'inside out' in his mind in a way that revealed something that felt true to him, to the patient, and to me as a reader. [...] Searles took his feeling that it was not right to read a letter not addressed to him – the 'inside', in the sense that it was his own personal response – and made it 'the outside'. By 'outside', I mean the context, the larger emotional reality, within which he was experiencing what was occurring between himself and the patient and, by extension, within which the patient was experiencing herself in relation to her daughter.

As Ogden (2007: 363) elaborates, this turning of experience inside out is 'far more subtle' than 'making the unconscious conscious'. It required 'Searles to make a transformation in himself in which context [his felt experience] becomes content [something to be thought about]' (Ogden 2007: 363). Moreover, Searles described this happening while he was talking, prompting Ogden to suggest that 'Searles was not saying what he thought; he was thinking what he said. That is, in the very act of speaking, inner was becoming outer, thinking was becoming talking, unthinkable context was becoming thinkable content, experience was being turned inside out' (Ogden 2007: 363).

In Ogden's (2007: 363) account, transactions between inside and outside are continuous and dynamic: 'like the surface of a Moebius strip, inside is continually in the process of becoming outside and outside becoming inside'. The metaphor of the Moebius strip is a way of thinking about psychoanalytic understandings of subjectivity, and the complex interplay between inter-subjectivity and intra-psychic experience within psychoanalytic practice.

The Creative Spaces of Psychoanalytic Practice

As I have begun to elaborate, spatial concepts infuse the language of psychoanalytic practice as well as psychoanalytic theory. Much of this spatial language moves with ease between practitioners who locate their work within different theoretical frameworks. For example, enormous emphasis is placed on therapeutic boundaries, including the times and spaces in which therapeutic work takes place, the kinds of contact permitted between clinicians and patients within and outside therapy sessions, and the principle of confidentiality, which places a boundary around communications between clinicians and patients (Bondi with Fewell 2003). Clinicians also attend carefully to the material spaces in which therapy occurs, valuing highly both consistency (in the sense of meeting in the same room in the same building with minimum alteration to the furnishings and other contents) and privacy (in the sense of a space protected from intrusion by others physically, visually and aurally). Within these spaces the spatial configuration of the analytic couple is accorded significance. Freud adopted the practice of sitting on a chair out of the line of vision of his analysand, who lay on a couch. Chair and couch have been configured differently by others and, in weekly (rather than more frequent) modes of practice, clinician and patient often sit more or less (but not directly) face-to-face in chairs of equal height.

These apparently practical details about physical spaces are invested with meaning in ways that connect back to Freud's (1926e/2002: 106) portrayal of

> the I [Ego] as a kind of façade of the It [Id], a foreground or if you like an outer
> layer or shell. [...] We know that shells owe their particular qualities to the
> modifying influence of the external medium to which they are exposed. [...] The I
> is situated between reality and the It, the actual mental realm.

In psychoanalytic practice, clinicians and patients necessarily interact through the medium of their 'shells' as well as in relation to what lies underneath those shells. The work is often about the dynamic interplay between surface and interior, between the 'I' and the 'It'. As the example from Searles illustrates, movements between these operate inter-personally as well as intra-psychically. To do this work clinicians provide an 'external medium', one into which their patients bring the 'particular qualities' of the 'shells' they inhabit. The external medium of therapy is carefully demarcated from the other environments and its consistency is designed in part to help the analytic couple to see the nature of the complex adaptations or habits of engaging with the world (inner and outer) that bring the patient to therapy. Consistency is not the same as rigidity, and clinicians also represent their capacity for thoughtfulness in the care with which therapeutic spaces are designed. The environments made available to patients include the psychoanalyst's mind, which is itself hidden beneath clinician's outer layers or shells. I would suggest that clinicians symbolize their capacity to think, and to serve as container to their patients (Bion 1963), in part through the interior designs and spatial configurations of therapeutic spaces.

Another way of framing this account is to describe psychoanalytic practice as operating in an intermediate area between inside and outside, to which Winnicott (1971) appealed in his concept of 'potential space'. On this account, therapy can be understood as taking place in 'an area of illusion', which provides an 'intermediate area of experience, unchallenged in respect of its belonging to inner or external (shared) reality' (Winnicott 1971: 14). According to Winnicott this area is the space of play, creativity and cultural experience. It is what enables meanings to be shared and co-created. One way of understanding psychoanalysis is as a body or bodies of theory and practice dedicated to enabling, exploring and enriching this intermediate space. In this sense, psychoanalysis is intrinsically geographical in its concerns.

Conclusion

Nearly a century ago Freud advanced a multidisciplinary vision for psychoanalysis. Although he did not refer explicitly to geography as a potential partner for psychoanalytic theory and practice, he did reference geographical concerns. Drawing on his essay in defence of lay analysis, I have identified two different aspects of Freud's geographies, contesting one and endorsing the other. On the one hand, I have argued against his universalist aspiration for psychoanalysis, insisting instead that neither theory nor practice are ever context-free. I have made the case that psychoanalysis is intrinsically situated, shaped in and by the places in which it is practised and the relationships between these places. From the earliest days, psychoanalysis has travelled from one context to another. Rather than leading to homogenization, such travels have enriched psychoanalysis through the constant recontextualization of ideas.

One the other hand, Freud realized that spatial ideas were vital to his thinking and this has continued to be that case for psychoanalysis ever since. Without much, if any, explicit contact with the work of geographers, psychoanalytic writers have relied strongly on spatial concepts and in so doing have developed highly spatial ways of thinking and practice. Psychoanalysis has become a rich source of non-Euclidean conceptualizations of space especially in relation to the distinction between inside and outside. I have suggested that psychoanalysis might be thought of as working to produce new geographies, especially across distinctions between inside and outside.

Acknowledgements

An earlier version of this chapter, written for a different audience, appears in Cullen, Bondi, Fewell, Francis and Ludlam, 2014.

References

Baranger, W. and Baranger, M. 2008. The analytic situation as a dynamic field. *International Journal of Psychoanalysis*, 89(4), 795–826.

Bion, W.R. 1963. *Elements of Psychoanalysis*. London: William Heinemann.

Bondi, L. with Fewell, J. 2003. 'Unlocking the cage door': the spatiality of counselling. *Social and Cultural Geography*, 4, 527–47.

Burston, D. 1996. *The Wing of Madness: The Life and Work of R.D. Laing*. Cambridge MA: Harvard University Press.

Clarke, G. 2006. *Personal Relations Theory: Fairbairn, Macmurray and Suttie*. London: Routledge.

Cullen, K., Bondi, L., Fewell, J., Francis, E. and Ludlam, M. 2014. *Making Spaces: Putting Psychoanalytic Thinking to Work*. London: Karnac.

Cushman, P. 1996. *Constructing the Self, Constructing America*. Cambridge MA: Perseus.

Fergusson, D. 2012. Persons in relation: the interaction of philosophy, theology and psychotherapy in 20th century Scotland. *Practical Theology*, 5, 287–306.

Flyvbjerg, B. 2001. *Making Social Science Matter*. Cambridge: Cambridge University Press.

Freud, S. 1901b/2002. *The Psychopathology of Everyday Life*. London: Penguin. (The New Penguin Freud, translated by A. Bance.)

Freud, S. 1926e/2002. The question of lay analysis. *Wild Analysis*. London: Penguin, 95–159. (The New Penguin Freud, translated by A. Bell.)

Freud, S. 1927a/2002. Postscript to 'The question of lay analysis'. *Wild Analysis*. London: Penguin, 163–70. (The New Penguin Freud, translated by A. Bance.)

Freud, S. 2002. *Wild Analysis*. London: Penguin. (The New Penguin Freud, translated by A. Bance.)

Gay, P. 1989. *Freud: A Life for Our Time*. London: Papermac.

Grosskurth, P. 1986. *Melanie Klein: Her World and Her Work*. London: Hodder and Stoughton.

Haraway, D. 1988. Situated knowledges: the science question in feminism and the privilege of partial perspective. *Feminist Studies*, 14(3), 575–99.

Harvey, D. 1989. *The Condition of Postmodernity*. Oxford: Blackwell.

King, P.H.M. and Steiner, R. 1991. *The Freud/Klein Controversies in the British Psycho-Analytical Society, 1941–5*. Routledge: London.

Lakoff, G. and Johnson, M. 1980. *Metaphors We Live By*. Chicago: Chicago University Press.

Leader, D. 2008. *The New Black*. London: Penguin.

Massey, D. 2005. *For Space*. London: Sage.

Miller, G. 2008. Scottish psychoanalysis: a rational religion. *Journal of the History of the Behavioural Sciences*, 44(1), 38–58.

Ogden, T. 2007. Reading Harold Searles. *International Journal of Psychoanalysis*, 88(2), 353–69.

Parker, I. and Revelli, S. (eds) 2008. *Psychoanalytic Practice and State Regulation*. London: Karnac.

Roazen, P. 2001. *The Historiography of Psychoanalysis*. New Brunswick, NJ: Transaction Publishers.

Searles, H.F. 1965. *Collected Papers on Schizophrenia and Related Subjects*. London: Hogarth Press.

Searles, H.F. 1990. Unconscious identification, in *Master Clinicians: On Treating the Regressed Patient*, edited by L.B. Boyer and P. Giovacchini. New York: Aronson, 211–26.

Wallerstein, R.S. 1998. *Lay Analysis: Life Inside the Controversy*. Hillsdale, NJ and London: The Analytic Press.

Winnicott, D.W. 1965. *The Maturational Processes and the Facilitating Environment*. London: Hogarth Press.

Winnicott, D.W. 1971. *Playing and Reality*. London: Tavistock.

Chapter 3

Consulting Rooms: Notes Towards a Historical Geography of the Psychoanalytic Setting

Felicity Callard

Introduction

For reasons that I shall never know, the psychotherapist whom I see for intensive psychoanalytic psychotherapy in London has moved her consulting room six times since I first met her in 2002. If I add other psychoanalytic consulting rooms in which I have been assessed and/or treated, the number of rooms in which I have been interpellated as a psychoanalytic patient is at least 10 (in two countries). I have long been interested in how the relationship between the external and internal world is conceptualized, constituted and experienced (for example Callard 2003, Callard and Margulies 2011). Such serendipitous exposure to such a variety of interiors could not but make me curious about how to begin to conceptualize and to narrate the relationship between the psychic work of analysis, and the spatial work of the particular setting in which an analysis unfolds. This chapter comprises preliminary reflections on that question.

At first blush, to thread one psychoanalytic therapy across seven different rooms might well be interpreted as to attack, or at least to undermine, the 'establishment of [a] secure setting, together with reliable and predictable adherence to it by the psychoanalyst' (British Psychoanalytical Society 2007). Robert Langs, for example (who could be regarded as exemplary of a wide spectrum of psychoanalysts on the matter of changing rooms), argues that 'the ideal therapeutic environment calls for a single setting without variation. Even a necessary move by the therapist of his or her office ... is traumatic to the patient (and usually for the therapist as well)' (Langs 1982: 354). While I do not wish to gainsay the anxiety that I experienced during at least some of the moves of consulting room, I wish to hold at bay both a too-rapid invocation of 'traumatic' sequelae, and, indeed, a too-rapid naturalization of the 'ideal' 'single setting without variation'.

As I came to discern shapes, atmospheres and choreographies – psychic and bodily – that variously opened and closed within each new room on whose couch I lay, I became increasingly curious about the relative paucity of literature that I had come across that might help me to understand the potency and the particularity of settings in which psychoanalysis takes place. The frequent psychoanalytic privileging of the *concept* of the 'secure' or 'stable' setting often occluded specific consideration of the environmental, architectural and socio-spatial characteristics that might help to underpin or enable such stability. If we put our assimilated psychotherapeutic assumptions to one side, several overlapping questions come into view: how did psychoanalysis come to be materialized in the form of a spatial (and temporal) dispensation in which a relatively immobile person, who is usually horizontal, talks to a therapist – who is also relatively immobile, and usually positioned on a chair behind her – in the same space, usually, and with the furniture not moving, day after day (week after week, year after year)? How, moreover, did such a dispensation come to be understood as 'secure' by those overseeing and enabling it? Which processes – material, psychic, epistemological and institutional – do we need to understand to answer these questions?

'The physical environment is not critical'

There are limits to how far one is able to progress in answering those questions if one cleaves simply to formulations provided by psychoanalytic institutes and exegeses of psychoanalytic technique. The American Psychoanalytic Association, for example, on its website page that addresses questions about psychoanalytic treatment, stated:

> Q. The Analyst's Office: How important is the physical environment in which psychoanalysis takes place, considered to be?

> A. The physical environment in which a psychoanalysis is conducted per se is not critical other than it should be a relatively quiet place where both analyst and patient are comfortable and can speak in private (American Psychoanalytic Association 2009–13).

Lewis Wolberg, in his monograph on psychoanalytic technique, argued:

> The physical surroundings are the least important factors that enter into psychotherapy. If the therapist has the proper didactic, personality and experiential equipment, he will be able to do good psychotherapy in almost any kind of setting (Wolberg 1967).

André Green defined the 'material setting' as those 'material arrangements which govern the relations between analysand and analyst (payment of missed sessions, co-ordination of vacations between patient and analyst, length of sessions, mode of payment, etc.)' (Green 2005: 32). Green made no mention of how the physical environment might govern relations between analysand and analyst. The psychoanalyst Lee Kassan interviewed 60 therapists, mostly in and around New York City. The final version of his interview schedule comprised 100 questions. While his questions addressed procedural specificities (for example, 'Do you allow smoking? Eating? Coffee or other beverages?'), he posed not a single question about the physical space or furniture of the consultation room (Kassan 1996).

This literature leaves us with the impression that the 'security' or 'stability' of the psychoanalytic setting resides largely in certain kinds of practices and behaviours on the part of the *analyst* – in relation to the space that she oversees – rather than by dint of characteristics of the *space*, or distribution of material artefacts within the space itself. The threshold that the analyst needs to cross in ensuring that she provides an appropriate physical environment appears to be relatively low. Why this general disregard, or dismissal, of the importance of the material space in which psychoanalysis takes place? One indispensable line of investigation returns us to the sites at which the practice of psychoanalysis emerged. Andreas Mayer has explored the 'peculiar way' in which the 'objects or the actual material components that make up the psychoanalytic setting' were lost or forgotten (Mayer 2006: 38). Through tracing the path that Freud took out of the laboratories of hypnosis and towards his installation of a specifically psychoanalytic couch, Mayer tracks the 'fade-out of the object world that surrounded the patient in the [psychoanalytic] consulting room' (Mayer 2006: 59). The agency and visibility of this external object world and setting was bracketed, in favour of an intense psychoanalytic focus on excavating and rendering discernable the inner object world.

Freud described, for example, in 'On beginning the treatment' the patient who, at the start of a psychoanalysis, maintains that he 'cannot think of anything to say' (Freud 1913: 137). Sometimes he can be persuaded that he has overlooked thoughts that were occupying his mind:

> He had ... been occupied with the picture of the room in which he was, or he
> could not help thinking of the objects in the consulting room and of the fact that
> he was lying here on a sofa ... These indications are intelligible enough: everything
> connected with the present situation represents a transference to the doctor ...
> (Freud 1913: 138).

The focus towards which these sentences drive is *the transference to the doctor*.
It is the transference that needs to be analysed, understood, and addressed;
the materiality of the objects in the consulting room – their objectality, their
position in relation to the patient – is not of central importance. Furthermore,
the patient's thoughts and feelings about the room in which he lies are not to be
taken as robust knowledge about the actual qualities and suitability of the room,
objects and couch. These thoughts and feelings are a result of the transference;
they have not – at base – been elicited by the room, the objects, or the sofa.
The couch, on such a model, is the instrument through which 'to isolate the
transference and to allow it to come forward in due course sharply defined as
a resistance' (Freud 1913: 134). It is a device that facilitates the disinterring of
the transference and the anatomization of the patient's psyche; it is not, *per se*, a
central element of the treatment.

Much of the psychoanalytic literature that has followed Freud bears witness
to this 'fading' of the prominence of the physical setting in the service of a
distillation and bringing to the fore of the transference. There are of course
differences in how each 'branch' of psychoanalysis has organized and understood
the physical setting, the objects within it, and the patient's reactions to that
setting and those objects. I am unable to address these differences here. That
said, Donald Meltzer described how the analyst needs to work out a 'style' of
analytical work (which includes the room, alongside the analyst's demeanour
and clothes), such that she is able to *'preside* over the setting in a way which
permits the evolution of the patient's transference' (Meltzer 2008 [1967]: xiii).
Hyman Spotnitz noted the '[s]parse consideration given the couch in
professional literature', guessing that this might be because 'this traditional item
of office equipment has commonly been viewed as extraneous to the analytic
endeavor' (Spotnitz 1978: 9). René Spitz described how, if there is 'transference
readiness' in the patient, the setting 'becomes a stimulus, a cue, a particularly
favourable configuration for the provocation of transference' (Spitz 1956: 382).

In scientific practice, a stimulus or cue is used to elicit the phenomenon
of interest, not that which needs to be analysed itself. (Indeed, once the 'cue'
or 'stimulus' has been decided upon, the scientist can afford to forget about

its particularities, since what it elicits is usually imagined to be a property of the phenomenon of interest, not of the experimental *circuit* that links the phenomenon to cue.) In clinical psychoanalytical writings, we can discern how the physical environment – or elements within it – is commonly invoked in the service of clarifying or exemplifying how the patient's inner world has responded to the 'stimulus' or 'cue' that it provides. The Lacanian Bruce Fink distinguished 'the hysteric' from 'the obsessive' through her relationship to the couch: the hysteric dislikes the couch since she 'cannot easily bear to speak to a blank wall ..., needing to feel the Other's gaze upon her' (Fink 1997: 134). The 'blank wall' is interpreted by the hysteric as an entity that cannot provide the gaze of the Other; the specificity of its materiality – its 'blank wall-ness' – is not central. Brett Kahr described a 'hugely narcissistic patient' who took several days to notice that Kahr had redecorated his consulting room (Kahr 2011a: 673). Carpelan described a patient whose 'narcissistic need of making the analysis on his own conditions' led to him 'moving the cushion and folding it double' (Carpelan 1981: 153). The state of the patient's internal world, then, is made manifest by the lack of response to the alteration in 'cue' (Kahr's patient), and by an attempt to fine-tune the specifics of the stimulus in the latter (Carpelan's patient).

To reconstitute and bring to light the work that the material, physical components of the psychoanalytic setting accomplish, then, demands a double gesture. First, one must bring into the foreground the shapes and textures of that realm that have been sloughed off as a mere backdrop to the analytic endeavour. Second, one must decide how those elements, largely disavowed or occluded within psychoanalytic practice, might, in fact, be intricately bound up in the work of psychoanalysis. Is everything within the psychoanalytic setting to be considered as important? Important for what, for whom, and in what way? How have those elements – their relation to one another, and their ability to act as good, poor or excessive 'cues' for the transference – shifted and transformed since the emergence of psychoanalysis?

Towards a Historical Geography of the Psychoanalytic Consulting Room

Historians of psychoanalysis are beginning to redress the lacuna in our knowledge of the history of the couch, that most characteristic element of the psychoanalytic setting (e.g. Marinelli and Sigmund Freud Privatstiftung 2006). But we are far from having a comprehensive historico-geographical analysis of the physical environment beyond the couch. As Volker Welter has argued, 'the allegedly passive placement of the patients on the couch and the methodological focus on the inner spaces of the mind' have 'made it easy to consider the couch and the chair as the location of the psychoanalytic process which apparently happened independently from any other spatial environment' (Welter 2012: 98).

Meanwhile, in the psychoanalytic journals, there is a small, oblique literature that emphasizes the varied textures and atmospheres of the psychoanalytic setting. Paul Roazen argued that, 'The nature of the consulting room, the taste of the decorations, as well as the meaning that certain artefacts of the analyst's suggest, are often overlooked as an aspect of the therapeutic process' (Roazen 1995: 46). De Chumaceiro noted that, 'The consulting office inevitably reflects the analyst's culture, taste, and mental health' lamenting that '[t]oo few, too intermittently, are writing about this important issue' (de Chumaceiro 1996). Kahr has argued that '[c]linicians have spent so much time concentrating on the *internal* furniture in the minds of our patients that we have written very little about the actual *external* physical atmosphere that each practitioner creates' (Kahr 2011a: 675). Some psychoanalysts have offered normative prescriptions regarding the physical components of the psychoanalytic setting (e.g. Wolberg 1967; Langs 1982). These provide a fascinating entrée into the changing mores of psychoanalytic practice, as well as the kinds of spaces deemed to be appropriate (as an ideal if not necessarily in practice) for psychoanalysts to undertake their craft. The edited collection *Between Sessions and Beyond the Couch* by Joan Raphael-Leff (2002), and Brett Kahr's 'Letter from London' bulletins (e.g. Kahr 2005, 2006, 2007, 2008, 2011a, 2011b) offer short, first-person reflections by psychoanalysts on elements of the physical world that they consider of importance to psychoanalytic practice.

What would it take to fill out the historical geography of the psychoanalytic consulting room? Below, I offer preliminary thoughts vis-à-vis how we might examine in more detail some of those sloughed-off elements. The list is incomplete and foreshortened; its items are more a function of my own fantasies and reflections elicited by the consulting rooms that I have inhabited than an argument for those items' pre-eminence over others'.

Design of the Consulting Room

The historical and geographical specificities of psychoanalytic consulting room design remain, to a significant extent, to be uncovered. Important exceptions include Diana Fuss's rich essay on Freud's Berggasse consulting room (Fuss 2004) and Volker Welter's monograph on the architectural designs of Ernst Freud,

Sigmund Freud's son (Welter 2012). Both Fuss and Welter consider the consulting room in relation to the building in which it is located, as well as the complex ways in which concepts of 'inside' and 'outside' and 'public and private' could be turned inside out in relation to these rooms and the practices conducted therein. Psychoanalysis has been practised in a variety of rooms and buildings, including private apartment buildings (such as Freud's), specialist clinics (such as Freud's free clinics; see Danto 2005), inpatient settings, office suites and houses. The design of such spaces can of course elicit fantasies in analysts, patients and architects – for example, of the apartment dweller or (English) homeowner. Design can also materially constrain and direct the ways in which the psychoanalytic dyad inhabit the room, affect the placement of artefacts in the room, and dampen down, or amplify, extraneous noise. (Winnicott, when describing Freud's clinical setting, wrote that 'the work was to be done in a room ... that was quiet and not liable to sudden unpredictable sounds, yet not dead quiet and not free from ordinary house noises' (Winnicott 1954: 285).) And what of effects – and affects – enabled by waiting rooms (Kassan 2008, Kieffer 2011), doors, corridors, exits, stairs, gardens, and the streets outside?

The complex entanglement of the so-called sphere of the 'psychic' and the sphere of the 'material' should push us to move beyond a flat-footed enumeration of numbers of doors and the presence or absence of a waiting room. How might we explore the archives of memories, bodily practices and architectural histories that ghost a patient's – and an analyst's – traversal across or through any one of these features, and affect her reactions to them? How, moreover, might we conceptualize and narrate the difference between undertaking an analysis in Berggasse 19 in comparison with a psychoanalysis in Tehran (Homayounpour 2012)? How – to return to my own speculations unleashed by my psychotherapist's moves in London – might the political economy of housing bear on the geographical location, size, room characteristics, the analyst's sense of 'security', and the longevity of tenure of psychoanalytic consulting rooms?

Furniture, Objects, and the Rhythms of Comportment

Intricate work by historians of science and cultural theorists has allowed us to gaze with new eyes at some of the most striking features of Freud's own psychoanalytic practice – for example, his collections (Forrester 1997), including his plaster cast bas-relief of Gradiva (Mayer 2012), his mirror (Fuss 2004) and his use of the couch (Marinelli and Sigmund Freud Privatstiftung 2006). This work has demonstrated the complex ways in which material and psychic spaces and distances within the consulting room – between the bodies, minds, material objects and 'internal objects' (of both analyst and patient) – can interweave with, as well as undo, one another. This literature encourages us to consider configurations of the couch, the analyst's chair and the door in psychoanalytic consulting rooms that were not Freud's. What were these configurations, how great has the variability been, and does this variability affect the practice of psychoanalysis? Welter has uncovered a variety of placements of couch and chair in both Germany and England, and characterizes these as 'isolated, little-known experiments with the spatial setting of psychoanalysis' (Welter 2012: 110). For example, the psychoanalyst John Rickman discussed different configurations of couch and patients with trainees in the 1940s through the use of a small model of a couch, with paper strips representing the walls (Welter 2012: 108). The psychoanalyst Joseph Lichtenberg, reflecting in the 1990s on mid-twentieth-century consulting rooms, recalled that a couch, at that historical juncture, '[sat] against the wall longways' (Lichtenberg 1995: 283). But when one of his analysands started scratching the plaster away from wall, he decided 'to break with tradition and place the couch several feet from the wall' (Lichtenberg 1995: 284). Paul Roazen, writing in the 1970s, tied the position of the couch to the relative gravity accorded to psychoanalysis by different national and regional traditions:

> Freud's forebodings about what would happen to his ideas in America have been in some measure fulfilled. For example, in the consulting rooms of present-day British analysts, the analytic couch is prominently displayed, sometimes in the very centre of the room. When one moves across the Atlantic to New England, the analytic couch, still a distinct entity, is more likely to be inconspicuous, placed against a wall. In Chicago an analyst's couch might be used for social purposes as well as therapeutic ones ... (Roazen 1976: 191).

Notably, analysts have associated the position of their chair in relation to the couch with the variable weight they give to hearing and sight. Lichtenberg, when he moved his couch several feet from the wall, discovered that this allowed him 'to place [his] chair behind and to the wall side of the couch, enabling [him] to see a patient's face with greater ease' (Lichtenberg 1995: 284). Braatøy, writing in the mid-twentieth century, commended the steady flow of information about the patient's affective state that could be gathered through observing her face, respiration and movements on the couch. He countered the tendency he saw for psychoanalysts around him to privilege *listening*; lamented the loss in psychoanalysis of the clinical skill of acquiring information by direct visual impressions through observing a patient's movement or lack of movement; and privileged the insights of the early Freud, arguing that '*looking* and *utilizing visual information* was an essential basis for Freud's discoveries in *Studies in* [*sic*] *Hysteria*' (Braatøy 1954: 110). Braatøy contrasted his own position with that of his analyst, Otto Fenichel, who, he reported, 'sat a low chair behind the head of the couch where he could not see [Braatøy's] face' and justified this by maintaining that it was through *listening* to dynamics of the patient's speech and silence that he could 'accurately gauge the emotional tension in them' (Braatøy 1954: 110). There remains ample work to be done (see Figlio 2002 for a fascinating, brief exemplar) on how diverse spatial and temporal configurations and technics encourage the production, circulation and interpretation of affect through and between analyst and analysand.

The positioning of furniture and other physical objects in the consulting room undoubtedly affects both patient's and analyst's comportment and bodily (im)mobility. The psychoanalytic literature is, unsurprisingly, not silent on the question of placing the patient on the couch (in comparison with seating her on a chair). Psychoanalytic writers have considered the way in which the couch facilitates regression (e.g. Winnicott 1954), the risk of placing certain kinds of patients on the couch, and patients' varied reactions to the couch (e.g. Kulish 1996). What interests me, particularly, is the comportment and behaviour of the patient as she approaches, gets on to, lies on, and gets off the couch. We should recall that Freud himself mentioned patients' bodily habits in relation to the couch. He averred that 'A clever young philosopher with exquisite aesthetic sensibilities will hasten to put the creases of his trousers straight before lying down for his first hour', and 'A young girl will at the same juncture hurriedly pull the hem of her skirt over her exposed ankles'. Freud argued that these 'first symptoms or chance actions' may 'betray a complex that governs [the patient's] neurosis' – seeing the philosopher as a 'former coprophilic' and pointing to the young girl's 'narcissistic pride in her physical beauty' as well as her 'inclinations to exhibitionism' (Freud 1913: 138). But what of the ways in which class and gender inflect the mores that govern how patients interact with particular kinds of furniture? And what of the varieties of couch that exist (see the essays in Marinelli and Sigmund Freud Privatstiftung 2006) – in both reality and memory – at any one historical moment? Freud's couch, when seen by a patient for the very first time, is likely to have carried varied and rich connotations – sparked by other couches known through personal acquaintance, visual representations and/or fantasies. Those connotations, I suggest, could not but have inflected how the patient approached and positioned herself on Freud's couch.

There is, then, a complex choreography of the consulting room, which enfolds the patient, the analyst and the props that either or both make use of. Consider the response that Lee Kassan received from one therapist in his empirical study of therapists' practices in response to the question, 'How do you end the session?':

> I've got everyone trained, just like Pavlov. Nearly all of my patients lie on the couch. My chair makes a loud squeak when I lean forward and they get up. I don't have to say anything (Kassan 1996).

A silent analyst moves; a noisy chair then moves; a patient (speaking? silent?) then moves: the psychoanalytic session is broken. What might we learn if we paid more attention to the spatial as well as temporal distribution of sounds and silence – deliberate and spontaneous, those connected and unconnected to one another – across animate and inanimate entities in the consulting room?

Or consider Bion's essay 'On hallucination' (Bion 1958). There, he recounts a virtuosic choreography that links him, his schizophrenic patient and various elements of his consulting room:

> While I close the door he goes to the foot of the couch, facing the head pillows and my chair, and he stands, shoulders stooping, knees sagging, head inclined to the chair, motionless until I have passed him and am about to sit down. So closely do his movements seem to be geared with mine that the inception of my movement to sit appears to release a spring in him. As I lower myself into my seat he turns about, slowly, evenly, as if something would be spilled, or perhaps fractured, were he to be betrayed into a precipitate movement. As I sit, the turning movement stops as if we were both parts of the same clockwork toy (Bion 1958: 349).

How might we understand the complex meshing of the psychic and the bodily, the mobile and the immobile, the agentic and the passive in Bion's account? Do we miss elements within this intricate dance for four (patient, analyst, couch, chair) if we regard the psychoanalytic setting as merely a neutral 'cue' for the provocation of the transference? How might this dance both revivify and memorialize earlier dynamics from the patient's life *and* be enabled by the particular spacings and rhythms of door ... chair ... couch?

I have largely focused on those most prominent physical elements of the psychoanalytic setting. But what of more mundane objects, such as the ashtray and cigarette (Paul Roazen writes that Freud, with at least one patient, 'regularly laid out a cigarette and match for the patient before the beginning of a session' (Roazen 1976; from an interview with Sándor Radó), the box of tissues (Kahr 2008), the coat rack, and the waste bin? These objects can also profoundly shape a patient's – and analyst's – bodily comportment, both through the actions she might take in relationship to them, and through their ability to influence the path taken in and out of the room. Their historical geography remains largely unwritten.

Often, when I read psychoanalytic literature that mentions physical elements of the setting, I am struck by the need to ensure that those elements do not cause excessive perturbation or excitement. If the setting is a 'cue' for the provocation of the transference, it must be a cue that is not, in itself, *over*-obtrusive. Langs, for example, advised that there should be nothing on the desk that is 'self-revealing', such as papers or books (Langs 1982: 364); Wolberg warned against disturbing pictures, gaudy draperies and embellishments (Wolberg 1967: 438). Vokan recalled that his consulting room 'was lighted only by a floor lamp; it was unpleasant to have the ceiling light shine down on my patients as though they were being forced to face an inquisitor' (Vokan 1984: 8). What counts as too obtrusive, disturbing, gaudy, or self-revealing has both a history and geography that is both psychic and material. We should recall, too, that Freud's own consulting room (with its collections, its photographs and books) could hardly be said not to be 'self-revealing'.

Others

While psychoanalysis is embedded in today's culture as a process that involves two people, the psychoanalytic consulting room is not always empty of all other living entities. These include maids and pets. Freud's maid would frequently greet patients, announce them to Freud (Blanton 1971: 44, 80; H.D. 1985 [1970]: 96), and retrieve the patient's hat and coat and give them to him or her on departure (Jones 1955: 424). Freud's beloved chows were also sometimes part of the psychoanalytic setting. One entry in Sidney Blanton's diary of his psychoanalysis with Freud described how there was, during the session, 'a rattling of the door', upon which 'Freud got up, opened it, and his chow dog came in' (Blanton 1971: 67). The attachment psychotherapist Tirril Harris described being in the middle of a session when she 'suddenly saw, ..., staring fixedly straight down at the couch, Ellie the tabby, perched on top of the tall book shelves, a Carollian Cheshire Cat but decidedly without the grin' (Harris 2002: 22). While Harris felt herself become paranoid, the patient did not, apparently, notice Ellie.

Harris further recounts how one of her patients left a previous therapist because her request that the cat not be present during her sessions 'was responded to merely with interpretation not with agreement' (Harris 2002: 23).

Why, when and where do living entities move from being accepted as part of the setting into protrusions that are no longer acceptable? Do they, their movements, and their animation or stillness, re-route the psychic energetics that pass between analysand and analyst into a three-way flow? How should our analysis move between cultural and historical mores (for example, the presence of Freud's maid and his chow could clearly, within a certain class and cultural context, be un-remarkable) and patients' reasons (psychic? somatic? social? cultural?) for not wanting other entities in the room? How do we explain a metamorphosis from an 'other' that can be uncommented upon into an unwelcome or over-intrusive presence?

Conclusion

I have attempted to think about a scientific and clinical practice that is founded upon two bodies and two minds meeting regularly, in largely the same spatial configuration, for a number of months or years. I hope that my argument might allow the physical and socio-spatial elements that comprise that practice – their history, geography and peculiarity – to provoke more curiosity from geographers and those in proximate disciplines. How those socio-spatial elements might *matter* for the theory and practice of psychoanalysis – psychically, phenomenologically, and epistemologically – is a question that I think we (as psychoanalysts, analysands, historians and social scientists) have tended not to address in a sustained way. We do not have a comprehensive understanding of the geographical and historical variation of those elements: what precipitates or enables those variations, and what allows some of those elements to become congealed and resistant to alteration? The institutionalization of psychoanalysis has undoubtedly resulted in the rigidification of some of the socio-spatial elements of and procedures within the psychoanalytic setting. Freud himself, we are told, would, in the middle of a psychoanalytic session, get up to let his chow in, go out of the room to urinate, light a cigar, confront a patient face to face, and occasionally rap on the couch (Roazen 1976: 139–41, from interviews with Edoardo Weiss, Edith Jackson and Smiley Blanton; H.D. 1985 [1970]: 23). Such mobility and noise make the comparative immobility and silence of many of today's spaces of psychoanalysis strikingly apparent.

Psychoanalysis has produced, over the course of more than a century, spatial distributions of bodies, setting and material artefacts that it has imagined as enabling and not excessively perturbing its therapeutic work. That therapeutic work is psychic work that takes place *right there*, in the midst of that bodily and object world. Yet, at the same time, that psychic work is envisaged as relatively 'free' of the socio-spatial materiality of that setting. The creation of that 'stable' spatial dispensation – in which the transference can be envisaged as, once provoked, capable of shining forth, largely unclouded by the intricacies of the physical, object world – is a work of significant magnitude. Psychoanalytic geography has much to contribute to tracing that achievement.

Acknowledgements

I thank my two psychoanalytic therapists (and their rooms), without whom this chapter would not – for many reasons – have been written.

References

American Psychoanalytic Association. 2009–2013. Ask a psychoanalyst: treatment FAQs. American Psychoanalytic Association. Available at: http://www.apsa.org/About_Psychoanalysis/Ask_a_Psychoanalyst/Treatment.aspx [accessed: 16 April 2013].

Bion, W. 1958. On hallucination. *International Journal of Psycho-Analysis*, 39, 341–9.

Blanton, S. 1971. *Diary of My Analysis with Sigmund Freud [with Biographical Notes and Comments by Margaret Gray Blanton; Introduction by Iago Galdston, MD]*. New York: Hawthorn Books.

Braatøy, T. 1954. *Fundamentals of Psychoanalytic Technique*. New York: John Wiley & Sons.

British Psychoanalytical Society. 2007. Psychoanalysis today. Available at: http://www.psychoanalysis.org.uk/psatoday.htm [accessed: 22 April 2013].

Callard, F. 2003. Conceptualisations of agoraphobia: implications for mental health promotion. *Journal of Public Mental Health*, 2(4), 37–45.

Callard, F. and Margulies, D. 2011. The subject at rest: novel conceptualizations of self and brain from cognitive neuroscience's study of the 'resting state'. *Subjectivity*, 4(3), 227–57.

Carpelan, H. 1981. On the importance of the setting in the psychoanalytic situation. *The Scandinavian Psychoanalytic Review*, 4(2), 151–60.

Danto, E.A. 2005. *Freud's Free Clinics: Psychoanalysis and Social Justice 1918–38*. New York: Columbia University Press.

De Chumaceiro, C.L.D. 1996. The analyst's consulting room. *American Journal of Psychoanalysis*, 56(2), 257–38.

Figlio, K. 2002. Freud's eyes. *Between Sessions and Beyond the Couch*, edited by J. Raphael-Leff. Colchester: CPS Psychoanalytic Publications, University of Essex.

Fink, B. 1997. *A Clinical Introduction to Lacanian Psychoanalysis: Theory and Technique*. Cambridge, MA: Harvard University Press.

Forrester, J. 1997. Collector, naturalist, surrealist. *Dispatches from the Freud Wars: Psychoanalysis and its Passions*. Cambridge, MA: Harvard University Press.

Freud, S. 1913. On beginning the treatment. *The Standard Edition of the Complete Psychological Works of Sigmund Freud, Volume XII*. London: Hogarth Press and Institute of Psychoanalysis, 121–44.

Fuss, D. 2004. Freud's ear. *The Sense of An Interior: Four Writers and the Rooms That Shaped Them*. New York: Routledge.

Green, A. 2005. Setting – process – transference. *Key Ideas for a Contemporary Psychoanalysis: Misrecognition and Recognition of the Unconscious*. London: Routledge.

H.D. 1985 [1970]. *Tribute to Freud: Writing on the Wall/Advent*. Manchester: Carcanet.

Harris, T. 2002. Pets behind the couch, in *Between Sessions and Beyond the Couch*, edited by J. Raphael-Leff. Colchester: CPS Psychoanalytic Publications, University of Essex.

Homayounpour, G. 2012. *Doing Psychoanalysis in Tehran*. Cambridge, MA: MIT Press.

Jones, E. 1955. *Sigmund Freud: Life and Work. Volume 2: Years of Maturity, 1901–1919*. London: The Hogarth Press.

Kahr, B. 2005. Letter from London: on patients who remove their clothing in sessions. *American Imago*, 62(2), 217–23.

Kahr, B. 2006. Letter from London: the handshake. *American Imago*, 63(3), 359–69.

Kahr, B. 2007. Letter from London: the ten-minute gap. *American Imago*, 64(4), 567–74.

Kahr, B. 2008. Letter from London: tissues. *American Imago*, 65(2), 299–308.

Kahr, B. 2011a. Letter from London: on painting the consulting room. *American Imago*, 67(4), 669–75.

Kahr, B. 2011b. Letter from London: the bookshelf. *American Imago*, 68(1), 127–34.

Kassan, L.D. 1996. *Shrink Rap: Sixty Psychotherapists Discuss Their Work, Their Lives, and the State of their Field*. Northvale, NJ: Jason Aronson.

Kassan, L.D. 2008. Encounters in the waiting room. *Annals of the American Psychotherapy Association*, 11(3), 20–23.

Kieffer, C.C. 2011. The waiting room as boundary and bridge between self-states and unformulated experiences. *Journal of the American Psychoanalytic Association*, 59(2), 335–50.

Kulish, N. 1996. A phobia of the couch: a clinical study of psychoanalytic process. *Psychoanalytic Quarterly*, 65(3), 465–94.

Langs, R. 1982. *Psychotherapy: A Basic Text*. New York: Jason Aronson.

Lichtenberg, J. 1995. Forty-five years of psychoanalytic experiences on, behind, and without the couch. *Psychoanalytic Inquiry*, 15(3), 280–93.

Marinelli, L. and Sigmund Freud Privatstiftung, Wein. 2006. *Die Couch: Vom Denken im Liegen*. München: Prestel.

Mayer, A. 2006. Lost objects: from the laboratories of hypnosis to the psychoanalytic setting. *Science in Context*, 19(1), 37–64.

Mayer, A. 2012. Gradiva's gait: tracing the figure of the walking woman. *Critical Inquiry*, 38(spring), 554–78.

Meltzer, D. 2008 [1967]. *The Psycho-Analytical Process*. London: Karnac.

Raphael-Leff, J. (ed.) 2002. *Between Sessions and Beyond the Couch*. Colchester: CPS Psychoanalytic Publications, University of Essex.

Roazen, P. 1976. *Freud and His Followers*. London: Allen Lane.

Roazen, P. 1995. Reflections on psychoanalysis, creativity, and Jackson Pollock. *American Journal of Psychoanalysis*, 55(1), 41–51.

Spitz, R.A. 1956. Transference: the analytical setting and its prototype. *International Journal of Psycho-Analysis*, 37(4–5), 380–85.

Spotnitz, H. 1978. Foreword, in *The Couch: Its Use and Meaning in Psychotherapy*, edited by H.R. Stern. New York: Human Sciences Press.

Vokan, V.D. 1984. *What Do You Get When You Cross a Dandelion with a Rose? The True Story of a Psychoanalysis*. New York and London: Jason Aronson.

Welter, V.M. 2012. *Ernst L Freud, Architect: The Case of the Modern Bourgeois Home*. New York and Oxford: Berghahn Books.

Winnicott, D. 1954. Metapsychological and clinical aspects of regression with the psycho-analytical set up. *Through Paediatrics to Psychoanalysis: Collected Papers*. London: Tavistock Publications, 1958, 278–94.

Wolberg, L.R. 1967. *The Technique of Psychotherapy*. London: William Heinemann Medical Books.

Chapter 4

"Worlding" Psychoanalytic Insights: Unpicking R.D. Laing's Geographies

Cheryl McGeachan

Introduction

The theoretical landscape of Scottish psychiatrist and psychotherapist Ronald David Laing's written work appears as a complex weave of ideas from phenomenology, existentialism, psychoanalysis and humanism, knotting them in intricate and unusual ways. Laing has been declared, since his death in 1989, a "divided self" (Clay 1996), a "trickster" (Westcott in Mezan 1972), an acid Marxist (Mullan 1997) and, alongside Foucault, Szasz and Goffman, one of the four horsemen of the anti-psychiatric apocalypse (Sedgwick in Clare 1982). His life and work nonetheless remains underexplored in the geographical literature to date. Born in Glasgow in 1927, Laing became fascinated with the intricate connections between body and mind. Studying medicine at Glasgow University in the late 1940s, and training in psychiatry in Army facilities and NHS long stay mental hospitals across Britain during the early 1950s, Laing became entranced by the patients who he encountered – particularly those diagnosed with psychotic disorders – and disturbed by the care that many of them were receiving. Laing moved to London to train in psychoanalysis at the Tavistock Clinic of Human Relations in 1956, under the supervision of Marion Milner and Donald Winnicott, beginning a highly influential period of his life when key texts such as *The Divided Self* (1960), *The Self and Others* (1961), and *Sanity, Madness and the Family* (1964) were drafted (during or shortly after his time there). Intriguingly, it appears that his time at the Tavistock, rather than enticing him further into psychoanalytic thought and practice, turned his attention back to the "psychotic" patients who he had met in psychiatric practice, but also to the existential and phenomenological insights that inspired his earlier thinking, causing an interesting fusion to emerge.

This chapter aims to build upon previous work on Laing that has situated his experiences (McGeachan 2013a, 2013b), but to adjust the focus in order to think more explicitly about the relationships that emerge between Laing's theories and therapeutic practices with seriously disturbed individuals and their often deliberate geographical resonances; in short, to think about Laing's geographies. This chapter hence attempts to consider not only the geographies integral to these theories and practices, but also to highlight, through an analysis of some of the case-study material presented in these key texts, Laing's inherently spatial approach in attempting to understand seriously disturbed, often schizophrenic, individuals. Beginning with an introduction to the existential and phenomenological traditions from which Laing drew considerable inspiration, this piece investigates the foundations of Laing's work with his patients and introduces his complex relationship to psychoanalytic thought. Using the case of "Mrs R", it then seeks to demonstrate Laing's insistence on "worlding" psychoanalytic insights, such as the unconscious, through seeing them set squarely in everyday social and familial spaces. Moving to unpick Laing's particular concern with "ontological insecurity" through the case of "magical camouflage", this chapter reveals the attention paid to the situated psycho-dynamics of his patients and their worlds in connection with Scottish psychoanalytic thought. In conclusion, it suggests different Laing-inspired pathways of connection between space, psychoanalysis and mental health geographies.

Laing as Existential Phenomenologist

Laing's desire to understand "psychotic" individuals who he encountered within the context of their own immediate situations arguably drove him away from the approach of Freudian psychoanalysis, with its desire to explain phenomena in terms of essences (Rycroft 1968: 46), and more into the terrains of phenomenology and existentialism. For Laing (1972: 32) the "unconscious" remains that which "we do not communicate, to ourselves or to one another", and is therefore inherently linked to a person's experience of themselves and "others" in the everyday world as "we may convey something to another, without communicating it to ourselves". This focus upon the nature of a person's experience of their own world, of "others" and of themselves, through an existential–phenomenological approach drove Laing (1990: 25) to explore "what the other's 'world' is and his [*sic*] way of being in it". Laing (1990: 19) notes:

> We all know from our personal experience that we can be ourselves only in
> and through our world and there is a sense in which "our" world will die with
> us although "the" world will go on without us. Only existential thought has
> attempted to match the original experience of oneself in relationship to others in
> one's world by a term that adequately reflects this totality. Thus, existentially, the
> concretum is seen as a man's *existence*, his *being-in-the-world*.

Various twentieth-century philosophers, such as Sartre, Merleau-Ponty
and Heidegger, have drawn heavily on aspects of the phenomenological
method, insist that in order "to understand human existence, we need to
put to one side abstract hypotheses, analytical procedures and philosophical
theories, and instead focus on human existence as it is actually lived"
(Cooper 2003: 11). It is these often varied streams of thought that Laing expands
upon in his own therapeutic approach, particularly with schizophrenic individuals
(see Laing 1990). From this perspective, human beings are not "fixed, static,
substance-like objects that can be studied in the same way that atoms or
tables can", but rather human existence is "fundamentally dynamic in nature,
that it is a flux (Merleau-Ponty 1962), an unfolding event (Guignon 1993),
a path (Jaspers 1963) or a process" (Cooper 2003: 12). This kind of claim
demonstrates that "existence is not located *within* the individual, but *between*
the individual and their world" (Cooper 2003: 18, emphasis in original).
MacQuarrie (1972: 58) argues that "[t]he existentialist begins with concrete
being-in-the-world, and out of this initial unity self and world arise as
equiprimordial realities", and it is from this position of being-in-the-world,
of one's standing out towards the world, that Laing began to think about the
extremely disturbed patients who he was encountering in mental hospitals and
private practices across Britain.

This focus upon an individual's being, as expressive of their mode of
being-in-the-world, led Laing to consider the role of the therapist in this
existential–phenomenological approach, bringing him back, once again,
to consider the Freudian endeavour. Although Laing acknowledges Freud's
distinctive influence, he was also eager to demonstrate his critique of
and general scepticism about psychoanalytic interpretation, despite his
experimental attempts to utilise Freudian inspired methods, such a dream
analysis, during his early career (see Beveridge 2011). Throughout *The Divided
Self*, Laing develops a distinction between "explanation" and "understanding"
that is central to his thought, demonstrating one aspect of Laing's divergence
from Freudian theory and practice (see Miller 2004). This particular way

of looking and treating individuals in his care has strong resonances with the Scottish psychoanalytic traditions, as demonstrated by the work of Ian Suttie and John Fairbairn, that presents the human personality as born into communion with others, with the aim of therapy being to restore, preserve and promote genuinely interpersonal relations (Miller 2008). Laing argues that, for "psychotic" patients in the therapeutic setting, "explanatory models actually stand in the way of simply understanding what is being said and done by a patient" (Miller 2004: 42). They encourage the therapist to look at the patient's actions as "signs" of a "disease", which then categorises them in an already constructed list of defined conditions (Laing 1990: 33). Physical diagnosis by inspecting patients for external signs such as inflammations, or obtaining articulations of inner symptoms such as pain, is problematic for Laing because this approach to the patient automatically summons explanation rather than understanding (Miller 2004: 42). Laing (1990: 33) evidences his distinction between explanation and understanding with an example of how a therapist may attempt to explain a patient's behaviour in the therapeutic encounter:

> If I am sitting opposite you and speaking to you, you may be trying (i) to assess any abnormalities in my speech, or (ii) to explain what I am saying in terms of how you are imagining my brain cells to be metabolizing oxygen, or (iii) to discover why, in terms of past history and socio-economic background, I should be saying these things at this time.

Explanations can indeed be made in any one of these ways, but Laing (1990: 33) proposes that "not one of the answers that you may or may not be able to supply to these questions will in itself supply you with a simple understanding of what I am getting at". Therefore, for Laing, the sense of the patients' words will remain eternally un-grasped by scientific explanation (Miller 2004: 42).

Laing's desire to take an "understanding" approach towards his "psychotic" patients does not at first seem inhospitable to psychoanalytic interpretation, but throughout his published case studies it appears that Laing was reluctant to "interpret" his patients psychoanalytically. Laing's relationship to psychoanalysis was dynamic and interchangeable, often stitching together ideas from Freud, Jung, existential psychoanalysis and ideas from his Scottish predecessors. In some ways, Laing felt that psychoanalytic theory could be depersonalising, since viewing the individual as a victim of unconscious processes may overlook that first and foremost this patient is a person (Beveridge 2011: 73).

Mrs R

One case study that illustrates this tension is the case of "Mrs R" found in *The Divided Self*. Laing noted that the presenting difficulty faced by Mrs R was a dread of being in the street, commonly labelled as the condition "agoraphobia". However, he observed that, on closer inspection, this was not necessarily the case as, while Mrs R's anxiety arose when she began to feel on her own in the street or elsewhere, "she could *be* on her own, as long as she did not feel that she was really alone" (Laing 1990: 54; emphasis in original). Laing believed it necessary to understand Mrs R's experience from her own understanding of it, and he therefore found it essential to outline her current personal context. In short, Mrs R was an only child and always felt that her parents were too engrossed in each other ever to take notice of her. She longed to be significant to someone else in whatever capacity she could, and at the age of 17 she married the first man who really took notice of her. Shortly, however, he was posted abroad. Unable to go with him, Mrs R felt a sense of severe panic, but not depression, at this separation, but this feeling was broken by the sudden illness of her mother. She moved back home to help take care of her mother, and for the next year she had never been, as she put it, "so much herself". There was no return of her sense of panic until after her mother's death, when the prospect of leaving the place where she had finally come to mean so much became a reality. Once again, it was not sadness Mrs R conveyed, as there was a distinct absence of grief at her mother's death, but fear at the thought of being increasingly alone in the world. After her mother's death, she went to join her husband abroad for a few years until she became restless and unsatisfied, leading to the disintegration and eventual break-up of the marriage. Mrs R then returned to London where she lived in a flat with her father and became the mistress and model of a sculptor for a few years until she was 28, when she entered therapy with Laing.

Mrs R's initial diagnosis of agoraphobia was connected to the way in which she reacted and felt towards social spaces. When speaking of the street, Mrs R observed:

> In the street people come and go about their business. You seldom meet anyone who recognizes you; even if they do, it is just a nod and they pass on or at most you have a few minutes' chat. Nobody knows who you are. Everyone's engrossed in themselves. No one cares about you (as quoted in Laing 1990: 55).

Her anxiety was clearly at being in the street alone or feeling on her own in this social space, for if she went into the same places with someone else she felt no anxiety. Different spaces evoked diverse emotions, and Laing (1990: 55) found that, although she was often alone in her father's flat, it was different as she never felt *really* on her own because to her "everything was familiar". Laing (1990: 56) observed:

> There was her father's chair and his pipe rack. There was a picture of her mother on the wall looking down on her. It was as though all these familiar objects somehow illuminated the house with the presence of the people who possessed and used them or had done so as part of their lives.

Laing brings attention to the micro-spaces of this familiar place in order to capture their importance in understanding Mrs R's own experience, as it was indeed (as stated) not that she could not be alone, it was that she could never *feel* like she was really alone, a state of being consistently played out in different settings throughout her life. Laing (1990) argued that, in order to understand Mrs R, we need to comprehend the experience of threatened existence that he designates "ontological insecurity". Hence, he believed that the central experience of Mrs R is her difficulty in experiencing her own existence. If Mrs R is not in the presence of another person who knows her, or she cannot evoke a person's presence in their absence through the likes of familiar furnishings, "her sense of her own identity drains away from her". Laing (1990: 56) noted that, just like Tinker Bell in J.M. Barrie's play *Peter Pan*, in order for Mrs R to exist "she needs someone else to believe in her existence".

Interestingly, Laing (1990: 56) argued that "the central or pivotal issue in this patient's life is not to be discovered in her 'unconscious'; it is lying quite open for all to see". He admitted that there were many things about herself that she did not realise, and so she was therefore in this sense "unconscious" of who she was; he believed that she would not find a greater self-consciousness through a Freudian interpretation (Miller 2004: 46). Laing (1990: 56) accepted that there was an obvious psychoanalytic interpretation of Mrs R's anxiety which regarded her "as unconsciously [and] libidinally bound to her father with, consequently, unconscious guilt and unconscious need and/or fear of punishment". The supporting evidence for this interpretation was "her failure to develop lasting libidinal relationships away from her father … along with her decision to live with him, to take her mother's place, as it were, and the fact that she spent most of her day, as a woman of twenty-eight, actually thinking about him".

However, Laing (1990: 57) suggested that "one cannot transpose her central problem into the 'unconscious'" as this would be yet another manoeuvre in order *not* to encounter the patient. In the case of Mrs R, Laing (1990: 57, emphasis in original) reflected:

> Her fear of being alone is not a "defence" against incestuous libidinal phantasies or masturbation. She had incestuous phantasies. *These phantasies were a defence against the dread of being alone*, as was her whole "fixation" on being a daughter.

Laing asserted that it would be "a mistake to translate her problem into phases of psychosexual development, oral, anal, genital" (Laing 1990: 57), since this Freudian interpretation would only obscure what was going on in this woman's life in terms of her everyday existence. For Laing (1990: 58), it was Mrs R's lack of ontological autonomy – the fact that she "could not be herself, by herself, and so could not really be herself at all" – which was of crucial significance and not the Freudian elements of repressed and deviant psychosexual development.

"Worlding" Psychoanalysis

Utilising such approaches, based on existential and phenomenological foundations, allowed Laing to concentrate on the unique experiences of these individuals, such as Mrs R, as set within their worldly contexts, and led him to consider the different spaces and environments that impacted upon their existence. During his time spent in psychiatric institutions, Laing became acutely aware that these disturbed individuals had to "live on" (Laing 1990: 65) in, and through, the many different societies, communities, institutions and family environments from which they came, and back into which they might be sent, and he therefore became increasingly concerned to widen his thoughts about these spaces and places. Laing (1972: 37, emphasis in original) observed:

> In so far as we experience the world differently, in a sense we live in different worlds. "The Universe is full of men [*sic*] going through the same motions in the same surroundings, but carrying within themselves, and projecting around them, universes as mutually remote as the constellations" (Mourier 1952: 5). Yet *the* world – the world around me, the world in which I live, *my* world – is, in the very texture of its mode of being-for-me, not exclusively my world, but your world also, it is around you and him [*sic*] as well, *one* world, *the* world.

Laing recognised the importance of investigating the relationships that these individuals were having, on a daily basis, at once with both the everyday spaces of the world around them and the people encountered within these landscapes. For Laing (1972: 135), in order to understand the "position" in which his patients lived, it was necessary to investigate the original sense of place in the world in which they lived, for "the space, geometrical and metaphorical, of both adult and child, is highly structured by the influence of others, one way or the other, all of the time". Moreover, Laing resisted the temptation to focus explicitly upon the spectacular displays of "madness", and instead turned the majority of his attention to the everyday situated psychodynamics of existence in order to tease out the complex interplays between his patients and their worlds.

One particular concern that emerged predominantly through Laing's earlier work, that chimes with the previously mentioned Scottish psychoanalytic tradition, detailed how people are involved in, and deal with, the issues arising from an existential position of what he labels "primary ontological insecurity" (1990: 39). His notion of ontological insecurity revolved around the feelings of a precarious and threatened sense of existence, and the ontologically insecure individual was seen as constantly engaged in a battle somehow to save the "self" from slipping out of existence. He argued that:

> If a position of primary ontological security has been reached, the ordinary circumstances of life do not afford a perpetual threat to one's own existence. If such a basis for living has not been reached, the ordinary circumstances of everyday life constitute a continual and deadly threat (Laing 1990: 42).

These threats come in a wide variety of shapes and forms, but for many with an already sound sense of ontological security, they appear so mundane that they simply vanish into insignificance.

A case study used by Laing to highlight the anxieties and threats felt by those individuals in an ontologically insecure position centred on a 12-year-old girl who employed a form of "magical camouflage" in an attempt to escape from her frightening environment. This girl recalled to Laing (1990: 110) how, in order to reach her father's shop, she would have to take a long walk through her local park. She stated that this was a walk rarely enjoyed and, especially as the nights grew darker and the scenery began to take on a more eerie quality, she felt increasing frightened when embarking upon the route. In order to combat this fear, she decided to play a game with herself that could help to pass the time:

> It struck me that if I stared long enough at the environment that I would blend
> with it and disappear just as if the place was empty and I had disappeared. It is as
> if you get yourself to feel you don't know who you are or where you are (quoted
> in Laing 1990: 110).

For this girl, being visible left her exposed to the risk of attack, but she believed that, by becoming invisible, she would be protected from any external threats. By attempting to blend herself into the landscape through the reduction of differences, this girl was trying to make herself indistinguishable from anything around her. However, the girl noted that the problem for her arose when she began to blend with the landscape without encouraging it. This would occur as she simply walked down the street, and she would become so frightened of disappearing that she would have to repeat her name over and over again in order to bring herself "back to life" (Laing 1990: 110). Laing speculated that this girl's game demonstrated a type of defence mechanism used regularly in certain schizophrenic conditions, given that being like everyone else – being *incognito*, being nobody (having nobody) – are all ways of protecting the self from annihilation. The fact that this girl was able to lose her sense of identity so easily in a game, leaving her desperate to bring herself back from the landscape, led Laing to question her ontological foundation. He suggested that it was highly probable that she initially came from the position of ontological insecurity, partly prompting her anxiety in the first place, and was therefore in effect using "her source of weakness as her avenue of escape" (Laing 1990: 111). Laing (ibid.) added that:

> In blending with the landscape, she lost her autonomous identity, in fact she
> lost her self and it was just her "self" that was endangered by being alone in the
> gathering dusk in an empty expanse.

For Laing, this young girl expressed a common feature of the ontologically insecure individual, in that, when the threat to the individual is loss of being, then one of the commonest forms of defence is precisely to lapse into a state of non-being.

Laing related that, just like the case of the 12-year-old girl, in order to save one's "self" from the continual threats present in daily existence, ontologically insecure individuals carefully devise complex strategies enabling them to live on through their everyday social worlds. Laing's interest in the lived experience of these un-embodied individuals led him to consider their

interactions with others and the world. In so doing, he quickly became aware
of the many devices and strategies employed in an attempt both to function
and to maintain relationships in everyday "normal" existence. Within the
scission that occurs between the self and the body of these individuals, Laing
found that two elements appear to highlight the lived consequences of this
split. One such element Laing (1990: 78) labelled the "inner self", associated
with the psychical withdrawal "into" one's self and "out of" the body:

> The "inner self" is occupied in phantasy and in observation. It observes the
> processes of perception and action. Experience does not impinge (or at any rate
> this is the intention) directly on this self, and the individual's acts are not self-
> expressions. Direct relationships with the world are the province of a false-self
> system (Laing 1990: 94).

A "divided self" is created in that the "inner self" remains detached and
hidden from others and the world, leaving the "false self system" to act as a
shield protecting the inner self from harm by exposure. This complex strategy
means that "the self's relationship to the other is always at one remove"
(Laing 1990: 80), since the self can never be revealed directly in the individual's
gestures or actions and neither can it ever experience anything spontaneously.
Although the inner self is preoccupied with phantasies, memories,
thoughts and experiencing the automatic nature of action through the false
self system, it is far from "sleepy" and is often thinking and observing with
exceptional intelligibility (Laing 1990: 78). By creating this division the
un-embodied individual feels that they become liberated in that, no matter
what is occurring between the world and the false self system, the inner
self can always remain apathetic and indifferent. In phantasy, the self can
be anything, go anywhere, or have anyone it likes and thus be completely
free – but *only* in phantasy (Laing 1990: 84). In reality, Laing (1990: 80)
reckoned that these individuals become engaged in a tragic struggle because,
by developing a strategy to protect their self from destruction, one predicated
on preventing the self from having a direct relationship with real people and
real things in the world, they inevitably begin to lose the self's own sense of
realness, aliveness and identity. Arguably for Laing, within this concept there
is a wilful disentangling from "geography" (physical and social); an ultimately
destructive state of being that can only be remedied by *re*-earthing someone
and connecting them back to their immediate geography and hence the
importance of "the place".

Laing (1990: 85) proposed that, in many schizophrenic conditions, it is the destructiveness in phantasy, caused by the creation of a closed circuit between phantasy and reality, that – quite contrary to the desired effect – leads to the individual's inner world and self becoming nothing but ruins and allowing "real toads [to] invade the imaginary gardens and ghosts [to] walk in the real streets". In fostering this division, these individuals are creating a microcosmos within themselves, but Laing (1990: 74–5) worried that this private and intra-individual world becomes no feasible substitute for the only world that there really *is*: the shared world.

Conclusions: Towards Laing's Geographies?

> The greatest psychopathologist has been Freud. Freud was a hero. He descended to the "Underworld" and met there stark terrors. He carried with him his theory as a Medusa's head which turned these terrors to stone. We who follow Freud have the benefit of the knowledge he brought back with him and conveyed to us. He survived. We must see if we now can survive without using a theory that is in some measure an instrument of defence (Laing 1990: 25).

This consulting of Laing's theoretical work to divulge the geographies present within them, draws to attention the possibilities for future engagement with Laing's work by academic geographers in uncovering different connective sinews between space and psychoanalytic thought. This way of inquiring into Laing's theories opens new and differently developed insights into psychoanalytic thinking, since his tendency – following an existential–phenomenological approach – to "world" psychoanalytic concepts, such as the unconscious and phantasy, particularly within the micro-social environments of family and home, departs from much of the previous work that has been conducted on figures such as Freud and Lacan within the psychoanalytic geographies literature (see Pile 1996). In the previous quotation, Laing teams the word "hero" with reference to the "underworld", a term he often deploys when describing patients who he has encountered, thereby positioning them as people condemned to a world beyond the horizon, a place populated by haunting darkness and unimaginable terrors. However, Laing charts a different "underworld" terrain from that of Freud, since he comes to explore the *psychotic* patient's experience rather than the preferred psychoanalytic choice of the *neurotic* individual. References are often made to the "underworld" of the unconscious realm and it is clear that, despite his cynicism, Laing was undoubtedly intrigued by Freud's conception of the unconscious as the undoubted pivot around which psychoanalysis orbits, as shown in the case of Mrs R. It appears within this passage that for Laing, the greatness of Freud lies less in the intricacies of his psychoanalytic theory, and more in his willingness to enter the "underworld" of experienced mental ill-health and to "meet" with the horrors he found there. Laing's rejection, at times, of Freudian interpretation, in favour of an existential-phenomenological approach, leads to a distancing of his own work and practice from that of the Freudian schools, yet he remains inspired by Freud's "descent" and impressed by his survival.

This chapter has been an initial attempt to introduce the possibilities of working through Laing's geographies by investigating some of the patient case studies covered in his early work, and to demonstrate the spatial resonances that appear when his theoretical work is inspected through a geographical lens. Whether drawing from Scottish psychoanalytic traditions, phenomenological musings, or existential theorising, Laing was continuously focussed upon the creation and development of placed interpersonal relations. Being with someone, viewing them from their own experience, seeing them as a *person* and not a thing and attempting to understand them within the context and spaces of their own life – worlds full of people, often strange family socio-spatial dynamics – are all crucial components of the therapeutic encounter for Laing. This is what relates back to the meaning by Laing's "worlding" of psychoanalysis, and indeed too of psychotherapy: if the former for Laing "worlds" the problematic immediacies of everyday lives lived in, with and often against proximate others, usually intimate others, then the later for Laing "worlds" possible solutions in alternative everyday communal, shared, genuinely inter-human (not professional analysis/analysand) relations enacted in all manner of (non-psychiatricised) spaces. By unpicking Laing's geographies, this chapter has sought to initiate further discussion over what Laing could mean for a recasting of psychoanalytic geographies which is more "worlded" in everyday spaces and places, more attuned to the psychotic – particularly schizophrenic – individual and therefore more tethered to the work on mental health geographies. Laing's own deep interest, to put it simply, for everyday social contexts and also the experiences of severely "disturbed" individuals arguably sets a framing for a rather different knotting together of the psychoanalytic, the psychotherapeutic and the concern for mental ill-health in human-geographical inquiry.

References

Beveridge, A. 2011. *Portrait of the Psychiatrist as a Young Man: The Early Writing and Work of R.D. Laing, 1927–1960*. Oxford: Oxford University Press.

Clare, A. 1982. Four horsemen of the apocalypse. *New Society*. Papers of Ronald David Laing, Special Collections, University of Glasgow. MS Laing T196.

Cooper, M. 2003. *Existential Therapies*. London: Sage Publications.

Guignon, C. 1993. *The Cambridge Companion to Heidegger*. Cambridge: Cambridge University Press.

Jaspers, K. 1963. *General Psychopathology*. Manchester: Manchester University Press.

Laing, A. 1994. *R.D. Laing: A Biography*. United Kingdom: Sutton.

Laing, R.D. c.1960/1990. *The Divided Self: An Existential Study in Sanity and Madness*. England: Penguin Books.

Laing, R.D. 1961. *The Self and Others: Further Studies in Sanity and Madness*. London: Tavistock.

Laing, R.D. 1972. *Self and Others*. Great Britain: Penguin Books.

Laing, R.D. and Esterson, A. c.1964/1990. *Sanity, Madness and the Family: Families of Schizophrenics*. England: Penguin Books.

MacQuarrie, J. 1972. *Existentialism*. USA: Penguin.

McGeachan, C. 2013a. (Re)remembering and narrating the childhood city of R.D. Laing. *Cultural Geographies*, 20(3), 269–84.

McGeachan, C. 2013b. Needles, picks and an intern named Laing: exploring the psychiatric spaces of army life. *Journal of Historical Geography*, 40, 67–78.

Merleau-Ponty, M. 1962. *The Phenomenology of Perception*. London: Routledge and Kegan Paul.

Mezan, P. 1972. After Freud and Jung, now comes R.D. Laing. *Esquire*, 77, 160–78.

Miller, G. 2004. *R.D. Laing*. Edinburgh: Edinburgh Review.

Miller, G. 2008. Scottish psychoanalysis: a rational religion. *Journal of the History of Behavioural Science*, 44, 38–58.

Mullan, B. 1997. *R.D. Laing: Creative Destroyer*. London: Cassell.

Pile, S. 1996. *The Body and the City: Psychoanalysis, Space and Subjectivity*. London: Routledge.

Rycroft, C. 1968. *A Critical Dictionary of Psychoanalysis*. England: Penguin Books.

Chapter 5

Mapping Trauma: Topography to Topology

Virginia L. Blum and Anna J. Secor

On February 24, 1984, a sniper fired successive rounds of ammunition at an elementary school playground from a building across the street (Pynoos and Nader 1989). One child and one passerby were killed, and 13 other children and one playground attendant were injured. During subsequent interviews with 113 children from the school whose exposure to danger ranged from high to nonexistent, researchers were struck by a pattern of spatial memory whereby those whose risk was highest recalled themselves further away from the scene and those whose risk was lowest "increased their life threat by (1) bringing themselves closer to danger, or (2) imagining the danger moving closer to them" (Pynoos and Nader 1989: 240). This place of relocation was in fact what the authors termed a "safe location," the zone most proximate to danger and yet just beyond risk (237). It was the imaginary place where experienced trauma was warded off (for the most exposed children) and registered (for the least exposed). All of these children spatialized their experience of trauma by asserting the ways in which material space (where they were physically located during the event) intersected with psychic space (where they remembered being). It is this psycho-material spatiality of trauma that is the subject of this essay.

To demonstrate how trauma works to fold both space and time, we will juxtapose this contemporary schoolyard shooting to a very early case from Freud's *Project for a Scientific Psychology* (1895). Emma first came for treatment as an adult who was phobic about entering shops alone. Analysis initially revealed a scene from when Emma was 12 years old and had gone alone into a shop. She noticed two shop assistants laughing at what she imagined were her clothes, and she rushed from the store in fright. She confessed that she found one of the stop assistants sexually attractive. "Further investigation now revealed a second memory (Scene II), which she denies having had in mind at the moment of Scene I. On two occasions when she was a child of eight she had gone into a small shop to buy some sweets, and the shopkeeper had grabbed at her genitals through her clothes" (1895: 353–4). When Scene II (the earlier scene) becomes pathogenic due to the deferred action of Scene I (the later scene), Emma develops a compulsion: she refuses to enter shops alone. While this might make sense if she was seeking protection, we learn that even a child companion suffices. Thus company of any kind provides a sort of talisman against a repeat not only of the assault, but the sexual release traumatically/unconsciously linked to the assault, which Emma retrospectively imagines she invited. "Here we have a case of a memory arousing an affect which it did not arouse as an experience, because in the meantime the change [brought about] in puberty had made possible a different understanding of what was remembered"(1895: 356). Jean Laplanche points to how the two events of the Emma case reiterate the diphasic nature of sexuality itself (infantile and pubertal). He describes "the seesaw effect between the two events [in which] [n]either of the two events in itself is traumatic" (1976: 41). Trauma is what happens when the two "scenes" converge in defiance of linear time and topographical space.

The premise of this chapter is that although the "scene" of trauma lacks a determinate time and place (it is, in a sense, unlocalizable), it is nevertheless spatial. But how so, since place is exactly what gets drained of specificity in the case of the traumatic neuroses? Trauma, a flood of intolerable stimuli, could be said to happen out of place or sequence. Freud writes that "dreams occurring in traumatic neuroses have the characteristic of repeatedly bringing the patient back into the situation of his accident, a situation from which he wakes up in another fright" (Freud 1920: 13). This observation raised a major question for Freud, since to feel traumatized by an event in battle or a horrific accident makes sense, but when we relive the trauma in another time and place, what principle is in operation?

It is through repetition phenomena that we can begin to understand the spatiality of trauma. In attempting to account for repetition phenomena that are inexplicable from the vantage point of the pleasure principle, Freud (1920) theorized the death drive, that which was "beyond" the pleasure principle and served primarily masochistic ends. Freud identified three phenomena that led him to revise his first instinctual dualism (between sex and self-preservation) to his second (life vs. death): 1) certain kinds of painful repetitions in children's play (e.g. the mother's absences or any event that highlighted the child's helplessness); 2) the traumatic neuroses in general (e.g. dreams that painfully throw soldiers back into the heat of battle); and 3) repetition in analysis in combination with the dreams of analysands. A central element of repetition in analysis is the patient's unwillingness to give up their painful symptoms

(Freud 1937). Thus, the resistance to cure is more than simply clinging to the secondary gain provided by one's symptom; it is the symptom itself, masochistically flourishing in the cycle its own never-ending reiteration.

Psychologically intolerable events, in combination with their retroactivity (*après coup*, as Lacan put it, after Freud's *Nachträglichkeit*), unfold in a repetition that is experienced simultaneously as once-removed and yoked interminably to the traumatic event. This event needs to be relocated again and again, in series of scenes, in order for trauma to sustain itself. Kathryn Stockton describes it this way: "Freud developed this view ... as a way to explain how a trauma encountered in childhood—more precisely, received as an impression—might become operative *as* a trauma, never mind consciously grasped as such, only later in life through deferred effect and belated understanding, which retroactively cause the trauma, putting past and present ego-structures side-by-side, almost cubistically, in lateral spread" (Stockton 2009: 14). We will show that trauma is *topological*, which is to say that the "origin" of trauma is not a single event localizable in time and space, but rather a topological constellation in which ordinary ideas of space (such as distance or location) are distorted and subject to ongoing transformations. The topological structure of trauma, we will argue, is at once cause and effect of psychical repetition phenomena.

When we use the term topology, we are following Lacan, whose work became increasingly topological as he attempted to map the structure of the subject without being limited to surfaces that are fully graphable in three dimensional space (Lacan 1975, 1976, 1997). Topology refers to a branch of qualitative mathematics that understands space in a non-Euclidean framework. In Euclidean geometry, Cartesian coordinates allow location to be defined in terms of positions along intersecting axes. This is *topography*: mappable, graphable, measurable space. But topologically speaking, a space is not defined by the distances between points, but rather by the characteristics that it maintains in the process of distortion and transformation (bending, stretching, squeezing, but not breaking). Topology thus deals not with measurable distances or locational coordinates, but with surfaces and their properties of boundedness, orientability, decomposition, and connectivity. For Lacan, the relational structures defined by topology allowed him to represent some of his basic insights about the structure of the subject, such as how heterogeneous elements (e.g. the ego and its objects) can be both non-identical and continuous, just as the interior and exterior of a Mobius strip are both distinct and constantly in the process of becoming one another (Lacan 2006: 486, fn).

Topographical vs. Topological Space: *Studies in Hysteria*

Freud's earliest ideas about the etiology of hysteria focused on the role of trauma as the precipitating cause of hysterical symptoms. Yet, the traumas that afflict the hysterics of his early work with Josef Breuer are not usually dramatic, singular events, like a schoolyard shooting or the experience of war. Instead, as in the case of Emma, the traumas of the hysterics are partial, multiple, and "psychical." As Breuer and Freud write, "In the case of common hysteria it not infrequently happens that, instead of a single, major trauma, we find a number of partial traumas forming a group of provoking causes" (1893: 6). Such multiple and partial traumas abound in moments that call forth "distressing affects" such as fright, anxiety, or shame. Further, as a precipitating cause of hysterical symptoms, trauma is not distant from its effects, but instead is a "determining process [that] continues to operate in some way or other for years ... a *directly* releasing cause" (1893: 7, emphasis in the original). They liken this trauma to a foreign body lodged within the patient; long after its entry, it is still at work. Here, we can see the connection between this early idea of traumatic hysteria and the post-First World War version in *Beyond the Pleasure Principle*: in each case, the effects of trauma are notable for their recurrence. Indeed, Breuer and Freud conclude from their studies, "*Hysterics suffer mainly from reminiscences*" (7).

In the formation of hysterical symptoms, the spaces of the body and domestic life are subject to topological transformations. While for Emma, the space in question is a store, for the *Studies in Hysteria* case study, Fraulein Elisabeth von R., the young woman's legs become a map of her psychic constellation. The particular location on her right thigh from which her pains radiate turns out to have been the "place that her father used to rest his leg every morning, while she renewed the bandage around it, for it was badly swollen" (1893: 148). Every further psychical trauma becomes attached to fresh pains in other regions of her legs, "zones of pain" with corresponding fantasies. Like the children in the schoolyard shooting example, Elisabeth remakes space—in this case, the space of her body—to correspond with the unconscious fantasy. Her vagina is relocated to her thigh, her father's penis to his leg. The anatomy of the body (a kind of topographical map) is reconfigured topologically.

While the somatic mapping of trauma might be the most recognized spatial/anatomical conversion of hysteria, hysterical symptoms also topologically transform domestic and everyday spaces. In *Studies on Hysteria*, it is notable that in most cases the outcome of the onset of hysterical symptoms is the confinement of these women to the very domestic spaces within which the traumas of their lives have been staged. In other words, they become unable to leave the scene of the trauma, a "scene" they now sustain on their bodies. The immobilizing symptoms of hysteria (paralysis, taking to bed) become a kind of resistance to the suppression of the traumatic scene, a refusal to evacuate or to move to a "safe location." Freud's work is thus to overcome this refusal in order to transform, topologically, the space of trauma into a qualitatively different space, a safe location. In order to make this transformation, the logic of the traumatic repetition must be disrupted; topologically speaking, the spaces of the body or the home (or in the case of Emma, the shop) must no longer be experienced as the same. A new topological cut or connection must be made in order to escape the repetitions of the traumatic constellation.

How topological repetition happens to begin with is dramatically illustrated in Breuer's case of Anna O., who experiences a temporal fold that reveals the material contours of her hysterical neurosis. In 1881, while being treated by Breuer for a series of symptoms (paraphasia, paralyses, disturbances in vision, somnambulism), Anna O. day by day re-experiences the corresponding events of 1880. Significantly for Anna O., in 1881 she is living in a different house than the one of 1880. Indeed, Breuer notes that during the first period of her illness, Anna's greatest fear is being removed from her home (the scene of her father's illness and death), and that following the move there is some improvement in her condition. Yet, when Anna O. is reliving 1880, she also experiences her new location as materially the same as her old one: "She was carried back to the previous year with such intensity that in the new house she hallucinated her old room, so that when she wanted to go to the door she knocked up against the stove which stood in the same relation to the window as the door did in the old room" (1893: 33). Anna O.'s room is not incidental to her unconscious fantasy; it is the material substance of her psychic state and of her traumatic repetition. Her family may have thought that Anna O. could be moved to a safe location, but the hysteric refuses, performing a topological twist (as on a Mobius strip) to re-place herself within the scene of the trauma, to repeat precisely that which she should not want to repeat.

The importance of recognizing the topological aspects of trauma can be illustrated by a short case study. Freud recounts that, while vacationing in the Eastern Alps, he hiked to the top of a mountain where he encountered a young woman named Katharina who tells him that she has been suffering from shortness of breath and hallucinations of a dreadful face. Freud narrates Katharina's story as he uncovers it, a tale that includes her coming upon the scene of an uncle copulating with her cousin. This sight activates Katharina's understanding of previous scenes in which her uncle had been making sexual advances on her, and these earlier advances become the traumatic kernel releasing her hysterical symptoms. While Freud's account of the case is fascinating in its own right (demonstrating most clearly the oscillating temporality of trauma), what is of particular significance for us here is the footnote that Freud added in 1924:

> I venture after the lapse of so many years to lift the veil of discretion ... The girl fell ill ... as a result of sexual attempts on the part of her own father. Distortions like the one which I introduced into the present instance should be altogether avoided in reporting a case history. From the point of view of understanding the case, a distortion of this kind is not, of course, a matter of such indifference as would be shifting the scene from one mountain to another (Freud 1893: 134, fn 2).

Freud's two possible dislocations—one from the father to the uncle, the other from one mountain to another—illustrate the difference between topological and topographical space. The original distortion of identity that Freud performs in the telling of the case study, turning the father into the uncle, fundamentally changes the constellation of Katharina's trauma (and not incidentally, delays Freud's recognition of the Oedipal constellation). By changing the uncle into the father, we would argue, what Freud actually changed was the relational structure of Katharina's trauma; he changed, in other words, the psycho-topological space of the case. Looking back on his own narrative, Freud regrets this manipulation. A geographical move, he suggests, from one mountain to another, would have done a better job of disguising the case while leaving the coordinates of the trauma intact. Indeed, this topographical displacement would have reproduced Katharina's real life experience: Her mother moved with her to a different mountain after learning of the father's transgressions. This move, of course, did not succeed in relocating Katharina psychically, since she carried the traumatic scene with her through her hysterical symptoms, suggesting that Katharina remained intractably affixed to the scene of trauma regardless of her physical location. Like Anna O. reliving the previous year in the previous house, Katharina could not be moved.

In fact, another way to read Freud's re-evaluation of his own telling of this case is in terms of the attempted production of a "safe location." Drawing on the Pynoos and Nader (1989) schoolyard shooting study, analyst Jack Lindy defines the safe location as "a safe place from which to tell to the story" (Lindy 1989). For Lindy, who specializes in treating traumatized war veterans, a "safe location" is what the analyst needs to identify and occupy (alongside the patient) in order to have access to traumatic materials without putting the patient at risk of re-traumatization. That trauma is simultaneously "scenic" and indeterminately located, that the site of analysis itself can be imagined as a kind of safe viewing platform from which to access psychically explosive memories, suggests the centrality of spatiality to understanding trauma. But this is not a topographic spatiality even though topographic space is seemingly invoked through spatial metaphors; moving Katharina to another mountain (a topographical adjustment) does not change the psychic constellation in the way that shifting her father to her uncle does. Here we can see that, in his presentation of the case, Freud is attempting to find a safe location for Katharina and, at this early stage in his thinking (before he had theorized the Oedipus complex) perhaps himself as well.

Safe Locations/Topography to Topology

We now return to the two cases with which we opened: the schoolyard shooting and Emma. These cases are in some ways dissimilar. One trauma is catastrophic while the other is only partially conscious. Yet both cases involve trauma, memory, and the transformation of space; in fact, both cases involve maps, but of very different varieties. By juxtaposing these two cases and these two maps, we show how the reminiscences of trauma in fact are spatial transformations, taking us away from the certain cartography of the topographic map into the realm of topology.

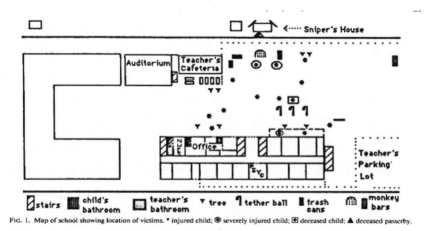

FIG. 1. Map of school showing location of victims. * injured child; ⊛ severely injured child; ⊞ deceased child; ▲ deceased passerby.

Figure 5.1   Map of schoolyard from Pynoos and Nader (1989)

Source: Reprinted from Robert S. Pynoos and Kathleen Nader, Children's Memory and Proximity to Violence, *Journal of the American Academy of Child & Adolescent Psychiatry*, 28(2), 236–41, Copyright (1989), with permission from Elsevier.

Pynoos and Nader, in their analysis of the children's initial recall of the shooting, focus on what appears to them to be the children's distortion of space, which they contrast to a veritable map (Figure 5.1). They describe three levels of spatial distortion corresponding to varying degrees of exposure, from the most exposed to the least. We can observe from their discussion of these three levels that the children most exposed to danger, the most directly in the line of fire, react the most topologically (though of course the authors do not themselves use this term). Write Pynoos and Nader, concerning the first level, "For example, one girl, who had actually been only feet away, placed the fatally wounded child yards across the playground, much closer to the sniper. She remembered the neck injury of the girl who was shot next to her as occurring only after the girl was at a distance. Like other uninjured children, she segregated her injured playmates into one area of the playground, clustered near the deceased girl" (1989: 237). This girl reconfigures the schoolyard around her own spatial immobility. Entirely dependent as she is on psychic space for producing a safe location, she performs a radical topological distortion on the space of the schoolyard.

Other children, who are able to put topographical distance between themselves and the danger, only partially recruit topological space. In danger but nevertheless able to take protective action, these children typically focus on the safest location in their trajectory away from the dangerous event. Pynoos and Nader elaborate: "For example, one child who had felt protected by the outdoor cafeteria divider several feet from her, saw the deceased girl fall and an adult attendant shot in the foot. She then ran to the safe side of the school and went through a safe exit gate. In her initial recall, she placed herself at the exit gate" (237). This child, with considerably more mobility, put herself on the "safe side of the school" in her initial recall. Her memory of events thereby references a material space that is in fact subject to psychic distortion through a reversal whereby she calls on her ultimate "safe location" as a defense against the traumatic memory of actual physical danger.

The least exposed students increased their proximity to the violence through both temporal and spatial folding. Pynoos and Nader again: "A boy who had been away on vacation said that he had been on his way to the school, had seen someone lying on the ground, had heard the shots, and then turned back" (238). Other children who were not at school imagine the sniper alive and terrorizing their neighborhoods. As Pynoos and Nader put it: "They bring the threat closer to home" (238). Curiously both the boy who had been on vacation and the girl who ran away from danger wind up at the same "safe exit gate," which thus figures at the intersection of safe and unsafe, psychic and material, topographical and topological spaces.

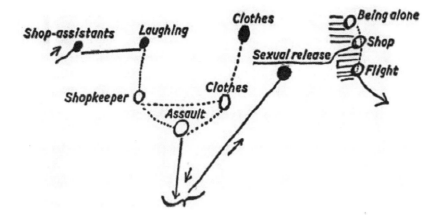

Figure 5.2   Emma's map, Freud (1895)

These children's proximity to the event is at once psychic and material. A psychic topology is helping some to mitigate the trauma while for others, further removed, the spatial folding that brings them in closer to the event reflects their subjective sense of exposure. Most of the children, those who had been nearby and those who had been nowhere close, put themselves in the same place psychically, in one crowded safe location, the vantage point from which they could relive the catastrophic events. The children's topological transformations of the schoolyard produced a solution to traumatic events. In the end, however, Pynoos and Nader leave us with a sense of a veridical measurable material space being radically distorted by trauma, whereas, as we will show, Freud suggests conversely that the intersection of psychic and material space is the (always already) condition for the origin of trauma.

The case study of Emma is brief, comprising only about three pages, and lacks a full discussion of her treatment. Yet, Freud includes in his discussion a graph, or perhaps a map, of Emma's pathology (Figure 5.2). It is a peculiar figure, consisting of circles, some of them blacked in, and lines, some of them dotted. Unblacked-in circles and dotted lines are elements and branches of association that are closed off from consciousness, while the blacked in dots and the solid lines are conscious elements and associations. The map represents the conscious and unconscious elements of the two scenes (shopkeeper, assault, clothes, sexual release, laughing) and the symptom formation (being alone, shop, flight) as a conscious–unconscious network. Interestingly, aside from the conscious connection between the shop assistants of the later scene and their laughing, the conscious elements are disjointed from one another, connected instead by unconscious associations (dotted lines) to the elements of the unconscious scene. In fact, "The whole [unconscious traumatic] complex (unblacked-in [circles]) is represented in consciousness by the one idea clothes," which serves as the symbol of the scene of the assault (Freud 1895: 355). This lack of connection amongst the conscious elements of Scene I (the later scene) and their unconscious connection to the nodes of Scene II (the earlier scene) provides Freud with analytic leverage on Emma's case: "Thought operating *consciously* has made two false connections in the material at its disposal," he writes, referring to the connections made by Emma between the laughter of the shop assistants and her clothes, and the attractive shop assistant and her sexual arousal (355). The diagram does not display these "false connections." As for "sexual release," its conscious connecting branch bypasses the entire diphasic scenic structure of the trauma. Instead, it originates (as indicated by a directional arrow running up the line of connection) from a bracket-like squiggle that is also the terminus (indicated by an arrow running down from the unconscious complex) of the assault. The bracket represents the site of Emma's memory. Freud leaves the case of Emma here with the observation that the sexual release "is linked to the memory of the assault; but it is highly noteworthy that it was not linked to the assault when this was experienced. Here we have the case of a memory arousing an affect which it did not arouse as an experience, because in the meantime the change [brought about] in puberty had made possible a different understanding of what was remembered" (356). In short, this peculiar diagram allows Freud to map the psychic space of Emma's trauma, to present it as a network in which the important information is the set of elements, the ways in which they are connected, and their quality of consciousness or unconsciousness.

Freud's map is thus a kind of network topology of Emma's pathology. A basic idea of network topology is that, so long as you do not alter a graph by taking apart or joining together any elements—that is, so long as you do not make a cut or an addition—distortions such as bending, stretching, folding do not change how the figure can be analyzed. In other words, a circuit can be redrawn in many ways, but so long as it has the same number of nodes connected in the same way, it remains the same topological figure. The ur-story of network topology is the problem of the Bridges of Königsberg, in which the eighteenth-century residents of the city became preoccupied with the problem of how to complete a circuit traversing all seven of the bridges that connected their city once and only once. The mathematician Leonhard Euler, by abstracting the city map into a graph, finds that the problem persists because the basic properties of a circuit are determined by the number of nodes and how they are connected (see Blum and Secor 2011).

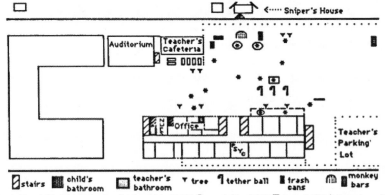

FIG. 1. Map of school showing location of victims. * injured child; ⊛ severely injured child; ⊞ deceased child; ▲ deceased passerby.

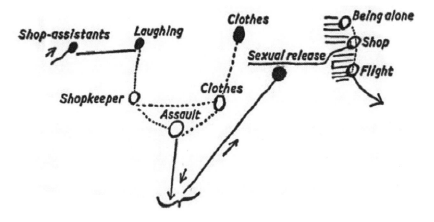

Figure 5.3   Two maps of trauma, side by side

This idea of recurring sameness works well for thinking about Emma's pathology. The store for Emma is embedded within a circuit that, no matter the manifest differences (across time and space), continues to reiterate the self-same relationships amongst its elements.

Understanding Emma's map in this way helps explain her particular solution to the traumatic impasse. If topological sameness—the repetition of the relational matrix that Freud maps—is the problem for Emma, topological difference seems to be a provisional solution. A new person, like a new blacked-in dot with new lines of conscious connection, fundamentally alters the open circuit of the trauma. By bringing someone along with her, Emma makes an addition intended to break the traumatic equivalence between the spaces. Her topological intervention is at once material and psychic. And yet, it is still a pathological solution, inhibiting her daily movement.

The case of Emma is especially rich because it not only illustrates trauma as a network topology, but also reiterates the role of material spaces within the topological constellations of trauma. In the Pynoos and Nader example, topographical locations were reconfigured by the children's defensive operations against the traumatic breach. Through their psychic intervention, the children re-mapped the traumatic event and found for themselves a safe location. In the case of Emma, the location of the shop (any shop) becomes a dangerous location; indeed, once the unconscious connections are made between the two scenes, dangerous locations proliferate for Emma.

Conclusion

Let us now examine the Pynoos and Nader and Freud maps side-by-side (Figure 5.3). The Pynoos and Nader map insists on and even produces a distinction between material and psychic space. It is a straightforward topographical map that is intended to put in relief the distortions involved in the children's recall. Thus, it is a map invested in the precedence of material Euclidean space over the crumpled and folded version produced by the children. Arguably, the Pynoos and Nader map is a re-stabilization of space thrown into disarray by trauma. Freud's map, on the contrary, brings everything onto the same plane, as though to instantiate the equivalence between material and psychic space. In contrast to the spatial certainty of the Pynoos and Nader map, Freud's is anxiety-inducing in its defiance of topographical space. For Freud, the unconscious is an atemporal apparatus that calls forth alternative spatialities, and is consequently what manages zones of safety and danger. Indeed, it is through the topological operations of the unconscious that materially safe locations become psychically dangerous and dangerous spaces are reimagined into safe locations.

In his 1930 work, *Civilization and Its Discontents*, Freud compared the archeology of the unconscious to that of the city of Rome: "Now let us, by a flight of imagination, suppose that Rome is not a human habitation but a psychic entity with a similarly long and copious past—an entity, that is to say, in which nothing that has once come into existence will have passed away and all the earlier phases of development continue to exist alongside the latest one" (Freud 1930: 70). Let us read this famous passage topologically. Freud makes his point about the atemporality of the unconscious through a spatial example, but not because it provides a sensible illustration. On the contrary, it is materially impossible for previous structures to co-exist on the same site. With this analogy, in which psychic space is founded upon material space and yet exceeds it, Freud forces us to conceptualize a different kind of spatiality, one that goes beyond topography to the topological. Indeed, for Lacan, topology was the key to understanding the workings of psychic space. It allows us to imagine psychic structures interpenetrating in ways that cannot be accomplished without topological foldings, like the Cubist "lateral spread" to which Stockton refers.

Such a psychotopological approach models alternative spatialities that we otherwise apprehend as mere distortions. By pursuing trauma back to Freud's early work on hysteria, we have shown that trauma—whether conscious or unconscious, whether domestic or on the battlefield—by its very nature defies temporal linearity and the Cartesian grid. Instead, trauma works as a topological constellation, a set of unconscious coordinates that upends the passage of time and the verities of space.

References

Blum, V. and Secor, A. 2011. Psychotopologies: closing the circuit between psychic and material space. *Environment and Planning D: Society and Space*, 29(6), 1030–47.

Breuer, J. and Freud, S. 1893. Studies on hysteria. *Standard Edition*, 2.

Freud, S. 1895. Project for a scientific psychology. *Standard Edition*, 1, 281–391.

Freud, S. 1920. Beyond the pleasure principle. *Standard Edition*, 18, 1–64.

Freud, S. 1930. Civilization and its discontents. *Standard Edition*, 21, 64–145.

Freud, S. 1937. Analysis terminable and interminable. *Standard Edition*, 23, 209–54.

Lacan, J. 1975. Seminar XXII (1974–75), R.S.I. *Ornicar?*, 2–5.

Lacan, J. 1976. Seminar XXIII (1975–76), Le Sinthome. *Ornicar?*, 6–11.

Lacan, J. 1997. *The Seminar of Jacques Lacan: The Psychoses*, translated by Jacques-Alain Miller and Russell Grigg. New York: Norton.

Lacan, J. 2006. *Écrits*. Trans. B. Fink. New York: Norton.

Laplanche, J. 1976. *Life and Death in Psychoanalysis*, translated by Jeffrey Mehlman. Baltimore: Johns Hopkins University Press.

Laplanche, J. and Pontalis, J.B. 1973. *The Language of Psychoanalysis*. New York: Norton.

Lindy, J.D. 1989. Transference and Post-Traumatic Stress Disorder. *Journal of the American Academy of Psychoanalysis*, 17(3), 397–413.

Pynoos, R.S. and Nader, K. 1989. Children's memory and proximity to violence. *Journal of the American Academy of Child and Adolescent Psychiatry*, 28(2), 236–41.

Stockton, K.B. 2009. *The Queer Child: Or Growing Sideways in the Twentieth Century*. Durham: Duke University Press.

PART II
Psychic Life and its Spaces

ROMA - Villa Pamphili - Terrazza

Chapter 6

Geographies of Psychic Life

Joyce Davidson and Hester Parr

Introduction

What is psychic life, and why should it be of concern to geographers? These questions may be especially pertinent given that there has been a long tradition in geography, successfully challenged by feminist and critical thinkers, to restrict the focus of study to decidedly *non*-intimate matters, such that bodies, emotions and even homes, were long considered beyond the geographical pale. Thanks to a range of critical approaches that draw on interdisciplinary theoretical resources we are now well aware that the 'geographies closest in' (Longhurst 2001; Davidson and Milligan 2004) exert an enormously significant impact on every aspect of our lives. The space of the psyche might be considered 'closest' of all, significant in terms of its impact on identity formation, and at least as complex and intertwined as the body. So, while not traditionally considered a legitimate part of geographers' terrain, some geographers have begun to look at what constitutes psychic life.

   In what follows, we use 'psyche' and 'psychic life' to refer broadly to the unconscious (acknowledging that there are various traditions within psychoanalytic and phenomenological thought which define this differently). We begin by briefly sketching the relational contours of psychic geographies before turning to methodological questions of how geographers have investigated dimensions of psychic life. Here we explicitly address how geographers have struggled with the influence (and promise) of psycho-dynamic and psycho-therapeutic practice and consider methods that move beyond the linguistic. Turning away from *why* and *how* questions, we then introduce some examples of research that examines different manifestations of psychic life in the city: first, to show how different approaches to thinking about the psyche can privilege playful and political experimentation emphasizing voluntary 'drifting', and second to explore how more problematic and disruptive psychic inhabitations and mobilities manifest in urban environments. The oppositions we draw through these examples are intended to illustrate the complex nature of unconscious life and its insistent insurgence into everyday places and spaces.

On the Geographies of Psychic Life

In discussing psychic life we may immediately elaborate something of why geographers might have avoided or neglected this area until recently. In part, this is related to the 'otherness' of the unconscious as research material; otherness that, as Parr and Philo (2003: 285) explain, is derived from the *substance* of what is entailed and related to a 'domain, full of "deeper" drives, passions and repressed psychic materials returning in "distorted" form', which 'inevitably unsettles those geographers who feel more comfortable dealing with the conscious, self-aware and apparently self-directing human being who makes rational decisions on the basis of available information'. Holding aside the false dualisms implied here, psychic life is thus depicted as potentially containing disruption and danger. To use psychoanalytic vocabulary, psychic landscapes are often 'uncanny' (Wilton 1998). This term refers to something which is familiar but unsettling, and leads us to ask whether analysis of psychic life is all about evoking slightly familiar, deeper, 'distorted' aspects of selves which have some kind of distinctive spatial expression.

This question is not easy to answer, and if we look at how geographers have engaged with what we might call aspects of psychic life, we see a history of encounter ranging from the psychological measurement of spatial behaviours (for a summary see Gold 2009) to cognitive studies (Kitchin and Freundschuh 2000) to psycho-social enquiry (Sibley 1995) to emotional geographies (Davidson, Bondi and Smith 2005; see also Thien 2011) to 'more than representational', 'pre-cognitive triggers' and 'enduring urges' (Lorimer 2005: 84). Psychoanalytic and post-humanistic theories of self and self-development have contributed a particular dimension to understanding the interior geographies inherent in psychic life (Pile 1995; Bondi 1999; Callard 2003; Kingsbury 2003). Other work circulates around the psycho-geographies of cities (Pile 2005; Pinder 2005), which we discuss later. This partial list begins to convey the very different ways in which geographers have sought to engage with interior geographies.

So, to what does 'psychic life' refer? Although psychic life is impossible to define precisely, we argue it is connected to vaguely articulated (or alternatively, too precisely delineated) notions of mind, spirit, emotion and (un)consciousness.

Our objective is not to produce an exhaustive literature review, but rather to write *through* aspects of existing work on psychic life, demonstrating that one of the most vibrant examples of human geography research at present is that which drops its disciplinary safeguards and confronts anxiety (Davidson 2003), affect (Anderson 2006), boredom (Anderson 2004b), emotion (Bennet 2004), memory (Thien 2005), love (Wylie 2005), and play (Bingley 2003), and asks 'what of anger, disgust, hatred, horror, stress, isolation, alienation, fear, terror, dread, decay, loss, denial?' (Lorimer 2005: 90). In listing these studies, we do not limit psychic life to these bounds, but rather use these references as a starting point in order to ask: what geographical insights can thinking about psychic life expose?

Explaining what the geographies of psychic life might entail means initial recourse to some now classic examples of work on the psychic dimensions of social and spatial life by David Sibley (1995, 2003) and Robert Wilton (1998). Sibley and Wilton work with ideas which emerge from Freudian psychoanalysis and psychoanalytic theory in order to explicate how reflecting on the psyche and theories of the self can serve to connect the unconscious, emotions and the social and material world.

Using object relations theory, developed through the work of theorists such as Donald Winnicott and Melanie Klein (see Bondi 2007 and Kingsbury 2004 for succinct overviews), Sibley posits that early childhood development structures the constitution of the world into 'good' or 'pure' and 'bad' or 'dirty' objects. These social stereotypes act as a catalyst for deeply held unconscious feelings that surface as we exercise social and spatial choices in adulthood, for example, who we choose to keep company with or exclude, keep close or at a distance. Moreover, this explanatory potential 'scales up' in Sibley's account in ways relevant for understanding aspects of xenophobia, social phenomena given spatial expression through, for example, the rigid policing of national borders to exclude 'alien others' (Sibley 1995: 108). In these psycho–social–spatial arguments, then, 'separation is a large part of the process of purification – it is a means by which defilement or pollution is avoided' (Sibley 1995: 37).

In a similar vein to Sibley, Wilton (1998) employs psychoanalytical concepts of the uncanny (or *unheimlich*; Freud 1919) and the abject (Kristeva 1982) to address questions of difference and how particular dimensions to psychic life are spatialized around what is constituted as 'other'. In his research, Wilton finds that plans for facilities to house socio-culturally defined 'others' (in this case, individuals with AIDS) disrupt the social order of a community, creating anxieties and resistance among neighbourhood residents. Objections relate to perceived threats to community and – more significantly – individual boundaries. That is to say, residents worry about contagion through proximity to bodies considered sufficiently impure and potentially polluting to threaten the integrity, the very basis of embodiment and identity.

The work of Sibley and Wilton requires taking seriously the notion that psyches as well as selves are socio-spatial phenomena (see also Butler 1997). Several other critical and cultural geographers have recently contributed to understandings of psychic life in such respects. Kingsbury (2008), Pile (2005) and Pinder (2005) (discussed further below), have stressed the need to extend our vision of unconscious affects beyond the realm of experience of identifiable individuals, to show how they (and their psyches) have socio-spatial repercussions, shaping wider socio-cultural and material environments.

How We Know Psychic Life

Qualitative methods of a kind typically used in social geography research are designed to ask questions about the experiences of others. They allow us to conduct in-depth, sometimes formal, often intimate interactions, intended to create opportunities for participants to reveal something of what the world is like for them, always on the understanding that we can never *really* be where they are or step into their shoes. By soliciting and attending closely to first-hand accounts of a matter of shared interest, we thus hope to gather or 'co-construct' meaningful insights that we might then re-present to interested others. Such methods have been more or less central to the practice of human geography throughout its history. Importantly, however, the way these methods are conceived and executed changes over time, making it 'hard, though perhaps not impossible, to imagine what a radically new form of qualitative research practice might look like' (Davies and Dwyer 2007: 257).

As geographers begin to think and write about unconscious realms, perhaps the primarily *different* dilemma we face is that of handling uncommonly intangible phenomena. Traditional methods are arguably intended to work with what participants tell us, how they (*say* they) think and feel about any given focus of research. Yet, with psychic life, there is clearly so much more than can be *consciously* thought or felt, and questions continually arise about how we might 'get at' this peculiarly unwieldy material.

These methodological and epistemological challenges are witnessed in contemporary research. Bennett (2009: 248), for example, refers to research relationships, a key concern for feminists. She states, 'I am also intrigued by how far [the] empathetic psychic space of a (research) relationship can stretch as feelings "grow" or "develop" beyond meetings through dreams, reflecting, writing and relating experience to others'. We can of course never control for such phenomena, but we might at least aspire to better understand what they do and mean. Bennett (2009: 249) adopts 'practices that explore how our fantasies and defences affect fieldwork, analysis, and writing'. Simultaneously, this prompts uncertainty for Bennett (ibid.) in terms of how to exercise 'empathy' and be 'emotionally present' in 'non-judgemental' ways as this involves 'taking' from a therapeutic context into a research situation. Clearly, although investigating psychic life or making sense of its manifestations does not mean importing methods from psychoanalysis wholesale, many researchers echo Bennett's (2009: 244) sense of the 'hurdles that geographers face when they engage with practices developed in a psychotherapeutic setting'. Thomas (2007: 538), for example, highlights one important aspect of the challenge facing geographers when she writes: 'it has been difficult to juggle the benefits of psychoanalytic theory with the conundrum of how to do so without psychoanalyzing individual interviewees when examining their articulations'. However, as Paul Kingsbury (2009: 482) explains, there may be more similarities between procedures in each profession than we are aware:

> much of critical human geographical research in general, is replete with processes that are comparable to free association, transference, and analytic listening. Think, for example, of the free association-like meandering pronunciations and spontaneous ramblings voiced during unstructured interviews. Think, for example, of the powerful transferential bonds that often develop between the researcher(s) and researched during interviews, ethnographies, and focus groups. Think, for example, of the degree to which geographers, especially feminist and poststructuralist geographers, attempt to foster data collection techniques and conditions that are comparable to analytic listening: attendance to self-reflexivity, mindful of multiple viewpoints and meanings, recognition of the situatedness and partiality of knowledge, vigilance towards power dynamics, and appreciative of the ineluctable instability of insider/outside and researched/researcher distinctions.

The similarities Kingsbury refers to here are, however, largely *unacknowledged*, and he insists that 'extensive critical assessments of the validity, value, and potentiality of psychoanalytic methods in human geography are rare' (ibid.).

In fact, Kingsbury (ibid.) argues that 'geographers have found psychoanalytic concepts much more valuable than psychoanalytic methods', but by attending more closely to the latter, Kingsbury continues, they 'may begin to formulate exciting and truly radical research projects wherein psychoanalytic methods are as equally relevant and valuable as the psychoanalytic concepts that they ultimately depend on'.

Bingley (2003) is amongst those who have begun to take up this challenge. Bingley has employed 'tactile' methodologies that draw her psychotherapeutic and geographical training together to investigate 'sense of place' in non-traditional ways. Working with groups, Bingley (2003: 330) organized workshops 'where methods drawn from art therapy and humanistic psychotherapy allowed participants to express their experience at a non-verbal, sensory level'. In particular, she used 'sandplay' to provide a way of 'getting beyond' habitual responses to explore meanings ordinarily inaccessible in everyday (conscious) life and thought. It is crucial to note, however, that Bingley's innovative approach was never used in isolation from conventional methods; Bingley (2003: 340) worked – i.e. talked – with her participants to jointly make sense of what they had made, and so meanings (research findings) are co-constituted in context as 'space is made for reflection and the emergence of the unconscious process into conscious awareness'.

This important aspect of the research process might then reasonably be described in time-honoured terms as focused group discussions, albeit ones with a different – therapeutically informed – dynamic and activities-based twist. Talk – then text, via transcripts – is at least as important to Bingley's research as performative act and artefact which, while pivotal to her method, could never stand alone as primary source materials. Artistic activities and their products can be observed, but to make *sense* that is shared, their meanings must be generated with, rather than imposed on, participants. This leaves feminist and other established methodologies in a place of still crucial importance. For Bingley (2003: 340), 'using psychotherapeutics' does not constitute a radical methodological departure, but 'simply offers a greater scope for opening up existing fields of exploration'.

Bingley's methods for investigating aspects of psychic life are clearly effective and potentially valuable, but we would question whether such methods are suitable for all. Any approach capable of stirring up psychic flows and bringing unconscious material to the surface should give us cause for caution, for what resources might those of us untrained in psychotherapeutics have to help smooth over that which we've troubled? While similarly trained and experienced in therapeutic methods, Liz Bondi's approach is perhaps more readily, safely accessible to typically trained geographers. Bondi (2003, 2005, 2006) draws existing connections between certain psycho-analytic/-therapeutic and feminist approaches closer still, and according to Kinsgbury's (2009: 483) recent assessment, her 'work on empathy and identification is one of the most incisive and extensive theoretical assessments of the potential benefits of using psychoanalytic methods in geography'. Focusing in particular on Bondi's approach to psychoanalytic understandings of identification and empathy, Kingsbury emphasizes that this approach is intended to theoretically enhance and enrich existing methodologies, those already acutely sensitive to questions 'about how positionality and power infuse the dynamics between the researcher and the researched'. Using insights from psychoanalysis need not mean abandoning existing methods, but can rather involve continuing to work to refine them. This serves to enrich our research, but also, and importantly, to protect (especially psychically sensitive) research participants.

Turning to one last alternative attempt to investigate unconscious/non-cognitive life, geographers have recently engaged with non- (or more-than-) representational approaches (Lorimer 2005; Thrift 2007). Geographers whose work falls under the umbrella term of Non-Representational Theory (NRT) tend to favour performance and activity over proclamations and products as foci for study, arguing that ineffable events provide (or perhaps represent?) more immediate embodied engagement with the world beyond, beneath or before language (Nash 2000; and see Philo 2011). That is to say, NRT develops a focus on what can be *shown* over what can be said. According to Davies and Dwyer (2007: 259), NRT practitioners 'seek ways of going beyond words, or indeed are suspicious of words'; they stress what people do over what they *say* they do, which leads to 'direct' study of such events as dance (McCormack 2005) and music (Anderson 2004a). Such research emphasizes the 'how' and the 'now' of performance, the ephemera of immediate experience arguably inaccessible via traditional 'textual methodologies' (Anderson, Morton, and Revill 2005). We would, however, and following James Hillman (1991: 28), caution against the turn away from language that characterizes much recent and influential work in this field, and suggest that words, too, are performances:

> As one art and academic field after another falls into the paralyzing coils of obsession with language and communication, speech succumbs to a new semantic anxiety. Even psychotherapy, which began as a *talking cure* – the rediscovery of the oral tradition of telling one's story – is abandoning language for touch,

cry and gesture. We dare not be eloquent ... Our semantic anxiety has made us forget that words, too, burn and become flesh as we speak.

Words are at risk of being taken-for-granted. While we agree that actions do, indeed, often speak louder than words – think also of tears, obscene gestures or even 'inactions' such as demonstrative, *meaningful* silences – such embodied expressions also often require contextual interpretative frameworks in order to make *sense* and can be just as representational (and limited) as expressions 'straightforwardly' verbal. Unconscious affects will always be excessive, elusive and resistant to interpretation and representation – such limitations are integral to the nature of representation (Smith et al. 2009: 12) – but to lose sense of the import of language would be to risk losing something of inimitable value, a cornerstone of communication, which is what researchers *do*.

Psychogeographies and the Psychodynamic City

Having explored something of *why* and *how* geographers understand aspects of psychic life, we turn now to consider some examples of work which explicitly explore it, and in very different ways to that discussed above. We begin with geographies of the city. Cities, according to urban social geographers, are concentrations of dreams, fantasies, memories, (un)conscious journeys, play and struggle. As an easily recognizable geographical entity, the city is perhaps a good place to start to tell some stories about these aspects of psychic life. There are different ways to tell the stories of the city: focusing on the psychic life of the city itself (Pile 2005), or on the psychic dimensions to everyday lives within the city. Research on psychogeographies (see Coverley 2006: 10) offers a useful starting point for thinking about how lives and cities are intertwined and interdependent.

In some of our comments above about psycho-social geographies, there is a risk that the psyche becomes a deterministic blue-print for spatial organization, especially with regards to questions of social difference. Research on psychogeography shows how some people quite deliberately try to resist this taken-for-granted imprinting in an effort to 'shake up' the psychic dimensions of the city. For example, Pinder (2005) traces the complex history of 'the situationists', a grouping of activists and artists intent on forms of urban revolution and the circulation of utopian ideals. Although there is much to say about this history and its implications for thinking about geography, our focus is to appropriate some aspects of thinking about utopian geographies of the city in order to relay how some groups voluntarily sought to engage in 'an experimental investigation of the free construction of daily life' (Debord 1963, quoted in Pinder 2005: 5).

In the late 1950s, groups of situationists and associated avant-garde activists deliberately sought to investigate and change urban spaces through new kinds of geographical research and action, including that labelled 'psychogeography' (Pinder 2005: 128). Part of the general motivation for this approach was bound up with a wilful reclamation of urban space in terms of 'desire, encounter and play' (ibid.: 150), including mobile 'drifting' (called 'the *dérive*'). This practice, and others like it, were intended as an 'oppositional mode of living in the (capitalist) city' (ibid.: 152), and activists used the term psychogeography to 'investigate different ambiences and zones in cities, and to attend to the relationship between social space and mental space and between urbanism and behavior'. A lived psychogeographical approach might engender a new map(ping) of the city whereby cartographies of unfettered desire and fluidity characterize movement. However, as Pinder argues, in fact the maps produced by situationists often indicated 'active and conscious' senses of behaviours (ibid.: 155). Indeed, the outworkings of various strands of situationism included thinking and architectural drawings, maps, various forms of art work as well as practices, all deliberately designed to comprise an 'irrational embellishment of the city' (ibid.). The contradiction between these *consciously* designed efforts to disrupt the city and also create irrational form stands in stark contrast to *less voluntary* examples of the embodiment of psychic disruption detailed below.

The story of psychogeography, and more broadly the situationists and associated movements, is orientated around urban experimentation and new relationships with mental and social space which supposedly allow 'spaces and times to be thought and lived otherwise' (Pinder 2005: 265). These themes have also been present in other work which has constructed the psychic life of cities as 'real'. This term is associated with the work of psychoanalyst Jacques Lacan, and refers to that which falls outside the symbolic order. For Lacan (1991: 164), the real is a powerfully affective and meaningful presence in our lives, but at the same time, it (or at least its *meaning*) is somehow disturbingly absent, unreachable; it is 'this something faced with which all words cease and all categories fail, the object of anxiety par excellence'. Pile's recent work on the city (1996, 2005) shows how he understands this entity as a 'state of mind and body' (1996: 210), as he illustrates a psychoanalysis of urban space, which he contends, 'contains the psychodrama of everyday life' (ibid.: 246). Analysis of city life, Pile (2005: 2) says, should be expanded to include 'shadows, irrationalities, feelings, utopianisms' and other elusive or 'unspeakable' and 'real' phenomena. Geographies, particularly those associated with city spaces, are psycho-dynamic, meaning that they are imprinted by, contain, shape and disrupt human psyches and psychologies. Geographers, Pile argues, can gain by using psychoanalytic theory to help explain this precisely because the spatialities of everyday life are so difficult to articulate. It is needed, he argues, to deal adequately with 'the complex psychodynamics of place' (ibid.: 100). Pile's (ibid.: 3) work excavates a related, but very different psychogeography of urban space, one that is 'phantasmagoric' in orientation, and concerned with 'occluded spatialities' which are ghostly and dream-like. These descriptors and claims are ones informed by early Freudian psychoanalysis and clearly seek to locate aspects of human psychic life as real, in real cities. Pile (ibid.: 156) discusses the 'grief work' of cities (see also Rose 2009) where 'dark histories' and the 'tradition of dead generations ... weighs so heavily on the lives of city dwellers'. For many, 'the city is haunting because it gathers together so many ghosts: there are so many reasons to be haunted' (ibid.: 151). There is so much we cannot know about city spaces – about who lived (and died) here before us, or about how they lived (and died) (ibid.: 147) – that these spaces become intensities of uncertainty, associated with 'spooky' happenings, legacies of terror and the uncanny.

Disruptive Psychic Life and Traumatic Geographies

To understand geographies, and particularly city geographies, as psychodynamic and phantasmagoric, brings questions of irrationality, emotion, memories and psychologies to the fore of analysis. Here we highlight less deliberate psychogeographies of mobility, whereby disruptive aspects of psychic life entail tenuous, stressed relationships in and with city spaces. These are also stories of the real city, but ones lived out by marginalized and disenfranchised city dwellers experiencing psychic trauma.

Caroline Knowles (2000) writes of 'post-asylum geographies of madness' (see also Wolch and Philo 2000) and charts the lives of deinstitutionalized psychiatric patients. Here lives 'are not static, fixed in place, but in the process of many journeys from one place to another' (Knowles 2000: 83). Individuals, often diagnosed with schizophrenia and coping with a variety of psycho-social challenges, find themselves wandering the city streets daily in search of shelter and warmth. The semi-permanent 'walking exile' of a life in motion challenges the (positive) radical analysis of the potential of the *dérive* (and see Cresswell 1997 on alternative imaginings of 'the nomad'). What psychogeographies are at play here? Knowles (2002: 161) is blunt in her answer concerning the psychic disruption we commonly call madness:

> It is the most shifting of personal landscapes and raises questions about the nature of identity and existence itself. It is about the rapid retreat of the certainties of the taken for granted and that formed the basis of being in the world. It is an experience that [leaves] people shaken about how and who to be in the world.

Is it not this flux which psychogeographers seek and through which they might revision the city?

Looking closely at accounts of homelessness and mental illness, we see that there are huge populations of people who have lived this flux, *involuntarily*, and who battle its results. Desjarlais' (1997: 127) critical phenomenology of street and shelter life for people who are homeless and mentally ill emphasizes how continual momentum and felt compulsions lead to a 'blunting' of existence: 'For many the sensorium of the street involved a corporal existence in which a person's senses and abilities to make sense soon became dulled in response to excessive and brutal demands on these'. Part of this story of dislocation and negative mobility is purportedly related to a lack of 'integrative narrative', a characteristic of the 'dreamy, disconnected' life accounts of people diagnosed with schizophrenia (Desjarlais 1997: 5). For people who already experience challenging forms of psychological disorientation, the city arguably offers little solace (although see Parr 1999 on delusional geographies). In accounts of the experience of psychic disruption in the city, the struggle for consensual reality dominates individual stories, though often in very distinctive ways:

> Most of the time, I can be walking down the street and hear thousands of voices and I feel terrible, like I'm not really there (quoted in Parr 1999: 683).

> You mishear things, out of synchronisation with other people, out of sync. You're outside. Things keep jumping into your mind. You feel like an animal, you feel like you're in touch with the universe, y'know you are outside yourself, in touch with nature. You go along with the momentum of the illness, it's just a different way of thinking – you see and hear the world differently (quoted in Parr 1999: 683).

Through more or less negative experiential accounts of psycho-social disruption we also learn more about the importance of boundaries, and the potential disadvantages of endless atmospheric and sensory mobilities. Arguing for recognition of the need for psychological boundaries for coherent subjectivity is not new (see Glass 1985; Kirby 1996; Hekman 2004), but sensitive work on the geographies of panic shows how our everyday experience of the city is also dependent on these (Davidson 2003). Analysis of agoraphobic life worlds highlights the city as a space of anxious contradiction, a geography of irrational affect. Again, this disrupts a romantic visioning of psychogeographical exploration, with the voices of agoraphobic women speaking of the city as a place where 'confusion proliferates on every level' (Williamson 1994, in Davidson 2003: 62):

> Your heart starts thumping, you feel like you're choking in your throat, you can't swallow and you feel all dizzy and giddy, and like if it's in a shop, or the church or what, you feel you want to run (quoted in Davidson 2003: 58).

While we seek to qualify the frames of reference for psychogeographical exploration as including negative spatialities, we also want to emphasize the hopeful possibilities engendered by disruptive psychic life experience. In her discussion of agoraphobic lifeworlds, Davidson (2003: 67) reminds us that panic is like excitement, and that 'to open oneself up to excitement, to learn to endure and even enjoy the potentiality of panic without giving oneself over to it completely is the phenomenal freedom to which the agoraphobic aspires'.

Returning cautiously to a position whereby psychic disruption may in itself be a process through which new and better social and spatial experiences are enabled is not to align ourselves (just) with the playful whims of psychogeographers, but rather to entertain the possibility that somewhere in delusional or anxious psychic experience lies hope and possibility of *connection*. This is not always about a radical collective politics of hope (Harvey 2000) in which new utopian city visions are rescued and redrawn (and see Pile's 2005 comments on this), but an understanding that (un)conscious engagements with material spaces may be an important part of a 'therapeutic' and psychological search for a sense of boundedness for those who reluctantly occupy transient and distressing psycho-mobilities. For those in delusional states, for example, by physically locating themselves in crowded parks and city malls, the movement, crush and performances of bodies may be(come) meaningful in transitional realms of dislocation, the flow being reminiscent of both material reality and fantastical states (see Parr 1999). For people seeking consensual reality, then, this reminiscence may be important in trying to locate senses of boundedness. As Pile (2005: 3) warns however, structures of feeling that emerge from and in cities are always 'contradictory, mobile, changing and changeable'. Mapping and anchoring psychic life in cities is clearly a risky and complicated endeavour.

Conclusion

Using work influenced by psychoanalysis, we have shown how concerns about relatedness (e.g. self and other) have dominated geographical accounts of psycho-social forms and structures. 'Relating' has also been a key theme of methodological exploration into deeply felt 'placing' in the world, and we have shown the radical ways in which some geographers have sought to expand their tool-kit of 'how to know' the social psyche. Relating to (and connecting with) the world through sand, dance, music and so on provide just some examples of the exciting mediums through which geographers are beginning to encounter psychic life. In providing some examples of contemporary research on psychic life we explored different aspects of relating to cities: we reviewed particular attempts to artistically disrupt perceived constructions of city life, and we contrasted writing on such playful mobilities with research that painfully reveals the traumatic material of dislocated psychic lives. The latter strategy reflects both our interest in emotionally challenging or atypical lifeworlds, but also gestures towards the promise inherent to exploration (and indeed experience) of disturbed and distorted psychic landscapes.

Acknowledgements

This is an edited and revised version of the following chapter: Hester Parr and Joyce Davidson 2011. Psychic life. *A Companion to Social Geography*, edited by Vincent J. Del Casino Jr, Mary E. Thomas, Paul Cloke, and Ruth Panelli. Oxford: Blackwell Publishing, Chapter 16.

References

Anderson, B. 2004a. Recorded music and practices of remembering. *Social and Cultural Geography*, 5(1), 3–20.
Anderson, B. 2004b. Time-stilled space-slowed: how boredom matters. *Geoforum*, 35, 739–54.

Anderson, B. 2006. Becoming and being hopeful: towards a theory of affect. *Environment and Planning D: Society and Space*, 24(5), 733–52.

Anderson, B., Morton, F. and Revill, G. 2005. Practices of music and sound. *Social and Cultural Geography*, 6(5), 639–44.

Bennett, K. 2009. Challenging emotions. *Area*, 41(3), 244–51.

Bingley, A.F. 2003. In here and out there: sensations between self and landscape. *Social and Cultural Geography*, 4(3), 329–45.

Bondi, L. 2003. Empathy and identification: conceptual resources for feminist fieldwork. *ACME: International Journal of Critical Geography*, 2, 64–76.

Bondi, L. 2005. The place of emotions in research: from partitioning emotion and reason to the emotional dynamics of research relationships, in *Emotional Geographies*, edited by J. Davidson, L. Bondi and M. Smith. Aldershot: Ashgate, 231–46.

Bondi, L. 2006. Is counseling a feminist practice? *Geojournal*, 65(4), 339–48.

Bondi, L. 2007. *Psychoanalytic Theory*. Online paper archived by the Institute of Geography, School of Geosciences, University of Edinburgh.

Butler 1997. *The Psychic Life of Power: Theories in Subjection*. Chicago: Stanford University Press.

Callard, F. 2003. The taming of psychoanalysis in geography. *Social and Cultural Geography*, 4(3), 295–312.

Coverley, M. 2006. *Psychogeography*. Harpenden: Pocket Essentials.

Cresswell, T. 1997. Imagining the nomad: mobility and the postmodern primitive, in *Space and Social Theory: Interpreting Modernity and Postmodernity*, edited by G. Benko and U. Strohmayer. Oxford: Blackwell.

Davidson, J. 2003. *Phobic Geographies: The Phenomenology and Spatiality of Identity*. Aldershot: Ashgate.

Davidson, J., Bondi, L. and Smith, M. (eds) 2005. *Emotional Geographies*. Aldershot: Ashgate.

Davidson, J. and Milligan, C. 2004. Embodying emotion, sensing space: introducing emotional geographies. *Social and Cultural Geography*, 5(4), 523–32.

Davies, G. and Dwyer, C. 2007. Qualitative methods: are you enchanted or are you alienated? *Progress in Human Geography*, 31(2), 257–66.

Desjarlais, R. 1997. *Shelter Blues: Homelessness and Sanity in a Boston Shelter*. Philadelphia: University of Pennsylvania Press.

Glass, J. 1985. *Delusion: Internal Dimensions of Political Life*. Chicago: University of Chicago Press.

Gold, J.R. 2009. Behavioural geography, in *International Encyclopedia of Human Geography*, edited by R. Kitchin and N. Thrift. Oxford: Elsevier.

Hekman, S. 2004. *Private Selves, Public Identities: Reconsidering Identity Politics*. Pennsylvania: Pennsylvania University Press.

Hillman, J. 1991. *A Blue Fire*. New York: Harper Collins.

Kingsbury, P. 2003. Psychoanalysis, a gay spatial science? *Social and Cultural Geography*, 4(3), 347–67.

Kingsbury, P. 2004. Psychoanalytic approaches, in *A Companion to Cultural Geography*, edited by J.S. Duncan, N.C. Johnson and R. Schein. Blackwell: Oxford, 108–20.

Kingsbury, P. 2008. Did somebody say jouissance? On Slavoj Žižek, consumption and nationalism. *Emotion, Space and Society*, 1(1), 48–55.

Kingsbury, P. 2009. Psychoanalysis, in *International Encyclopedia of Human Geography*, edited by R. Kitchin and N. Thrift. Oxford: Elsevier, 480–86.

Kirby, K. 1996. *Indifferent Boundaries: Spatial Concepts of Human Subjectivity*. New York and London: Guilford Press.

Kitchin, R. and Freundschuh, S. (eds) 2000. *Cognitive Mapping: Past, Present and Future*. London: Routledge.

Knowles, C. 2000. *Bedlam: On the Streets*. London: Routledge.

Kristeva, J. 1982. *Powers of Horror: An Essay on Abjection*. New York: Columbia University Press.

Lacan, J. 1991. *The Seminar of Jacques Lacan: The Ego in Freud's Theory and in the Technique of Psychoanalysis, 1954–1955*. London and New York: Norton.

Longhurst, R. 2001. *Bodies: Exploring Fluid Boundaries*. London and New York: Routledge.

Lorimer, H. 2005. Cultural geography: the busyness of being 'more-than-representational'. *Progress in Human Geography*, 29(1), 83–94.

McCormack, D. 2005. Diagramming practice and performance. *Environment and Planning D: Society and Space*, 23(1), 119–47.

Nash, C. 2000. Performativity in practice: some recent work in cultural geography. *Progress in Human Geography*, 24(4), 653–64.

Parr, H. 1999. Delusional geographies: the experiential worlds of people during madness and illness. *Environment and Planning D: Society and Space*, 17(6), 673–90.

Parr, H. and Philo, C. 2003. Introducing psychoanalytic geographies. *Social and Cultural Geography*, 4(3), 283–94.

Philo, C. 2011. Discursive life, in *A Companion to Social Geography*, edited by V.J. del Casino, M. Thomas, P. Cloke and R. Panelli. Oxford: Blackwell Publishing, 362–84.

Pile, S. 1996. *The Body and the City: Psychoanalysis, Subjectivity and Space*. London: Routledge.

Pile, S. 2005. *Real Cities: Modernity, Space and the Phantasmagorias of City Life*. London: Sage.

Pinder, D. 2005. *Visions of the City*. Edinburgh: Edinburgh University Press.

Rose, G. 2009. Who cares for which dead and how? British newspaper reporting of the bombings in London, July 2005. *Geoforum*, 40(1), 46–54.

Sibley, D. 1995. *Geographies of Exclusion: Society and Difference in the West*. London: Routledge.

Sibley, D. 2003. Psychogeographies of rural space and practices of exclusion. *Country Visions*, edited by P. Cloke. Prentice Hall: Harlow, 218–31.

Smith, M., Davidson, J., Cameron, L. and Bondi, L. 2009. Geography and emotion – emerging constellations, in *Emotion, Place and Culture*, edited by M. Smith, J. Davidson, L. Cameron, and L. Bondi. Aldershot: Ashgate, 1–20.

Thien, D. 2005. Intimate distances: considering questions of 'us', in *Emotional Geographies*, edited by J. Davidson, L. Bondi and M. Smith. Aldershot: Ashgate, 191–204.

Thien, D. 2011. Emotional life, in *A Companion to Social Geography*, edited by V.J. del Casino, M. Thomas, P. Cloke and R. Panelli. Oxford: Blackwell Publishing, 309–25.

Thomas, M. 2007. The implications of psychoanalysis for qualitative methodology: the case of interviews and narrative data analysis. *The Professional Geographer*, 59(4), 537–46.

Thrift, N. 2007. *Non-representational Theory: Space, Politics, Affect*. London: Routledge.

Williamson, J. 1992. I-less and Gaga in the West Edmonton Mall: towards a pedestrian feminist reading, in *Anatomy of Gender: Women's Struggle for the Body*, edited by D.H. Currie and V. Raoul. Ottawa: Carleton University Press.

Wilton, R. 1998. The constitution of difference: space and psyche in landscapes of exclusion. *Geoforum*, 29(2), 173–85.

Wolch, J. and Philo, C. 2000. From distributions of deviance to definitions of difference: past and future mental health geographies. *Health and Place*, 6(3), 137–57.

Wylie, J. 2005. A single day's walking: narrating self and landscape on the South West Coast path. *Transactions of the Institute of British Geographers*, 30(2), 234–47.

Chapter 7

A Distributed Unconscious:
The Hangover, what happens in Vegas and Whether it Stays There or Not

Steve Pile

Introduction: A More Than Repressed Unconscious and the Unrepressed City

The opening scenes of *The Hangover* (2009) show the wedding preparations of a very rich household, which we assume is located somewhere in California because of the particular combination of sunshine and style. It all looks beautiful. Seemingly to reinforce the perfection of the happy day, the accompanying song is the ice creamy 1898 Neapolitan classic, *O sole mio*, the first line of which (in English) is "What a beautiful thing is a sunny day". *The Hangover*'s version of *O sole mio* is – entirely against expectation – not even remotely as romantic. Written and performed by El Vez (the stage name of Mexican-American Robert Lopez, the Mexican Elvis), this song is about gang warfare:

> It's now or never
> please no more gangs
> people are dying
> don't you understand
> *manaña*
> will be too late.
> It's now or never
> let's stop the hate.
> It's now or never
> stop throwing signs
> don't be a victim
> just use your mind.
> (Lyrics reproduced by kind permission of El Vez.)

Surely, this is a strange opening for a romantic comedy? Yet, we will see that El Vez's song is actually the perfect introduction to movie: not only does what is said contradict what is shown, its darker side is also hidden in the bright sunshine of familiarity. But, the audience has little time to register the intended irony; the song is quickly drowned out by voicemail messages for Doug, Dr Stewart Price and finally Phil – none of whom answer their phones. The bride-to-be, Tracy Garner, is exasperated and worried: where are they? Helpfully, her father, Sid, seeks to reassure her. The men are in Vegas so, he reasons, they are probably gambling; gambling means they have probably lost track of time; and, if they are winning, they certainly wouldn't break their lucky streak by answering Tracy's calls. Then she gets a call from Phil. Tracy angrily despairs: "Where the hell are you guys? I am freaking out". Phil delivers the bad news: "Yeah, listen ... we fucked up ... the bachelor party ... the whole night ... it's a ... things got out of control ... and ... er ... we lost Doug. We can't find Doug". Danzig's song *Thirteen* blasts into the movie. It opens "Bad luck wind been blowin' on my back", but the standout line is "I was born in the soul of misery". At this point, you would hardly guess that this movie was going to win a Golden Globe Award for best Musical or Comedy (on 17 January 2010).

The premise for the film is quickly established. The friends have five hours to find Doug and get him to the wedding on time. Will they make it? First, of course, they must find Doug. It is in the unfolding search for Doug that the comedy – which is mainly situational and slapstick, but also the product of the stupidity and crudity of the characters, rather than them being clever or witty – transpires. The movie is funny, but I had thought no more about it until Virginia Blum perceptively observed, over pizza and merlot, that the film was like a psychoanalytic session. I take this insight to be an open invitation to reconsider the film from a psychoanalytic perspective, but I also want to think about it spatially.

The Hangover, for me, affords an opportunity for thinking spatially about the unconscious: that is, for showing that the unconscious as both *external* (as discussed in the introduction to this book) and also *distributed* spatially. That is, there appears to be an opportunity here for thinking about, on the one hand, the spatial production of the unconscious and, on the other, the unconscious production of space. This, then, is the purpose of this chapter. I will use the various weddings presented in *The Hangover* to think through the folds and whorls of the unconscious and space. Such an analysis demands that there is a concept of the unconscious that is both social and spatial and not, on the contrary, simply confined to the secret recesses of the psyche.

Freud's Topographical, Dynamic and Economic Understandings of Psychical Processes

Freud's first fully developed account of the unconscious appears in 1915 (although his first attempt to outline the concept of the unconscious was published in 1912). *The Unconscious* is best known for spelling out three different aspects of the unconscious. To begin with, Freud argues, it is important to consider the psyche as having a *topography*. Psychic topography has three different systems: the conscious, the preconscious and the unconscious. For Freud, it is important to understand not only in which system a psychical act takes place but also how psychical acts move, or do not move, between systems. His concern is not only with psychical material, but with its psychic location and with its mobility or lack of mobility in the topography of the mind (see 1915: 56–7). To understand the forces that move psychical acts, or prevent their movement, within the psyche, Freud argues that it is necessary to supplement the topography of the psyche with a *dynamic* understanding of psychical processes.

To explain the dynamism of psychical processes, Freud adds a theory of drives to his model of the psyche. Famously, these drives are bundled around two opposing (yet related) poles. For our purposes, it is helpful to think of these bundles crudely, as *sex* and *aggression*. Psychodynamics, from a Freudian perspective, involve both the affectual forces associated with the drives within the psyche, and also the interaction between affectual and emotional forces within and between systems. To account for the ways these forces work within the psyche and between systems, Freud adds an *economic* perspective. Using this idea, Freud seeks to understand how the psyche makes investments in particular ideas and gains a return from that investment. In other words, he tries to discover the fate of "quantities of excitation" within the psyche (1915: 64). Freud's main concern, however, is not with "quantities of excitation" in general, but with a particular excitation: that is, with what he calls *libido*, or the sexual investment associated with the sexual drives. What is critical is whether the fate of the sexual drive is to be repressed or not. In repression, "the idea representing a drive [is] not removed or destroyed, but prevented from becoming conscious" (1915: 49). Bluntly, it is both the persistence of the idea that re-presents the (sexual) drive *and* its repression that causes his patients to become so sick. In the case of a child with an animal phobia, this will cause anxiety "in two situations, first when the repressed love impulse becomes intensified, second when he perceives the feared animal" (Freud 1915: 65).

Freud's example of the phobic child is almost certainly the Wolfman (Freud 1918; see also Campbell and Pile 2010; and Pile 2014). In this case, simply put, the four-year-old Wolfman represses how his sexual drives have become entangled with his mother and father by hiding an idea, about sex between his parents, behind an even more intense image, that of frightening wolves – as wolves constantly threaten to gobble up little children. So, as an adult, the Wolfman experiences neurotic anxiety not only in relation to sex, but also in relation to animals. Thus, unable to deal with the fate of his sexual drives, the Wolfman represses his sexual affects and emotions – but in such a way that causes him to become sick.

Yet, Freud's analysis opens up the unconscious to the Wolfman's world. Thus, what makes these sexual drives so painful and unacceptable for the Wolfman is determined by his relationships both with his family (including his sister) and also other adults (such as his nurse). More than this, the fate of the Wolfman's drives is also determined by his relationship to his animal world (not only wolves). What Freud opens up is an account of the unconscious that is more than psychical, more even than familial and social, it is also distributed through relationships to other things *and* through the Wolfman's worlds. Alongside family and social mores, alongside his internal psychodynamics and animal phobias, the Wolfman's neuroses are also formed in relation to his wealthy family's country estate and large house (see Campbell and Pile 2010).

This chapter is less about psychical systems than about the fate of the ideas that represent the sexual and aggressive drives. This chapter is even more about the ways in which these fates of unconscious ideas whorl and fold with supposedly external spaces. Importantly, let us be crystal clear that the unconscious is comprised of more than just repressed ideas. Freud is clear about this: "the repressed does not constitute the whole of the unconscious. The unconscious is the more extensive; the repressed is one part of the unconscious" (1915: 49). It is by extending our understanding of the unconscious beyond repression, that we can more clearly see a *distributed* unconscious, both producing and produced by its worlds. In this chapter, our setting is Las Vegas – a city long associated with its supposed lack of repression of people's desires – yet, what happens in Vegas is meant also to stay there, as if Vegas functioned as the location for America's repressed unconscious.

What Happens in Vegas? When the Fates of Drives Become (All Too) Real

The plot of *The Hangover* centres on a bachelor party gone badly wrong. Doug Billings is marrying Tracy Garner. Doug is being taken to Las Vegas for one last bachelor weekend. His best friends are Phil Wenneck, a high school teacher, and Stu Price, a dentist. Doug persuades Phil and Stu to let Tracy's brother, Alan, accompany them. Before they set out, Sid and Doug talk about the trip. Sid reminds Doug that "what happens in Vegas stays in Vegas". Doug laughs, uncomfortably. Then, with a face that suggests bitter personal experience, Sid adds, "except for herpes, that shit will come back with you". They drive to Vegas in Sid's beloved Mercedes. They arrive in Vegas just as day turns to night, and the boys' desire to take advantage of Vegas' many delights increases as they take in the bright neon lights of the city's hotels. At Caesar's Palace, Phil decides that they should spend the night in a $4,200-a-night villa (on Stu's credit card). The view of Vegas from the suite is intoxicating. On the rooftop of Caesar's Palace, the boys toast their friendship and the night ahead (Figure 7.1).

The next morning, Stu, Alan and Phil painfully stir from unconsciousness to find their expensive suite in chaos. Amongst the wreckage of the night before, the hung-over men discover various empty bottles and cans, a smashed TV, a smouldering chair, underwear, a sex doll, a blow up pig in the Jacuzzi, a chicken … a baby … and, as Alan goes to the bathroom, a tiger. Stu is missing a tooth. Worst, Doug is nowhere to be found. And they cannot remember what happened in Vegas.

Figure 7.1   The "Wolf Pack" on the roof of Caesar's Palace, the night before
Source: *The Hangover* 2009. Directed by Todd Phillips (USA: Warner Bros).

The dream-like quality of the day's residue that the three hung-over men find in the suite does indeed suggest a psychoanalytic interpretation. Each element seems to be a clue to the story of the night before, yet the elements are bizarre, contradictory and seemingly unconnected: a chicken, a tiger *and* a baby?! In fact, the film-makers designed the scene in the hotel suite by gathering party anecdotes from the film-crew. They took the "morning after" stories and created a composite image, in a method that parallels, in many ways, condensation and displacement in dream work (Freud 1900). The effect is surreal – and, in effect, the unexplained presence of the chicken serves (on reflection) to remind the audience that there's never a full interpretation of what happens in Vegas, just as the interpretation of dreams can constantly unfurl new meanings for dream elements. Similarly, just as the psychoanalytic session proceeds from the clues that dream elements provide to the discovery of the hinterland of meaning that is associated with each element, so Doug's friends must now use their interpretative skills to follow the clues left over from the night before to discover his whereabouts. As they follow the clues, a hazy picture of a forgotten bachelor party emerges.

Las Vegas, of course, is the setting proper for the bachelor party. The image of Vegas as a "sin city" has been carefully nurtured since the 1960s, built on the twin pillars of sex and gambling. The city seems free – offering "free" pleasures and "free" money, spiced with liberal amounts of alcohol and other drugs (including testosterone). The often-repeated expression "what happens in Vegas stays in Vegas" seemingly lifts the restrictions of normal moral behaviour, yet also puts a firm boundary around this amorality. In the city, anything goes, but outside the city whatever happened must remain, if not forgotten, then at least unspoken. Yet, as Sid's warning about herpes demonstrates, what happens in Vegas must leave no trace – such as marriage certificates, tattoos, photographs, sunburn and missing teeth – otherwise what happens will come home with you. Vegas is paradoxical, then: offering the freedom to act out your fantasies, but only if you follow the rules set by the inevitable return to real life. Perhaps unsurprisingly, it is this tension, or contradiction, between "reality" and "fantasy", so intense and visible in Vegas, that has caught the attention of architectural and urban theorists (Venturi, Brown and Izenour 1972; Hannigan 1998). Indeed, what happens (before and after the bachelor party) to Phil, Alan and especially Stu traverses the fine line between the fantasy that sin city is fun, sexy and consequence-free and its somewhat scarier, repercussive reality.

In the pool area of Caesar's Palace, Phil, Alan and Stu make their first efforts to recall the night before. In a scene where Alan makes the baby simulate masturbation (twice), various tanned fat-free young women in skimpy bikinis are arbitrarily shown, and Stu vomits at Phil's feet, normal social conventions are crudely transgressed, without apparent humour. Amongst all this, the trio attempt to reconstruct the sequence of events. They remember the rooftop toast, the dinner at the Palm, then craps at the Hard Rock. That's the last they recall of the night, and Doug. At a loss, they check their pockets, discovering an $800 ATM receipt at the Bellagio time stamped at 23.05 and a valet ticket for Caesar's clocked at 05.15. On Phil's wrist, there's a hospital tag. Less of a chronology, the men now have a preliminary map of the night before. Their first stop is the hospital, where they discover that their inability to remember is due to taking "roofalin" (the movie's slang for rohypnol). Rohypnol has gained notoriety as the date-rape drug, so even though the hospital confirms that Phil has not been physically raped, both Phil and Stu nonetheless seem to feel psychologically raped.

The hospital doctor gives the trio their next clue, apparently one member of the group got married at the Best Little Chapel (Figure 7.2). It turns out that it is Stu who got married. So, they leave to find his new wife, Jade, who is also the mother of the baby. As they drive away, their car, a stolen police car, is attacked by two men, wielding an iron bar and a baseball bat. "Where is he?", one of the men yells. Phil hits the accelerator and speeds off.

Figure 7.2   **The Best Little Chapel. The Chapel was built for the film on a vacant lot (at 1236 Las Vegas Boulevard South) next to the Talk of the Town strip club, whose signs can be seen in the background. The location is near the Little White Wedding Chapel, which is famous for many celebrity "quickie" marriages**

Source: *The Hangover* 2009. Directed by Todd Phillips (USA: Warner Bros).

Clueless and dejected, they decided to confess to Tracy that they have lost Doug, but before they can call they are sideswiped by a large black SUV. A small Asian man, Mr Chow, approaches their wrecked car, accompanied by two henchmen. He demands that Phil, Stu and Alan return his money, $80,000 dollars, in cash, or he will kill their friend, who he has captive. On a promise that Alan can "beat the system", the men head for the Riviera casino to win the money at the blackjack tables. To everyone's amazement, it turns out that Alan is a blackjack savant. Quickly, they win $82,400, before the casino cottons on and they make a sharp exit.

With real hope in their hearts, they head for their desert rendezvous with Mr Chow. The men exchange the money for Doug, but when they take off the hood they find, to their horror and dismay, that it is not their Doug, but another Doug – in fact, the drug dealing Doug who sold the bad drugs to Alan. It is only then that Phil calls Tracy to tell her that they have lost Doug, and that the wedding is not going to happen. It is then that the actual clues to Doug's whereabouts finally fall into place. Like a good dream analyst, Stu connects the dots differently. Thanks to something the wrong Doug says, "roofies" makes Stu think of ending up on the roof. Stu realizes where the right Doug is: on the roof of Caesar's Palace.

Finally, they rescue a thoroughly sunburnt, and furious, Doug. They have three and a half hours to drive to the wedding. Of course, they make it, just in time. Only Doug's red skin suggests anything is awry and that their perfect wedding is not exactly as it should be. After the wedding, Alan shows the other three men photos taken on Stu's camera, showing them exactly what did happen in Vegas. The four agree to look at the photographs *one time* only, afterwards they will "delete the evidence". The last picture on the camera shows the four men, in blue wedding suits, at the Best Little Chapel.

So far, we have seen Phil, Stu and Alan follow clues in an attempt to find the secret to Doug's whereabouts. In some ways, this can be seen as analogous to the interpretation of a dream. The various elements of the dream act as clues, which lead to further clues. As the various webs of meaning are traced out, so the riddle to the dream's core concern can be discovered, but only with forensic and painstaking attention to detail. That said, the clues in *The Hangover* also trace out a psychogeography of Las Vegas, entwining desire and fear, sex and money, lost and found. Las Vegas, in some ways, becomes a map of the unconscious. This is not simply, or only, a repressed unconscious, however. Las Vegas contains elements that are overlooked (such as the relationship between the roof and the roofies) as well as destroyed and forgotten (rendered unavailable to memory by the roofies – where did the chicken come from?).

The night seems to have been wild and unrepressed, taking in luxury hotel rooms, drugs, alcohol, strippers, a stolen police car, gun fire, gambling, encounters with celebrities, prostitutes, and a sex act in hotel lifts. These are all "unconscious", but none are truly repressed. Rather, they are forgotten or overlooked or tantalizingly just out of reach or on the tip of the tongue or require considerable effort to be recovered. Yet, it is through these non-repressed unconscious elements that the repressed unconscious can also find *forms* to express itself. If nothing seems to be repressed in Vegas, then this is only because the repressed unconscious finds ample opportunities to find forms for itself via the non-repressed unconscious. To get at this, I will focus on "'marriage" in the film, for this provides ample opportunities for other unconscious ideas to surface.

The Distribution of Unconscious Material: A Tale of Two Weddings, Three Women and Four Men

Tracy and Doug are, evidently, the perfect couple, ready and willing to turn their perfect wedding into a perfect marriage. Sure, Tracy is "freaking out", but her anger and anxiety are entirely appropriate under the circumstances. Tracy stands in marked contrast to Stu's girlfriend, Melissa. When Doug, Phil and Alan pick up Stu, Melissa is crossly barking orders at Stu. He has to take his Rogaine, and not forget to use it. He must call as soon as he gets to the hotel. She does not want to be kept waiting. Her voice is sharp and mean-spirited. Old misdemeanours are brought up, as Melissa ensures that Stu knows she will be monitoring him. Stu sighs and complies. Melissa doesn't want Stu going to some strip club. Stu reassures Melissa that they are going on a harmless trip to wine country. There will be no bachelor party behaviour – and definitely no strippers. Melissa despairs: "It's just boys and their bachelor parties, it's gross ... not to mention it's pathetic, those places are filthy ... and the worst part is that little girl grinding and dry humping the fucking stage up there, that's somebody's daughter up there". Stu parrots Melissa: "that's somebody's daughter up there".

During the drive to Vegas we learn about Phil's life. He left his wife and kid behind, and is really happy to do so. Phil hates his life. He'd rather stay in Vegas than go back. Phil turns to Doug: "You know what, Doug, you should enjoy yourself. Come Sunday, you're gonna start dying. Just a little bit. Every day". Nonetheless, marriage is in the air. At the hotel, Stu informs Phil and Doug of his intention to propose to Melissa, and shows them the ring he intends to give her – it's his Grandmother's, the ring having made it all the way through the Holocaust with her. Phil is dismayed: "it's a big fucking mistake ... she beats him". "That was twice", Stu replies "and I was out of line". "Wow", Phil responds "he's in denial". It's clear that Melissa is Stu's superego: constantly and vigilantly policing his behaviour, his desires and his emotions. Of the four, Stu seems the most strait-laced. So, it is almost a relief to discover that it is Stu that gets married at The Best Little Chapel, yet this is tempered by the "shock" (and "joy") that his wife, Jade, works as an "escort", both a stripper and a prostitute. Indeed, of the four, it is Stu that is wildest, seemingly freed of his superego, his denials and his repressions.

Stu's impulsive, garish and unplanned marriage to Jade is a direct contrast to the carefully choreographed, stylish and thoroughly planned marriage between Doug and Tracy. Yet, of the two, it is Stu's marriage that seems to be the most fun, the most about love. Although the "style" of the wedding conforms to the image of the tacky Vegas "quickie", with tawdry suits, a bride in a cowboy outfit, and a bunch of kitsch souvenirs, Stu looks like he is having the time of his life; Stu seems to be in love and, as Phil observes, happy. Jade seems to have released something suppressed in Stu that Melissa simply oppresses. While Stu's marriage is the apparent product of unbridled desire, Doug's seems to be more of a corporate merger between rich families. Yet, it is to the idea of the "perfect" wedding that Stu returns. The sober Stu is horrified to find that he has married an "escort"; Jade must be found, not just as a step towards finding Doug, it is also as a step back from marriage – Stu wants to divorce her as quickly as he can.

In the end, after they have found Doug, Jade tells Stu that what they did was stupid – and a relieved Stu agrees, as Jade hands back Stu's holocaust ring. Sweetly, Stu suggests that they should meet up for a dinner the next weekend, but we know he still has to confront Melissa. During a tirade of accusations from Melissa, Stu finally snaps and (to everyone's relief) he publically dumps her. Here is another contrast between Stu and Doug. As Doug arrives at the wedding, Tracy angrily asks why he is so late and why his skin is so red. Doug says it's a long story, apologizes and, importantly, promises never to put Tracey through anything like this again.

Despite appearances, there is a single thought underlying Stu's relationship with Melissa, Stu's marriage to Jade, Phil's relationship with his unnamed wife (even while he greets her passionately when reunited at Doug's wedding), and Doug and Tracy's wedding. This single thought is that marriage is castration and, worse, the end of life. The film displays a consistent fear of women throughout, either that they are directly castrating (e.g. Melissa) or desire for them will overwhelm men and cause them to castrate themselves (e.g. Jade) (Figure 7.3). Tracey even has both effects on Doug: his "wild side" is muted at the same time as he mutes himself.

Of course, male fears of emasculation and castration do not necessarily have to be repressed – and this is why it is important to recognize, along with Freud, that the unconscious is always more than a product of repression and the mechanisms through which repression is maintained. In fact, a whole series of morally repugnant and socially unacceptable thoughts run through the film *The Hangover* – and, of course, this is exactly why it is so funny. What we witness is exactly how gross and stupid men are, and this liberates the audience to laughter. Yet what the movie does is cover over the disturbing idea that marriage-is-death and women-are-castrators, by the reassuring idea of the proper marriage: Tracey and Doug get their perfect wedding; we see that marriage-weary Phil loves his perfectly beautiful wife and cute son; and there is real hope that Stu might now get the girlfriend/wife he really deserves. So, is all well that ends well?

Figure 7.3 **Alan bets Stu that he is not a good enough dentist to pull out his own tooth. Stu wins the bet, but of course his display of "balls" to Jade is also a symbolic castration; a symbol that Melissa instantly recognizes, as only she is allowed to castrate him**

Source: *The Hangover* 2009. Directed by Todd Phillips (USA: Warner Bros).

Conclusion: "that shit will come back with you" –
Thinking Beyond the Spaces of Repression

Barely noticeable, the sign on the Best Little Chapel reads "The Weddings Last" (Figure 7.2). Stu's marriage to Jade lasts less than a day. As we know, from apocryphal marriages, such as Britney Spears' to Jason Alexander, Vegas marriages do not last. They are moments of madness that are not meant to leave Vegas. They are not really meant to happen in the first place. It is this tension between what happens and what is not meant to happen that provides the latitude and longitude for the Vegas map of unconscious materials. The key locations are Caesar's Palace (suite, poolside and rooftop), the Bellagio and Riviera casinos, the strip club, the car, the vacant lot and the marriage ceremony. Each location does more than simply allow unconscious material to be re-presented, however. Each location is over-determined by unconscious desires and fears. Thus, hotels and casinos are produced by an intoxicating mix of pleasure and danger (Figure 7.1), while strip clubs and weddings hold together a contradictory blend of sex and money (Figure 7.3), just as cars and vacant lots are sites of possibility and violence. Strangely, when put together, these conform to Freud's description of the key features of unconscious processes.

For Freud, unconscious processes are distinguished by: the privileging of psychic reality; the mobility of psychical investments; ambivalence and the absence of contradiction; and, also, timelessness. *The Hangover*, in a variety of ways, displays all these features. More than just a set of locations, Vegas is a map of psychical reality; it is a psychogeography of desire and fear. Put another way, we should be clear that repressed unconscious material is also geographical, producing and produced by its (only seemingly) external worlds. As the weddings show, contradictions and ambivalences are not just held, they are flaunted and indeed provide opportunity for the very funniest moments. And, all the while, *The Hangover* re-presents, at various points, the ways in which the men's desires and fears intensify or abate as they search for Doug. In particular, we see Stu's wild desires turn into something sweeter, yet running through the same object: Jade (named, after all, after a precious stone). There is one more thing, though.

I have indicated that, when released from the idea that the only process that makes anything unconscious is repression, we can see that there are many different kinds of unconscious material and that these are also productive of spatial relationships. This is not to blunt Freud, but to remind ourselves that he did not make the mistake of thinking that the unconscious was comprised of only repressed material. Indeed, it would be impossible for repressed unconscious material to make it out of the unconscious if it were not for non-repressed unconscious processes. If the evidence never made it out of Vegas, all would be forgotten. All is not forgotten, *The Hangover* warns. What happens in Vegas gets out. It is not an unrepressed city. As the missing tooth shows, there is evidence (even if it is in the form of something that is not there). So, if Vegas were a map of the unconscious, we would be forced to conclude that the unconscious is the product of the relationship between all kinds of unspoken and un-thought ideas, but always filtered through social forms of expression. If these ideas appear to have no spatial form, we should remember that the entire film is devoted to putting lost Doug back into in his proper place: into the ideal marriage – the one which masks the thought that marriage-is-death, that women castrate, that men castrate themselves.

But shouldn't we remember Alan? He ends up alone, no longer part of the "wolf pack", nor paired off with a desirable woman. Alan, thus, is a sign that if there is one thing worse than death by marriage, it is death by masculinity.

References

Campbell, J. and Pile, S. 2010. Telepathy and its vicissitudes: Freud, thought transference and the hidden lives of the (repressed and non-repressed) unconscious. *Subjectivity*, 3(4), 403–25.

Freud, S. 1976 (1900). *The Interpretation of Dreams*. Harmondsworth: Volume 4, Penguin Freud Library.

Freud, S. 1984 (1912). A note on the unconscious in psychoanalysis. *On Metapsychology: The Theory of Psychoanalysis*. Harmondsworth: Volume 11, Penguin Freud Library, 50–57.

Freud, S. 2005 (1915). The unconscious, in S. Freud, *The Unconscious*. Harmondsworth: Penguin Books, 47–86.

Freud, S. 2002 (1918). From the history of an infantile neurosis [The 'Wolfman'], in S. Freud, *The 'Wolfman' and Other Cases*. Hardmondsworth: Penguin Books, 203–320.

Hannigan, J. 1998. *Fantasy City: Pleasure and Profit in the Postmodern Metropolis* London: Routledge.

Pile, S. 2014. Beastly minds: a topological twist in the rethinking of the human in nonhuman geographies using two of Freud's case studies, Emmy von N. and the Wolfman. *Transactions of the Institute of British Geographers*, 39(2), 224–36.

Venturi, R., Brown, D.S. and Izenour, S. 1977 (1972). *Learning from Las Vegas: The Forgotten Symbolism of Architectural Form*. Boston: revised edition, MIT Press.

Chapter 8

"Or does it explode?"
Psychoanalytic Geographies of Violence and Creativity in a Small Mexican City

Karen Rodríguez

Langston Hughes ends his well-known poem, *A Dream Deferred*, with an ominous question. After passing through the possibilities of what happens to a dream never materialized—a desire never symbolized into words, music, art or action—he famously wonders, "or does it explode?" Suppressed dreams (or unsublimated desires) as Hughes, psychoanalysts and others tell us, lead to all sorts of violence (whether to one's own psyche and body, or to society) and to aggressions that can be physical, emotional or ideological. We see Hughes' "explosions" in cities as urban residents' searches for expressivity manifest themselves in occurrences that range from violent and destructive to artistic and reparative, causing both radical interruptions and subtle shifts across the urban landscape. If cities are, as geographer Nigel Thrift (2004: 57) writes, "roiling maelstroms of affect," the geographies of these urban sublimations and frustrations become significant on multiple planes.

While geographers increasingly explore the relationships between affect, politics, and the often violent experience of urban space, psychoanalysts are also concerned with the rising aggressions, frustrations, and desperation they too observe, paying attention now to a scale that extends far beyond the individual on the couch. Julia Kristeva takes up this question of percolating desires and aggressions from a more hopeful angle by inquiring into what happens when desires *do* get sublimated and symbolized. In *Hatred and Forgiveness* (2011) she boldly posits creativity as an antidote to contemporary violence. For Kristeva, creativity is synonymous with the ability to question and to imagine otherwise. It lies at the core of our human nature and, indeed, marks us as alive and still responding to that which is external, whether subtly and personally, or socially in outright revolution. She argues that it is the sublimation of desire and aggression into symbolic form that allows individuals to assert themselves in a world of others—to both connect with and challenge the social order. Following her work, this chapter argues that how different urban groups harness (or fail to harness) this human potential can provoke shifts in the psychic and spatial geographies of affect and violence, re-choreographing how people understand themselves, their others, and the spaces in which they meet.

The chapter explores the ways in which creativity offers a marginalized *barrio* (neighborhood) in the small Central Mexican city of Guanajuato a chance to rearrange its psychic and spatial relationships with the larger city, both fitting into and challenging things at once, and, hopefully, averting more violence. While it is far too early to say that the affective and spatial issues have been resolved, what we can note is the opening of potential. Drawing on a choreographic metaphor, as well as geographic and psychoanalytic theory, I would like to suggest that the city may be lightly shifting its center of gravity, re-choreographing relationships and freeing up the urban imagination as aggressions that cross the local and national contexts are sublimated. These shifts support Kristeva's argument for creativity as a route to social change even as the larger Mexican scenario pushes the theory to its limits. As the city alters its traditional, overly binary geographies of creativity and violence, the potential for a more dialogic choreography between city residents that is open to creative improvisation and that provides for new ways of being in urban space is revealed.

Times of Caution: National and Local Choreographies

The barrio I examine here hovers at the edge of Guanajuato, a rather bucolic university city of about 160,000, located in the exact center of Mexico. The city is known for its intense colonial-era beauty, its heavily Catholic and class-oriented nature, and its occasional adversity to change, which then dialogue in complex ways with its artistic focus and vibrant university life (Rodríguez 2012). The idea that national-level violence could enter into our colorful, bowl-shaped "bit of heaven," as locals are apt to label this city, intrudes greatly upon the city's notion of self.

Indeed, despite international news reports that depict all of Mexico as unilaterally dangerous, Guanajuato remains a quiet and safe city. Protected by a lack of big business and a chaotic, curvy topography that impedes high-speed getaways, Guanajuato has maintained itself at the margin of organized crime issues and sustains its identity as an important tourist destination.

Figure 8.1   Mexico map showing Guanajuato

Rather paradoxically, however, Guanajuato faces the task of being vigilant about who and what enters into its space even as it opens up to draw in tourists, to develop the university's national and international connections, and to attract prestigious visitors, including, in March of 2012, Pope Benedict XVI.

This entails a tightly controlled looking outward that often leaps over the marginal and peripheral spaces of the city, which are much less quaint and much less safe than the city's preferred self-image acknowledges. This not-seeing of certain urban spaces is choreographed into a not-passing-through. Tourists and other visitors are moved through the curvy downtown space along routes that direct them to shady plazas, key monuments, and popular museums, and away from any less attractive areas. Similarly, despite the existence of many inexpensive and free cultural events, those groups who are *not* part of the mainstream do not participate in these opportunities. Left out of the city's creative life, these many unseen, unvisited neighborhoods represent a threat to Guanajuato's colonial charm and quiet calm as gang violence, drug use, and other problems grow steadily. Because as local inhabitants know but are reluctant to acknowledge, the distance from gang membership to organized delinquency is not so great. Should these at-risk barrios decide to take up a serious relationship with the narco-business world, the consequences would be grave indeed, and certainly upset the careful balance of safety and threat.

In the summer of 2011, a non-governmental organization named Espacios Posibles (which translates as "Possible Spaces," a rather fortuitous choice in both geographic and psychoanalytic terms) introduced a range of artistic projects into the troubled barrio of La Venada in an attempt to recuperate and renovate urban space. Because this barrio is so geographically close but so affectively distant from the main downtown area whose image represents city identity (and is hereafter referred to as the *centro*), I wondered how introducing creative work into this downtrodden space might not only alter internal aspects of the neighborhood, but also set up the possibility for new relationships with *other* neighborhoods. How does (or might) creativity provide a way to change existing urban choreographies in this small city, and how could these displacements allow Guanajuato to engage these marginalized areas that are so essential to its continued associations of safety and tranquility? Could we find some applied support for Kristeva's assertions? Could creativity allow this barrio to challenge the status quo while simultaneously connecting with the mainstream?

The Intersections Between Choreography, Geography, and Psychoanalysis

Choreography, geography, and psychoanalysis share several broad concerns. First, each is preoccupied with the relationships between inside and outside, center and periphery, self and other. Choreographers think about the relationship between the dancer and the surrounding space, the dancer and other dancers on the stage, as well as the dancer's center of gravity and the relationship of body weight to this. Classical ballet enlisted a Cartesian geometry and understanding of the body in space in which the dancers and their movements could be plotted and understood in terms of coordinates and distances from main axes. Traditionally, the dancer's body followed this fixed path designed by a choreographer. Contemporary dance, however, conceives of a body that both initiates and responds to things in space in a more democratic sort of conversation where not everything is resolved, and where both chance and improvisation play a role in what the dancer ultimately does. (One can refer to the work of choreographers such as Merce Cunningham or William Forsythe, for example.) In different ways, then, both traditional and modern choreography work with these spatial/corporal relations and the balances established between the dancer's body and that which is external.

Geography is also concerned with the balance between what is internal or contained, and what is external and outside of a constructed boundary. It enquires into how things fit into spaces—physical, psychic, or otherwise; who is included or excluded; and how relationships arise between things or people both within and with a space. Since the 1970s, geographers having been using a choreographic vocabulary, asking how our urban movements are choreographed, enabled or limited by different structures, architectures, and affective contexts (Merriman, following Derek McCormack 2010: 428). Drawing from a historical base of Baudelaire's flâneur, Charles Simmel, Walter Benjamin, Michel de Certeau, Lefebvre, and others, they too question how much agency we have in space and where we find resistance, creativity, and possibilities to improvise. In the process, they have effectively unbounded cities—cities are no longer viewed as finite containers in what Thrift labels as a "nested hierarchy moving from global to local" (2004: 59). Rather, space is now understood as "a product of practices, trajectories, interrelations" (Massey 2004: 5). Similarly, cities have been defined as complex and interactive networks of social relations, activities, and processes, unified through psychic and social inscription (Grosz 1992: 243). In other words, a city—like a dancer— exists as an infinite series of ephemeral moments of balance in a larger context of change.

Like a staged dance or a city, the human subject can also be posited as a set of flows and movements, and psychoanalysts argue that the subject is, precisely, constituted through his or her changing relationships with the exterior environment and with others. As analyst Robert Langan observes, from conception to birth to a lifetime of relationships with exterior sources of physical and affective elements vital to our continued existence, "We exist as an exchange—of outside and inside" (2000: 70). And psychoanalysts, he continues, explore this porous boundary between the subject and his or her others, and the ever-changing balance between them. Julia Kristeva would concur; she conceives of the subject as ever *"en procès,"* which translates doubly as both "in process" and "on trial," threatened and refortified by these contacts with the exterior world which leave us in a state of permanent becoming. As she notes, "Even the soundest among us knows, just the same, that a firm identity remains a fiction" (1989: 257). Our subjectivity maintains its own ephemeral and changing balance, one that is deeply affected by changing cultural and political contexts, as recent clinical work has shown (Layton et al. 2006; Dimen 2011).

Finally, each of these three disciplines is concerned with both establishing and challenging the balances at hand. Choreographer William Forsythe, building upon the earlier work of Rudolf Laban, challenged the field of dance by asking what would happen if we re-imagined the center of gravity of the dancer as *not* in the body's center? While Laban imagined a Vitruvian body from which emanated a kinesphere of endless planes with the human body acting as their shared axis, Forsythe played with the "multiplication and displacement of the kinesphere" of Laban (Aguilar Alejandre 2010: 4); any point, now—even an elbow or an ear or another dancer's body—could act as the center of gravity, which provided movement with infinite points (or lines, or planes) of origin, opening up new possibilities for the dancer's trajectory and interactions across the stage.

We can think very similarly about cities as we ask how new flows and movements can shift urban centers of gravity. How does renovating an impoverished neighborhood with cafés and galleries re-center a city's creative life and change the flow of bodies and resources? How does an influx of violence re-choreograph us and alter the ways we previously moved through space? How do developments in a neighboring city spill over to change the local? As geographers move away from understandings of cities as containers with a rigid boundaries, they ask us to conceive of more flexible urban representations "that can take more of the world in" (Thrift 2003: 99). This not only accounts for the flow of people, products, media messages and emotions at larger levels, but also frees up the potential of space, permitting us to think differently about how we inhabit both who we are and where we are (104). What needs to happen, according to Thrift (2003) is that we must "unblock" space, which we can do by thinking about the flows and transferences, translations and differences that travel through a space, thus de-containing it and allowing for new rhythms to run through it.

In much the same way, psychoanalysts are also concerned with unblocking stagnant and limiting ideas in order to free up a person's potential and change their habitual ways of being. For Kristeva, the analyst's task lies in re-opening the subject's psychic space that has been foreclosed by media images that tell him what to think or imagine, and by totalitarian regimes (familial or political) that do not permit questioning. She roots our potential to imagine and question both the personal and the social in the *chora*, a term she borrows from Plato and which she posits as a rhythmic space from which our capacity to symbolize emerges (1984). Often erroneously confused with the womb, the chora is an unlocatable structure or semiotic "disposition" (1973) which permits the discharge of drives and affect into symbols in a rather Forysthian way: freely, multiply, improvising, always falling, interrupting and participating in the larger social order. By listening to the subject and not responding with closure, rejection, or violence, the analyst effectively re-opens this psychic space—reconnects the subject with his or her chora—which then permits the subject to imagine alternative ways of being and to speak into the symbolic, interrupting the status quo by participating. This process is, Kristeva writes, "a wager on rebirth" (2002: 286).

If effect, each field supports the idea that limits can be challenged and crossed and that instability may lead to more creative possibilities. Dancers unblock Cartesian space and experiment with new centers of gravity. Geographers and city planners unblock urban spaces and change the way people move through, experience, and make sense of the urban area. And psychoanalysts help patients unblock resistances and change their relationships to themselves and others. In all cases, unblocking that which limits us on our paths through cities, across the stage, and through our fears and desires enables us to move towards change.

Espacios Posibles and La Venada

Espacios Posibles creates art-based community projects which aim to transform the public spaces of gang-ridden barrios from insecure sites into safer, more pleasant nodes of sociality. Espacios begins its projects by asking the particular gang to choose an art activity, offering a wide panorama of options such as theater, dance, clown work, storytelling, and even the formation of a hip-hop group in one case. To mention another example, gang youth in a particularly dangerous barrio of the neighboring big city of León studied and staged a short version of *Hamlet* through which they were able to relate the violence of Shakespeare's plays to their own lives. One participant stated that before the theatre project, his life consisted of construction work,

Figure 8.2   The neighborhood of La Venada

smoking marihuana, and waiting for the day to end, but with the play, he suddenly had rehearsals—something new to do and something to think about (L. Saravia, personal communication, November 15, 2011). When the play ended, he returned to high school and, in his words, "changed my life." With this recent success in mind, the project moved into Guanajuato's barrio of La Venada in June, 2011.

The barrio now referred to as La Venada sits just above a middle class neighborhood. The sort of urban poverty found here matches other barrios in town where one finds not so much material poverty as a social poverty. The area is known as having a heavy incidence of domestic violence, alcoholism and drug use, as well as problems with both school desertion and un- and under-employment (L. Saravia, personal communication, November 19, 2011). With failing families, schools and employment structures, affective relationships and everyday routines have been increasingly structured around gang membership. Young men from about 14–30 years old belong to several different gangs, although they have identified a particularly notorious outside gang, the Pollos Negros, as their common enemy. Unlike the Pollos Negros who can be quite visible in local news and social media, La Venada's gangs seem to be fairly unknown and unseen outside of their immediate space. Their activities revolve around marihuana use, glue sniffing, minor assaults and robberies which, in the opinion of the Espacios leader, are committed not out of need, but out of frustration and generalized anger at not being seen or acknowledged (L. Saravia, personal communication, November 15, 2011).

Figure 8.3   Participants painting a house in La Venada

These factors conspire to construct La Venada as exceedingly distant from mainstream Guanajuato, although the area is only a 10-minute bus ride away from the centro. Young people from La Venada do not go to the centro to work and often cite residents' rejection when they say they are from La Venada. Tellingly, a stray balloon from the Three Kings' Day celebration drifted into the university patio this year; on the traditional tag which provides children space to request a toy from the Kings was a message from a little boy from La Venada. In his note, he asked for a toy truck and then ended with "vivo ayá en la venada" (original spelling errors maintained): "I live *out there*, in La Venada." In the child's mind, he is already outside ... other. The situation of social marginalization, internalized by La Venada's residents, already seems poised to repeat itself for the current generation.

Interior Voyage Toward the Self

Kevin Lynch (1960) argues that a city's legibility is defined by paths, districts, edges, landmarks and nodes. Guanajuato's centro is full of these things—monuments, churches, plazas, and so on—but La Venada had no such readability. The small plaza was rundown and unused. The edges of the neighborhood are poorly defined as houses trail off into unregulated areas in the mountain. While the city centro counts on a main plaza as a creative and sensorial site in which local culture and everyday life are reproduced, La Venada had no such "secret garden," to use Julia Kristeva's poetic term for the space of psychic life (1995: 27). It had no chora-like space that might permit creativity and change, no site in which to revive, reimagine, or make meaning. Violence, rather than creativity, seemed to dominate. While previous Espacios groups had chosen other options (with other sensory components), perhaps then it is not surprising that the La Venada participants voted for heavily visible, aesthetically beautiful projects, attesting to their desire to be seen in a city which renders them either invisible or ugly. They chose to paint their houses bright colors, to revive the decayed plaza, and to paint a mural with the help of a professional artist.

This beautification was accompanied by an internal journey. The mosaic design for the plaza's renewal centered on the deer symbol for which the barrio is named. Along with the attending artist, the youths involved made up a new origin myth as well. In the new myth, a passing miner fell in love with a beautiful woman who transformed into a deer at night, and from this relationship, the barrio of La Venada was born. It is well-known that in times of crisis people retell their founding stories and re-narrate who they are in an effort to reassert their subjectivity, be it group or individual (Todorov 1984; von Franz 1995). This return to origins constituted a creative interior voyage of sorts that allowed La Venada to re-draw a boundary around its own subjectivity or sense of self. Kristeva refers to this as "self-love in aesthetic sublimation" (2011: 164). By creating the mosaic, La Venada, the

> subject of sublimation ... overinvests [its] own means of expression (language, music, painting, dance, etc.), which is confused with a real object, when it does not replace it and become a veritable object of self-love. *The self loves itself in its outsize creations* ... [my emphasis] (2011: 164).

In short, this expression permitted a return to the self, a reparation of the ego, and a renewal of faith in the expressive act. The new myth asserted both a spatial and psychic center of gravity from which to extend outward, and it permitted *La Venada* to re-join the other of the mainstream city by participating in its visual beauty, its mining identity, and its symbolic visual language. This narcissistic repair then led to some unexpected exterior flows that could potentially reconnect the barrio to the dominant areas of the city in new ways and re-choreograph everyone's usual modes of moving through the city.

The Potential for New Flows and Movements

The first unexpected flow was the movement of La Venada children down to the main university gallery in December where they displayed their photos and paintings created in the Espacios project in an exhibition entitled "Soñando en La Venada" (Dreaming of La Venada) which seems to nicely capture what is bubbling up from the barrio unconscious. This marked not only a new physical movement for the children of the barrio, but also a new imaginative moment as they found themselves participating as artists in the city's downtown spaces, something no one had ever dreamed of. The event was covered in the local newspapers and quite literally "re-wrote" a new portrayal of La Venada residents, showing how the mainstream Other of the centro was also shifting its view of La Venada.

The second movement, still in the discussion stages, involves a proposal to take city residents and tourists up to La Venada which would also dismantle (or at least decrease) the social distance between the barrio and the centro. This too would radically alter existing choreographies in the city. However, an even more surprising proposal emerged that would reimagine the distance not between La Venada and the centro, but between the gangs of La Venada and the Pollos Negros. Some of La Venada's gang members began to talk about going to one of the Pollos Negros' territories in anger and dumping "a ton of trash" there. Espacios Posibles proposed that instead they deposit "a ton of flowers" (L. Saravia, personal communication, November 15, 2011). Gangs of young men leaving each other flowers? Amazingly, the idea took hold and went under discussion ... Whether or not this ever comes to the pass, the fact that one gang actually imagined this sort of unusual pilgrimage to another gang's neighborhood testifies to the opening up of new ways of thinking, relating, and acting.

Potential for Shifts of Gravity

If the dance of urban areas is held together by affects "like love and hate, sympathy and antipathy, jealousy and despair, hope and disappointment" (Thrift 2003: 103–4), a psychic shift can radically alter the careful choreographies between different city spaces. The Espacios effort has the potential to alter how local residents know and experience place. For those of us at the university with a center of gravity based in the centro, perhaps we realize that the violence is closer than we think when we meet gang members. Much more importantly, however, for those in the more peripheral barrios, it becomes apparent that peace is closer than *they* think. As works of art, gang members, and tourists change their usual paths of circulation, we begin to live relationships of nearness and farness differently (Grosz 2001: 129) and re-adjust our urban centers of gravity.

Sociologist Richard Sennett (2006) has argued that the critical imagination of the city is weak indeed, as cities around the world conform to uniform models of capitalist development, which closely parallels Kristeva's assessment of the contemporary human subject. However, what we are seeing here is something deeply creative with rather staggering possibilities in terms of social impact. The *Hamlet* actor in Espacio's previous project gave himself permission to imagine himself and his space otherwise. In a video interview posted online, he says:

> Before we were just a gang, but now we're "pure culture"—rap, theatre, and 2-to-3 other things. Our 3 blocks ... are pure culture. The gangs above and below our areas fight, but we're not involved anymore. Everyone respects us; everyone treats us well now (my translation, Testimonio Instantes Clandestinos: http://www.youtube.com/watch?v=QfjherC6uus&feature=youtu.be).

Notably, spatial analysis has everything to do with subjectivity in this example. Creativity provokes a shift in how the gang members experience themselves, others and the local physical site. This same psychic transformation is playing out in La Venada. As violence decreases and self-esteem rises, people's everyday movements through this particular neighborhood are re-choreographed, opening up the way for new flows, new ideas, new ways of being in and conceptualizing urban space.

National Level Potential

The local barrio is traversed by processes that simultaneously exist at the national level, but the context of greater Mexico takes us beyond troubled youth in search of affective ties to their neighborhood and city. This larger context of violence brings in more complex flows of live and dead bodies, drugs, guns, money, barbaric violence and human tragedy. This "public security" crisis, as the media labels it, reveals humanity close to its breaking point. Kristeva has argued that we have both formed a passion for death and lost all passion as we are numbed out of reaction to the violence, an argument we can certainly find fitting for Mexico where violence becomes the norm and where the media coverage has made it into a spectacle (2011: 94).

Figure 8.4   *Espacios Posibles* poster

With a stream of soap operas and songs glamorizing the narco-business and young children aspiring to be organized crime leaders, Mexico would seem to find itself at a crucial intersection. Kristeva suggests provocatively that:

> ... the more we work out/work through our signs (instead of throwing stones, as in guerrilla warfare, one would throw paint, as in a Pollock drip painting, or throw words out to one's analyst who would reconstruct their meaning), the more passion will be clarified without being extinguished (2011: 94).

She is encouraging the subject (individual or collective) to harness passion, anger, the desire to dream large, to create and to speak back, and to channel all of this into signs and symbols instead of violence. Is creativity-as-cure realistic for a problem this overwhelming and complex? While we may reach the limits of the choreographic metaphor and this excursion into French psychoanalytic theory and British geographic theory, La Venada nonetheless provides a hopeful start. If the psychic and spatial leap from the barrio to narco-violence is short (and filled with connections, rather than a void), the potential to leap from barrio solution to larger-scale strategies for harnessing the country's violence may also be feasible.

Kristeva advocates passionately for the revival of creativity which she fears may be disappearing in our increasingly robotized lives. For her, the sublimation of desire and aggression into symbolic form allows individuals to take up a relationship with the social while simultaneously challenging the status quo in a non-violent manner. We see in Guanajuato a cautious *essai*, a serious yet playful attempt to re-choreograph the potential space between the self and other of La Venada and the centro. In the opening of both psychic and physical space, the possibility of rewriting existing relationships and restoring an atmosphere of possibility and trust is revived. If the *Hamlet* actors constructed the stage as a safe space to try out new ways of being in the city, the La Venada gang members re-imagined the larger city space as a site in which to be differently. By re-choreographing their own responses to frustrations and longings related to the larger urban context, they effectively unblocked city space and shifted the city's traditional balance toward something much more democratic and dialogic, resisting habitual geographies of violence and creativity and opening up new possibility. These new choreographies allowed for both initiated and responsive moves, permitted chance and improvisation, and simultaneously rebalanced the city, however temporarily, widening existing representations and understandings of space. In the case of La Venada, the sublimation of aggressions through creativity provoked a surprising potential for deep change.

As Nigel Thrift writes, cities may be "oceans of hurt resulting from the undertow of the small battles of everyday life," but they are also "reservoirs of hope resulting from a generalized desire for a better future" (2005: 147). As the city of Guanajuato shifts its center of gravity ever so slightly in response to La Venada's creative work, we find hope that there is, indeed, still room in urban spaces for resistance and imagination. If desires for a better future could be sublimated as exemplified by the gangs in this essay, perhaps the local and national desire for (or dream of) peace will not, in the words of Langston Hughes, fester, stink, sag or explode. And perhaps our fundamentally creative nature will, as Kristeva posits, safeguard our urban humanity in these challenging times.

Acknowledgements

The author would like to thank Lucila Saravia, head of the Espacios Posibles project, for her insight into the work being done with the residents of La Venada and for generously sharing unpublished data about the barrio.

References

Aguilar Alejandre, M. 2010. Embodied architecture. *International Review: Mind, Land and Society*, 36–7.

Dimen, M. (ed.) 2011. *With Culture in Mind*. New York: Routledge.

Grosz, E. 1992. Bodies/cities, in *Sexuality and Space*, edited by B. Colomina. Princeton, NJ: Princeton Architectural Press, 241–54.

Grosz, E. 2001. *Architecture from the Outside. Essays on Virtual and Real Space*. Cambridge, MA: MIT Press.

Kristeva, J. 1973. The system and the speaking subject, in *The Kristeva Reader*, edited by T. Moi (1986). New York: Columbia University Press, 25–33.

Kristeva, J. 1984. *Revolution in Poetic Language*. New York: Columbia University Press.

Kristeva, J. 1989. *Black Sun: Depression and Melancholy*. New York: Columbia University Press.

Kristeva, J. 1995. *New Maladies of the Soul*. New York: Columbia University Press.

Kristeva, J. and A. Rice. 2002. Forgiveness: an interview. *PMLA*, 117(2), 278–95.

Kristeva, J. 2011. *Hatred and Forgiveness*. New York: Columbia University Press.

Langan, R. 2000. Someplace in mind. *International Forum on Psychoanalysis*, 9(1–2), 69–75.

Layton, L., Hollander, N. and Gutwill, S. (eds) 2006. *Psychoanalysis, Class and Politics: Encounters in the Clinical Setting*. New York: Routledge.

Lynch, K. 1960. *The Image of the City*. Cambridge, MA: MIT Press.

Massey, D. 2004. Geographies of responsibility. *Geogr. Ann.* 86B(1), 5–18.

Merriman, P. 2010. Architecture/dance: choreographing and inhabiting spaces with Anna and Lawrence Halprin. *Cultural Geographies*, 17(4), 427–49.

Rodríguez, K. 2012. *Small City on a Big Couch: A Psychoanalysis of a Provincial Mexican City*. Amsterdam: Rodopi.

Sennett, R. 2006. *The Open City*. Berlin. Available at: https://www.lse.ac.uk/collections/urbanAge/01_introduction/intro_investigation_H+N.html [accessed: August 2013].

Thrift, N. 2003. Space: the fundamental stuff of human geography, in *Key Concepts in Geography*, edited by S. Holloway, S. Rice and G. Valentine. London: Sage, 95–107.

Thrift, N. 2004. Intensities of feeling: towards a spatial politics of affect. *Geografiska Annaler*, 86B(1), 57–78.

Thrift, N. 2005. But malice aforethought: cities and the natural history of hatred. *Transactions of the Institute of British Geographers*, 30(2), 133–50.

Todorov, T. 1984. *The Conquest of America: The Question of the Other*. New York: Harper & Row.

von Franz, M.-L. 1995. *Creation Myths*. Boston: Shambhala.

Chapter 9

"Tehrangeles," CA:
The Aesthetics of Shame

Nazanin Naraghi

Introduction

The Arab Mind, a book first published in 1973 was, in the words of journalist Seymour Hersh, "the bible of the neocons on Arab behavior" (Copjec 2006: 12). A chapter of particular interest to the pro-war conservatives was on Arabs and sex. This chapter speculated that because of sex segregation and veiling, sex was a "prime mental preoccupation in the Arab world" (Copjec 2006: 13). This guesswork led to as *The New Yorker* reported in 2004, two themes that interrogator strategists employed at the *Abu Ghraib* torture prison, "Arabs only understand force" and "the biggest weakness of Arabs is shame and humiliation" (Copjec 2006: 13). The sinister and sexually humiliating photos of military personnel and prisoners that emerged from Abu Ghraib are a testament to these tactics.

Joan Copjec argues shame is tragically misunderstood to be a "primitive" affect that depends on the approval or disapproval of one's ancestors while guilt is a "sophisticated" self-regulating internal system of morality. According to Copjec, the world has crudely been divided into "shame" and "guilt" cultures, wherein "shame" cultures are less advanced than "guilt" cultures. She suggests these divisions "are improperly defined as types of cultures; for what they define, rather, is a subject's relation to her culture" (2006: 13). Culture understood as all of the things (nationality, race, family, ethnicity) that we inherit from our ancestors, "the manner in which we assume this inheritance, and the way we understand what it means to keep faith with it, are, I argue, what determine shame or guilt" (2006: 13).

Joan Copjec's analysis of a scene in celebrated Iranian filmmaker, Abbas Kiarostami's "The Wind Will Carry Us" (1999) illustrates shame as an affective response that allows one to "experience oneself as a subject" (Copjec 2006: 15). Copjec understands shame to be an, "unassumable object which sticks to us like a semi-autonomous shadow" (Copjec 2006: 21) and is "our sense of an inalienable and yet unintegratable surplus of self" (2006: 23). Copjec deftly argues, with the support of Kiarostami's film and the system of modesty known as *hejab* that greatly affected Iranian film, Iranians largely keep faith with their inheritance through the irreducible process of shame. This chapter following Joan Copjec's psychoanalytic investigation of shame asks: what is the relation Iranian migrants in Los Angeles have to their culture? Do the traumas of migration affect how Iranian migrants have kept faith with their inheritance?

I investigate these questions through the work of Iranian artist and graphic designer Houman Mortazavi. Mortazavi produced a series of controversial images that appeared on the streets of "Tehrangeles," CA. The popularized portmanteau refers to the Iranian-American neighborhood in Santa Monica and Westwood Los Angeles, CA. The satirical images were discovered by passers-by and newspaper readers throughout 2003 in the form of advertisements in the local paper, fliers on storefront windows, and stickers on utility poles. Mortazavi's images produce an encounter with an Iranian migrant character named Souleyman "Simon" Ordoubadi. The artist describes Simon as "the embodiment of my own alter ego going through a torture test. But he is also our collective unconscious let loose in the wilderness. He is us when nobody is watching" (2004: 23). Mortazavi's suggestion that he is releasing the collective unconscious of Iranians onto the streets of Los Angeles and that his character is "us" when no one is watching is directly related to the main investigations of this chapter, the trauma of migration and the complex affect of shame.

The Successful Migrant

For Mortazavi, his character of the displaced, confused, incomplete, split and tragic character of "Souleyman/Simon" (the Anglicization of one's name is a common and significant practice amongst Iranian-Americans) is in stark contrast to the whole, modern, stable and westernized Iranian migrant that I suggest dominates imaginings of Iranian-Americans in Los Angeles. For Mortazavi, members of the Iranian diaspora in Los Angeles work to promote their entrepreneurial and westernization efforts with what he considered amateur graphic design, ego-driven and image based advertising, and often times incorrect and nonsensical use of the English language. Consider the ongoing campaigns of two of the Iranian diaspora's commercially successful fashion designers, Bijan and Amir. Significantly, known only by their mononyms both have, at least professionally, disconnected from their familial cultural inheritance.

Bijan and Amir have consistently used prominent images of themselves on overbearing billboards along the famed Santa Monica Boulevard. These imaginary and ego dominant images have become part of the civic landscape of Los Angeles and in turn part of the psyche of Iranian-Americans in Los Angeles.

The haunting images of these successful men lord over the city with a forceful determination to promote happy and successful imaginings about Iranian migrants. Mortazavi took to the streets of "Tehrangeles" with his images of Simon. Mimicking the ego-driven advertising of Bijan, Amir, and others, his character began appearing on telephone poles and bus stop posts. Simon was changing the landscape of "Tehrangeles" with his visage by introducing an uncanny element, an out of place figure (depressed, confused, defeated) that at first glance seemed entirely in place (typical Iranian-American entrepreneur).

Iranian-American subjectivity has been centered or anchored by the dominant discourse of the successful and often entrepreneurial migrant. The powerful discourse of the "successful" Iranian migrant comes with a cost. Alenka Zupančič, points out that there is a marked and significant shift from the "pull yourself up by your boot straps" rhetoric to something much more ominous, she argues that "success is becoming almost a biological notion, and thus the foundation of a genuine racism of successfulness" (Zupančič 2008: 6). In order to fit into the success trope in the "contemporary ideological climate" as Zupančič writes "it has become imperative that we perceive all terrible things that happen to us as ultimately something positive-say as a precious experience that will bear fruit in our future life" (2008: 5).

If everyone is under pressure to turn their hardships into experiences that make them "better" or more "equipped" people then in effect the traumatic dimension of those experiences is reduced. In other words, integrating or domesticating trauma within the symbolic universe gives trauma meaning rather than allowing it to exist without allocating meaning. The disastrous effect of this is that when the traumatic experiences or "terrible things" are forced to serve a purpose that is meant to make you stronger the person who can't be stronger is ostracized or understood to be innately corrupt. What happens to the person "who dares to raise her voice and say that as a matter of fact, she is not happy, and that she can't manage to—or, worse, doesn't even care to—transform all of the disappointments of her life into a positive experience to be invested in the future" (2008: 5)?

The question becomes how could you not want to be happy? The assumption is the person is unwell "thus 'naturalizing' the differences and features produced by the sociosymbolic order rather than how traditional racism has worked which is taking biological features and giving them social meaning" (2008: 5). Although education and income reflect "success" in terms of adhering to the expectations of the Other (whether the Other is the host country, parents, or homeland) there are experiences associated with migration that are often left unaccounted for in statistical and imaginary analyses. What has led to the "successful" assimilation of Iranian-Americans to the United States?

Migration to the West

The dominant discourse that circumscribes Iranians into the language of migration is that Iranian-Americans are a "model minority" group and have largely embodied the proper paths to complete the transition from migrant to citizen (Mostofi 2003: 684). Classic assimilation theory supports the "model minority" categorization by suggesting that education is one of the essential indications that "should lead to a decline in home country ties, insofar as it facilitates swifter integration and mobility in the host society" (Guarnizo, Portes, and Haller 2003: 1215). Bozorgmehr and Douglas' study found that Iranian-Americans are amongst "the most educated ethnic groups in the United States," 37 percent of male Iranians living in the United States have a graduate or professional degree while 23 percent of female Iranians living in the United States hold an advanced degree (2010: 18).

Ali Mostashari, one of the founders of the Iranian Study Group, a collection of researchers assembled in 2002 by leaders in the Iranian community to gather statistical information on Iranian-Americans, comments on the pre-migration status of many Iranian-Americans: "these were people who could make it to the U.S. and sustain themselves in the U.S. It was a pre-selection, not your typical immigration where people come mainly for financial reasons" (www.payzand.com/news/04/jan/1191.html). Iranians that immigrated to the United States from Iran post-revolution were largely the product of Pahlavi era Iran, father and son monarchs, both of whom cultivated and strongly supported westernization, modernization, and urbanization (Dabashi 2001). The majority of Iranian migrants who left Iran post revolution were entrepreneurs or professionals that potentially held anti-Islamist sentiments (Mostofi 2003: 683). Iranian migration to the United States is generally divided into two broad waves, pre- and post-Revolution.

With the support of the state, pre-revolution migrants left the rapidly industrializing Iran of Shah Mohammad Reza Pahlavi to gain North American university educations. At the height of student migration in 1980, one in six international students was from Iran, translating to 50,000 Iranian born students in the United States at that time (Bozorgmehr 2006: 11). The second wave of Iranian migrants to the US is marked by the Iranian/Islamic Revolution of 1978–79, which brought with it the ascendancy of Islamic ideals to the political landscape and the instatement of Muslim clerics to positions of governmental power. The numbers of Iranians admitted to the United States steadily increased throughout the 1980s during the devastating Iran–Iraq war (1980–88) reaching a high point in 1989 (Bozorgmehr 2010). Although Iranians came to all parts of the United States, Southern California became a significant hub and is where the largest number as well as the most ethnically, linguistically, and religiously diverse population, which includes but is not limited to Jewish, Baha'i, Assyrian and Armenian Iranians reside (Mostafi 2003; Bozorgmehr 2006).

The numbers reflecting the heterogeneous Iranian population in Southern California are difficult to gage because of inconsistent participation of Iranian/Iranian-Americans in population research potentially due to residing in the country illegally. The 1990 US Census showed 74,000 (Naficy 1993: 25) Iranians in Southern California while currently there are estimates upwards of a million first, second, and third generation Iranians in the Greater Los Angeles Area (Mostofi 2003: 685).

Arguably, the project of modernity did not end for migrant Iranians with the revolution and the formation of the Islamic Republic of Iran but rather shifted in context and strategy. It certainly didn't end for Iranians who migrated to the West. Large numbers of Iranians who left Reza Shah's modernized Iran on the cusp and after the shift in power were groomed, prepped, and prepared to continue the trajectory of modernity, westernization, and urbanity. Following, Mostafi and Bozorgmehr the Iranians who left Iran and came to Los Angeles were positioned to complete the project of the modern Iranian subject. James Clifford has argued that diaspora "involves dwelling, maintaining communities, having collective homes away from home (and in this it is different from exile, with its frequently individualistic focus)" (1994: 308). He goes on to say that the "diasporist discourses reflect the sense of being a part of an ongoing transnational network that includes the homeland not as something simply left behind, but as a place of attachment in a contrapuntal modernity" (1994: 311). Ghorashi and Boersma (2009) argue that diaspora is the relationship members have to concepts such as homeland and return.

Rather than the traditional notion that the diaspora has a shared desire (based on collective suffering) to always want to return to homeland,

Ghorashi and Boersma suggest that Clifford's definition prompts an understanding of homeland not as a place of return but "a source of shifting and ambivalent attachment" (Ghorashi and Boersma 2009). This consideration of diaspora brings to the fore the concepts of loss, excess, and trauma. How have Iranian migrants dealt with the loss of homeland, with the "shifting and ambivalent attachment" to homeland, and the excess of trauma associated with migration processes? Mohsen Mobasher (2006) draws on cultural trauma theory as developed by Alexander Eyerman et al. (2004) to explain what he calls a "national and religious identity crisis among Iranian immigrants" (2006: 102). His study is focused on Iranian migrants in Houston, Dallas, and Austin, Texas. Mobasher suggests that there has been "a double cultural trauma affecting both the home society and host society" and this double trauma has prompted varied responses by migrants from Iran, including feelings of shame and disassociations from their home country.

As this chapter seeks out to investigate artist Mortazavi suggests that the idealization of Iranian migrants specifically in Los Angeles as completed modern western subjects dismisses the traumas of migration and its subsequent complex affective responses. Before beginning a discussion of shame and Mortazavi's work I first turn to a discussion of shame's "sister" affect, anxiety.

Anxiety

Mortazavi is not concerned with images of Iranian-Americans as a "model minority group." Rather Mortazavi's images dwell within the disturbing points where shame emerges. These points are where the trauma of migration and assimilation, the censorship of intimacy, and who "us" is when nobody is watching come forth. Before delving into the "paradox of shame" (Copjec 2006: 15) we must look closely at anxiety. With migration comes the responsibility of breaking with the past, the wisdom of our ancestors, and established knowledge systems. Modernity is founded on the same concept. Paradoxically, the modern subject and migrants often find themselves bound to culture, nationality, and religion and there are no shortage of wars and outbreaks of violence to provide evidence for this claim.

Specifically, in Los Angeles identity labels such as Iranian-American (this title intimates acceptance of the current Islamic regime), Persian-American (return to a pre-Islamic period) or political affiliations such as monarchist, constitutionalist, or Islamist are part of everyday separations and sources of conflict. In my research I interviewed members of households divided by allegiances to Islam and Khomeini and loyalties to Reza Shah and imperialist sentiments. Modernity and geographical/temporal breaks did not dissipate these loyalties. Modernity undermines the authority of our ancestors and this process of undermining the truths that came before us demands that we confront the "unfinished past" of our ancestors. Copjec suggests, "the theorization of this unfinished past is concentrated, in the West, around the concept of anxiety" (2006: 17). Heidegger, Kierkegaard, and Freud to name a few became concerned with theorizing anxiety. If modernity put a "zero in the denominator of our foundations," if culture, religion, ethnicity, and so on were eradicated with modernity, a radical break with both space and time, why did these remnants of the past have such a tenacious grip, as Mortazavi's work suggests, on in this case the Iranian migrant community in Los Angeles?

While in Iran I interviewed a woman in her late fifties who had decided to stay in Iran as the revolution was underway even though she had the opportunity to board a plane and never return like many others. Under Reza Shah's Iran, what she argued was a police state and imperialist pawn, she worked for a government institution, disliked her job, and made little money. For her, whatever type of change was to come was welcome. She described that, during the tumult that unfolded in the years between 1978 and 1979, *confusion* and *anxiety* were the order of the day. She boldly stated no one knew anything, no one had any idea what was going to happen, as she put it "Generally, we were all blind. Some people knew more than others. But most were swept away in the tide. It felt so good to wipe the past away and start over without knowing what was to come next" (2010). She embraced Khomeini and *hejab* wholeheartedly because for her transformation had come, the answer had finally arrived.

During our interview she smiled as a woman of experience does and said she became a full supporter of Khomeini, marching in the streets, yelling his name, and parading his image throughout Tehran. She confessed she didn't know much about him or what his plans were but not knowing what was to come next gave her a simultaneously exhilarating and terrifying feeling. Several years into Khomeini's Iran and the outbreak of insufferable war (Iran–Iraq War 1980–1988) she felt weighed down again. The liberating transformation had turned into a heavy burden, a suffocating debt. She confided that now they wait, they wait for the next change in power. Freud, Heidegger, and Kant understood anxiety not as dependent on an actual condition, like loss, but on a "condition that is not" in other words "anxiety is the experience not of a loss that has happened but the experience of awaiting some event, something that has not happened" (2006: 18).

Interviews with an Iranian family, living in Santa Monica near the heart of "Tehrangeles" since the late 1980s, revealed their anxiety about what would be next for Iran. This family was ideologically split politically the patriarch was a secular monarchist while the matriarch was a supporter of Khomeini and the Islamic Republic. Their son claims to despise Iran and all cultural associations with Iran and identifies as an ex-national. His resentment and disassociation, my research has found, is a common response amongst the Iranian diaspora in Los Angeles. The patriarch of the family is waiting for Reza Shah and the constitutional monarchy to be reinstated, while the matriarch would like to see Khomeini's original ideals returned, their son much to the dismay of both his parents was in favor of a US or Israeli military invasion.

Each interview I conducted with this family both as a unit and independently revolved around these manifestations of anxiety. The patriarch and son no longer had any ties financially or materially to Iran but they consistently spoke of Iranian politics and its people in every interview. The son, a man in his mid-40s, was preoccupied with unsavory Iranian behavior (behaviors that Mortazavi formalizes in his work) in Los Angeles, while his father was preoccupied with the invasion of mullahs in Iran. The patriarch fled Iran in 1980, leaving behind his beautiful home and his stable bureaucratic job with the Department of Transportation. The ejection from his job was a trauma that he has not come to terms with and he continues to fantasize that one day his pension will be returned to him. Copjec writes, "anxiety is this feeling of being anchored to an alien self from which we are unable to separate ourselves, nor to assume as our own, of being connected to a past that, insofar as it had not happened, was impossible to shed" (2006: 18).

Modernity as a process suggests that the modern subject chose or made a decision to break with the past. Once that decision was made there was no one else to blame but oneself for the outcome of that decision, no authority to curse. Iranians experienced a transformation in their destiny as a people and a country that produced a break with the past. The authority of ancestral decisions and actions was undermined whether it was the long reigning monarchy system or Islamic ideals. Can the break ever be complete and total? For some in the Iranian-American community in Los Angeles, I have observed there isn't a sufficient enough distance from the past for others there is a deep sentimental attachment to the past both lead to the same, some point in the past that continues to have a bearing on the present. Iranians in Los Angeles are bearing as jouissance "the injustice that horrifies us" in other words "jouissance is the affective result of our relation to ancestral desire" (2006: 20).

As Mortazavi's work illustrates the break with ancestral ties has produced a crisis of how to live for Iranian-Americans in Los Angeles, a scrambling for authority, truth, and guidance. As Copjec goes on the observe "in the moment of anxiety, we are gripped by our own jouissance as the very object-cause of our actions, but the experience is of being parasitized by an alien object so suffocatingly close we cannot discern what it is" (2006: 19). Copjec argues that Giorgio Agamben understood that potentiality and actuality are distinct experiences and if this is so then there must exist the possibility of impotentiality. Psychoanalysis gives the name jouissance to the capacity for impotentiality, and Copjec suggests that if we believe in jouissance then we must believe in the "speculative notion of the death drive ... anxiety can be understood as the affect that registers our encounter with the death drive" (2006: 19).

Death is an unknown that can never be known until actualized but the potential for death is constant, pressing, and sticks to one relentlessly. Anxiety is the affect that registers our encounter with the death drive and the jouissance we experience in anxiety is the burden of ancestral desire that we bear. The attachment we have to the incomplete, unactualized past we are born into is experienced as impotentiality, jouissance, and the paralyzing effect of anxiety. Lacan insists that anxiety is "not without object" even if what presses on us with anxiety has no material object, it is still not nothing.

Shame is incomprehensible without understanding anxiety and "what is fundamental to both affects is this non-actualized, unassumable object which sticks to us like a semi-autonomous shadow" (2006: 21). Fleeing from anxiety leads one to want to take that unshakable feeling and to find comfort in the social. To turn that alienating feeling into a shared experience we seek out to find an image of ourselves in others to assuage the incomprehensible and unassumable thing that sticks to us. Anxiety as Copjec points out is "rarely experienced in the raw; something like the 'stem cell' of affects, it is more often encountered in another form, in one of the 'social affects' of guilt or shame" (2006: 22). Which according to Mortazavi do Iranians in Los Angeles turn to as the way in which they "keep faith with their inheritance"? (2006: 13).

Houman Mortazavi: The Rise and Fall of Simon Ordoubadi

As I will show in a moment, according to Mortazavi's caustic images Iranian-Americans in Los Angeles have no shame. Unabashed self-promotion, underhanded business practices, doing as one is told, and obsession with demonstrating wealth, good looks, and degrees are all practices that Mortazavi suggests are perpetuated throughout the Iranian-American community. In stark contrast to how shame functions, these externalized social behaviors encourage a process of deferment to the Other, "all Iranians go to UCLA," "dentistry is the best profession," "Mercedes or BMW are the best cars," "lying in business is normal everyone does it." Copjec describes shame as an affect that allows one to "experience oneself as a subject." In other words, when one experiences shame there is nowhere to turn but to the deepest and often times uncomfortable well-springs of one's subjectivity.

Shame doesn't allow for an externalization or an anchoring of the self in the social but rather forces one to engage their subjectivity in a real and potentially jarring way. Thus, shame, paradoxically, is both an isolating experience and a basic social response. Iranian filmmaker Abbas Kiarostami developed a "cinema of restraint" as an aesthetic response to the strict Islamic rules of modesty enacted after the 1979 Islamic Revolution. His camera, in the most intimate moments, between for instance potential lovers, always hangs back and allows for privacy because of how censorship laws and Kiarostami's aesthetic decisions inform one another. Audiences around the world will see and experience their intimate moment, from a distance. Out of necessity, imagination, and shame he asks the audience to share in their singular experience without demanding, as Hollywood films often do, transparency, clarity, and the insatiable pornographic desire to see it all.

Mortazavi's aesthetic project investigates the complex affect of shame amongst Iranian migrants in Los Angeles by suggesting that there is none. In Mortazavi's art process (process as opposed to art object because the art object itself is disposable), he explores the interior, intimate, and personal processes of Iranian migrant failure, the trauma of loss of homeland, and the "searing pain" (2004: 15) associated with the unintegratable affect of shame. Unlike Kiarostami, Mortazavi's acerbic images and text deriding Iranian-American advertisements, business practices, and obsession with self-image is meant to point out the lack of shame rather than the presence of shame.

Iranians in Los Angeles, generally speaking, have gone to great lengths to avoid the experience of shame, primarily because as Zupančič argues, there is no space for "unintegrateables" like shame and trauma, in advanced capitalist societies. As Zupančič points out, turning trauma into a positive experience as advanced capitalism demands drains the trauma of its irreducible quality, shame being an affect that allows one to experience this irreducibility. For Iranians to assimilate, to become Iranian-Americans, the traumas of migration and the "unintegrateables" have successfully been reduced. My suggestion is that Mortazavi became curious about why many Iranian-Americans in "Tehrangeles" are deeply fearful of the singular experience of shame. If shame is that which sticks to us like a "semi-autonomous shadow," in other words a raw reminder of the past and future that never was then it is clear why Iranian-Americans would avoid the experience. If the West has decided that "the biggest weakness of Arabs is shame and humiliation" (2004: 13) then shame as an Iranian-American becomes an Achilles Heel. Mortazavi in a combination of vulgarity and sensitivity points out there are real repercussions to this attempt to be rid of shame.

Mortazavi writes, "one of the worst if not, if not the worst, fear of any standard-issue Iranian is *beaberouey* (disgrace). Anything that threatens your reputation is to be avoided like the plague, just as you are expected to do anything to enhance your image. So: fame good, poverty bad, education good, being overweight bad, and all because of the way it makes you look" (2004: 19).

As Figures 9.1 and 9.2 illustrate, Iranian men and women in Los Angeles are well-known for their groomed appearances. Mortazavi and as my research has found many Iranians in Los Angeles are embittered by the image-based behavior and practices of Iranians in Los Angeles. Mortazavi suggests that Iranians in LA are deferring to the Other to find their self-image, resulting in dissolvable guilt rather than unshakable shame. In other words, rather than face the real of their subjectivity they turn to one another for affirmation of their behavior. In this scenario, self-reflection and the opacity of the unconscious is dismissed while deferral to the Other for answers and the crude clarity of expensive cars prevails.

Figures 9.1 and 9.2   Iranian men and women in Los Angeles
Source: Photographs by author.

Figure 9.3   Houman Mortazavi's "Who Cares? I Cares"

For Mortazavi his characters, images, and words demonstrate that the promise of assimilation had failed for many. Simon Ordoubadi appears as four recurring male Iranian characters—businessman, politician, inventor, mystic and a desperate combination of all of them—focusing attention on issues of Iranian masculinity. Simon/Souleyman was not the same as the regal and smiling figures of successful fashion moguls, Amir and Bijan. Amir and Bijan gave Iranian-Americans figures to look up to, be inspired by, and emulate. Instead Simon reflected back characteristics of Iranian migrants that were less than appealing. Simon appeared as desperate, frustrated, confused, manipulative, dogmatic, idiotic, and goofy. All of which for the modern, western, urban Iranian subject was intolerable. It was reported that many of the advertisements were angrily torn down, people called in to local papers and asked that the advertisements be pulled, and Mortazavi said that he had received threatening phone calls. The enraged response to Mortazavi's tongue-in-cheek images speaks to the nerve that they struck (see Figure 9.3).

Figure 9.3 is part of Mortazavi's 2003 series. Simon sits with his hand over his heart, head tilted to the side and forward—the body language that Iranian men often use when they are humbling themselves although there is almost certainly manipulation in this universal gesticulation.

The politician in the "Who Cares? I Cares" confronts the viewer with out of context images and Iranian English idiosyncrasies such as, unnecessary plurals like "cares," an Iranian flag next to Omar Khayyam the Persian Renaissance man and an American flag next to Abraham Lincoln both pictured with the number one next to them. The political ad is in support of Souleyman Ordabadi for United Nations representative (not a position elected by popular vote) and makes statements written in Persian like "no one attends to you like your kind," "voting for another equals betraying Iran," and "remember your friends in the next election." The Iranian migrant characters that Mortazavi experiments with are not the images of success and happiness that Iranians are comfortable seeing in the landscape of their community. The characters reflect back a blind spot, the failures and misfires that so many Iranian migrants experience. Mortazavi investigates what happens to the migrant that doesn't fully assimilate and who doesn't smoothly transition to the new sociosymbolic order. His characters are depleted, display unnecessary bravado, or clownish good nature and reflect back to the Iranian American community a blind spot.

In Figure 9.4 Simon looks exhausted, depleted, and the bittersweet copy "I don't need your vote" suggests he is both resentful that he has to sell himself as worthwhile and simultaneously embodies the Iranian-American quality of inflated self-importance. Clearly, in order to win a public election one must garner votes. The advertisement includes the montage of out of context images, a bald eagle, a man and a woman mimicking Ordoubadi's gesture, and more naïve and manipulative text like "electing another is like betraying Iran." Mortazavi's images and text speak to Mobasher's claim that Iranians migrants are experiencing a "national and religious identity crisis" (2006: 102).

Figure 9.4   Houman Mortazavi's "I Don't Need Your Vote"

The viewer reads taglines like "today unity ... tomorrow revenge" or, in another advert, "inventor of 'especial' blend of spirituality, business, and politics." Many Iranian-Americans wouldn't necessarily see this advertisement as strange. As Mortazavi points out in regards to Tehrangeles, "there aren't many successful attempts at ingenuity in Tehrangeles. Quantity always trumps quality. You can see huge billboards in Westwood with big bold Farsi typos ... it's as if their only goal is to have their own photos printed somewhere to remind themselves that they exist" (2004: 20).

To answer the primary question of this chapter, how do Iranians keep faith with their inheritance? Mortazavi's work suggests that, for many Iranian-Americans who have migrated to Los Angeles, shame has been replaced by avoidance, in other words, guilt. Iranian-Americans who migrated to Los Angeles began to keep faith with their cultural inheritance via guilt primarily because the cultural inheritance of Iranian migrants (family, nation, ethnic ties) was interrupted and for many dissolved altogether. Mortazavi's description of Simon as "the embodiment of my own alter ego going through a torture test. But he is also our collective unconscious let loose in the wilderness. He is us when nobody is watching" (2004: 23) speaks to the irreducibility of shame; shame as that which doesn't require approval or disapproval from one's ancestors but rather an experience that requires no external force at all.

References

Bozorgmehr, M. 1997. Internal ethnicity: Iranians in Los Angeles. *Sociological Perspectives*, 40(3), 387–408.

Clifford, J. 1994. Diasporas. *Cultural Anthropology*, 9(3), 302–38.

Copjec, J. 2002. The strut of vision. *Imagine There's No Woman: Ethics and Sublimation*. Cambridge, MA: MIT Press.

Copjec, J. 2006. The object-gaze: shame, hejab, cinema. *Filozofski Vestnik*, 27(2), 11–29.

Dabashi, H. 2001. *Close Up: Iranian Cinema Past, Present, and Future*. London, UK: Verso.

Ghorashi, H. and Boersma, K. 2009. The "Iranian diaspora" and the new media: from political action to humanitarian help. *Development and Change*, 40(4), 667–91.

Lacan, J. 1978. Of the gaze as *Objet Petit a*. *The Four Fundamental Concepts of Psychoanalysis*. New York, NY: W.W. Norton and Company.

Massey, D., Alarcon, R., Durand, J. and Gonzalez, H. 1987. *Return to Aztlan: The Social Process of International Migration from Mexico*. Berkeley, CA: University of California Press.

Mobasher, M. 2006. Cultural trauma and ethnic identity formation among Iranian immigrants in the United States. *American Behavorial Scientist*, 50(1), 100–117.

Mortazavi, H. 2004. *Project Misplaced: The Rise and Fall of Simon Ordoubadi*. Printup Graphics.

Mostofi, N. 2003. Who we are: the perplexity of Iranian-American identity. *The Sociological Quarterly*, 44(4), 681–703.

Naficy, H. 1993. *The Making of Exile Cultures: Iranian Television in Los Angeles*. Minneapolis, MN: University of Minnesota Press.

Roudinesco, E. 1997. *Jacques Lacan*. New York: Columbia University Press.

Zupančič, A. 2008. *The Odd One In: On Comedy*. Cambridge, MA: MIT Press.

Chapter 10

Psychoanalysis and the Geography of the Anthropocene: Fantasy, Oil Addiction and the Politics of Global Warming

Stephen Healy

We have a serious problem: America is addicted to oil, which is often imported from unstable parts of the world. The best way to break this addiction is through technology.

President George W. Bush, State of the Union Address, January 31, 2006

For decades, we have known the days of cheap and easily accessible oil were numbered. For decades, we've talked and talked about the need to end America's century-long addiction to fossil fuels. And for decades, we have failed to act with the sense of urgency that this challenge requires.

President Barack Obama, June 15, 2010

Denial in addiction is not a linear course, either. The addict may be in denial at some times, and facing reality at others, so addiction in denial may be fluid especially in the beginning stages of recovery.

Drug and Alcohol Rehab Now, 2010

Introduction

"Addiction" connotes a dangerous dependency with severe, potentially fatal, consequences. In the United States "oil addiction" is regarded as an economic, geostrategic, and ecological challenge. The ecological consequence of oil addiction that receives the most attention is anthropogenic global warming. Just as the consequences of alcohol abuse, from DUIs to cirrhosis, are symptoms, global warming is a symptom of oil addiction (Roelvink and Gibson-Graham 2009; Speth 2009). For geographers interested in demonstrating the usefulness of psychoanalytic insights, talk of addiction has two implications.

On the one hand it is discouraging. "Addiction" is casually deployed in popular discourse, encompassing everything from heroin to social media use, appearing to render the concept theoretically impotent. On the other hand use of the word addiction does indeed imply a connection between global warming, the habituated pattern of fossil fuel use—from individual auto-driving to a fossil fuel based agriculture—and the human desires and drives that animate this abuse. Even the pattern of casual admission followed by denial speaks to the similarity between oil addiction and other addictions.

In this chapter, drawing largely on work of Lacanian clinicians and Stavrakakis's (2007) Left Lacanian theorists, I argue that it is important to take oil addiction seriously if we are to address the ecological challenge of global warming. Contemporary Lacanian theory asserts that the addict's relationship to substance or habit is mediated through language and fantasy and is thus open to analytic intervention (Loose 2011). This chapter is an intervention into "oil addiction" that attempts to understand the fantasies animating the politics of global warming: fantasies of carbon markets solving the problem, fantasies of adapting to climate change through sustainable cities, and fantasies that climate change is a hoax perpetrated by people with a nefarious agenda. Psychoanalytic theory allows us to understand the underlying architecture of these disparate familiar fantasies and their connection to addiction. Certainly they are palliative fantasies that promise an "easy fix," but more centrally, each fantasy is connected to addiction in so far the promised solution allows the subject to avoid entering the social bond of language, confronting and assuming responsibility for their own desires in relation to others. Entering into relation with others is precisely what is required to shift our relationship with oil and to address the challenge of global warming.

This chapter proceeds as follows. In the first section I will briefly define the psychoanalytic concept of fantasy, noting two recent efforts by geographers, Swyngedouw (2010) and Davidson (2012), to apply the concept to global warming politics and policy. In the second section, I argue that oil addiction and its symptom must be contextualized in relation to the contemporary society of enjoyment described in psychoanalytic theory, with its unbearable command to enjoy and the culture of toxo-mania (addiction) that emerges in response (e.g. McGowan 2003; Baldwin et al. 2011; Salecl 2011). In the third section I consider two familiar fantasy formations in connection with global warming: fantasies which imagine climate change as a catalyst for a sustainable future centered on carbon market solutions and sustainable cities and a paranoid fantasy which regards climate change as an elaborate hoax. In spite of their differing politics I argue, following Loose (2011), that both fantasies are integral to an addictive "administration" of enjoyment. If "oil addiction" is indeed an addiction, and global warming its symptom, then an intervention would entail a confrontation with the society of enjoyment itself.

In the concluding section I suggest ways in which the psychoanalytic process of traversing fantasy might allow for a different relationship with oil addiction and the politics of global warming. Swyngedouw (2010) and Davidson (2012) call for a properly political response to climate change, characterizing many current efforts as depoliticized "acting out." Though they fall short of describing what a properly political response might look like, their arguments suggest a familial resemblance to the Lacanian treatment of addiction. The Lacanian approach to the treatment of addiction underscore the challenge of wresting the addict from the hypnotic qualities of discourse and shocking them into a new relationship with language and a new level of responsibility for their own desires. If the addict-fantasy formation makes use of language in order to evade responsibility, a post-fantasmatic politics of oil and climate change would inaugurate an entirely different politics centered upon the social bond—a shared confrontation with the problem and with one another. I conclude with a brief sketch of the Transition Town and Solidarity Economy movements as examples of a post-fantasmatic response to climate change.

Psychoanalytic Geographies

In psychoanalysis, fantasy is a concept central to clinical intervention (Wright 1999; Stavrakakis 2007). Geographers have used this concept of fantasy to understand a wide variety of topics: the political economy of tourism (Kingsbury 2005), soccer fanaticism (Proudfoot 2010), city space as dreamscape (Pile 2005), racism in institutional settings (Thomas 2007), and the narcissistic attachments of pet owners to beloved animals (Nast 2006). More recently Swygnedow (2010) and Davidson (2012) have used fantasy to analyze the politics of global warming.

Certainly, the psychoanalytic concept of fantasy encompasses the common sense understanding of the term as daydreaming wish-fulfillment. What psychoanalysis adds to this common sense is use of the term to understand the relationship between discourse, individual subjects, and society in which fantasy's power is found in language's failure to provide coherence. Operating in an imaginary register, composed of images and speech fragments, fantasy provides coherence for the subject in the form of a compensatory explanation, locating a symptom that explains why he is unhappy or why society is full of conflict (Wright 1999; Stavrakakis 2007).

The integration of fantasy into social science theory, method, and analysis has political implications. As Kingsbury (2008) points out, the Lacanian project remains committed to a radical notion of enlightenment—not a repressive normalization, nor the development of a functioning ego, but according dignity to the patient as they nominate their "truth" by recognizing how fantasy structures and delimits their understanding of reality. The patient may come to the clinician wishing to restore the potency of a fantasy that no longer provides coherence (e.g. when the parent who is to "blame for everything" has died) but the analyst's goal is for the patient to traverse their fantasy in order to assume greater responsibility for their own desires. In this sense psychoanalysis is a performative discourse: the aim is to transform subject/society by (provoking) a new understanding (Healy 2010). I would like to attend to the political fantasies that surround global warming and their connection to "oil addiction." Pursuing this social analysis requires us to situate it within the context of what psychoanalytic theory terms the "society of enjoyment."

Society of Enjoyment

When Freud was developing psychoanalytic theory crossing the threshold into the symbolic realm of speech meant renouncing unlimited enjoyment. Civilization was understood as a repressive process that produced symbolic law and order, confining enjoyment largely to the imaginary (Freud 1994 (1930)). Contemporary psychoanalytic theory describes an inversion of the law from prohibition to enjoyment developing over the course of the twentieth century. Following Lacan, McGowan (2003) and Salecl (2010) offer an explanation for why this happened revolving around the development of the discourse of capitalism (Salecl 2011: 64). In this formulation what distinguishes contemporary capitalist society from earlier eras, where personal sacrifice and values like thrift functioned as injunctions of the superego (conscience), is the requirement for greater levels of consumption:

> The superego commanding enjoyment and the epoch of global capitalism exist in
> a symbolic relationship. Those who are under the sway of the command to enjoy
> become perfect global capitalist subjects. They constantly seek the new products

that the global capitalist economy proffers in hopes of obtaining more enjoyment. And on its side, the structure of global capitalism makes it easy for the subject to work on heeding the command to enjoy (McGowan 2003: 34).

The proliferation of opportunities for enjoyment, and the demand that one enjoy, leaves those of us in thrall of the discourse of capitalism in a dilemma: what to enjoy? At first glance this question appears to have an easy answer—we are free to enjoy what we wish. But, the danger is that when we imagine we are completely in charge of our enjoyment the structure of fantasy changes from an explanatory compensation for our lost enjoyment to a space for believing we can "somehow recover our lost jouissance (enjoyment)" (Salecl 2011: 64), that total enjoyment is possible. Technological and social organization allows some of us to enjoy everything: climate controlled environments, boundless mobility, and instant connection to distant others. If necessary we can consult with experts to ensure we are enjoying properly. The delusion of total enjoyment is dangerous to the psyche because it instills unreasonable expectations and inexorably generates an anxiety as the subject encounters enjoyment's spatio-temporal limits. First, while enjoyment may be infinite as technology melts all that is solid into air and a blur of motion, the body remains "riveted to being," finite and mortal (Copjec 2006: 101). Second, choice always in implies loss, no matter how perfectly the subject chooses, there will always be other things that we have not chosen that seem worthy of our attentions.

Along with Copjec (2006) and Nusselder (2009), Salecl (2011) argues that the further development of social media, smart phones and other devices, what Žižek (2004) refers to as "reality of the virtual" and Lacan named the allethosphere, serve to exacerbate the subject's dilemma. They engender a need to be continuously connected to our sense of choice and to what others are choosing. Naparstek (2011) sees the society of enjoyment encapsulated in a phrase born of Rave culture—"the impossible is nothing!" When the subject encounters limits the aim is to try harder and do more: more work, more self-help, more dieting, more yoga, etc. For Salecl (2011) even "renunciation," becoming a vegetarian for example, comes to function as source of enjoyment in the form of an internalized prohibition. For a great many, the gulf between promised freedom and ultimate limitations of enjoyment creates unbearable anxiety. Subjects respond with a new levels of "toxic mania and excess—alcohol, drugs, shopping, workaholism," (Salecl 2011: 65).

Loose (2011: 2) observes that while Lacan did not speak frequently on the subject of addiction he was prescient in his observations in the early 1960s about the rise of a medical model and the proliferation of the pharmacological responses to an increasing array of conditions just as the society of enjoyment was taking shape. Lacan predicted that this medical model would lead, not just to a rise in addiction but a generalization of addiction, what Loose (2011) refers to as addictification.

For Loose addiction is defined both by an engagement with a substance or habit, taking "the toxic route of the body," but also an attempt at avoiding the other.

> Addiction is a choice for jouissance that is administered independently of the structure that determines the social bond with other people. With this definition I am not implying that the social bond with other people does not play a role in the aetiology and experience with addiction. Rather what I want to emphasize here is the fact that the effect the addicts pursues is something that takes place to a large degree independent of the Other (Loose 2011: 5).

Loose's conception of the addict adds to our understanding of the society of enjoyment a different relationship between the imaginary and the symbolic, one where entering the symbolic does not have to mean a renunciation of unlimited enjoyment, or having to consider others in relation to one's own pleasure. Rather than Freud's "satisfaction in love and work" the addict is able to achieve enjoyment via the *administration* of a substance. Loose acknowledges the agency of the addict in choosing to the short cut to satisfaction through the toxic body, avoiding "the less immediate, and thus less satisfactory, root of the social bond." (Loose 2011: 7) The addict's short-cut explains why addiction is difficult to treat, for psychoanalysis also depends upon the social bond.

Addictification generalizes this process so that almost anything can be used as a short cut to enjoyment that avoids encounters with others. Loose uses the example of a patient who experiences incredible excitement and depression when her cellphone is not charged. Naparstek (2011) observes that the recreational use of Viagra allows for a different relationship with sexual performance.

Lacanian clinicians and theorists assert that the society of enjoyment increasingly compels us to engage in life's daily realities as addicts. Substances and habits help us to administer the anxieties (and pleasures) that surround our choices of enjoyment. In turn this administration produces and depends upon the imaginary coherence of the fantasy that we can either sustain this level of enjoyment indefinitely or modulate it at will. This is obvious when one thinks about conventional addicts; administering a shot of heroin is taking a dose.

The addict believes he is in control of the dose and that he has no problem, or that he can quit when he wishes, or that moving to a new location, getting a new job or girlfriend will allow him to quit (what 12 step movements refer to as a geographic "cure"). In each of these fantasies the addict "solves" his own problem without recourse to others. These fantasies are as much a part of addiction as the addictive substance itself.

There is a material connection between oil consumption, the society of enjoyment, and the consequences of combustion whether or not it is an overstatement to name this an "addiction." The Hirsch Report (2005), commissioned during the Bush administration, begins with the truism that oil is the lifeblood of modern civilization. It clearly describes US dependency upon oil and the consequences of diminishing extraction rates as the world passes peak oil production. As popular writer Richard Heinberg (2005) puts it, the 150 year "party" of cheap oil may be over and what we have left to burn are unconventional oils and coal likely to make the climate situation worse. To put it more bluntly, peak oil is the end of a bender and climate change is our collective hangover. There are parallels between the way we talk about oil dependence and its climatic consequences, and the fantasies central to addiction. In the section that follows I detail fantasies of global warming and climate denial with these parallels in mind.

Fantasies and Global Warming

Case One: An Easy Way Out

Recent efforts by Swyngedouw (2010) and Davidson (2012) make deft use of psychoanalysis to understand the fantasies that surround global warming and possible responses to climate change. Both authors argue the specter of a climate induced "dystopic urban future" (Davidson 2012: 15) or a coming ecological apocalypse (Swyngedouw 2010: 216) animate popular climate change discourse, generating a desire for an immediate response.

Swyngedouw notes that what has accompanied the rise of this populist apocryphal sentiment is the emergence of post-political approaches to governance which gives license to a class of experts to solve the problem

> Nurturing of the promise of a more benign retrofitted climate exhausts the horizon of our aspirations and imaginations ... In other words, we have to

change radically but within the contours of the existing state of the situation (Swyngedouw 2010: 219).

Swyngedouw goes onto argue that this apocryphal populism fixates on expert lead control of carbon dioxide. CO_2 becomes the fetish, or in Lacanian parlance "the objet petit a" that simultaneously expresses our deepest fears and desires for change" (220). Most national and international attempts to control CO_2 emissions focus on turning the emission of CO_2 into a commodity that has transaction costs associated with it, either through a carbon tax or through the creation of carbon markets (Swyngedouw 2010: 222). These markets are post-political in the sense that they are a product of expert administration and not political debate. They obscure other solutions, legitimate the existing economic and political order, all while allowing manufacturers to pass the final costs of carbon dioxide onto consumers.

Writing in a similar vein Davidson (2012) notes that this sense of emergency legitimates new "sustainable" approaches to urban planning. Sustainable cities are a topic of discussion amongst planning experts legitimated and impelled forward by a sense of crisis. Visions of the sustainable city are responsible for "mediating the relationship between climate change science and public policy" (Davidson 2012: 15). In developing his argument throughout the paper Davidson points out it is easy to see these plans, particularly in an age of municipal austerity, taking the form of a gentrified response to climate change: some places will get nice landscaping while others will be subjected to the next Katrina. In his view they are a kind of "acting out" an adaptive response for some communities to climate change while preserving, intact the larger set of practices that give rise to ecological challenges in the first place.

> These would include the continued pursuit of economic growth without necessary reductions in carbon emissions, carbon neutral scheme standing alongside coal-fired power stations, extensive suburban expansion with policies advocating reduced auto transit (Davidson 2012: 14 15).

As with Swyngedouw's analysis of carbon market fetishism the sustainable city has now become the ideal of expert-led urban planning and yet idealizing one thing and doing another requires another twist in the fantasy of the sustainable city—cynical investment. According to Davidson, it is really the psychic distance cynicism creates that allows fantasy to function effectively. On the one hand fantasy creates a space for acting out a utopian, gentrified "sustainable city" while on the other hand leaving intact the usual processes that contribute to urban and economic development, and fossil fuel consumption, as usual. All that is required, Davidson argues, is that someone believes in sustainability sincerely for the planner to act-out sustainably, keeping at bay the traumatizing recognition of the impotence of these half measures.

Case Two: There is No Problem

In May of 2012 the Heartland Institute placed a billboard outside of metro-Chicago as part of an advertising campaign for its upcoming Seventh International Conference on Climate Change. The initial billboard, featuring Ted Kaczynski, the infamous Luddite una-bomber, was removed after several sponsoring organizations including State Farm and Verizon withdrew annual support (Fischer 2012).

Similar billboards were planned to feature the faces of Charles Manson, Fidel Castro, and Osama Bin Laden (Lakely 2012). The billboard is an attempt to suggest that belief in global warming is something confined to the fringe of society.

> The point is that believing in global warming is not "mainstream," smart, or sophisticated. In fact, it is just the opposite of those things. Still believing in man-made global warming—after all the scientific discoveries and revelations that point against this theory—is more than a little nutty. In fact, some really crazy people use it to justify immoral and frightening behavior (Lakely 2012).

In their press release the Heartland Institute takes issue with the "scientific consensus" around global warming, arguing that it is a vast overstatement repeated by a complicit mainstream media.

Figure 10.1   Heartland Institute billboard

The Heartland Institute senior researcher physicist Fred Singer and his fellow physicist and mentor the late Fred Seitz, have intervened in a number of scientific controversies motivated by the belief that the science had become politicized: debates around the connection between smoking and cancer, second hand smoke and cancer, industrial activity and acid precipitation, and man-made chlorofluorocarbons and ozone depletion (Oreskes and Conway 2010). In each case the argument was that junk science had mistaken correlation for causation along with the implication that the research proving this causal connection was motivated by an anti-corporate agenda.

Fred Seitz wrote the forward to the Nongovernmental International Panel on Climate Changes 2008 position paper, "Nature, Not Human Activity Rules the Climate" published by the Heartland Institute. Seitz argues that the NIPCC offers a valuable "'second opinion' on the 'global warming' issue, we do not currently have any convincing evidence or observations of significant climate change from other than natural causes" (Singer 2008: iii). Singer, in his editorial introduction is more diplomatic in his remarks insisting that the NIPCC is playing the valuable role of the "skeptic" in relation to the dominant opinion and that our understanding of the climate can only be advanced by exploring ideas that run contrary to consensus. There is a point here, of course. Normal science has on more than one occasion failed to initially consider propositions that have upended consensus when they were finally heard. Indeed Lacan points out scientific discourse, what he terms university discourse, depends upon the generation of hysterical reaction—the voice of dis-identification—in order to advance (Lacan 2007).

What emerges then is a very contradictory intervention on the part of the Heartland Institute. On the one hand the Heartland Institute pays for a pointedly controversial billboard equating climate scientists with "crazy and immoral people." On the other hand the Heartland Institute representatives are astonished by the climate science community's lack of interest in engaging rational debate. Reading these two seemingly contradictory interventions together perhaps serves to illuminate their rhetorical function: the climate skeptic appears as a rational person open to reasoned debate while the climate scientist, in refusing to respond, is revealed as a close minded ideological militant worthy of caricature.

In every controversy the Heartland has weighed in on, it positions itself as a defender of free market capitalism. It joins with others in decrying the IPCC as part of a UN socialist conspiracy (Oreskes and Conway 2010: 247–2520). What follows from this attribution of a nefarious motive to climate scientists is an exculpation of human guilt in relation to global warming. The climate conspiracy is proof for Singer that human activity and fossil fuel combustion has no impact on climate. At other points in the NIPCC Singer contends that CO_2 is increasing naturally but that the effects of increased atmospheric CO_2 will be benign, even largely beneficial to economies around the world (Singer 2008: 23–7). From a psychoanalytic perspective, part of what alerts us to the fact we are dealing with fantasy is not the absence of logic but the surplus of explanations, a fantasy whose conservative political function leaves in place the supremacy of markets, technological innovation and individual choice. In its defense of free markets the Heartland Institute is, in fact, defending the society of enjoyment which prioritizes pleasure over consideration of others. In so doing, they are nothing if not consistent, recently publishing a paper that suggested a smokeless tobacco product called Snus would be more effective than government regulation in curbing the ills of smoking (Bacon 2011).

Fantasy in the Society of Enjoyment, Addiction and the Traversal of Fantasy

According to Davidson (2012) the notion of the sustainable city as a response to climate science is recognizable as a palliative fantasy in part because it pacifies the subject. No sacrifice is required, only trust in the architects that transform crisis into an engineered utopia. Likewise Swyngedouw (2010) identifies in the politics of global warming a fetishist fantasy around the market regulation of CO_2 in which imagined international cooperation radically changes economic and social organization while simultaneously leaving the system itself in place. If there is a politics of fantasy at work in the utopian, easy, post-political solutions to climate change there is in equal measure a fantasy at work in denying that we have a problem. The Heartland Institute asserts that climate change does not exist, or that it does but it's largely natural, or that it does but its effects will be benign. This surplus of explanations reveals a deep investment in preserving social and economic order against any disturbing incursion.

Loose (2011: 7), following Lipovetsky (2005), argues that the society of enjoyment rests upon "three elements: the market, technocratic efficiency, and the individual." This trinity roughly corresponds with each of the fantasies that animate the politics of global warming—fantasies that carbon markets will solve the problem, that expert design will solve the problem, or that there is no problem apart from any force that constrains individual choice in the market place, but, to return out our initial question, what connects them to addiction?

I think one answer to this question is to note a resemblance. All three of these fantasies, deployed in the context of debates around global warming, are continuously repeated. Each of these fantasies mobilize what Lacan referred to as the hypnotic quality of discourse, placing the subject in the thrall of a repetitive speech act which insists that our problems are easily solved or that there is no problem to solve (Loose 2011: 31). The rhythm imparts a consistency as the symbolic becomes imaginary. Whether it is the promise of an easy solution, "we'll quit tomorrow," or denial "what problem?" the point here is that the imaginerization of speech avoids collective confrontation with the issue and the social bond that confrontation creates. Could it be then that the "post-politics" of carbon markets described by Swyngedouw, the promises of an easy cure in the form of the utopian city described by Davidson, and the denials issued by the Heartland Institute, are simply a vacillation between admission and denial common to all addicts?

If the politics of fantasy that surrounds global warming sustain our oil addiction we are left with a stark picture. It is an understatement to say that addicts are notoriously difficult to treat. The failed war on drugs and the long term success rates of all approaches to drug treatment are testament to this (Flor 2011: 61).

What then does psychoanalysis offer in the way of an intervention in relation to addiction? For Loose (2011) the process is complicated by how addicts tend to relate to enjoyment and the ego ideal—they want to enjoy life too much and they expect to be able to do it perfectly. In this sense addicts are the perfect subjects of the society of enjoyment. Freud famously observed that the point of analysis was to allow for the patient to experience ordinary unhappiness in love and work. For the addict this is always a step down. According to Loose, Lacan's attempt at a general understanding of how patients can assume responsibility for their own desire in the context of a society of enjoyment has particular implications for the treatment of addicts. We cannot return to a society of prohibition; just saying "no" doesn't work. It is equally unacceptable to abandon the addict to the tyrannical rule of enjoyment. According to Loose, Lacan's answer lay in recognizing that the nomination of desire can represent the subject symbolically, it can consolidate their imaginary identity, or it can position them in relation to the real—to the limits of symbolization. It was his conclusion that exposing the addict to the void of the real, "real nomination" would help the addict to attenuate their belief in an idealized enjoyment, traversing the fantasy that structures addiction and, in so doing, enter into relation with others and the social bond that implies.

What might 'real nomination' look like for the oil addict, in a practical and political sense? The Transition Town movement, inspired by the popular writings of Robert Hopkins (2008), seeks to create locally resilient post-carbon eco-municipalities that can continue to function socially and economically. Accepting both anthropogenic climate change and peak oil as reality the more than 300 transition towns seek to enroll citizens in a democratic and participatory approach to surviving the end of the oil-age. Fittingly, Hopkins offers a guide for composing citizen groups capable of researching and implementing an Energy Action Descent Plan in 12 steps.

Similarly, solidarity economy movements have sprung upon around the world seeking to build economies based on principles of mutual aid rather than competition, democratic social inclusion, and non-capitalist economic development. These movements seek to build ecologically resilient communities while injecting social justice into collective considerations of ecological challenges. In the United States both these social movements are in their incipient stages and yet their response to climate change seems quite a bit different than the fetishism described by Swyngedouw or the "acting out" critiqued by Davidson. Solidarity NYC's recent policy statement pointed out how super-storm Sandy underscored the need to considered economic justice in responses to ecological challenges. Their position is that NYC needs to minister to the social and economic vulnerabilities that attend climate change now, and in making this point many solidarity economy practitioners mobilized a cooperative civil response to the effects of Sandy well-ahead of any municipal initiatives (Solidarity NYC 2013). Both of these movements reject "easy solutions" in favor of the ordinary unhappiness that attends a political process of building more ecologically and economically resilient communities. Rather than avoid social bond through fantasies of quick fixes, geographic cures or denial, they have entered into the social bond by figuring out what to do when the answers are not obvious. What the formation of this social bond seems to imply is a collective reworking of our relationship with the society of enjoyment, one in which subjects may be in a position to be accepting of social, ecological and personal limits on individual enjoyment. Indeed, following Roelvink and Zolkos (2011) we might see these movements as engaged in the "embrace" of climate change, a kind of hitting bottom in our relation to oil addiction as a precondition for moving beyond it.

References

Bacon, J. 2011. New anti-smoking campaign encourages tobacco use. *USA Today* [Online: USA Today]. Available at: http://content.usatoday.com/communities/ondeadline/post/2011/10/new-anti-smoking-campaign-encourages-tobacco-use/1#.UIlI58XA9oE [accessed: 4 July 2013].

Baldwin, Y., Malone, K. and Svolos, T. (eds) 2011. *Lacan and Addiction: An Anthology*. London: Karnac.

Bush, G.W. 2006. State of the Union Address [Online, 31 January]. Available at: http://georgewbush-whitehouse.archives.gov/stateoftheunion/2006/ [accessed: 24 August 2012].

Copjec, J. 2006. May '68, the emotional month, in *Lacan: The Silent Partner*, edited by S. Žižek. New York: Verso, 90–114.

Davidson, M. 2012. Sustainable city as fantasy. *Human Geography*, 5(2), 14–25.

Drug and Alcohol Rehab Now. 2010. Denial and addiction [Online: Drug and Alcohol Rehab Now]. Available at: http://www.drugalcoholrehabnow.com/denial-in-addiction.htm [accessed: 24 August 2012].

Fink, B. 1995. *The Lacanian Subject: Between Language and Jouissance*. Princeton NJ: Princeton University Press.

Fischer, B. 2012. Scott Walker and Ted Kaczynski in the heartland [Online: PR Watch]. Available at: http://www.prwatch.org/news/2012/06/11578/scott-walker-and-ted-kaczynski-heartland [accessed: 18 August 2012].

Flor, R. 2011. Knows no's nose, in *Lacan and Addiction: An Anthology*, edited by Y. Baldwin et al. London: Karnac, 59–72.

Freud, S. 1994 (1930). *Civilization and Its Discontents*. New York: Dover Publications.

Glynos, J. 2008. *Ideological Fantasy at Work: Toward a Psychoanalytic Contribution to Critical Political Economy*. Paper to the 58th PSA Annual Conference, Swansea, UK, April 1–3, 2006.

Hamilton, C. 2010. *Why We Resist the Truth About Climate Change*. Paper to Climate Controversies: Science and Politics Conference, Museum of Natural Sciences, Brussels, October 28, 2010. Available at: http://www.clivehamilton.net.au/cms/mediawhy_we_resist_the_truth_about_climate_change.pdf [accessed: 25 October 2012].

Healy, S. 2010. Traversing fantasies, activating desires: economic geography, activist research, and psychoanalytic methodology. *Professional Geographer*, 64(4), 496–506.

Heinberg, R. 2005. *The Party's Over: War and the Fate of Industrial Society.* Gabriola Island, BC: New Society Publishers.

Hirsch, R., Bezdek, R. and Wendling, R. 2005. *Peaking of World Oil Production: Impacts, Mitigation, and Risk Management.* MacClean VA: Science Applications International Corporation/US Department of Energy.

Hopkins, R. 2008. *The Transition Handbook: From Oil Dependency to Local Resilience.* White River Junction, VT: Chelsea Green Publishing.

Kingsbury, P. 2005. Jamaican tourism and the politics of enjoyment. *Geoforum*, 36(1), 113–32.

Kingsbury, P. 2008. Did somebody say jouissance? On Slavoj Žižek, consumption and nationalism. *Emotion Space and Society*, 1(1), 48–55.

Lacan, J. 2007. *The Other Side of Psychoanalysis: The Seminar of Jacque Lacan Book XVII.* New York: W.W. Norton & Company.

Lakely, J. 2012. *Do You Still Believe in Global Warming? Billboard Hits Chicago* [Online: The Heartland Institute]. Available at: http://heartland.org/press-releases/2012/05/03/do-you-still-believe-global-warming-billboards-hit-chicago [accessed: 28 August 2012].

Lipovetsky, G. 2005. *Hypermodern Times.* Cambridge: Polity Press.

Loose, R. 2011. Modern symptoms and their effects as forms of administration: a challenge to the concept of dual diagnosis and to treatment, in *Lacan and Addiction: An Anthology*, edited by Y. Baldwin et al. London: Karnac, 1–39.

McGowan, T. 2003. *The End of Disatisfaction? Jacques Lacan and the Emerging Society of Enjoyment.* Albany: State University Press of New York.

Naparstek, F. 2011. New uses of drugs, in *Lacan and Addiction: An Anthology*, edited by Y. Baldwin et al. London: Karnac, 39–58.

Nast, H.J. 2006. Loving ... . Whatever: alienation, neoliberalism and pet love in the twenty-first century. *ACME: An International E-Journal for Critical Geographies*, 5(2), 300–327.

Norgaard, K. 2011. *Living in Denial: Climate Change, Emotions and Everyday Life.* Cambridge, MA: MIT Press.

Nusselder, A. 2009. *Interface Fantasy: A Lacanian Cyborg Ontology.* Cambridge, MA: MIT Press.

Obama, B. 2010. Remarks by the President to the nation on the BP oil spill [Online, 15 June]. Available at: http://www.whitehouse.gov/the-press-office/remarks-president-nation-bp-oil-spill [accessed: 24 August 2012].

Oreskes, N. and Conway, E. 2010. *Merchants of Doubt: How a Handful of Scientists Obscured the Truth on Issues from Tobacco Smoke to Global Warming.* New York: Bloomsbury Press.

Pile, S. 1993. Human agency and human geography: a critique of the "new models" of the self. *Transactions of the Institute of Royal British Geographers*, 18(1), 122–39.

Pile, S. 2005. *Real Cities: Modernity, Space and the Phantasmagorias of City Life.* London: Zed Books.

Proudfoot, J. 2010. Interviewing enjoyment, or the limits of discourse. *Professional Geographer*, 64(4), 507–18.

Robbins, P. and Moore, S. (Forthcoming). Ecological anxiety disorder: diagnosising the politics of the anthropocene. *Cultural Geographies*.

Roevlink, G. and Gibson-Graham, J.K. 2009. A postcapitalist politics of dwelling. *Australian Humanities Review*, 46, 145–58.

Salecl, R. 2011. *The Tyranny of Choice*. London: Profile Books.

Singer, F. 2008. *Nature, Not Human Activity, Rules the Climate*. Chicago: The Heartland Institute.

Solidarity NYC. 2013. *Growing a Resilient City: Possibilities for Collaboration in New York City's Solidarity Economy* [Online: Solidarity NYC]. Available at: http://solidaritynyc.org/wp-content/uploads/2013/02/Growing-A-Resilient-City-SolidarityNYC-Report.pdf [accessed: 4 July 2013].

Speth, G. 2009. *Bridge at the End of the World: Capitalism, the Environment and Crossing the Bridge from Crisis to Sustainability*. New Haven CT: Yale University Press.

Stavrakakis, Y. 2007. *The Lacanian Left: Psychoanalysis, Theory, Politics*. Albany: State University of New York Press.

Swyngedouw, E. 2010. Apocalypse forever? Post-political populism and the spectre of climate change. *Theory, Culture & Society*, 27(2–3), 213–32.

Thomas, M. 2007. The implications of psychoanalysis for qualitative methodology: the case of interviews and narrative data analysis. *The Professional Geographer*, 59(4), 537–46.

Wright, E. 1999. *Speaking Desires Can be Dangerous: The Poetics of the Unconscious*. Cambridge: Polity Press.

Žižek, S. 1997. *Looking Awry*. Cambridge, MA: MIT Press.

Žižek, S. 2000. *Tarrying With the Negative: Kant, Hegel and the Critique of Ideology*. Durham, NC: Duke University Press.

Žižek, S. 2004. *Organs Without Bodies: On Deleuze and Consequences*. New York: Routledge.

Zolkos, M. and Roelvink, G. 2011. Climate change as experience of affect. *Angelaki*, 16(4), 43–57.

PART III
The Technologies of Becoming a Subject

Chapter 11

When 1+1 Does Not Equal 2: Childhood Sexuality and Laplanche's Enigmatic Signifier

Mary E. Thomas

Children's geographies as a field rarely considers psychoanalytic thought. In fact, as Chris Philo (2011: 125) notes, the field more generally insists on a child's autonomy and assumes that each child is a "capable and knowledgeable actor to whom we must always listen." Louise Holt similarly claims that the concept of the "sociological child" (after James et al. 1998) undergirds geographers' advocacy for the "competency" of child actors (Holt 2011: 2), so that scholarship can push against predominant understandings of children as anything from socially and culturally marginal to unknowing, frivolous, and apolitical. She rightly questions the modernist notion of agency on which children's geographies stand (see page 3, where she points to Susan Ruddick's [2007] work to do so), as well as the centrism afforded to children's experiences at the expense of examining the constraints of children's lives and agency. In these assessments of children's geographies and their welcome critiques of the subdiscipline's child-centrism, the child as a subject is not afforded a complexity that psychoanalysis might bring to it.

Perhaps the potentials of psychoanalysis could most obviously be directed toward children's contemporary sexual subjectivities. Chris Philo, in an editorial in the journal *Children's Geographies*, cleverly questions the ways that child-centrism falls apart at the mention—or perhaps threat would be a more accurate word—of childhood sexuality. The inciting issue that Philo takes up is whether children can consent to sexual relations with adults (this example is taken from discussion aired on a radio broadcast between Foucault, Jean Danet, and Guy Hocquenghem in 1978). While Foucault was interested in questioning the ways that adult–child sexual activity has become criminalized, Philo turns the issue on its head by asking how the child-centrism of children's geographies would fare with a hypothetical situation of a child-initiated sexual encounter with an adult, with no evident trauma to the child (Philo 2011: 125). Philo predicts that scholars of children's geographies would "retreat" from the celebrated child actor when he or she becomes evidently sexual–agential, since that sexuality could be quite "discomforting" for the adult researchers (126). His tone, I think, teases those children's geographers who want to advocate for children's "voices" but then who might run screaming for the hills by what they hear when children talk about sexuality.

Despite his ironic teasing, to Philo the "adultist" position must win out; he suggests that the going discourse on children's sexuality is that "adult society knows best" (125). He calls this stance "adultist" since it assumes that children's own perspectives or desires are rendered either unknowing or warped toward adult malfeasance. He even invokes his own status as a parent to mark his concern and presumably his moral obligation to protect the child (even when protecting a kind of child-only space for sexuality, away from adults, see 124). Yet, he surprised me by ending his editorial with these words:

> I am convinced that there is a major *dilemma* to be faced here, and, to clarify my own position, my feeling is that it indeed signals the limits to how far we should go with child-centric children's geographies, suggesting instead that there are moments when it is imperative to remain more conventionally Foucauldian, not being "seduced" by children's own voices but instead retaining a (thoroughly and reflexively critical) sense of the adult *discourses*—the understandings and prescriptions derived from informed adult agents (scholars included)—which cannot but "see further and deeper" than is ever possible for the children themselves (126; emphasis in original).

I'm surprised with this ending for several interrelated reasons. First, Philo's account plays with words to insinuate that adults can be seduced by child-centrist accounts, yet adults can and should maintain mastery of the sexual over children. While he is manifestly questioning the intellectual seduction—the appeal of the child-centrist approach over time in the development of the field and the grasp it continues to have on researchers—his choice of wording reads to me an obviously sexual double entendre. The effect of the wordplay is an acknowledgement of the potential for adult sexuality intruding in the research encounter. How "we" study sexuality, thus, becomes an issue of morality and ethics. It is impossible to fathom an adult researcher discussing the sexual seduction of a research project with children (let alone being seduced by a child, even only through fantasy), as prevalent and expected social-cultural mores take us immediately to criminality and abuse. Thought and action have been too woven together when it comes to adult–child sexual relations, and "relations" as a term itself insinuates social-embodied interaction rather than transference, association, or other psychic processes. There is no space to consider the adult researcher's sexuality, conscious or unconscious, within these socio-intellectual, moral, and ethical limits.

Second, I admit that whenever I see the words "reflexively critical" my guard goes up. This is not to discount the politics of methodology and the feminist advances in bringing embodiment and awareness to the research "encounter," but I do greatly worry that "reflexivity" becomes a roadblock toward bringing psychoanalytical thinking to geography. Of course, the debates about reflexivity and psychoanalysis go back over 20 years now (from Pile 1991 to recent work by Kingsbury, Pile, and Bondi). Geographers interested in both have argued persuasively that putting a term like reflexivity to use means acknowledging the fantasy of full knowledge, both of the self (researcher) and of the other (researched). I have not seen much of this psychoanalysis literature taken up by studies of contemporary children's geographies, however, so the hope for an underpinning psychoanalytic tone of Philo's caution might be lost on readers more sociologically interested in relationality. And again, Philo himself cuts down the psychoanalytic possibilities of critical reflexivity when he notes that it is of "informed adult agents" who themselves seem not affected by desire and unconscious sexuality. This leads to my final point.

Third, and most important, Philo's assumption that adults know more about sexual discourse than children confines sexuality itself to a very narrow range of meaning and activity. Sexuality is adult discourse. Children might engage with adult discourse, but childhood sexuality is merely reactionary to or absorptive of it. Thus, children's sexual subjectivities are sponge-like, soaking up adult discourse, and in turn children mimic it in their sex play. Sexuality in this account is discursive to a fault, so that children's theories of sexuality, the language they ascribe to various sexual "things" in idiosyncratic and unconscious ways, and the particular paths of their desire, are all completely wiped out. Simply put, the spatiality of the subject is exteriorized and reduced to what we see or hear: discourse.

Let me be clear that, in contrast, by "sexuality" I do not mean any sort of overt sexualization or sexual behavior. The tone of criminal lechery that attaches to any mention of child–adult sexuality is obvious in contemporary Western contexts that struggle with hypersexualized childhoods, abuse, pornography, trafficking, and even sexual enslavement. Philo himself calls the attachment of childhood with sexuality a "taboo" in academic inquiry (125) and questions when and where scholars should intrude on the spaces of children's sexuality. He points to the presumed spatiality of children's sexuality as bounded, contained in their own worlds of play, and he worries whether the adult research foraying into those spaces will irrevocably translate children's play into adult logic (a translation which may in fact, according to Philo, be grounded on adult discomfort, see page 126). Sexuality in such a scene is spatially reductive, agential and bound to the autonomous "person," and behavioral.

Rather, I suggest that children's geographies must broaden sexuality as a concept, away from the practices of identity and sexual activity, and beyond "discourse." To do so, psychoanalysis is a sure aid. *The Language of Psycho-Analysis* by Laplanche and Pontalis (1973) defines sexuality as a concept that "embraces a whole range of excitations and activities which may be observed from infancy onwards and which procure a pleasure that cannot be adequately explained in terms of the satisfaction of a basic physiological need" (418). Importantly, they note that the subject's sexuality does not result structurally or unilaterally, either from the development of physiological capacity, or through generalizable and influential relations (e.g. the completion of an Oedipus complex through a familial structure), or the combination of the two. Rather, sexuality is the infant's or child's own process as she or he grapples with how to "find a place in the phantasy universe of the parents" (421). The child subject forms an interiority, an unconscious, to deal with the messages that come its way that it cannot assimilate; the unconscious is therefore a topography of repressed and unresolved matter (see the entry on "unconscious" in Laplanche and Pontalis for their distinction between Freud's first and second topographies, 474–6). Childhood (or infantile) sexuality, to Laplanche and Pontalis, is thus both "endogenous inasmuch as it follows a course of development and passes through different stages, and exogenous inasmuch as it invades the subject from the direction of the adult world" (421). The infant/child subject forms its own theories, desires, and even its own "language" of sexuality, through unconscious processes that might be inaugurated through encounters with adults, but can never be reduced to the reality of those relations, times, or spaces.

Discourse, therefore, is never an effective term to describe the sense of any capacity to interpellate or determine subjects (this a common critique of Foucault from psychoanalytic scholars). "Discourse," too, misdirects our attentions away from subjects' sexualities toward the appearance of society and its social and even interpersonal relations (see Copjec 1994: 9). As scholars of children's geographies, "discourse" brings us to ethical arguments rather than psychoanalytic ones; Philo's is therefore a musing on how we *should* govern sexuality, not how we should conceptualize it or even research it. Understanding sexuality as discursive becomes, in this context, normative and subject-less.

When psychoanalysis turns to the adult other to frame childhood sexuality, it does so for different reasons that Philo suggests. To be sure, I'm not necessarily in disagreement with Philo's decision to tread carefully around childhood sexuality. His piece is a short editorial, not a theory of childhood subjectivity, and his purpose is to challenge scholars of childhood to push against the fantasy of a centered child; in that goal we are in complete agreement (Thomas 2011). I also agree with him that childhood sexuality is "invaded" by adult sexuality, but here I want to rethink Philo's use of the word "discourse," and instead I advocate opening up considerations of how adult sexuality interacts with children and childhood. Thus, while I agree with Philo that placing the child at the center of their own sexual discourse is a mistake, my reasons for decentering the child sexual subject are motivated by an interest in understanding subjectivity differently. I next turn to the theory of Jean Laplanche, to suggest that children's sexuality is not only formed through "an incursion of the [adult] other," it is also indelibly marked by the unconscious of adults—an unconsciousness that leaves adults even enigmatic to themselves. Thus, while Philo assumes that adults can "see further and deeper" than children can, I question the extent to which we should let this statement go. Children's geographies should not decenter the child only to center the adult. Laplanche tells us why.

The Adult Other

Laplanche's legacies for psychoanalytic thought are many, including the indispensable *The Language of Psycho-Analysis* with Pontalis, his remarkable essays on psychoanalytic interpretation, and his general theory of seduction. In this section I will contain my brief overview to the obvious necessities in understanding the enigmatic signifier and its role in the development of the child's unconscious. In the subsequent section I turn to sexual seduction, before finishing the chapter with concluding thoughts for children's geographies.

Laplanche, in the words of Nicholas Ray, "brought to bear the principles of psychoanalytic interpretation on the Freudian corpus itself ... [dismantling] the 'manifest' history of Freudian thought in order to track what he called 'the latent and partially unconscious history' running counter to it" (Ray 2012: 54).

Laplanche's reading was to mark a profound contradiction in Freud's work, which he argues tends Freud to a Ptolemaic resolution of the human subject, that is, to a notion of the subject as centered (to Ptolemy, the earth was the point around which celestial bodies revolved: a geocentric model). "Indeed," Laplanche writes, "if Freud is his own Copernicus, he is also his own Ptolemy" (Laplanche 1999: 60). Laplanche points to the shift from a geocentric to a heliocentric model of the universe, referring to the "Copernican revolution" that took man away from the center of the universe: "the Copernican revolution is perhaps still more radical in that it suggests that man, even as subject of knowledge, is not the central reference-point of what he knows" (56). Freud likened his "discovery" of psychoanalysis, Laplanche writes, to a Copernican revolution (60), and Laplanche carries that language and metaphor throughout his opus to mark the tendencies of Freud both simultaneously and contradictorily to center and decenter the subject. Thus, what Ptolemy and Copernicus stand for is the difference between a world centered on the subject (Ptolemy) and a subject who is not at the center of things (Copernicus).

Throughout Freud's metapsychology particularly, Laplanche suggests, is a tendency to domesticate the unconscious by re-centering the subject (1999: 67). He dates Freud's Ptolemaic "going-astray" to the abandonment of the seduction theory (even as he finds a "secret pathway" of seduction running through Freud hence). Thus, he argues that Freud forgets the primacy of the other in the development of the unconscious. Freud rather, Laplanche suggests, comes to assign a "mine-ness" to the unconscious that results *not* from attempts to interpret messages from an other, but from a sort of naturalization, genetic truth, or inner core that "belongs" to the subject. To Laplanche the unconscious is never one's own; it is not "your inner core that you fail to recognize" (66). The unconscious, to Laplanche, is Copernican because it is never its own reference point. If the Copernican revolution suggested that man "is not the central reference-point of what he knows" (56), the Ptolemaic tendency of Freud self-centers the subject. Laplanche refers to this as Freud's "going astray" by understanding the "self-begetting" of the subject over time, in part, by the naturalization of the Id, i.e. its supposed biological presence (see 86). (Laplanche also discusses the profound consequences of translation of Freud to English, which results, for example, in the mistake of Kleinians to "fail to make a basic distinction between drive and instinct"—see the interview of Fletcher and Osborne in *Radical Philosophy.*) There is nothing, in the theory of Laplanche, that allows any sort of independence of the unconscious, and indeed, the unconscious is no mere reaction to the fact of an other. His general theory of seduction proposed that the adult other's unconscious itself played a foundational role in the development of the child's unconscious (see Ray 2012 for a succinct summary). Laplanche states in an interview with Caruth that

> there is some strangeness in this seduction theory. For every one of us it is difficult to give an account of this strangeness, and to face it. Think of it in terms of grammar. In grammar, you say, the first person is the person who speaks. The second person is the person to whom I speak. The third person is the person of whom I speak. But who is *the person who speaks to me*? (Caruth 2001: para 140).

Why is it, Laplanche repeatedly asks, do we forget about the adult's unconscious in the effort to theorize the child's? In this argument, Laplanche distinguishes himself from Lacan (who insists that there is no other of the other, see Laplanche 1995: 667): the adult's unconscious is other to him or herself with its own foundational alterity. Thus, the adult other (or even in Lacan, the Other) is no mere "implantation" in the child which then sparks unconscious development. This is not just "subjectivism," which Laplanche faults Freud for sometimes suggesting by "reducing the other to the subject's perception of the other" (Laplanche 1999: 73) (he also faults Lacan for emphasizing trans-individual structures at the expense of the alterity of an other/person).

Laplanche emphasizes the alterity of unconscious via the seduction theory because, he writes, "it maintains the unconscious in its alien-ness" (1999: 62). As such, to repeat, the unconscious is never its own reference point. The message "is opaque to its recipient and its transmitter alike" (Laplanche 1995: 665). In the essay "The Unfinished Copernican Revolution," Laplanche insistently points to the method of psychoanalysis to highlight the impossibility of "the direct transposition or translation of one discourse into another" (Laplanche 1999: 63). This point is why Laplanche also rejects the symbolic reading of manifest content, say, of dreams. The unconscious is not the repository of memories; "the unconscious cannot be a mere hermeneutic copy of the conscious" (63). Laplanche firmly rejects the notion that psychoanalysis is a set of "codes" which unlock a generalizable human condition.

In "Psychoanalysis as Anti-hermeneutics" he therefore laments the unfortunate reduction of psychoanalysis to "a system of stereotypical interpretations to which it is too often reduced" (Laplanche 1996: 8). He connects this reduction to Freud's turn to symbolism and his inconsistent adherence to the analytic methods—especially in his later years with the shift in his attentions to myth and the Life and Death instincts (8). Laplanche believes that the anti-hermeneutics of psychoanalysis vitally belongs to its method, rather than its content:

> I will insist once again on the fact that the original discovery of Freud is that of a *method*. An unprecedented method, it is linked to something equally unprecedented, the foundation of the psychoanalytic *situation*. ... It is a strictly individual method, favouring an individual's way of connecting things, element by element, through "associations," to the detriment of all self-construction and self-theorization. The method is ana-lytic in the true sense of the term, associative-dissociative, unbinding. ... It is not that there is no question, with complexes and myths, of discoveries which are partly psychoanalytic. But these discoveries are wrongly situated: obscuring the unconscious in psychoanalytic theory, just as they obscure it in the human being. They are transformed into something which can be used by the human being to master enigmas (9–10; emphasis in original).

Myths and codes mislead us, as psychoanalytic thinkers. To Laplanche, it should not be up to the analyst to achieve a hermeneutical tidiness of meaning, separate of the psychoanalytic method. There is something here of the horse and the cart, whereby the worrying trend in psychoanalysis is to put the fact of the unconscious (the cart) in front of the horse, its development in childhood. When the fact of the unconscious becomes the rule of analysis, then the "heterogeneity of the unconscious to all systems" (1996: 11) is lost; the individual's own relation to the enigma is ignored, in other words the cart comes before the horse—indeed propels itself with no fuel. The method is abandoned with the desire for theoretical synthesis, Ptolemaicism re-centers the subject, and metapsychology no longer needs analysands (see page 12).

Laplanche writes, *"the only genuine, originary hermeneutist is the human being"* (1996: 10, emphasis in original). The human subject is *both* Copernican and Ptolemaic, in that it seeks synthesis and self-centeredness (Ptolemacism) yet it only can attempt to do so by contending with the alterity or alien-ness of its unconscious (Copernicanism). As Laplanche relates to Caruth, "it is in relation to the seduction theory that the subject builds himself as an individual. He Ptolemizes himself, being at the very beginning Copernican, that is, circulating around the other's message. He has to internalize this, and he builds an inside in order to internalize. ... That is the building of the psychic structure" (Caruth 2001: para. 30). The ego in Laplanche's theory is therefore always bound to the originary seduction—every following message is dealt with by the ego that is in place due to the original seduction.

The enigmatic message is what the child tries to contend with, as opposed to an understanding that the child enters into a relation with the adult who is self-evident. Laplanche clearly states that the messages from the adult are not enigmatic simply because they are "mysterious, hard to get at, or inexplicable" for the child (1996: 11); it's not that the child is just inexperienced or unable to understand because she or he has inadequate language or social skills. The adult's unconscious is "stirred up by the relation to the small child" and therefore messages "are enigmatic for the receiver only because they are enigmatic for the sender" (11).

> The agent of this proto-translation is not an adult man, situated here and now, a *cogito* or a *Dasein*. Heideggerianism, along with the entirety of hermeneutical thought, bears the seal of reflexive thinking—what I term Ptolemaic thinking, which is the mode of thought *par excellence* of the adult closed in upon himself. Originary translation is, then, performed by the child, the nursling baby. And let us add, for good measure: the baby that has no unconscious (11).

The "nursling baby" is rejected in the course of Laplanche's argument to be representative of a passive recipient of nutrition and dependency on adults, since of course Laplanche rejects Freud's understanding of the hungry baby in *The Interpretation of Dreams* as an "experience of satisfaction" (see Laplanche 1999: 76–7). This is sexual seduction, and the breast belongs to an adult woman who has an unconscious.

Sexual "Seduction"

It is a great shame, to Laplanche, that Freud's seduction theory became a kind of metaphor for pathological sexual abuse by adults of children. Sexuality in this concern is radically reductive and induces a facile adult–child relation through perversity alone. And not least, "seduction" conceptually thus cannot be put to use in a theory of unconscious development, despite the clinical, analytic lessons which insist, to the contrary, that sexuality be at the heart of generalizable psychic life (see, for a start, Laplanche and Pontalis's entry for "Sexuality" in *Language*, especially 420).

In the writings by Laplanche that I am utilizing for this chapter, there are several examples given to explain the primacy and sexuality of the enigmatic message. One is the breast-feeding of the baby (even though Laplanche admits it is perhaps an "archaic" example, see Laplanche 1999: 78), which I detail next. A second is the primal scene of the Wolf Man case study (and third, a rendering of "A child is being beaten," see 154–9). All of these examples serve Laplanche's goal to illustrate the "going-astray" of Freud's seduction theory by failing to bring the adult's unconscious into the scenes. In brutal brevity I will overview Laplanche's argument, especially the breast case, before finishing this chapter by turning back to the question of sexuality in children's geographies.

First, the breast (pun intended). Laplanche reconsiders Freud's theory of the birth of the wish based on the baby's need, in this case, to satisfy its hunger. The baby is hungry, it cries, it receives food, and through these steps learns wish fulfillment. Laplanche faults Freud for basing his concept of the sexual on biological need; the need for food, to Laplanche, is not what is important in this scene, nor is the "introduction of food" (1999: 77).

> The introduction of food simply triggers off the whole activity. Thereafter, the entire mode of functioning [in Freud's writing] is solipsistic. There is no longer any trace of the alien in what is to take place, either in the object or in the aim of the drive. ... what is missing from all this is a sign, something that "signals." A sign offered to the infant by the adult, delimited by the adult in the situation before the infant itself finishes the process of sampling. It is thus, and only thus, that one can conceive the intervention of sexuality in the experience of satisfaction (77–8).

For it is not the milk that the adult woman first brings, *but the breast*, and she "does so due to her own desire, conscious and above all unconscious. For the breast is not only an organ for feeding children but a sexual organ, something which is *utterly overlooked by Freud and has been since Freud*" (1999: 78, emphasis in original). Laplanche insists that we need not split the sexual breast and the nursing breast (see in the Caruth 2001 interview, starting para. 69, his discussion of women's sexuality and the breast, something Freud never ventured!). We need not even concentrate on whether or not a woman experiences sexual pleasure in nursing a baby—what is important to Laplanche is that "something passes from the nursing person to the child, as an enigma. ... And the most important thing is not the breast as a shape, as a whole, as an object, but the breast as conveying a message to the child. And this message is invaded by sexuality" (para. 72).

The woman nursing will have her own unconscious process about her breast, her own primary trauma that of necessity recurs unconsciously and remains enigmatic to her—and thus is simultaneous to the child's unconscious development (see paras 77–84 on the atemporality of the message). The alterity of the mother,

her own Copernicanism, passes to the child, who must try to make something of it—who must make an unconscious in order to attempt to make something of it.

The second "going astray" that Laplanche considers in his general theory of seduction is the case of the Wolf Man. Laplanche asks, "When the Wolf Man's father takes the child to watch animals copulating, are we really to imagine that nothing but an innocent stroll is intended?" (Laplanche 1995: 666). Here, Laplanche insists, is more than the "perceptual reality on the one hand and the child's fantasy on the other" (665). The child is trying to make sense of the enigmatic message of the other, which is of course impossible in the sense that there is no sense about it. The message is enigmatic, unreadable, undigestible, and then, restructured and repressed. And foremost to be considered, is "always at first in the direction from adult to child" (665).

While the primal scene of the Wolf Man is copulation, Laplanche carefully urges us to not restrict the sexual to genitals. In fact, Laplanche points to Freud's hint that the question of "origins and procreation" can just as easily come from the arrival of a younger sibling. This, too, is an enigmatic message from the other, and not "just a purely objective fact" (1995: 666). But the repression and restructuring of the enigma (through the development of the unconscious and psychic process) also, Laplanche argues, has to extend beyond the "fact" that the message comes from "outside" the child. He says, "even in the first moment it must be internalized, and then afterwards relived, revivified, in order to become an internal trauma" (Caruth 2001: para. 7; see more on afterwardsness or *Nachträglichkeit* and the breast in paras 16–17). Laplanche compares the child to the analysand when he suggests that transference and psychoanalytic method are the only ways to "master an enigma" (Laplanche 1996: 9). While the process of repression and unconscious development may be universal to Laplanche (and to psychoanalysts more generally), the meanings of sexuality are never synthetic: "where one follows the path of synthesis, one silences the unconscious" (10). What "discoveries" are there to make of children's sexualities, then?

Adult Sexuality, Child Sexuality

Philo is right that sexual discourse is adult discourse. The problem with a term like "discourse," however, is that it implies an evident meaning (even if that meaning is not straightforward or obvious). To add a Laplanchian psychoanalytic perspective, sexuality *by definition* is rife with struggles to interpret enigmatic messages and opaque others and failures to do so.

Sexuality in all its plurality always insinuates primary repression—the development of the unconscious—in the associations and dissociations that channel from attempts to achieve Ptolemaic stability in a Copernican state. The temporality of that primary situation is not a stepping stone back in time and place, a kind of mapping of the subject through memory, but a topological relation of messages made wholly unique in each individual's psychic process. "With the concept of *enigma*," Laplanche reminds us, "there can be no linear causality between the parental unconscious and discourse on the one hand and what the child does with these on the other" (Laplanche 1999: 160).

The argument that there is no adult sexual situation or discourse that is not also a message, that is not also born enigmatically, holds many challenges for children's geographies. At the very least, our questions, as scholars, posed to youth are themselves messages to youth: they are, to mimic Laplanche, questions posed by the other (Laplanche 1996: 11). The argument, however, cannot be reduced to the question of method alone, although I would agree with Laplanche that psychoanalytic method and theory must remain bound together.

Even returning to Philo's essay shows us that his concerns about examining childhood sexuality themselves are tightly intimate with method and theory. The issue, remember, to Philo is not just one of how to approach the fact of children's sexuality, the issue is how to do so through research. No matter how much we would "enjoy" the research itself would be, how "lovingly" we would refine methods to do so (Philo 2011: 26), we are discomforted by the adult sexual discourses that affect children and invade childhood.

Perhaps by starting with Foucault's comment on adult-child sexual relations, Philo's editorial can get nowhere else than caution. The behavioral and sociological, not to mention legal, situation of childhood sexual abuse is a dead end for psychoanalytic thinking. Laplanche says as much in an interview:

> The important thing for the analyst is the message and the way the message is treated. So even in the cruder cases of seduction, criminal cases of seduction, what is important for us is not how it happened—that's not our problem—but what was remaining of a message in this situation, and what could have been treated by the infant. What was being communicated by the act? (Fletcher and Osborne 2000: 38).

The point to take away from this example is not the question of "how far we should go with child-centric children's geographies" given that their "voices" are framed by adult discourses (Philo 2011: 126).

The question, to my mind, is why we continue to be so focused on a Ptolemaic voice to begin with. Is sexuality so dangerous a topic in children's geographies that we can't theorize it away from this voice? Maintaining the child-agent perhaps becomes a way to protect the child from our contaminations as adults—their "voice" and autonomy protects them conceptually, in other words, from our enigmatic messages. Just as vital to bring back in here is adult recoil from Copernicanism. In many ways, sure we "see further and deeper," as Philo puts it, than children do. In many other ways we do not. Is it not the quest of critical scholarship to figure out the difference and to decide what is at stake in the very positing of the distinction?

References

Caruth, C. 2001. An interview with Jean Laplanche. *Postmodern Culture* [online], 11(2): no page numbers. Available at: http://muse.jhu.edu/journals/postmodern_culture/v011/11.2caruth.html [accessed: 29 March 2007].

Copjec, J. 1994. *Read My Desire: Lacan Against the Historicists*. Cambridge: MIT Press.

Fletcher, J. and Osborne, P. 2000. The other within: rethinking psychoanalysis, an interview with Jean Laplanche. *Radical Philosophy*, 102, 31–41.

James, A., Jenks, C. and Prout, A. 1998. *Theorizing Childhood*. New York: Teachers College Press.

Laplanche, J. 1995. Seduction, persecution, revelation. *International Journal of Psycho-Analysis*, 76(4), 663–82.

Laplanche, J. 1996. Psychoanalysis as anti-hermeneutics. *Radical Philosophy*, 79, 7–12.

Laplanche, J. 1999. *Essays on Otherness*. London and New York: Routledge.

Laplanche, J. and Pontalis, J.-B. 1973. *The Language of Psychoanalysis*. New York: Norton.

Philo, C. 2011. Foucault, sexuality and when not to listen to children. *Children's Geographies*, 9(2), 123–7.

Pile, S. 1991. Practising interpretative geography. *Transactions of the Institute of British Geographers*, 16(4), 458–69.

Ray, N. 2012. Jean Laplanche, 1924–2012: forming new knots. *Radical Philosophy*, 174, 53–6.

Ruddick, S. 2007. At the horizons of the subject: neo-liberalism, neo-conservatism and the rights of the child. Part one: from "knowing" fetus to "confused" child. *Gender, Place & Culture*, 14(5), 513–27.

Thomas, M. 2011. *Multicultural Girlhood: Racism, Sexuality, and the Conflicted Spaces of American Education*. Philadelphia: Temple University Press.

Chapter 12

Towards a Psychoanalytic Geopolitics: The Militarization of Public Schooling in the USA

Ian G.R. Shaw, Jared Powell and Jessica De La Ossa

Introduction

What role the American school should play in society is a question as old as the institution itself. For former President Woodrow Wilson, the purpose of the school was to divide the population into different social segments. In his words: "We want one class of persons to have a liberal education, and we want another class of person, a very much larger class, of necessity, in every society, to forego the privileges of a liberal education and fit themselves to perform specific difficult manual tasks" (cited in Lapham 2012). Indeed, despite being perceived as a pathway for upward social mobility, public schooling continually reproduces the very social and economic inequalities it purportedly targets by channeling students through academic "tracks" (e.g. Bowles and Gintis 1976; Giroux 1981; Berliner and Biddle 1995; Mitchell 2003; Apple 2004; Lipman 2004; Kozol 2005).

Moreover, conventional public schooling encourages individuals to prioritize "high" performance over critical thinking, thereby generating consent for the status quo (Apple 1990, Chomsky 2003, Au 2009, 2011, Leahey 2013). This process is never completely successful of course (Giroux 1981), and as Paolo Freire (1972) has argued, a transformed public education *could* cultivate a critical consciousness of one's circumstances. However, in the century since Wilson articulated his vision of a hierarchical society, the federal government has not prevented its manifestation: US school systems are increasingly split between a dialogical, inquiry-based model in affluent white suburbs, and a didactic, militarized, vocational model in economically depressed areas inhabited by people of color (Kozol 2005; Lipman 2004, 2008).

This division is illustrated in the striking contrast between the pedagogical philosophies of Sidwell Friends School in Washington DC, where President Barack Obama sends his two daughters, and the Chicago Military Academy, one of four such academies operating while Obama's Secretary of Education, Arne Duncan, was CEO of Chicago's public school district (Kroll 2009). At Sidwell, the school's prevailing philosophy is to offer "students a rich and rigorous interdisciplinary curriculum designed to stimulate creative inquiry, intellectual achievement and independent thinking in a world increasingly without borders ... to be a school that nurtures a genuine love of learning ..." (Sidwell Friends School 2012). Sidwell's philosophy doesn't translate at the Chicago Military Academy, which prepares its students for academic success through a disciplined military environment. The school lists "Five General Orders" that must be obeyed by its students: (1) Be at the right place, at the right time, with the right materials. (2) Follow the orders of the faculty, staff, and cadet leaders appointed over me. (3) Refrain from loud and boisterous behavior. (4) Engage in no public display of affection. (5) Remain in uniform at all times (Chicago Military Academy 2012). Submission to authority is not simply a means for teaching at Chicago's Military Academy—it is a central aspect of *what* is to be learned. And yet, despite these authoritarian rules, which appear devoid of all pleasure and fantasy, we add a sixth, no less insignificant injunction that students follow at the Chicago Military Academy whether they know it or not: *Enjoy!*

In this chapter we explore how enjoyment is crucial to sustaining US nationalism and foreign policy. While much of the analysis in political geography and critical geopolitics on the so-called "war on terror" has focused on violent state practices (e.g. Gregory 2004), as well as more grounded accounts of oppression and occupation (e.g. Fluri 2009), there is a crucial element that helps explain the continuing allure of war and war-making, and that is the rituals and practices of enjoyment. We suggest there is a vital relay between the pain and suffering "out there" and the metastases of enjoyment and desire "at home"—particularly in an in increasingly militarized education establishment. This topology suggests the necessity of the sensual and playful at the very heart of some of the most outrageous excesses of nationalism. By focusing on the militarization of schools in the US, particularly through the Junior Reserve Officers' Training Corps (JROTC) program, the *psychoanalytic geopolitics* we put forward attends to the banal and enjoyable processes of war. In our analysis, military recruitment at schools and the targeting of young children should not be seen as a strange aberration taking place in an otherwise innocent sphere of social reproduction, but rather, a historical process that is instrumental to the American "war machine" (Deleuze and Guattari 2004). We therefore ask: what does it mean to think about military recruitment as a psychoanalytical technology? Our answer points towards the importance of enjoyment in nationalist ideology.

Paul Kingsbury has variously studied the relationship between nationalism and enjoyment—in particular, the seemingly banal manifestations of nationalism in things like car bumper stickers (Kingsbury 2007) and football matches (Kingsbury 2011; see also Kingsbury 2005; Proudfoot 2010). Using the psychoanalytical theory of Slavoj Žižek (1994, 2002) in particular, Kingsbury explains that "a crucial element at work in the emotional lures of nationalism, as well as other (fundamentalist) ideologies, is the enjoyment sought in and garnered from investments in and identifications with ideological fantasies" (Kingsbury 2008: 52). We also share the enthusiasm for Žižek's work as a vital lens for understanding the psychic economies of violence, nationalism, and geopolitical ideology. Mirroring critiques of textualism that would follow decades later in critical geopolitics (Müller 2008), Žižek (1989b: 10) argues that: "It is no longer sufficient to denounce ideological experience as artificial; to seek to demonstrate how the object proffered by ideology as natural and given is the product of a discursive construction, the result of a network of symbolic overdetermination; to locate the ideological text in its context, to render visible its necessarily overloaded margins." Instead, we must focus on what makes ideology enjoyable, fascinating, and sensual—suspending our interpretive twitches. To contextualize our argument, we begin with a history of the relationship between nationalism, militarism and public education in the United States, before exploring the relationship between enjoyment, the JROTC, and a psychoanalytic geopolitics.

Occupying the Classroom

Psychoanalysis can enrich the study of critical geopolitics through its complex understanding of the psychic and emotional geographies of nationalism. For new Lacanians such as Žižek, there are three interlocked ways of understanding nationalism: its Symbolic, Imaginary, and Real dimensions. As a symbolic concept, nationalism is understood as the product of a Hegelian "internal repulsion" that creates exclusions and outsiders in the maintenance of the nation (Žižek 1989a). Mertz asserts that "If racism is intranational that is simply because an intra-national symbolic exclusion must have already taken place before 'the Nation' as an entity opposable to other nations can exist. Racism and nationalism are related precisely in that racism is the prop needed to maintain an illusory nationalist subjectivity" (1995: 87). This symbolic (and racialized) universe of insiders and outsiders is likewise played out in the Imaginary. This process parallels the well-known Lacanian "mirror stage" (Lacan 2005). The patriotic citizen, like the early child, derives a sense of existential unity through identifying with an unbroken reflection—in this case, the very idea of the nation. Finally, the nation possesses a more-than-symbolic and more-than-imaginary dimension: a national "Thing" that eludes symbolism and language altogether yet nonetheless remains active in its constitution (Kingsbury 2008; Proudfoot 2010). Given that the nation has no positive existence then, it must continually be stabilized with a set of concrete rituals—a "*point de capiton*"—that provides a quilting point for a sliding chain of signifiers. In the militarized classrooms of the US, we find such a *point de capiton*, where libidinal energy is captured by the state and codified into law.

How, then, did nationalism become so entrenched within the American school system? How did we get to the bizarre situation where half a million young Americans dress-up in uniform and take lessons on science from military instructors? How did education become so utterly embroiled in defending the nation?

Federal legislation codifying the confluence of militarism and schooling extends as far back as the Morrill Act of 1862. Passed during the American Civil War, the Morrill Act provided each Union (Northern) state with 30,000 acres of federal land per Congressperson, with the provision that each state accepting this land must create at least one college teaching "agriculture and the mechanical arts," which, as the Act further stipulated, must include courses in "military tactics." After the war, the Act was extended to include the formerly Confederate (Southern) states. Six decades later, on the eve of America's entry into the First World War and in the midst of the so-called "preparedness controversy," the National Defense Act of 1916 expanded the size of the American military and gave President Woodrow Wilson new powers to assemble and deploy military force during a declared "emergency." It also created, under the aegis of the US Army, the Reserve Officers' Training Corps (ROTC) to teach military discipline and tactics in public colleges, and the Junior Reserve Officers' Training Corps (JROTC), which was intended to act as a feeder to the senior ROTC by teaching a version of its program in public high schools.

During the Cold War, education reform was used to increase the production of civilian laborers skilled in fields applicable to the US and Soviet arms race, especially research scientists, engineers, foreign language specialists, and "area" specialists. With the American foreign policy establishment shaken by the Soviet launch of the *Sputnik* satellite—and what this suggested about the American school system's capacity to contribute to the arms race vis-à-vis the Soviet educational system—the National Defense Education Act (NDEA) was signed into law in 1958. The NDEA diverted significant federal funds to the subsidization of educational loans and provided grants to states to be used as start-up money for new science, math, and foreign language programs in secondary schools. Less about creating soldiers than accelerating the militarization of civilian industries, the NDEA nevertheless strengthened the discursive relationship between militarism and public schooling by linking knowledge production with national defense. The ROTC Revitalization Act of 1964, signed by President John F. Kennedy significantly increased federal funding for both senior and junior ROTC programs and authorized the creation of Navy, Air Force, and Marines *Junior* ROTC programs to complement those of the Army. From a total of 294 "units" in 1964, the number of high schools offering JROTC curriculum now stands at 3,200, with over 513,000 cadets enrolled across the US (Schrader 2009).

During Secretary of Education Arne Duncan's tenure as Chief Executive Officer (CEO) of Chicago Public Schools from 2001–2009, the district became the most militarized in the United States in terms of per capita student enrollment in the JROTC. The district also opened four of what are now six high schools using an exclusively JROTC curriculum and program of instruction. Duncan has said of schools offering a militarized education: "I love the sense of leadership. I love the sense of discipline" and that "*for the right child*, these schools are a lifesaver" (Kroll 2009: online, emphasis added). While Duncan did not elaborate on who exactly the "right child" for JROTC programs might be, the Department of Defense has been somewhat more explicit, stating in 2006 that one of its primary goals was to "focus on at-risk youth" by maintaining a minimum number of JROTC units in "educationally and economically deprived areas" (Office of Management and Budget, 2006)—no doubt a euphemism for minorities and minority neighborhoods. Notably, the Obama Administration's most comprehensive articulation of its educational policy objectives to date, *A Blueprint for Reform* (US Department of Education 2010), lacks any indication that it will make a similar effort to extend pedagogical emphases on "creative inquiry," "independent thinking," "collective reflection," or a "genuine love of learning"—like those at Sidwell Friends—to schools in these "deprived" areas.

But while race and class certainly factor into the "tracking" of students among differential types of schooling, we look to frame the militarization of public schooling as part of a broader project of encouraging potentially counter-hegemonic subjects to invest in the nationalist fantasy presented by contemporary American imperialism. Fundamental to our argument is the contention that submission to authority *channels* rather than smothers enjoyment by locating it in violent fantasies of protecting the nation. The militarization of public schooling thereby becomes a kind of psychoanalytic geopolitics, a quilting point of nationalism. More specifically, we argue that the JROTC program is instrumental in the coding of desire around the enjoyment of military service and citizenship. As with most activities at any public school, the JROTC program does not seem especially enjoyable. In fact, its highly regimented system of discipline, order, and routine appears *antithetical* to enjoyment. And yet, this picture is incomplete. What is it about militarism that keeps students coming back for more? What is the emotional lure of gun tossing rituals and flag raising ceremonies? In the case of the JROTC, desire is coded around the creeds of military service. The national "Thing" exists as a product of the ritualistic support of the Nation (Kingsbury 2011)—and the enjoyment that is derived from such psychic and emotional investments.

Enjoy the War Machine!

Enjoyment is a funny old thing, and is one of the most important concepts in Lacanian psychoanalysis (Kingsbury 2008). For Lacan it has ambiguous and at times contradictory meanings. Lacan introduces the concept of enjoyment, or *jouissance*, in his seminar of 1953–54, where the term refers to orgasmic physical pleasure. In his later work it takes on a much darker meaning: as an unyielding, sadomasochistic drive that seeks an impossible fulfillment—a will to enjoy *regardless* of pleasure. While we tend to gravitate towards a definition of enjoyment as the existential pleasure accrued through imaginary investments, the *Žižekian* (2002) twist we give is to insist on the always-already politicization of enjoyment.

In the above section we explored the slow encroachment of militarism in the American school system. But its survival depends on more than what is written in the symbolic universe. Žižek is at pains to emphasize the *performative* nature of ideology. No idea can reign supreme without been actively lived in the subject's life: "... belief, far from being an 'intimate,' purely mental state, is always *materialized* in our effective social activity: belief supports the fantasy which regulates social reality" (Žižek 1989a: 36). Nationalistic ideology is no different: its survival depends on being lived and breathed in the most banal pockets of social life. The JROTC program is one such space where the future of American nationalism is negotiated. The formal justifications for the existence of the JROTC are usually tied to wider foreign policy and defense imperatives. But key to its widespread success is the intimate, personal, and emotional achievements that it advertises. The cadets are not simply "duped" into a regimented apparatus.

The JROTC program pivots on the idea of "building character" in its students by instilling a sense of citizenship, patriotism, leadership, and strength. Consider the following tenets from the Chicago Military Academy's (2012) Cadet Creed:

> I am an Army JROTC cadet. I will always conduct myself to bring credit to my family, country, school, and the corps of cadets. I am loyal and patriotic. I am the future of the United States of America. I do not lie, cheat, or steal and will always be accountable for my actions and deeds. I will always practice good citizenship and patriotism. I will work hard to improve my mind and strengthen my body. I will seek the mantle of leadership and stand prepared to uphold the Constitution and the American way of life.

Given the indeterminacy of the psychoanalytic subject, there is a sense of accomplishment in the very act of investing in such creeds. And this investment contains an enjoyable, non-symbolic dimension. In the words of two of the Directors of the Chicago JROTC: "It is also our intent to socially and personally develop our students through numerous competitive and non-competitive events such as summer camp, leadership camp, sports challenge, orienteering, local and national drill competitions, field trips, and more. This is an *exciting* program that offers students the opportunity to develop their academic and social skills while making a difference in their school, community, and Chicago" (Chicago Public Schools 2012: online, emphasis added). The JROTC program is thus more than its discursive allure, and more than its seemingly disciplinary set of technologies: it is *exciting*. The ideological power of the JROTC program is already on the side of unconscious reality itself, already on the side of jouissance.

JROTC programs are houses of enjoyment, productive of jouissance. But they are also vital in stabilizing the wider social field and channeling subversive desires to state-sanctioned ends. Technologies must exist to sanction and control the Real of jouissance, which "is a tremulous part of our emotional lives that constantly threatens to upset or even traumatically dissolve our sense of everyday 'reality'" (Kingsbury 2008: 50). To understand this necessity is to register the "dark side" of jouissance beyond the pleasure principle. Nationalism is founded on the relationships between the "big Other" (or *Big Brother*) which is a "symbolic" and "dead" realm, and jouissance, which is a non-symbolic life substance (Kingsbury 2008: 49). For the subject to exist they must renounce this lawless life substance and enter the symbolic. This split, which is homologous to the subject donating their existence and will to a Hobbesian Leviathan, leaves a space of castration which is then reinscribed in desire. To be symbolically castrated and "socialized" is thus predicated on a renunciation of the pre-Symbolic (and Real) of jouissance—which then returns in unexpected outbursts and events. This means that the de facto existence of nation is generative of its own obscene excesses: jouissance is both a condition and consequence of nation, and one that must be captured through a set of social practices that structure these internal inconsistencies.

There is therefore a kind of collective "war machine" that is generative of jouissance and constantly the target of apparatuses of state capture. The war machine is a transgressive and violent force that has destruction (and therefore creation) as its object, rather that war per se. Deleuze and Guattari (2004) recognized the libidinal power of the war machine to both challenge sovereign law and enforce it; the war machine is the space of the nomad, of smooth space, and of deterritorialization. So while the war machine is co-extensive with military institutions, it remains a dangerous "outside" of alterity and desire that the state fails to completely capture. Jouissance—what can be thought of as the very currency of the war machine—is a transgressive force that is not only anterior to the symbolic law; it is fundamentally sustained because of it. Jouissance is *beyond* war and peace, it is an extra-discursive and embodied force "that can disrupt people's pursuit of their individual and collective interest" (Kingsbury 2008: 51). When we start reducing enjoyment to *what* is enjoyed (i.e. splice it within the Symbolic) we misrecognize the simple, but no less significant *act* of enjoyment itself, which possesses a fundamental and dangerous autonomy.

Every political regime has written laws that demand the subject to forego jouissance in the name of a greater good such as nation. Yet such explicit laws—far from repressing this enjoyment—(re)institutionalize it in a sanctioned space of transgression. Such spaces, we find, are becoming more and more common in the paradoxical place that is the US school, which continues to find itself the target of regimes of military capture. Military academies exist for many complicated and diverse reasons, but a psychoanalytic explanation explores how these schools codify the dangerous excesses of jouissance. The JROTC offers a space where a form of "inherent transgression" is sanctioned. What is usually exceptional or prohibited in everyday life—from the institutionalization of violence to gun-tossing rituals—is experienced as jouissance. Jouissance can never fully be institutionalized of course, but its excesses and obscenities can be redirected and reinscribed. Indeed, the surplus of enjoyment is integral to enjoyment itself. If there is something completely irrational about the militarization of public education in the United States, then consider the obscene rationality of jouissance—of excess beyond reason: the ethical imperative to *enjoy*!

Conclusion: Towards a Psychoanalytic Geopolitics

For Deleuze and Guattari, "One of the biggest questions from the point of view of universal history is: How will the state *appropriate* the war machine, that is, constitute one for itself, in conformity with its size, its domination, and its aims? And with what risks?" (Deleuze and Guattari 2004: 641). In this chapter we have argued that configuring enjoyment at military schools is central to the project of maintaining US nationalism, and central to appropriating the war machine. There are lots of other forces at work too of course, including a sprawling military–industrial complex that invests billions of dollars in ensuring perpetual war, and a political oligarchy that is driven by the creeds of American exceptionalism. And yet, rational explanation only gets us so far. Rational explanation starts to stutter and stumble when dealing with the seductive and sensual qualities of war. We therefore ask, what are the unwritten rules and practices of geopolitical power? What is the Real of the "war on terror" beyond the self-evident expressions of destruction and occupation? In order to move past a cynical impasse that sees enjoyment as extraneous to empire, we must see its internal necessity "as a political practice locked within a violent imperial topos, rather than existing 'in-itself'" (Shaw 2010: 799). The registers of domination and power are not characterized solely by pain, anxiety, and death; they are legitimized and produced by topologies of desire, enjoyment and play.

In his seminal work, *Civilization and Its Discontents*, Sigmund Freud argued that there was a painful friction between society's prohibitions and the individual's pursuit of instincts. This inherent compromise instills a perpetual malaise at the very heart of civilization—a pathology that is bound to return. In his words, "our so-called civilization itself is to blame for a great part of our misery, and we should be much happier if we were to give it up and go back to primitive conditions" (Freud [1930]: online). The paradox that we are dealing with here is that the very repression of violence, of the war machine, of *Thanatos*, only leads to its reinscription as a symptom. And the militarized school is built on legitimizing the enjoyment of this symptom.

The JROTC's program of disciplined education and martial practices give jouissance an expressive, phallic form: it is neither the antipode of war or peace, pain or pleasure, but rather, it is the Real symptom of both—the ineluctable obverse of a pathological society. Our argument has been that the JROTC is a program instrumental for coding desire around the enjoyment of military service and citizenship. Students are invited to invest and identify within a nationalist fantasy. The war machine is not so much restrained as it is released by the US state apparatus, as libidinal energy is realized as pride, and enjoyment as gun tossing. In other words, the feeling of loss (not just of the loss synonymous with late capitalism in a crumbling American economy, but of the "void" that haunts the subject) is institutionalized in a military that can offer a form of completeness. This desire is realized around the fantasy of the ideal subject that blurs the line between citizen and soldier, classroom and battlespace.

Critical geopolitics can be far too serious, and in all its seriousness, is nowhere near serious enough. The role of emotion, humor, enjoyment, and desire are central forces in legitimizing violent geopolitical processes that cannot be captured by discourse (Proudfoot 2010). Our approach is therefore allied to work in feminist geopolitics and political geographies (see also Dittmer 2010: 34–6). This literature emphasizes why the personal, emotional, and embodied manifestations of global power is vital for understanding and challenging the abstract discourses of state elites and military officials, whose carefully crafted representations often work to erase the experiential (Hyndman 2007; Sharp 2007). As Fluri (2009: 264) writes, "Critical scholarship on political violence should include examinations of gender and the geopolitics of violence from below. It is within these informal places and sites below macro-scale political frameworks that require additional and further study in order to increase a nuanced understanding of the spatial, social and far reaching impacts of and resistance to local, state, and inter-state conflict." Similarly, Pain (2009) argues that discussions of "fear" in critical geopolitics are usually hierarchical and overlook the epistemological challenges posed by feminist scholars. She suggests that geopolitics takes into account *emotion* as a vital site of meaning-making, experience, and agency. In this chapter we have taken up the emotional challenge laid down by Pain and others—only instead of focusing on a geopolitics of fear—we explore fear's playful obverse.

A psychoanalytic geopolitics thus confronts us with a series of uncomfortable meditations, chief of which is the role of enjoyment in imperial topologies of violence. More generally, a psychoanalytic geopolitics places the banal practices of nationalism, such as military schooling, as vital existential anchors for ensuring the consistency and durability of nation. We cannot fully understand American imperialism "out there" in Afghanistan, Iraq, and beyond, without acknowledging the underlying ideological productions of enjoyment "at home." In the case of the JROTC, we find a set of psychoanalytic technologies instrumental for sustaining such enjoyment. It is not simply violence that acts as a supplement to the law of American imperialism, it is the overriding injunction to "enjoy." It is in the military school that enjoyment takes on a radical new meaning: *Enjoy the nation! Enjoy citizenship! Enjoy teamwork! Enjoy your symptom!* The paradox that we've wrestled with, therefore, is that militarized discipline is not simply suppressive of enjoyment but is functionally expressive.

There are lots of reasons why over half a million cadets are enrolled in the JROTC. In his 1995 autobiography, former Secretary of State Colin Powell wrote that "Inner-city kids, many from broken homes, found stability and role models in Junior ROTC. They got a taste of discipline, the work ethic, and they experienced pride of membership in something healthier than a gang" (quoted in Stodghill 2002). What unites these many human stories is not simply their socio-economic class or their appetite for "something healthier than a gang." It is jouissance: a political factor beyond pleasure and pain, war and peace, civilization and its many discontents. To recall the Chicago Military Academy's Cadet Creed once again, "I am the future of the United States of America."

References

Apple, M. 2004. *Ideology and Curriculum*. New York: Routledge Publishers.

Au, W. 2009. High-Stakes Testing and Discursive Control: The Triple Bind for Non-Standard Student Identities. *Multicultural Perspectives*, 11(2), 65–71.

Au, W. 2011. Teaching Under the New Taylorism: High-Stakes Testing and the Standardization of the 21st Century Curriculum. *Journal of Curriculum Studies*, 43(1), 25–45.

Berliner, D. and Biddle, B. 1995. *The Manufactured Crisis: Myths, Fraud and the Attack on America's Public Schools*. New York: Perseus Books Group.

Bowles, S. and Gintis, H. 1976. *Schooling in Capitalist America: Educational Reform and the Contradictions of Economic Life*. New York: Basic Books.

Chicago Military Academy at Bronzeville. 2012. *Cadet Code of Honor.* [Online]. Available at: http://www.chicagomilitaryacademy.org/creed.jsp [accessed: 21 September 2012].

Chicago Public Schools, 2012. *Cadet Leadership Challenge.* [Online]. Available at: http://www.cps.edu/Spotlight/Pages/spotlight339.aspx [accessed: 21 September 2012].

Chomsky, N. 2003. The Function of Schools: Subtler and Cruder Methods of Control, in *Education as Enforcement: The Militarization and Corporatization of Schools*, edited by K. Saltman and D. Gabbard. New York: Routledge, 24–35.

Deleuze, G. and Guattari, F. 2004. *A Thousand Plateaus*. London: Continuum.

Dittmer, J. 2010. *Popular Culture, Geopolitics, and Identity*. Lanham, MD: Rowman and Littlefield.

ESEA Blueprint for Reform. [Online]. Available at: www2.ed.gov/policy/elsec/leg/blueprint/blueprint.pdf [accessed: 6 July 2012].

Fluri, J.L. 2009. Geopolitics of gender and violence "from below." *Political Geography*, 28, 259–65.

Freire, P. 1972. *Pedagogy of the Oppressed*. Harmondsworth: Penguin.

Freud, S. 1930. *Civilization and Its Discontents*. [Online]. Available at: http://www.free-ebooks.net/ebook/Civilization-and-its-Discontents/html/13 [accessed: 21 September 2012].

Giroux, H. 1981. *Ideology, Culture, and the Process of Schooling*. Philadelphia: Temple University Press.

Gregory, D. 2004. *The Colonial Present: Afghanistan, Palestine, Iraq*. Oxford: Blackwell.

Hyndman, J. 2007. Feminist geopolitics revisited: body counts in Iraq. *The Professional Geographer*, 59(1), 35–46.

Kingsbury, P. 2005. Jamaican tourism and the politics of enjoyment. *Geoforum*, 36(1), 113–32.

Kingsbury, P. 2007. The extimacy of space. *Social & Cultural Geography*, 8(2), 235–58.

Kingsbury, P. 2008. "Did somebody say jouissance?" On Slavoj Žižek, consumption, and nationalism. *Emotion, Space and Society*, 1(1), 48–55.

Kingsbury, P. 2011. The World Cup and the national Thing on Commercial Drive, Vancouver. *Environment & Planning D: Society & Space*, 29(4), 716–37.

Kozol, J. 2005. *Shame of the Nation: The Restoration of Apartheid Schooling in America*. New York: Crown Publishers.

Kroll, A. 2009. *Fast Times at Recruitment High*. [Online]. Available at: http://motherjones.com/politics/2009/08/fast-times-recruitment-high [accessed: 3 July 2012].

Lacan, J. 2006. *Écrits*. New York: Norton.

Lapham, L. 2012. *The Servant Problem*. [Online]. Available at: http://www.laphamsquarterly.org/ [accessed: 5 July 2012].

Leahey, C. 2013. Catch-22 and the Paradox of Teaching in the Age of Accountability. *Critical Education*, 4(6), 1–19.

Lipman, P. 2004. *High Stakes Education: Inequality, Globalization, and Urban School Reform*. New York: Routledge.

Mertz, D. 1995. The racial other in nationalist subjectivations: a Lacanian analysis. *Rethinking Marxism*, 8(2), 77–88.

Morrill Act of 1862, 7 U.S.C. § 301.

Müller, M. 2008. Reconsidering the concept of discourse for the field of critical geopolitics: towards discourse as language and practice. *Political Geography*, 27, 322–38.

National Defense Act of 1916, Pub. L. 64–85, 39 Stat. 166 (1916).

National Defense Education Act of 1958, Pub. L. 85–864, 72 Stat. 1580 (1958).

Office of Management and Budget. 2006. *Detailed Information on the Junior Reserve Officer Training Corps Assessment*. [Online]. Available at: http://georgewbush-whitehouse.archives.gov/omb/expectmore/detail/10003233.html [accessed: 5 July 2012].

Pain, R. 2009. Globalized fear? Towards an emotional geopolitics. *Progress in Human Geography*, 33(4), 466–86.

Proudfoot, J. 2010. Interviewing enjoyment, or the limits of discourse. *Professional Geographer*, 62(4), 507–18.

Schrader, J. 2009. *Junior ROTC "more than a class" to Teens*. [Online]. Available at: http://www.usatoday.com/news/education/2009-12-31-jrotc_N.htm [accessed: 21 September 2012].

Sharp, J. 2007. Geography and gender: finding feminist political geographies. *Progress in Human Geography*, 31, 381–7.

Shaw, I.G.R. 2010. Playing war. *Social and Cultural Geography*, 11(8), 789–803.

Sidwell Friends School. 2012. *School Philosophy*. [Online]. Available at: http://www.sidwell.edu/about_sfs/school-philosophy/index.aspx [accessed: 21 September 2012].

Stodghill, R. 2002. *Class Warfare*. [Online]. Available at: http://www.time.com/time/education/article/0,8599,212638,00.html [accessed: 21 September 2012].

US Department of Education. Office of Planning, Evaluation and Policy Development. 2010.

Žižek, S. 1989a. *The Sublime Object of Ideology*. London: Verso.

Žižek, S. 1989b. The undergrowth of enjoyment: how popular culture can serve as an introduction to Lacan. *New Formations*, 9, 7–29.

Žižek, S. 1994. *The Metastases of Enjoyment*. London: Verso.

Žižek, S. 2002. *For They Know What They Do: Enjoyment as a Political Factor*. New York: Verso.

Chapter 13

"Welcome Home our Military Sisters": Sexual Difference and Female Veterans with PTSD

Deborah Thien

Introduction

In 2005, the United States Department of Veteran Affairs (VA) produced a video encouraging military health providers working at the National Center for Post-Traumatic Stress Disorder to "Welcome home our military sisters, reach out and give them the best care possible" (National Center for Post-Traumatic Stress Disorder 2005). I contend the "military sister" is a complex figure and her care more vexed than this straightforward call to healthcare providers can elucidate. The necessity of such an appeal gestures towards the ways in which care for women veterans with PTSD is compromised by their very state of "being female" (Simmons 2007: 86). I suggest that rather than being welcomed home, she is unhomed in the masculinist spaces of Post-Traumatic Stress Disorder (PTSD), itself embedded in the psycho-social-spatial norms of western culture. As an alternative framing, I place the military sister in the context of the feminist psychoanalytic theories of Luce Irigaray; I assess what is gained when the military sister is read within an (im)possible landscape of sexual difference, that is, a "culture [no longer] elaborated above all by one sex" (Irigaray and Grosz 2008: 134), and I explore what is lost, and for whom.

The first section develops an analysis of Irigaray's ideas. In particular, I consider her oft-critiqued notion of sexual difference, explain her insistence on impossibility, and evaluate her work's usefulness for a spatialized reading of gendered identity. The second section offers a discussion of the gendered, psychic terrain of Post-Traumatic Stress Disorder, including diagnostics and treatment. In the third section, I return to the military sister, herself. Employing Irigaray's framework of sexual difference, I examine the ways in which PTSD recruits a masculinized subjectivity that cannot recognize the military sister. I consider the ways in which this shapes her (lack of) mental health care. I suggest how the military sister not only the re-figures the masculinized conventions of soldering through her marked absence in the broader militaristic landscape, but also redraws the boundaries of Irigaray's (il)logic. Finally, I conclude with the suggestion that the military sister presents an unexpected challenge to the promise of sexual difference, resisting any easy categorization and refusing the deferral to an impossible new order.

Re-imagining Psychoanalytic Spatialities: Irigaray's Spaces of Alterity

Feminist, philosopher, psychoanalyst, Luce Irigaray has been described as offering one of the two most important approaches to feminism, embodiment, and sexual difference, alongside Judith Butler (Stone 2006). Irigaray was once, famously, Jacque Lacan's student but was expelled from his Freudian School in Paris in the 1970s. Her separation from him was made manifest in the *Speculum of the Other Woman* (Irigaray 1985), a work critical of both philosophy and psychoanalytic theory for their exclusions of women. Throughout her extensive body of scholarship, Irigaray's central project is to declare the impossibility of a subject position for women within such theoretical frameworks, to argue for the resulting lack of sexual difference in westernized culture, and to imagine a new conceptual and material reality. For Irigaray, this imagined world is founded in true alterity; that is, the existence of two truly different subject positions, instead of the singular (masculine) subject of western (broadly) thought.

Irigaray has faced much criticism, in particular, feminist criticism, for her emphasis on sexual difference as a "foundation of alterity" (Irigaray and Grosz 2008: 132). This is commonly due to interpretations of her work as essentialist (though she has also been critiqued for being elitist, naïve, and heterosexist). Indeed, political scientist and feminist theorist, Anne Caldwell remarks: "... Irigaray's insistence that sexual difference is the fundamental difference has become not the scandal to philosophy that she herself saw it, but a scandal to feminism" (Caldwell 2002). The "scandal" arises because

> [s]exual difference [is] taken to mean differences between men and women. But this is not what Irigaray means. She means an ideal, alternative, transformed sexual difference, not culturally impoverished relations between men and women

or existing differences in their status, equality or psychology. The latter indicate the absence of sexual difference in our culture (Deutscher 2002: 112).

In Irigaray's terms, then, sexual difference is about the recognition of otherness, or what she refers to, in conversations with feminist thinker, Elizabeth Grosz, as "the insistent question of the other" (Irigaray and Grosz 2008: 132); a question, she suggests, that has been critical since the nineteenth century in Western culture, but has been incompletely parsed "as a question relative to otherness within a single and unique world: the question of the other as child or mad, for example" (Irigaray and Grosz 2008: 132).

While she is dealing in an ideal realm, Irigaray has nonetheless sought to give matter to the possibility of a culture of difference (Irigaray 1996). For example, she has taken the mother–child dyad as a starting point for her revision of subjectivity as intersubjectivity (see Thien 2004; see also Whitford 1991 who notes the influences of feminist object-relations theory on this work). In *Je Tu Nous: A Culture of Difference* she analyses the mediating role of the placenta in the relationship between a maternal body and uterus. In conversation with a biologist, she explores the ways in which a mother's body necessarily and continuously recognizes an other in order to sustain both her own body and the foetus. From this, Irigaray reinterprets subjectivity as "autonomy-in-relation-to"; in so doing, she departs from both Freud and Lacan, each of whom render differentiation from the maternal figure (respectively, at birth and in early childhood) as a process of separation. For Irigaray, the intrauterine relationship is relationally constituted and negotiated; intersubjectivity, alterity, begins between mother and embryonic self, as two which can never be one. This is not to say that subjects do not always encompass others, but that being sexuate "would aid reconciliation with being not-whole", that is, "the self would not cannibalize either a negative or an ideal to the ends of self-reinforcement" (Deutscher 2002: 85). Indeed, a major contention Irigaray makes in her discussion of sexual difference is that in the absence of sexual difference, "woman is used by the male imaginary to deflect or mediate the death drives of *men* [...], but there are no social/symbolic forms which mediate *their* [women's] death" (Whitford 1991: 159). As such, they are denoted "sacrificial objects" instead of subjects capable of experiencing their own pain or trauma (159).

Irigaray's reworking of the symbolic order attempts to answer the question of the other in a conceptual move based on bodies as differently sexuate; her premise is that on these ideal terms, gender is always two, irreducible to one, and further that this reflects true difference (not simply one and its other).

Because of this necessary alterity, then subjectivity is also possible in multiple forms. Such intersubjectivity expressly accounts for "the dimension of gender as a means capable of protecting alterity" (Irigaray 2000). By emphasizing gender as theoretically internally incommensurate, foundationally different, an/other logic is produced. In this new symbolic order, sexual difference can be creative instead of impoverishing. This logic does not suggest that men and women are respectively variations on a theme. Irigarayan scholar, Deutscher, explains: "Sexuate genre would [also] be the conceptual structure allowing a woman to value another woman's possible difference" (Deutscher 2002: 88). That is, difference begets difference. However, in Irigaray's rendering, existing masculinist frameworks for subjectivity do not allow a true female subject position; sexual difference is impossible: "certain subjects come [...] to be represented as those who have not, or are not" (Deutscher 2002: 75). In re-imagining alterity, Irigaray undertakes the important project of acknowledging this conceptual lack and thus paradoxically the "trace" of (her) possibility for otherwise excluded identities. However, a paradox is an uncomfortable home, and a trace a ghostly place. For the military sister with PTSD, her challenge lies in resisting such a placement and instead embodying complexity through her very diagnosis and subsequent care (or lack thereof).

Gendered, Psychic Landscapes of PTSD

> [T]he effects of trauma within the military have shown that the impact is even greater than those people traumatized in the general community. And that may be because the military is seen in such a symbolic way. Many of the people are attracted to the paternalistic structure, and the promises for something better. The trauma then becomes a betrayal of that (National Center for Posttraumatic Stress Disorder 2005).

Post-Traumatic Stress Disorder (PTSD) is a psychiatric condition so well-known as to be ubiquitous. PTSD is featured in all kinds of popular culture representations, from the small screen (such as *Grey's Anatomy*) to the large (films like *Brothers* and *Jarhead*). A 2013 search of the *New York Times* website reveals 525 references to PTSD in the last 12 months. PTSD has been described as a "signature wound"—that is, a casualty that defines a war in terms of its human (potential) damage, instead of a more traditional emphasis on key events such as battles or campaigns (Terry 2009). This terminology has been particularly prominent in reference to US soldiers in Iraq and Afghanistan. 2007 Statistics from the US Department of Defense Task Force on Mental Health indicate that 30 percent of armed forces returning from Iraq and Afghanistan were diagnosed with PTSD—military psychiatrists report, it is not a matter of if, but when a combat veteran will have a reaction (Likierman 2008, cited in Bragin 2010: 317). This relentless exposure of/to PTSD has had the effect of rendering trauma itself a seemingly everyday occurrence and PTSD its straightforward consequence. However, this pervasiveness conceals a more involved spatialization that bears further examination. Combat-related PSTD, it has been claimed, "is an invention, not a discovery" (Howell 2010: 114), and one with a clear and insidious purpose: to place the problem of war "in the psyches of soldiers, instead of in the act of making war" (Howell 2010). Much energy has been devoted (one could also say, diverted) to trying to heal such wounded warriors. But what takes place when the psyches in question belong not to these readily visualized soldiers, but to the military sister? As with other forms of war-related injury (see Terry (2009) on what constitutes "significant injury" and Hyams et al.'s (2009: 121) table of diagnoses matched to major wars) the particularized terrain of PTSD is an ongoing complex accretion of militarist, medicalized, psychic, socio-political, and perhaps most especially, gendered contexts.

War-related trauma has had many names, from the lyrical "soldier's heart" to "shell shock," and on to increasingly clinical terms such as "war neurosis," "battle fatigue," "combat stress reaction." PTSD appeared in the Diagnostic Manual (DSM) of the American Psychological Association in 1980—these first diagnostic criteria arose from the treatment of and advocacy for American veterans of the Vietnam War. The originating codification of PTSD is significant because it "positioned veterans as victims of war, rather than as perpetrators or offenders" (Howell 2010: 121). The legitimating of the suite of symptoms associated with PTSD thus gave shape to a dominantly (un)masculine figure: the psychically wounded Vietnam veteran in need of both social and economic care. Not incidentally, this mirrored the psychically wounded America and the country's similar need for both psychic and fiscal repair following Vietnam and the attendant betrayals of patriarchal promises for protection and victory. Also, also importantly, this psychosocial account reveals the ways in which the diagnosis of PTSD is embedded within not just a western account, but also a particularly American socio-spatial and emotional logic.

While the militaristic context was (and is) paramount, the new PTSD diagnostics nonetheless also became a means of validation for an/other psychically wounded, if more shadowy figure. As Freedman argues, "feminist and trauma theorists were quick to notice that survivors of rape, domestic battery, and child abuse shared essentially the same symptoms as those seen in war veterans" (Freedman 2006: 106; see Herman 1992). These trajectories produced two distinctly gendered versions of the subject of PTSD: the masculine veteran, paradoxically unmanned as a consequence of his public and psychic recruitment in national discourses of war, and his other, the feminized victim of private violence, also paradoxical in Irigaray's terms, for her inability to be traumatized in her own right.

The diagnostic criteria for PTSD discussed in this chapter are based on the DSM-IV TR (this text revision of the DSM-IV was published in 2000; the DSM-V, the result of 14 years of revision, was released in May 2013), unless otherwise noted. The criteria include exposure to a traumatic event wherein the person has experienced, witnessed, or been confronted with events involving actual or threatened death or serious injury, or a threat to the physical integrity of oneself or others; circumstances, in other words, which involve intense fear, helplessness, or horror. In addition, the traumatic experience is repeatedly re-experienced despite efforts to avoid anything associated with the event, there is a tendency towards hyper arousal, and efforts are made to limit one's range of feelings—loving feelings are noted in particular (American Psychiatric Association 2000). The developed language of and treatments for PTSD reflect the dominant masculine terms of engagement, for example, "anxiety" is rewritten as "hypervigilance" (Karner 1995, see also Smith 2006: 188), a descriptor more suitable for soldiers in that it is a less feminized term. In addition, for the past 33 years, sexual assault has not been specifically included in the diagnostic criteria for what constitutes a traumatic event. This reflects the presumption that men, the primary subject of PTSD diagnostics, will not be victims of sexual assault. At time of writing (May 2013), a revised entry for PTSD in the just released DSM-V now includes sexual assault (American Psychiatric Association 2013). How that will affect the gender imbalances in diagnoses of PTSD is as yet unknown, but as women's PTSD numbers are already high, and as women are more likely to report military sexual assault, it seems probably that yet more military women will be diagnosed with PTSD.

Treatments for PTSD are based on and respond to specific and gendered notions of PTSD sufferers. Marissa M. Smith has examined group therapy for men with combat-related PTSD in an American VA setting (Smith 2006). Her analysis, based on 2.5 years of ethnographic fieldwork, suggests that masculinity becomes the "discursive framework" for the group therapy process:

"PTSD group therapy implicitly or explicitly posits the responses to stressors (e.g. combat trauma) as at least partially conditioned by societal expectations for creating the masculine self. Significantly, in therapy, masculinity is both a source of 'troubles' and a resource to overcome them" (Smith 2006: 202). As I have argued elsewhere, also analyzing a PTSD group therapy program for male veterans, efforts to resolve tensions between disordered (feminized) feelings and the hegemonic masculinity of military subjectivity have produced a profoundly psychically challenging therapeutic experience for many male veterans with PTSD (Thien and Del Casino 2012).

Studies of treatment programs for women with combat-related PTSD are few even though women statistically are twice as likely to be diagnosed with this psychiatric condition (Budden 2009). In part, this lack of attention to combat-related PTSD treatment programs for women can be explained by the American history of combat exclusion policies for women (the US Defense Secretary only recently lifted the ban on women in combat in January 2013). At least in principle, officially excluding women from combat should have limited women's exposure to the traumatic events proscribed by a PTSD diagnosis. Fiore explains: "Women [were] not permitted to serve in direct ground combat in the U.S. armed forces, so by military reasoning, they weren't likely to suffer from combat-related trauma. Except they do" (2011). The limitations are not only policy-driven, then, but also reflect interwoven psychosocial norms about masculinity, femininity, militarism and emotion. Thus the lifting of the ban on women in combat is not going to solve the conundrum of military sisters who are "missing in action" when it comes to PTSD care. These issues further complicate the care prospects for women veterans with PTSD. The military sister with PTSD not only offers a possible challenge to Irigaray's figuring of sexual difference, but also, in her very embodiment as a veteran with PTSD, she illuminates the narrow field of vision that is the psycho-social-military complex of PTSD diagnostics and care.

Sexual Difference: Another Welcome, Another Home?

In consideration of the emancipatory potential of Irigaray's radical ideas about sexual difference, and in light of the lack of place for military women with PTSD, I now want to imagine what is gained (or lost) when the military sister is read within the (im)possible landscape of sexual difference. To begin, it is clear that the military sister is not recognized in either of the two dominant faces of PTSD, that is, she is neither the masculinized "wounded warrior," nor his other, the feminized victim of privatized violence. In a culture that is lacking sexual difference, as per Irigaray's theorization, the warrior stands as the central or dominant figure, while the victim is the subject on the fringes whose identity is only elaborated through her relation to masculine subjectivity. In Irigarayan terms, anything (anyone) beyond that lies in (im)possible terrain, that is, in another cultural order wherein men and women hold unique subject positions.

The military sister, then, seems to occupy a paradoxical position. The female veteran with PTSD is a wounded warrior whose trauma is often diagnosed in relation to sexual violence (or military sexual violence). She is not present in the masculinist-oriented therapeutic spaces of veterans with PTSD, nor does she neatly fit into the shadowy worlds of that other PTSD sufferer, the feminized casualty of so-called domestic violence. What then of Irigaray's new cultural order? Does the military sister find a home here, occupying that ghostly place? Does she function as a trace of (im)possibility?

Military sisters may be ill considered in PTSD treatment, but they face the prospect of PTSD in startlingly high numbers (see Suris et al. 2007). The VA's literature on PTSD treatment puts this bluntly: "female gender is a risk factor for PTSD" (Goldzweig et al. 2006). In ever-greater numbers, the military sister with PTSD persists, if in diverse ways in relation to her brother soldiers (Conard and Sauls 2013). I suggest she is not a contradiction in terms (a paradox), rather, she is on her own terms. She is, in effect, another other.

What can it mean to be "another other"? As suggested above, while the military sister is clearly not at home in the masculinist spaces of PTSD diagnoses and treatments, she is also not simply the negative image to her brother soldier. Military sisters present very different demographics from male veterans: they tend to be younger, have more education, and are more likely to be racial minorities (National Survey of Veterans 2001). Roberts and colleagues (2011) conclude that the effects of PTSD on race/ethnic minorities in the USA (whether male or female) go largely untreated. While women veterans make up a growing proportion of the new users of VA health services, and while the VA is aware of this population, and has some programs in place to address health concerns of female veterans, their plans of care are complicated by the conceptual lack of place of these women as soldiers, or to put it another way, by the confined quarters of "being a soldier." These ideological gaps are made manifest not only in the slim care offerings directed towards this growing and internally diverse population, but also in the lack of uptake of this care.

Stories women tell about coming home from service are resonant with this lack of recognizable place:

> I felt very isolated when I came back, like I didn't fit in the family any more in some ways. They could do without me. [cries] So, it was hard when I came back (Leeann, National Guard, in National Center for Post-Traumatic Stress Disorder 2005).

> Trying to be a good mother is very hard. There's days when I don't even want to get out of the bed. But I know I have to for [my children]. They know there's something wrong with me. And they seem to understand, but there's times when they don't. And I don't know how to explain it to them (Patricia, Army Private, in National Center for Post-Traumatic Stress Disorder 2005).

As veterans, Leann and Patricia suggest, coming home is a difficult transition and socio-cultural process of translation for women with PTSD. Leann describes being unhomed, her place in the family lost; for Patricia, her ability to mother is compromised and her relations with her children altered. These familial issues are particularly salient for women who remain symbolically and material over-identified with home spaces. Alongside these uncomfortable new realities, their options for healthcare are limited or non-existent. Veteran Ruth More (Navy 2013) refers to her "double betrayal": first, by the supervisor who assaulted her, and second by the VA who failed to believe her or compensate her for her resulting health condition.

But this lack of recognizable place is not equivalent to no place at all. It is in the diverse and embodied details of military women's experiences of trauma and its aftermath where the military sister resides. Existing scholarship on gender and mental health is valuable here, in order to elaborate on why and how women and men differently experience psychiatric conditions (for example, Simmons 2007). In reference to PTSD, many possible reasons for a seemingly enhanced vulnerability in women have been posed, including the kinds of trauma men and women experience (for women, sexual trauma features; for men it may also feature but is more frequently disavowed). The VA's Fact Sheet on Women, Trauma and PTSD reports:

> The gender difference in susceptibility to PTSD may be at least partially related to the fact that women are more likely to experience sexual assault. Of potentially traumatic events, exposure to rape carries one of the highest risks

for PTSD. However, there is also some evidence that women are more likely to develop PTSD than men even when exposed to similar types of trauma (Vogt).

This evidence of gender-related reasons for why women seem to "contract" PTSD more readily includes: the pathologizing of women's experiences of interpersonal trauma, gendered measures of PTSD, and gender-biased reporting methods.

In addition, "women are more likely to blame themselves for trauma exposure than men. Interpersonal violence [...] may produce greater distress for women because women's sense of well-being and self-definition is more likely to be integrated with their capacity to develop and maintain relationships" (Vogt). Finally, research indicates that the availability of social supports is differentiated by gender, that is, that women report experiencing higher levels of stress due to their obligations to family and other kinds of care. Returning home is therefore fraught.

> Women need to come right to treatment before home to help them adjust. There needs to be a welcoming committee made of women just for women (Deb, Air Force, 2008).

As Deb notes, women need care and assistance before returning home to their noted and stressful obligations in order to successfully reenter their social worlds.

Some feminist scholars have argued that the key to the unlocking the gendered terrain of PTSD is in the working through of trauma, that is, in the individual processing of trauma at the everyday scale. This offers a helpful way to ground the military sister, in opposition to deferring her to her futuristic potential. Simmons elaborates on how PTSD is a daily process:

> Some feminists have theorized that the traumatic event itself is not the source of pathology in PTSD, instead, a series of sociocultural factors inhibit the adequate "working through" the trauma both at its time of occurrence, and the days, months, and years that follow (Simmons 2007).

As these factors include gender socialization and social roles, women are at a socio-cultural-spatial disadvantage in terms of the necessary material and symbolic space to "work through" their trauma. The resulting complexity of all these factors makes it difficult presently to truly welcome or care for the military sister, for all that the VA is exhorting its health providers to do so. But in the attention to the everyday scale of the military sister, her encounters with and experiences of PTSD, her presence is more firmly established.

Conclusions

The more the military sister is defined in the militarist, medicalized and gendered diagnostic terms of PTSD, this more this wounded warrior subject position empties out. That is, in Irigaray's terms, the militarized figure/figuring of PTSD has been and can only be profoundly masculine, in the symbolic terms of a culture built around a singular subjectivity. In this gendered psychodynamic terrain, "female gender" is a risk not for the long list of psycho-social factors at play, but due to its impossibility, due to its exceeding the possibilities of subjectivity. In this sense, the military sister is a psychosocial figure of loss, marking a profound cultural absence; perhaps, even more than PTSD itself, this lost figure could be the signature wound of our time and place.

Arguably, then, the military sister is the "trace," that is, she is an embodiment of Irigaray's "insistent question of the other." But what is lost for the military sister herself in such a placement? Casting her as the "trace" is to leave her nowhere, is to leave her "stranded in paradox" (Weir 1996: 111). Instead, the military sister claims more than a shadow otherness to her wounded warrior brother, and she is also more than an impossible trace—she is another other, one whose experiences (traumatic and otherwise) figure another kind of space for women and demand a recognition of her difference, not in the impossible world of true sexual difference according to Irigaray, but in the impossible world of sexual difference as it takes place in daily and embodied ways.

The military sister is a complex and emancipatory character in her own right—she is obscured by but therefore illuminates not only the masculinized conventions of soldering and the broader militaristic landscape, but also the bounds of Irigaray's (il)logic. She figures the question of the other, and yet, she does not rest easy in the place Irigaray would have her hold. That is, the military sister is not the kind of "other" Irigaray envisions, wherein "feminine identity is women's nonidentity" (Weir 1996: 106), nor is she part of Irigaray's impossible space, that other-world impossibility. The military sister is different from her solider-counterpart, but not as his empty set. Rather, she is distinctly and spatially different; in a space of her own, another other.

Ultimately, Irigaray's aim is to challenge feminine subjection in a repressive economy of singular subjectivity with the possibility of two subjects where neither is subjected to the other (Irigaray and Grosz 2008; Irigaray 1996). In doing so, she is declaring sexual difference as a "foreclosed conceptual possibility that has not yet been recognized as culturally significant" (Deutscher). In the "trace" of sexual difference that exists in its foreclosure, Irigaray finds her (im)possible politic, and it is here that the military sister could, in theory at least, be truly be welcomed home. Instead, the military sister presents an unexpected challenge to the promise of sexual difference, resisting her (dis)placement into otherness or "what could be" and thus refusing the deferral to an impossible new order.

References

American Psychiatric Association 2000. *Diagnostic and Statistical Manual of Mental Disorders: DSM-IV-TR*. Washington, DC: American Psychiatric Association.

American Psychiatric Association 2013. Posttraumatic stress disorder. [Online: American Psychiatric Association DSM-5 Development]. Available at: http://www.dsm5.org/Documents/PTSD%20Fact%20Sheet.pdf [accesssed: 25 March 2013].

Bragin, M. 2010. Can anyone here know who I am? Co-constructing meaningful narratives with combat veterans. *Clinical Social Work Journal*, 38(3), 316–26.

Budden, A. 2009. The role of shame in posttraumatic stress disorder: a proposal for a socio-emotional model for DSM-V. *Social Science & Medicine*, 69(7), 1032–9.

Caldwell, A. 2002. Transforming sacrifice: Irigaray and the politics of sexual difference. *Hypatia*, 17(4), 16–38.

Conard, P.L. and Sauls, D.J. 2013. Deployment and PTSD in the female combat veteran: a systematic review. *Nursing Forum*. DOI: 10.1111/nuf.12049.

Deutscher, P. 2002. *A Politics of Impossible Difference: The Later Work of Luce Irigaray*. Ithaca, NY; London: Cornell University Press.

Fiore, Faye. 2011. Female veteran fights an invisible injury. *Los Angeles Times*, April 9, 2011.

Freedman, K.L. 2006. The epistemological significance of psychic trauma. *Hypatia*, 21(2), 104–25.

Goldzweig, C.L., Balekian, T.M., Rolón, C., Yano, E.M. and Shekelle, P.G. 2006. The state of women veterans' health research. *Journal of General Internal Medicine*, 21(3), S82–S92.

Howell, A. 2010. The art of governing trauma: treating PTSD in the Canadian military as a foreign policy practice, in *Canadian Foreign Policy in Critical Perspective*, edited by J.M. Beier and L. Wylie. Don Mills, Ont.: Oxford University Press, 113–25.

Irigaray, L. 1985. *Speculum of the Other Woman*. Ithaca, NY: Cornell University Press.

Irigaray, L. 1996. *I Love To You: Sketch of a Possible Felicity in History*. New York; London: Routledge.

Irigaray, L. 2000. *To Be Two*. London: Athlone.

Irigaray, L. and Grosz, E. 2008. Sexuate identities as global beings questioning western logic, in *Conversations*, edited by L. Irigaray and S. Pluhácek. London; New York: Continuum.

Karner, T.X. 1995. Medicalizing masculinity: post traumatic stress disorder in Vietnam. *Masculinities*, 3(4), 23–65.

National Center for Posttraumatic Stress Disorder. 2005. *Women Who Served in Our Military: Provider Perspectives*. United States Department of Veterans Affairs.

Pile, S. 2010. Emotions and affect in recent human geography. *Transactions of the Institute of British Geographers*, 35(1), 5–20.

Roberts, A.L., S.E. Gilman, J. Breslau, N. Breslau, and Koenen, K.C. 2011. Race/ethnic differences in exposure to traumatic events, development of post-traumatic stress disorder, and treatment-seeking for post-traumatic stress disorder in the United States. *Psychological Medicine*, 41(1), 71–83.

Simmons, C.A. 2007. Speculation as to why women "get" PTSD more often than men. *Women & Therapy*, 30(1), 85–98.

Smith, M.M. 2006. Medicalizing military masculinity: reconstructing the war veteran in PTSD therapy, in *Medicalized Masculinities*, edited by D. Rosenfeld and C.A. Faircloth. Philadelphia: Temple University Press.

Stone, A. 2006. *Luce Irigaray and the Philosophy of Sexual Difference*. Cambridge; New York: Cambridge University Press.

Terry, J. 2009. Significant injury: war, medicine, and empire in Claudia's case. *Women's Studies Quarterly*, 37(1), 200–225.

Thien, D. 2004. Love's travels and traces: the "impossible" politics of Luce Irigaray, in *Geography and Gender Reconsidered: Feminist Geography after 20 Years*, edited by K. Browne, J.P. Sharp and D. Thien. Women in Geography Study Group: Glasgow, 43–8.

Thien, D. and Del Casino, V.J. 2012. (Un)healthy men, masculinities, and the geographies of health. *Annals of the Association of American Geographers*, 102(5), 1146–56.

Vogt, D. 2007. *Research on Women, Trauma and PTSD*. [Online]. Available at: http://www.ptsd.va.gov/professional/pages/women-trauma-ptsd.asp: US Department of Veterans Affairs [accessed: 1 February 2013].

Weir, A. 1996. *Sacrificial Logics: Feminist Theory and the Critique of Identity*. New York and London: Routledge.

Whitford, M. (ed.) 1991. *The Irigaray Reader*. Oxford: Basil Blackwell.

Chapter 14

Periscope Down!
Charting Masculine Sexuation in Submarine Films

Jesse Proudfoot and Paul Kingsbury

Introduction

The question of the Other's desire is central to submarine films. Whether in the confrontation between two captains in *U-571*, a submarine and a destroyer in *The Enemy Below*, or a captain and a CIA analyst in *The Hunt for Red October*, an uncanny number of submarine films stage the same scenario: a dyad of male protagonists attempting to locate the desire of the Other through the opaque signifiers of sonar pings, radio silence, screw propellers, depth charges, and strategic maneuvers. Aided by their well-disciplined all-male crews, submarine captains sound the depths behind these submerged signifiers, searching for their signifieds: "He changes course, has he detected me?" or "The sonar comes up with nothing, is he hiding on the seabed?" The opacity of signifiers in submarine films mirrors that of language itself, effectively dramatizing Jacques Lacan's emphasis on the alienated condition of living in signification. Thus the heroes of submarine films are above all hermeneuts. How else are we to understand Alec Baldwin in *Red October*, who somehow divines in the signifier of radio silence (literally, the signifier of nothing or the real) his adversary's desire to betray his country?

Submarine films, then, give flesh to fantasy, to the impossible desire we all harbor to understand the indeterminate desire of the Other through the murky waters of language. Submarine films begin with the question of the Other's desire insofar as they dramatize another fundamental symptom: the fraught masculine relationship to jouissance or what Lacan calls masculine sexuation. Specifically, submarine films illustrate the logic of masculine sexuation by depicting spaces held together by the bonds of phallic jouissance and sustained by the belief in a boundless jouissance that is not submitted to the phallic function.

Moreover, these spaces themselves are significant, for it is the claustrophobic intimacy of the submarine and concentration of bodies within it that allows us to see both how masculine sexuation operates and how the Lacanian account of sex cannot be reduced to language. This is the main concern of our essay, which is structured as follows. We begin by explicating Lacan's notion of sexuation and its revision of the Freudian account of sex difference. Here, we focus on how sexuation challenges historicist accounts of sexual difference and how geographers have yet to engage with this challenge. We then turn to submarine films to show how the cinematic space of the submarine sexuates crewmembers as masculine in two ways: via the universal shortcomings of phallic jouissance and an exceptional and boundless non-phallic jouissance. We briefly conclude by suggesting how sexuation can further psychoanalytic geographies.

From Castration to the Enjoying Substance

Lacan is renowned for "de-biologizing" Sigmund Freud's allegedly reductive theorizations about sexuality by emphasizing the role of language in the constitution of human subjectivity. In his later theorization of sexuality, however, Lacan goes beyond this well-known engagement with Saussurian linguistics and structural anthropology. The twentieth public seminar *Encore*, which took place at the Law Faculty on the Place du Panthéon in Paris between 1972 and 1973, is regarded as "the cornerstone of Lacan's work on the themes of sexual difference, knowledge, *jouissance*, and love" (Barnard 2002a: 1). Lacan introduces his "formulas of sexuation" to theorize sexuality as a matter of psychical position, which he distinguishes from both biology and culture. Specifically, sexuation formalizes "masculine" and "feminine" structures through predicate logic that eschews dominant classical, that is, post-Aristotelian logics of totalizability, harmony, and the grammar of language.

Lacan's formulas of sexuation are not only a fundamental concept in Lacanian psychoanalysis, they have also been central to numerous studies in the humanities and the arts and sciences that have explored, for example, capitalism and communism (Özselçuk and Madra 2005), virtual reality (Matviyenko 2009), and feminist media theory (Friedlander 2008). In geography, however, discussions of sexuation—Lacan's canonical statement on sexual difference—are virtually absent. When geographers address Lacan's understandings of sexuality, they typically focus on his pre-1960s writings that privilege visual identification with the (m)Other's desire and symbolic identification with the father.

As a result, geographers have yet to reckon with the extent to which *Encore* significantly revises Lacan's previous statements on sexuality.

From a Lacanian perspective, "sex is produced by the internal limit, the failure of signification" (Copjec 1994: 204) and therefore "only the failure of its inscription is marked in the symbolic. Sexual difference, in other words, is a real and not a symbolic difference" (Copjec 1994: 207). By claiming that sexual difference is rooted in the real, Lacan does not consider sexual difference as a prediscursive entity, but rather as a stumbling block for discursive practices. The formulas of sexuation define two ways in which language falters, corresponding to two different modes of "jouissance," which is Lacan's term for an extreme extra-discursive libidinal enjoyment that is aggressive and painful yet alluring insofar as it is something people feel compelled to pursue (Kingsbury 2008). On the one hand, there is masculine "phallic jouissance," which refers to ways of enjoying like a man (regardless of sex or gender) that abound in neurotic failure and disappointment. On the other hand, there is feminine "Other jouissance," which refers to enjoying like a woman (again, regardless of sex or gender). This Other jouissance, while equally fallible, is nonetheless capable of encountering the ineffable poetics of love or what Lacan called "*lalangue*" (Barnard 2002b: 183–4; Lacan 1998).

Much of Lacan's writing on sexuality revises Freud's concepts of the castration complex, the Oedipus complex, and the phallus. Briefly, according to Freud, humans only become sexed subjects once they are consciously aware of sexual difference. This realization is accompanied by the emergence of the castration complex wherein a boy unconsciously fears that his penis will be cut off by his father and a girl unconsciously believes that her mother has already castrated her. Furthermore, Freud argues that the girl will unconsciously want a penis (penis envy) and upon realizing that her penis-less mother cannot give her one, may turn to her father to provide a baby as a symbolic substitute for an absent penis. Crucially, such assumptions exemplify how in psychoanalysis, human sexuality is borne out of an infant's flawed sexual knowledge (Freud 1905: 194–7).

In Freud's account of the Oedipus complex, which begins around the age of three and ends around the age of five, boys and girls continue their different journeys through unconscious dramas of familial hostility and desire. The so-called "positive" form of the Oedipus complex consists of the following: for the male child, the sex upon which the Oedipus complex is modeled, the Oedipus complex is the culmination of the traumatic castration complex because in fearing the punishment of castration from his father, the boy stops coveting the mother and enters the latency period. For the female child, the castration complex inaugurates the Oedipus complex wherein her anger, directed toward a penis-less mother whom she blames for her own lack of a penis, results in the redirection of desires to her father (Freud 1927: 256). Freud's notions of the castration and Oedipus complexes, then, assert that children assign a great deal of value to the penis.

While Freud sometimes uses the term "phallic" and (less commonly) the "phallus" in ways that are synonymous to the penis, Lacan makes a sharp distinction between the penis and the phallus. For Lacan, psychoanalysis is not primarily concerned with the penis as a biological sexual organ, but rather its status as an imaginary and symbolic object in fantasy space. During the pre-Oedipal phase, Lacan situates the phallus as an imaginary object of desire that circulates between the mother and the child. The father plays the role of castrating agent for both male and female infants by making it impossible for them to identify with the imaginary phallus, that is, by forcing them to accept the impossibility of being a phallus for the mother. Girls *and* boys, then, assume castration by accepting that they cannot be the "unsymbolized, nonfungible, undisplaceable object" (Fink 1997: 175) of the mother's desire. Thenceforth, both sexes begin their different journeys of identifying with the symbolic phallus that inaugurates questions about sexual difference.

Lacan's writings on the phallus have generated a vast literature, especially in feminism and poststructuralism. Informed by these paradigms, geographers' evaluations of Lacan's writings on the phallus are typically negative. Exemplary are Virginia Blum and Heidi Nast (2000: 183), who, alleging the "*spatial* limitations of his theory ... [and] the unstated but nevertheless implacable limitations placed upon subjectivity," argue that Lacan's

> anti-biologism, his implicit condemnation of the prevailing insistence upon a corporeal innateness and inevitability of masculinity and femininity, leads him to the extreme: He locates subjectivity entirely in language—of which the body becomes merely an effect. Lacan's assertion that the symbolic order precedes the human subject, means, then, that subjectivity comes at the price of shedding the body altogether (Blum and Nast 2000: 197).

Asserting that Lacan locates the subject entirely in language, however, only tells half of the story. For Lacan, "there are actually two subjects ... the subject of the signifier and the subject of jouissance" (Fink 2002: 22). Geographers have traditionally focused on the former subject, which Lacan theorizes via the science of linguistics, at the expense of the latter subject that is aligned with the embodiments of jouissance and the drives. In *Encore*, which importantly is a homonymic pun on *en-corps* or "in-body," Lacan (1998: 15) coins the neologism "linguistricks" (*linguisterie*) in order to bring to the fore effects of language on the embodied "subject of the enunciation," as opposed to the linguistic "subject of the statement" that is the object of Nast and Blum's critique. For example, when *Crimson Tide*'s Captain Ramsey exclaims, "As commanding officer of the USS Alabama, I order you to place the XO [Executive Officer] under arrest under charges of mutiny!" the subject of the statement is the "I" in the sentence whereas the subject of the enunciation is he who is "breathing and [performing] all of the movements of the jaw, tongue, and so on required for the production of speech" (Fink 2002: 24). The distinction between these two subjects is consequential. Lacan (1998: 23) refers to the subject of the enunciation as the "enjoying body" (*jouir d'un corps*), wherein the body is an "enjoying substance" (*la substance jouissante*) that "enjoys itself only by 'corporizing' (*corporiser*) the body in a signifying way." Put simply, sexuation is Lacan's way of defining how a body enjoys in a signifying way.

The Formulas of Sexuation

Sexuation is an attempt to overcome the limitations of post-Aristotelian systems of knowledge that rely on the grammar of language. For Lacan, "language remained insufficient and an obstacle to explaining the questions that Aristotle raised" (Ragland 2004: 8), not simply because language is unstable, dynamic, and differential (the standard historicist critique) but because of the conflicts and deadlocks inherent to language itself—the fact that language can never entirely signify what we want it to. From a Lacanian perspective, then, because sex takes place where discursive practices fail, "sex is ... not an *incomplete* entity but a totally empty one—it is one to which no predicate can be attached" (Copjec 1994: 207).

In order to show how sex is the result of the inherent deadlock within language, Lacan jettisons the classical logic of class and attribute and turns to the logics of propositional function. In addition, Lacan revises the framework he developed in "The Signification of the Phallus" which sexed—via classical logic—the psychoanalytic subject as "being" (female) or "having" (male) the phallus (Lacan 1958: 575–84). Such a revision

> marks a conceptual difference: the two classes, male and female, are no longer
> formed by gathering together subjects with similar attributes as was the case with

the older terms. The principle of sorting is no longer descriptive, that is, it is not a matter of shared characteristics or a common substance. Whether one falls into the class of males or females depends, rather, on where one places oneself as argument in relation to the function, that is, which enunciative position one assumes (Copjec 1994: 215).

The above "function" is the "phallic function" that designates the impasses of language. Refusing the idea that sex can be adequately understood as a biological and/or cultural phenomenon, Lacan (1998: 10) desubstantializes sex entirely by asserting that our sexed being "results from a logical exigency in speech ... the fact that language exists and that it is outside the bodies that are moved by it." These exigencies are explained by two fundamental Lacanian concepts: castration and the real. Very briefly, castration refers to how the human subject's entry into a social world of language involves surrendering their access to jouissance. The latter concept, the real, refers to how language is inherently conflicted because it cannot accurately reflect or neutrally communicate our thoughts, intentions, or being. As Lacan (1990: 3) puts it: "saying it all is literally impossible: words fail." From a Lacanian perspective, when

> we speak of language's failure with respect with sex, we speak not of its falling short of a prediscursive object but of its falling into contradiction with itself. Sex coincides with this *failure*, this inevitable contradiction. Sex is, then, the impossibility of completing meaning, not (as [Judith] Butler's historicist/ deconstructionist argument would have it) a meaning that is incomplete, unstable. Or, the point is that sex is the structural incompleteness of language, not that sex is itself incomplete (Copjec 1994: 206).

Lacan's infamous claim that "there is no sexual relation" refers to how sex, in opposing sense, communication, and relation, can misfire in two ways: a masculine way and a feminine way. In the seventh meeting of *Encore*, "A Love Letter," Lacan (1998: 78) draws on predicate logic to schematize the lack of a sexual relation as formulas of sexuation:

$$\exists x\, \overline{\Phi x} \qquad \overline{\exists x}\, \overline{\Phi x}$$

$$\forall x\, \Phi x \qquad \overline{\forall x}\, \Phi x$$

The left side of the schema is masculine and the right side is feminine. The formulas consist of the following terms: Φ is the symbol for the phallic function; x is a variable usually designated as jouissance; and ∀ and ∃ are quantifiers wherein ∀ refers to universal quantifiers such as "*every, all, and none*" and ∃ refers to existential quantifiers such as "*some, one, at least, certain, most*" (Copjec 1994: 214). The quality of each proposition "is determined by the quality of its copula, either affirmative or negative" (Copjec 1994: 214); negative with a bar above the predicative term and positive without the bar. The formulas, then, can be read as follows:

Masculine

$$\exists x \, \overline{\Phi x}$$

There is at least one x that is not submitted to the phallic function.

$$\forall x \, \Phi x$$

Every x is submitted to the phallic function.

Feminine

$$\overline{\exists x} \, \overline{\Phi x}$$

There is not one x that is not submitted to the phallic function.

$$\overline{\forall x} \, \Phi x$$

Not all x is submitted to the phallic function.

The two formulas that comprise the masculine side appear contradictory: on one hand every x is submitted to the phallic function while at the same time, one x is not. Bruce Fink translates the male formulas as follows: "All of man's jouissance is phallic jouissance. Every single one of his satisfactions may come up short ... Nevertheless, there is a belief in a jouissance that could never come up short, the belief in another jouissance" (2002: 38). This translation is where our reading of submarine films begins: with the idea that masculinity itself is a fantasy, a neurotic relationship to an inaccessible jouissance, and this is nowhere more in evidence than aboard a submarine.

Submarines and Genre

When one watches submarine films, it quickly becomes apparent that they share a set of genre conventions in the same way as the western or horror film.

Just as the western would be incomplete without the "showdown" and the horror film incomplete without the protagonists "splitting up" in order to find the killer, the submarine film is almost unthinkable without the sub diving below "hull crush depth" or submariners listening anxiously to the sound of depth charges detonating overhead. Following the tenets of genre theory (Grant 2003), we elaborate a series of recurring conventions in submarine films that stage masculine sexuation, including the obsession with the military chain of command as a fetishization of the symbolic order, the tyrannical figure of the submarine captain, and the Oedipal structure of the relationship between the captain, executive officer ("XO") and crew. Our argument is that these seemingly hackneyed clichés perform an ideological function within the genre and illuminate key elements of Lacan's theory of masculine sexuation.

Interestingly, the most significant conventions in the genre have their roots in the naval dramas of the nineteenth century, predating submarines entirely. While sailing ships do not spatialize the containment within the phallic symbolic order quite as potently as submarines, it is essential to note that we nevertheless find antecedents of the submarine genre within these earlier masculine microcosms. Herman Melville's posthumously published novella *Billy Budd* is arguably the most important text in this lineage, setting down the central themes of law, military order, and the ever-present threat of mutiny (Melville 1924). *Billy Budd* tells the story of a young seaman impressed into service aboard a British warship during the French Revolutionary Wars. The charismatic Budd arouses the antipathies of a superior officer, Claggart, whose jealousy leads him to accuse the young seaman of conspiring to mutiny. In the confrontation that follows, Budd accidentally kills Claggart, which leads to the central drama of the novella, wherein the sympathetic Captain Vere must decide the fate of Billy Budd, of whom he is both fond and inclined to believe over Claggart. At the same time, Vere sees himself responsible to the law above all, which is unequivocal on the matter: any seaman who kills an officer during wartime must hang. Set against a backdrop of mutinies in the Royal Navy, Vere eventually chooses the law over the just and orders Budd's execution. Incredibly, Budd walks to the gallows without complaint, and even endorses the captain's fidelity to the law when he declares: "God bless Captain Vere" as the noose is put around his neck.

At the heart of Melville's novella lie fundamental questions about the law, authority, and the threat posed by mutiny. We understand these questions as castration anxieties (in the Lacanian sense) concerning the phallic function that grounds the symbolic order. These anxieties persist as the most enduring themes in contemporary submarine films: from *Billy Budd* to *Crimson Tide*, we find a genre that is intimately, perhaps even obsessively, concerned with phallic authority and the role it plays in regulating the masculine symbolic order.

∀x Φx: All of Man's Jouissance is Phallic Jouissance. Every Single One of His Satisfactions May Come Up Short

The symbolic order emerges most powerfully in submarine films' all-consuming fascination with the military chain of command: the rules governing rank, authority, and the division of labor. In some films, this fascination crosses over completely into fetishism, lavishing attention on the minutiae of military order and protocol, luxuriating in each performance of the chain of command. Tony Scott's *Crimson Tide* is both exemplary and typical in this respect, devoting considerable screen time to Gene Hackman's Captain Ramsey drilling his crew in the byzantine bureaucracy required to launch a nuclear strike. From the communication officer's reception of the order and the senior officer's concurrence that the order is properly formatted, to the XO's order to unlock the safe and compare the authentication codes, each elaborately stylized link in this chain is scrutinized with the attention of a lover to his beloved. Arguably the greatest pleasures offered by submarine films are these scenes where we observe the crew executing the complex, ritualized actions of their duties. Indeed, the genre is defined in many ways by scenes that depicting the submarine and its crew as an Oedipalized body-of-organs: the sonar man intercepts a new contact and relays its coordinates to the "con," the captain calls out the depth to the Chief of the Boat, who in turn orders the planesman to dive, and each order in turn is echoed by the crew in a syncopated call and response that gives submarine films their distinctive rhythm and cadence.

Such scenes call to mind Lacan's (1966: 700) argument that the jouissance one loses when one submits to the phallic function does not disappear but is transferred to the Other. What the men pursue in the compulsive repetition of missile launch drills is a thoroughly libidinized enjoyment of bureaucracy: a symbolic order where the "mere pittance of pleasure" (Fink 1997: 100) that remains for the castrated subject is only accessible through language and obedience to rules. *Crimson Tide*'s fetishistic treatment of these arcane military structures allows us to see this psychical structure at work, for what should theoretically be the most mindless, stultifying bureaucracy is depicted in quasi-pornographic detail; every command, every order, every instance of the law is treated as a love object.

Figure 14.1   Chain of command: cables and gauges as love objects.
Submarine U-505's control room, The Museum of Science
and Industry, Chicago

Source: Photograph by Jesse Proudfoot.

We can read this devotion to the chain of command as an expression of
submarine films' staging of masculine sexuation. The fantasy of military order
and the chain of command is a materialization of the obsessional neurotic desire
for the smooth functioning of the symbolic, for the perfect operation of the
pleasure principle. To live completely within the chain of command is in essence
to foreclose the question of desire by reducing it to demand, which is a key
element of how Lacan defines neurosis (Fink 1997: 63): the space of ambiguity,
or more accurately, lack that makes desire possible is effaced by the chain of
command's commitment to order and control.

Thus submarine films provide a window onto obsessional neurosis, which
is the paradigmatic masculine symptom because of the particular way that it
represses the lack in the Other. When systems function perfectly there is no
lack, no need for doubt, and no space for the terrifying uncertainty of desire;
the Other commands and the subject obeys. In this way, the Lacanian overtones
of the *chain* of command become clear: the chain of command is a metonymy
for the signifying chain itself and military order is the fantasy of perfect
signification and pleasurable repetition. Here we see dramatized a crucial aspect
of masculine sexuation: for every x who is subject to the phallic function in
submarine films, who accepts castration and submits to the law, the consolation

prize for surrendering jouissance is the phallic jouissance of the symbolic order. As Lacan puts it, "castration means that jouissance has to be refused in order to be obtained on the inverse scale of the law of desire" (1966: 700). Small wonder, then that submariners should enjoy the chain of command, mining it for the scant pleasures that remain.

$\overline{\exists}$x Φx: Nevertheless, There is a Belief in a Jouissance that Could Never Come Up Short, the Belief in Another Jouissance

What about the other side of masculine sexuation? And what about the jouissance that allegedly escapes the phallic function? If submarine films fetishize the symbolic order, it is only because they are grounded in the belief that someone enjoys outside of it; the constitutive exception of the Freudian primal father who masters the excess and holds the real at bay. Here, we turn to the genre's seemingly endless cast of steely-eyed patriarchs, from *Crimson Tide*'s Captain Ramsey to *Run Silent, Run Deep*'s Captain Lancaster. These men personify the fantasy of someone who, exempt from castration, is able to stand outside the symbolic order and access the jouissance that others have renounced. Submarine captains perform this role by behaving like Freudian tyrants, mercilessly drilling the crew and disciplining their bodies. Robert Wise's *Run Silent, Run Deep* is paradigmatic here, with Clark Gable's Captain Richardson driving his crew to exhaustion, commanding them to repeat the same surfacing and diving sequence until his repetition compulsion becomes the very structure of the film itself.

The captain's privileged position is nowhere more apparent than in the cliché of diving the ship below "hull crush depth," an iconic scene of the submarine film genre that captures the ideological role that the captain as *Urvater* plays in the psychic economy of the submarine. In Kathryn Bigelow's *K-19: The Widowmaker*, the despotic Captain Vostrikov calmly instructs his crew to dive the ship to suicidal depths while the crew nervously obey, sweat glistening on the foreheads of sailors listening anxiously to the metallic groans of distressed steel and the horrifying ricochet of bolts popping loose from the pressure. As the Chief of the Boat calls out the depth with increasing alarm ("280 ... 290 ... *300 meters*, Captain!"), Vostrikov calmly sips his tea, unperturbed by the mounting panic around him.

What such scenes show us is the position that the captain occupies with respect to the symbolic order of the ship. Diving the ship below hull crush depth is supposed to be impossible; according to accepted engineering knowledge it should not be able to go that deep. By doing so—and, crucially, by appearing indifferent to danger—the captain demonstrates to the crew that he stands outside of the symbolic and is not subject to its castrating effects. We could argue that the captain stares into the watery real and dares it to break through and flood the phallic submarine symbolic—shoring up its hull with his own imaginary bravado. Perhaps the surest sign that the submarine is a signifier for the phallic symbolic order comes from its opposite, as in Blake Edwards' 1959 comedy *Operation Petticoat*. Here, the submarine genre is inverted to comic effect when the captain of a bombed submarine is forced to take on women as passengers and eventually paint the submarine pink. The film's comedy is thus derived entirely from the castration of the phallic submarine.

The Captain Vostrikov scene also demonstrates how, rather than being drained of enjoyment, the *problem* with the symbolic is that it nevertheless still drips with reckless, terrifying jouissance. The captain's object-lesson is thus two-fold: by taking the ship where it should not possibly be able to go, he reminds the crew (and us as viewers) that their neurotic phantasies about the perfect functioning of the symbolic are just that, fantasies, while simultaneously positioning himself as the primal father who circumscribes the symbolic as an exception to the law of castration.

Figure 14.2   The intimacies of war: domesticity and weapons of destruction. Aft torpedo room of submarine U-505, Museum of Science and Industry, Chicago

Source: Photograph by Jesse Proudfoot.

Despite the elaborate displays of potency put on by captains in submarine films, it is essential to remember that the role of captain, like that of the father, can only ever be a role, a position, or *function*—it can never be synonymous with the individual who tries to occupy it. To be a father, Lacan reminds us, is to fulfill a function, to fulfill the phallic function of guaranteeing meaning and regulating jouissance. But while it is essential that someone fill this role, it is impossible for a living, breathing person to coincide with the position of the father in fantasy space. This idea is perfectly illustrated by *Run Silent, Run Deep* during a scene in which an accident occurs in the torpedo room.

During an enemy attack, chaos among the crew results in armed torpedoes malfunctioning and nearly detonating inside the ship. In a thoroughly uncharacteristic act, Captain Lancaster runs to the torpedo room to save his men. This is significant because up until this point in the film, Gable's character has ruthlessly governed the crew as a fearsome patriarch. When the accident occurs, he rushes to his men's aid not as the aloof captain who values the mission over the crew, but as a father concerned for his children. The narrative of the film makes clear the cost of this breakdown in the symbolic order: the captain is mortally wounded in the accident and dies by the film's end. What *Run Silent, Run Deep* suggests apropos the phallic function is that the structure must be upheld at all costs; when the patriarch abandons his position as patriarch, he becomes a man again, and is revealed to be nothing more than another fallible—which is to say, phallic—individual.

Submarine films are deeply concerned about the prospect of a failure of the phallus, as revealed by this line from *U-571*, when Harvey Keitel's CPO Klough rebukes the new captain for admitting to the crew that he does not know whether they will succeed:

> This is the navy, where a commanding officer is a mighty and terrifying thing, a man to be feared and respected. All-knowing. All-powerful. Don't you dare say what you said to the boys back there again, "I don't know." Those three words will kill a crew, dead as a depth charge. You're the skipper now and the skipper always knows what to do, whether he does or not.

What Klough's speech makes clear is that the fallibility of the phallus can never be spoken, for to do so would result in the collapse of the symbolic order and even, ultimately, death.

The dissolution of the symbolic is never so central to submarine films as it is in the threat of mutiny, a theme that, as we have already seen, dates back at least as far as Melville's *Billy Budd*. In *K-19*, crewmembers angry with Captain Vostrikov's authoritarian leadership stage a mutiny at gun point and install the XO in his place. In *U-571*, CPO Klough puts down an attempted mutiny by crewmembers unwilling to follow the new captain. Finally, the climax of *Crimson Tide* consists of a dramatic sequence in which the XO seizes control of the ship, citing the captain's violation of the chain of command, only to be ousted in a Thermidorian counter-revolution led by a cadre of officers loyal to the captain. Mutiny is such a preoccupation of submarine films that we could even argue that it is the necessary corollary of their fetishization of the chain of command. Mutiny, in effect, dramatizes the central question of the symbolic order: who is in charge? To contemplate mutiny is to restage the murder of the Freudian primal father, to refuse castration and seize jouissance. The enduring presence of mutiny as a theme is therefore the surest proof that submarine films are firmly ensconced in the space of masculine sexuation: even as we, along with the crew, take pleasure in the perfect operation of the signifying chain of command, we never stop dreaming of breaking free of our Oedipal prison, killing the captain and taking his place.

Mutiny haunts the submarine film like the repressed because it is the shadowy double of the genre's obsession with the symbolic. From *Billy Budd*'s veneration of the law to *Crimson Tide*'s fetishistic devotion to bureaucracy, these narratives obsess over what happens when the symbolic is called into question. And if the return of the repressed is the correct way of reading this repetition it is surely because mutiny in submarine films restages the murder of the primal father as a working-through of their profoundly Oedipal desiring-structure. Indeed, in every one of the films we examine, the structure is identical: a tyrannical captain-father is countered by an empathetic XO-mother with the antagonism between them played out for the crew *qua* child. Liam Neeson's XO Polenin could not make the point more explicit in *K-19* when he reminds Vostrikov that "the crew is a family; the captain is the father."

Conclusions

We hope this chapter, which should be read as a preliminary exploration, will incite belated work on Lacan's crucial notion of sexuation and its relevance to geographical inquiry. For us, submarines films neatly illustrate the logic of masculine sexuation because they depict spaces held together by the bonds of phallic jouissance and sustained by the belief in a boundless jouissance that is not submitted to the phallic function.

We believe there are at least three interrelated ways that geographers can build on and go beyond our chapter. To begin with, one might provide a similar introduction to how feminine sexuation is relevant to geographical inquiry. Second, one might extend the above theoretical analysis of sexuation. For instance, it is notable that we did not address the lower portion of Lacan's table of sexuation that depicts the masculine position having access to only one type of libidinal position and the feminine side having access to two libidinal positions (see Lacan's (1998: 79) "complete" graph of sexuation). In addition, while our chapter focused on sexuation as a theory of masculine sexuality, it somewhat neglected sexuation as theory of space insofar as submarine spaces sexuate its crewmembers as masculine through the spatial dramas of containment, exception, and concealment. Third, rather than simply use cultural artifacts such as submarine movies to elaborate the contours of a psychoanalytic concept; one might use a psychoanalytic concept such as sexuation to psychoanalyze socio-spatial phenomena. All of these tasks are a testament to the pressing promises that continue to define Lacanian geography.

References

Barnard, S. 2002a. Introduction, in *Reading Seminar XX: Lacan's Major Work on Love, Knowledge, and Feminine Sexuality*, edited by S. Barnard and B. Fink. Albany, NY: State University of New York Press, 1–20.

Barnard, S. 2002b. Tongues of angels: feminine structure and other jouissance, in *Reading Seminar XX: Lacan's Major Work on Love, Knowledge, and Feminine Sexuality*, edited by S. Barnard and B. Fink. Albany, NY: State University of New York Press, 171–85.

Blum, V. and Nast, H. 2000. Jacques Lacan's two-dimensional subjectivity, in *Thinking Space*, edited by P. Crang and N. Thrift. New York: Routledge, 183–204.

Copjec, J. 1994. *Read My Desire: Lacan Against the Historicists*. Cambridge, MA: The MIT Press.

Fink, B. 1997. *A Clinical Introduction to Lacanian Psychoanalysis: Theory and Technique*. Cambridge, MA: Harvard University Press.

Fink, B. 2002. Knowledge and jouissance, in *Reading Seminar XX: Lacan's Major Work on Love, Knowledge, and Feminine Sexuality*, edited by S. Barnard and B. Fink. Albany, NY: State University of New York Press, 21–45.

Freud, S. 1905 [2001]. Three essays on the theory of sexuality, in *The Standard Edition of the Complete Psychological Works of Sigmund Freud*, Vol. VII, edited and translated by J. Strachey. London: Vintage, 123–245.

Freud, S. 1927 [2001]. Some psychological consequences of the anatomical distinction between the sexes, in *The Standard Edition of the Complete Psychological Works of Sigmund Freud*, Vol. XIX, edited and translated by J. Strachey. London: Vintage, 243–60.

Friedlander, J. 2008. *Feminine Look: Sexuation, Spectatorship, Subversion*. Albany, NY: State University of New York Press.

Grant, B.K. (ed.) 2003. *Film Genre Reader III*. Austin: University of Texas Press.

Kingsbury, P. 2008. Did somebody say jouissance? On Slavoj Žižek, consumption, and nationalism, *Emotion, Space and Society*, 1(1), 48–55.

Lacan, J. 1990. *Television: A Challenge to the Psychoanalytic Establishment*. New York: Norton Press.

Lacan, J. 1998. *On Feminine Sexuality: The Limits of Love and Knowledge, 1972–1973*. New York: Norton.

Lacan, J. 1958 [2006]. The signification of the phallus, in *Écrits: The First Complete Edition in English*. New York: Norton, 575–84.

Lacan, J. 1966 [2006]. The subversion of the subject and the dialectic of desire, in *Écrits: The First Complete Edition in English*. New York: Norton, 671–702.

Matviyenko, S. 2009. Sensuous extimacy: sexuation and virtual reality. Taking on a gender identity in second life. *Proceedings of the Digital Arts and Culture Conference 2009*. University of California, Irvine.

Melville, H. 1924 [2009]. *Billy Budd and Other Tales*. New York: Signet Classic.

Özselçuk, K. and Madra, Y. 2005. Marxism and psychoanalysis: from capitalist-all to communist not-all. *Psychoanalysis, Culture and Society*, 10(1), 79–98.

Ragland, E. 2004. *The Logic of Sexuation*. Albany, NY: State University of New York Press.

Films

Crimson Tide (dir. Tony Scott, 1995).
K-19: The Widowmaker (dir. Kathryn Bigelow, 2002).
Operation Petticoat (dir. Blake Edwards, 1959).
Run Silent, Run Deep (dir. Robert Wise, 1958).
The Enemy Below (dir. Dick Powell, 1957).
The Hunt for Red October (dir. John McTiernan, 1990).
U-571 (dir. Jonathan Mostow, 2000).

PART IV
Social Life and its Discontents

Chapter 15

"Race," Imperializing Geographies of the Machine, and Psychoanalysis

Heidi J. Nast

In Freud the fetish is not only a "protection" against castration; it is also a "memorial" to it: the fetish may occlude recognition of castration, but it cannot erase it; sometimes the fetish reinscribes castration in its very form. The trauma is never undone, its threat never exorcized. And so it is with the machine: it may figure a new totality, a dynamic phallic body, but it cannot rectify the old fragmentation nor make good the originary castration of the subject. In this way the double logic of the prosthesis may replicate that of the fetish: the prosthesis cannot undo its reason for being; it may even underscore that the subject is defined in lack.

From Hal Foster's, "Prosthetic Gods" (1997: 14–15)

Introduction

The exclusive geographical placement of industrial machinery—what I henceforth refer to as "the machine"—was singularly important in securing and stabilizing the white working class male subject as an exceptionally productive one. Such spatial anchoring allowed the machine's profoundly superior technological abilities to be singularly claimed by, associated with, mapped onto, and incorporated into, the body of industrial man and nation. In so doing, both were categorically rendered phallic (exceptional) agents of progress and history.

The incorporation of the machine into the bodily ego of white industrial man was especially strategic to capitalism and empire building. On the one hand, identification with the machine served a compensatory purpose, allowing white working class male subjects to deny their filialized exploitation at the patriarchal hands of capital. It allowed them to work "as if" they were not castrated but superordinately powerful, especially physically so, particularly in relation to white women. On the other hand, machinic identification enabled all white subjects to assume ontological superiority over persons of color—enslaved, freed, or colonized, additionally allowing for a national imaginary in which whiteness could be identified with a supreme and supremely colonizing place.

Both bodily and national particularities of the machine-phallus stabilized the racialized and patriarchal political economies of capitalist societies and modern nation-states, as well as imperial social and psychical formations.

The geopolitical and psychical security afforded by supremacist national and bodily mappings was significantly challenged in the 1970s when de-industrialization and re-structuring began to gain strong international hold. The slow removal of one of the main historical props of white male subjectivity and nationhood—the machine—led some to armor themselves psychically against (racialized) others, accusing the latter of stealing their industrial jobs, or of stealing (migrating) illegally into the nation. I argue that such defensiveness must be seen not simply in terms of simple economic stresses related rationally to unemployment, but in psychical terms as anxieties unconsciously related to bodily and, as we will see, parental loss.

I make this argument in several steps using three machine-centric films to guide me. I begin by discussing how the exclusive siting of the industrial machine in Europe created the geographical conditions through which metonymic associations amongst European workers, European nations, and the machine could take hold. The machine's privileged and privileging geography allowed the machine's superior powers and energies to be mapped onto the white body, eventually permitting male workers in particular the means by which to celebrate a phallicism and strength they in fact did not have. I analyze this privileging in light of Buster Keaton's role in his 1926 film, *The General*, which takes place on steam-engine trains operating in the Civil War South. The machine-related themes raised by the film are then addressed in light how the growing efficiencies of nineteenth-century factory machinery became associated with a growing menagerie of "white" surplus workers. The first such workers were primarily children and women, whose social identities were managed in spatially distinct ideological ways. White children were withdrawn in part through the force of sentimentalization, which resituated them in the home and in places of public education. Soon thereafter, married (white) women were withdrawn and also re-placed into the home, where they carried out unremunerated reproductive labor.

I examine how white working class men dealt with their subordination by the machine and the rigors of factory by drawing on two iconic films, Fritz Lang's *Metropolis* (1927) and Charlie Chaplin's *Modern Times* (1936). I argue that, together, the films speak of distinct psychical registers of castration: on the one hand, the maternal and, on the other hand, the Symbolic (paternal). *Metropolis* portrays the machine as specially frightening and overwhelming, workers' fears calling to mind primary fantasies of maternal castration. *Modern Times*, by contrast, portrays the machine as something humanly manageable. Here, despite labor's subordination, workers willfully identify with the machine, the latter becoming a prosthetic device through which men imagine themselves wholly (as being the phallus) or in part (as having the phallus). Whereas the first instance involves ego armoring, the second involves incorporation of the machine into the bodily ego of the subject, a means of extending one's agency outward. For Lacan (2002), "being" and "having" the phallus creates a dynamic of desire that, in this case, permitted (white) male–male desires to circulate in ways that allowed workers to be simultaneously invested in, and subordinated to, capitalist interests.

The Geography of Industrial Machinery: Race and the Machine-phallus

Despite the presence of vast amounts of raw materials, energy sources (including coal), and cheap labor in nineteenth-century European colonies, the machine was located exclusively in Europe and white-settler colonies, far from the reach of colonized and enslaved hands. The latter, by contrast, carried out the most arduous, non-mechanized kinds of labor. The machine's *absence* marked the colonized body as one naturally fit for toil, an idea inaugurated centuries earlier by the Spanish and Portuguese in Latin America and by French, English, and white US settlers in the context of American and Caribbean slavery. Industrial bodies and nations consequently became marked as plenitudinous—exceptional bearers of progress and productivity. The coloniality and raciality of the machine came to operate similarly in the US, including what we generally consider to have been the non-mechanized antebellum South.

I call the latter to mind using a still image of Buster Keaton from his comedic film, *The General* (1926), set in 1861 Confederate Georgia on the eve of the Civil War. Here, Keaton sits awkwardly on the front edge of a moving steam engine train, holding askew a thick railway tie he has scavenged for fuel (Figure 15.1). The steam-engine was displayed and celebrated at early World Fairs as a dramatic measure of scientific and racial advancement, a stark contrast to the primitivized African villages and Orientalized mise en scenes (Adas 1989). The steam-engine train, emblematic of capital itself, was monumentally important in early nineteenth-century expansion of white-settler life and capital accumulation. Along with the telegraph, it accelerated US racial-imperial projects. What is generally less well known, however, is that many US railways were built with slave labor. Railway companies had regularly rented and purchased slaves since the 1830s when the building process began. Slave men graded thousands of miles of track, while slave women and children ran wheelbarrows, moved dirt, cooked, picked up stones, and shoveled. Their labor eventually became so important that it would be exported out of the south into all railway reaches of the US (Thomas 2011). Black men also labored onboard, carrying out the lowliest, most dangerous, and most backbreaking tasks, including those of firemen and brakemen. Despite the monumental productivity of slave labor on behalf of the train-machine, slaves were forbidden from assuming the most important position of all, that of the train engineer, even as the work involved for that post was next to none. By the Civil War the number of slaves in railway companies' employ rivaled that of the largest plantation owners (Licht 1983; Nelson 2006; Kornweibel 2010; Thomas 2011: 24).

Despite the ubiquity of slaves working in the fields and on the railway, *The General*'s characters are all white, even those playing "extras." The main protagonists include Confederate and Union officers, cavalry men, and foot soldiers readying themselves for battle. Buster Keaton plays Johnnie Gray, the central character that wants to be a soldier, but is forbidden from doing so because he is needed for his skills as a train engineer. The film's name comes from the fact that "Johnnie's" train bears the name of *The General*, these words engraved on the engine car's side. Johnnie is accidentally drawn into the war after Union forces unwittingly load his love interest, Annabelle Lee, onto a train bound for the battlefield. When Johnnie realizes this he jumps on *The General* to save her, finds her, and de-boards, lying in hiding until he can carry out his rescue plan. Within earshot of Union officers, he overhears details of an impending assault. Thus, after rescuing Annabelle, he races *The General* back to tell the Confederate generals all that he knows, in the process becoming a local hero (he is made an honorary Lieutenant) and winning the heart of Annabelle Lee.

In light of my discussion about the machine the honors bestowed on Keaton must be seen as somewhat strange in that Johnnie did nothing other than put wood into a large mechanical device. That is, it was not his labor that made a difference, but that of the *train*; the train made Johnnie's and, later, the Confederacy's success possible. The beam that Johnnie plies across his thighs thus belongs not to him, but to the train-engine, just as Johnnie belongs to larger Southern economic interests otherwise absented from the film. The same engine that fueled white settler expansion was likewise used to fuel the early industrial era in the US and Europe, to which I now turn (Figure 15.1).

Figure 15.1   **Buster Keaton awkwardly balances a railway tie across his thighs in his 1926 comedic film,** *The General*

Source: *The General*. 1926. Directed by Buster Keaton. USA: United Artists.

Machines, Men, and Nineteenth-century (White) Surplus Labor

Children and women were integral and important parts of the early industrial labor force precisely because machines made laboring easier (Marx 1915: 431). At first, Marx explains, capitalist interests recouped investments by imposing ever-longer working days and by employing entire families, the consequently bloated labor pool helping to keep wages low. The increasing productive capacity of the machine, however, eventually decreased the labor-time needed for social reproduction, permitting reductions in the length of the working day and the release of some workers to reserve pools of the unemployed (Marx 1915: v1, ch X). The first workers categorically released from the industrial workplace were (white) children (e.g., Freedman 1994). Their "surplus" status was managed politically and ideologically by sentimentalizing childhood and through mandates for public education, the latter effectively ensuring the scientific viability of industry's future. The second group released were white women, even though it was they who dominated some of the most important industries (especially textiles) and even though machines had continued to make factory work *less* rather than more strenuous; more feminine (see also Berg 1991). The "surplus" status of women—first bourgeois and middle class women and, later, the wives and mothers of the "respectable" working class—was ideologically managed and disappeared through cults of domesticity and (nuclear) family. Cultural productions of sentimentality and domesticity therefore mitigated what would have been not insignificant losses to some white working class subjects and households (Welter 1966; Zelizer 1994; Bartoletti 1996).

The spatial and ideological folding of children's and women's labor into the hidden (domesticated) space of the home could not have happened without the invention of the nuclear family and of the "family wage." Male workers were singularly identified with the latter, the term advancing them as those most naturally disposed toward familial caretaking and able to carry out related obligations (Barrett and McIntosh 1980; MacKenzie and Rose 1983; Boydston 1990; Connell 1995). Such re-positioning blocked many white women and children from having formal (exchange) value of their own and consequently from having full economic and social lives (Coontz 1993; Connor 1995).

The "privileging" of the white working class (biological) paternal to provide for the family and access related markets became a basis for (white) pride, helping to structure, manage, contain, and canalize the *emotional* life of the white working class as well as racialized others. Working class (white) men could now feel proud of a wage that otherwise marked them, in relation to capitalist interests and the machine, as castrated or feminized (du Bois 1965). The naming of the family wage as such additionally made manifest the *procreational* objective of the wage, that is, to streamline reproductive concerns into patriarchally structured productive ones. The efficiencies to be had made from such this blending made other kinds of sex (including masturbation) socio-economically injurious and wasteful by comparison.

The masculinity of workers, however, must be seen as having been distinct from that of the industrial capitalist (Nast 2002). Whereas the former assumed phallic force through the family wage, biological paternity, and identification with the machine, the phallic authority of the capitalist rested on control over the economic means of imagining and realizing industrial projects, a very different kind of conception that *de-emphasized* the body (see Wigley 1991). Indeed, in making biological reproduction the concern and preserve of the white working class, the bourgeois subject was free to invest in, elaborate, and obsess over the abstractions involved in accumulating and planning for profit.

**Figure 15.2   Workers ascend the stairwell into the all devouring world of
the machine and industrial production**

Source: *Metropolis*. 1927. Directed by Fritz Lang. Germany: UFA.

Primary Castration and Early Industry

The intensity with which the machine disciplined and cadenced the working
class body had psychical consequences that varied across time and place, an
intensity that began even earlier with the clock. E.P. Thompson (1967) is the
first scholar to substantively engage with the geographical unevenness with
which abstract, syncopated clock time came to replace the event-driven agrarian
renderings of "natural" time in England during the seventeenth and eighteenth
centuries. The clock, he says, helped to create a temporal regime that disciplined
and coordinated not only the factory floor, but all aspects of commercial and
industrial life.

The clock's disciplinary force and presence in *industrial* times was palpable,
its authoritative and at times punitive dimensions assuming, for some, sexual
proportions. Thompson (1967: 57) tells us, for instance, of a humorous English
essay from 1760 in which virtuous matrons are said to have kept clocks in their

bedrooms as "exciting to acts of carnality," while female street walkers haled male clients by asking if they'd like their "clock wound up." Over 150 years later, the most phallic clock of all—Big Ben—would figure prominently in Virginia Woolf's *Mrs. Dalloway* (1925: 100), the sadistic qualities of clock time notable throughout, as evident in the following:

> Shredding and dicing, dividing and subdividing, the clocks of Harley Street nibbled at the June day, counseled submission, upheld authority, and pointed out in chorus the supreme advantages of a sense of proportion ...

Indeed, by the nineteenth century, the clock's authority ruled the factory floor, modern time's abstractions becoming pivotal to industry's elaboration. Fritz Lang powerfully portrays the physical and psychical force of the clock-machine nexus in his 1927 expressionist film, *Metropolis*, the opening scene of which sets time's sinister tone: a group of downtrodden (white) workers, heads hanging low, walking lock-step toward an elevator that will descend into a darkened machine-laden landscape cadenced by the clock. Here, industry overwhelms: the machines are monumental, as is the human-sized clock against whose hands a worker eventually dies, his arms outstretched as though on a crucifix. In one scene, the machine appears as a gaping-mouthed, human-eating monster (Figure 15.2).

The machine's immensity presses, holds, and infantilizes workers in ways that terrorize and are a measure of worker defeat. Following Ettinger's (2006) work on primary unconscious fantasies, the overwhelming, devouring abilities of the machine resonate with those of the all-powerful fantastical maternal against which the infant feels powerless. As Ettinger (2006: 106) explains, maternal castration is about three primary fantasies—not-enoughness, devouring, and abandonment—even if Freud and Lacan never formulated these characteristics specifically in maternal castration terms. She writes that while "Freud remarks [on] 'the surprising, yet regular, fear of being killed (devoured?) by the mother' (Freud 1931: 227) and Lacan remarks that 'there is no other real relation with the mother than that which all present psychoanalytical theory puts in relief, that is, the relation of devouring' (Lacan 1994: 380)," neither made the "radical step of realizing that these phantasies correspond in each and every criteria to the requirements of primal phantasy." Workers, here, are thus not oppressed or castrated in an oedipal sense but, from the position of capital, are overwhelmed and, hence, infantilized.

That said, the most horrible machine-monster of all is a robot-woman of *human* proportions: the *maschinenmensch* Maria, created by the scientist Rotwang and factory owner Joh Fredersen to replace a human Maria who has been rallying workers to strike. Rotwang has the "real" Maria kidnapped and sets out to replace her, too. In this way, he scientifically supplants the maternal; she, as woman (in the name of the Virgin Maria), has the singular human capacity to biologically replace (reproduce) human labor. In one scene, human Maria, seemingly lifeless and stretched out in a glass incubator, has various of her bodily parts tethered by electrical wires to those of her not-yet awakened robotic double, robot Maria. Robot Maria's eventual incarnation marks capitalism's end game: the total machinic replacement of humanity, including the maternal that ordinarily replaces old labor naturally with the new (see O'Brien 1993). The robot is therefore a unique modality of machine that embodies capitalism's drive to eliminate humanity's productive *and* reproductive capacities. Capitalist industrial conception is here made complete. Or, as Huyssen (1981–82: 227) puts it:

> just as the technological artifact is considered to be the quasi-natural extension of
> man's natural abilities (the lever replacing muscle power, the computer expanding
> brain power), so woman ... is considered to be the natural vessel of man's
> reproductive capacity, a mere bodily extension of the male's procreative powers.

Metropolis' foreboding is consequently not just about subordinating workers through machinic infantilization and annihilation (as meted by paternal law); it is about how—through the quest for profit—competitive and misogynist desires to reduce, control, displace, and eliminate the biological-maternal (and hence humanity itself) are exposed. In replacing mother *and* child, the basis of future labor, industrial capitalism manifests its defining drive toward death.

Secondary Castration and Fordism

> Man has, as it were, become a kind of prosthetic God. When he puts on all his
> auxiliary organs he is truly magnificent; but those organs have not grown on to
> him and they still give him much trouble at times.
> Sigmund Freud, *Civilization and Its Discontents* (1930), cited in Foster (1997).

Metropolis was released nearly a decade after the First World War just as "the technology cult of the *Neue Sachlichkeit* and its unbridled confidence in technical progress and social engineering" was unfolding in the Weimar Republic (Huyssen 1981/82: 223). Some have claimed that the film's dystopic view is ahistorical in nature, having more to do with the machine-gun's invention and its unprecedented contribution to the First World War's bloodshed than to the miseries associated with the industrial machine per se. Indeed, by 1927 machines had become not only more efficient (total fertility rates correspondingly going into decline) but less formidable. Rising wages and consumption levels meant that workers had access domestically and professionally to electric lights, cars, tractors and harvesters, calculating machines, sewing and washing machines, and so on. The vernacularization, professionalization, and increasingly individual and largely male ownership of these smaller scale devices allowed the machine to assume a different psychical tenor and thus enter a different psychical register.

**Figure 15.3   Charlie Chaplin on the Fordist assembly line where he
eventually goes insane**

Source: *Modern Times* © Roy Export S.A.S. Scan Courtesy Cineteca di Bologna.

Rather than the working class being overwhelmed by machines that evoked primary fantasies of maternal castration, the machine had become psychically pliable, enough so as to enter the oedipal, Symbolic register. To the degree that the machine no longer physically over-determined one's life and death, it could be laughed at.

This shift is evident in Charlie Chaplin's *Modern Times* (1936); a comedic film produced 10 years after *Metropolis* to portray the inanity of US factory life, in this case after the Great Depression. Chaplin plays the protagonist, a frail, undersized, dim-witted worker who is having a hard time dealing physically and mentally with the de-humanizing repetitiveness of Fordist factory life (Figure 15.3).

His debility is made plain in a number of ways. In one of the film's first depictions of the factory floor, we find him working on an assembly line, incapable of following the regimented pacing with any grace. He yawns, loses his place—disturbing everyone down the line, and is easily distracted. At one point, Chaplin slips away for a bathroom cigarette break. But just as he strikes a match (on his buttocks) to light up, the factory owner appears on an oversized screen on one of the bathroom walls, paternalistically commanding him to return to the line. Panic-stricken, Charlie rushes out of the bathroom. Even so, he dawdles before slipping back into his place. Standing obnoxiously close to the overseer who has replaced him, Chaplin coquettishly files his nails with a metal rasp, the overseer snapping at him to re-enter the line. Later, when he and the other men go on lunch break, Chaplin cannot get his shoulders or hands to stop violently twitching, his arms involuntarily convulsing as if he is still at work.

Unlike the *Metropolis* and despite Chaplin's despair, the workers of *Modern Times* show little evidence of being downtrodden. In a clear reference to *Metropolis*, the film's opening scene shows the workers walking along a downward-sloped path en masse into the factory. Yet, they do not move in lock-step but in disorganized fashion, like feckless sheep; the analogy is made plain through a fade-in in which Chaplin features as a single black sheep amongst many white ones scrambling into the chute. While at the assembly line, the workers operate in concert, using wrenches, hammers, and other tools to carry out mind-numbingly repetitive tasks. All of them, save Chaplin, are engaged and invested. The tools they hold and wield, and the machinic world in which they operate, seem to be part of their human bodily nature. Here, "worker productivity" becomes seen as the summative efforts of machine *and* human, even as the former subordinates and dwarfs the latter's contributions (Szasz 1958). Like the "family wage," which allowed working class men to bolster their position prosthetically, identification with the extraordinary and growing achievements of the machine are incorporated into the bodily ego of "man."

It is precisely this psychical identification of man with machine that Chaplin works comedically to disrupt. He does this most famously in a scene where his wrench gets stuck on a nut-like part and he is carried along the conveyor belt into the gear-filled bowels of a colossal machine. The machine's interiority is not cast as something that digests and devours, however, but as a theater for the absurd—and as something that can be shut down with unwitting human ease. In causing havoc, Chaplin points to the vulnerability of the machine and to masculinity's artifice, his comrades' near hysteria over the work stoppage speaking of the fragility of their machinic identification.

Around the corner from the assembly line stands a different kind of masculine subject whose machinic desires Chaplin likewise confronts. This is the well-built, shirtless lieutenant-worker whose job it is to stay close to a large television console where the factory owner occasionally appears to issue him commands about the pace at which assembly work should proceed. Upon appearing, the worker salutes him and listens, proceeding hence to a control station, within which there are dramatically large levers and dials that he accordingly adjusts. The muscle-bound bareness of the man is bemusing, for he does no physical labor. That he is expected to present his bared self in front of the *screen*—the ironic embodiment of the all-seeing disembodied capitalist—speaks to the importance of male–male desire within the workings of capitalism; the capitalist gazes approvingly at the armored or hardened machine-like bodily-subject who, in turn, looks at the capitalist, desiring to be desired (approved of, valued, hired) as such.

The looks exchanged belie a singular truth: that what the capitalist ultimately desires (banks on, invests in) is the machine (*constant* capital), not the human (*variable* capital); machinic desire being that on which the lieutenant's armored livelihood depends. Chaplin explodes this second instance of the masculine (the armored ego) when his character unexpectedly goes insane. Pirouetting across the factory floor like a ballerina, he leans on the lieutenant's large levers, using them as a barré on which to practice and coyishly lean. He proceeds to push and pull on them and to turn the many dials, Chaplin's puny size belying the fact that no physical strength whatsoever is needed to carry out the lieutenant's job. Later, he squirts the lieutenant with lubricating oil—as if the latter is indeed the phallus/machine. Yet, despite his desire to *be* the machine, the lieutenant is disgusted at the goo, making plain the fact that he is all too human (Figure 15.4).

Figure 15.4 **After Chaplin's character goes insane he pirouettes and**
dances on the shop floor, taking a lubricating can and
spraying the muscle bound lieutenant

Source: *Modern Times* © Roy Export S.A.S. Scan Courtesy Cineteca di Bologna.

Modern Times thus interrupts two identification processes through which working class masculine subjectivity took shape in early industrial nation-states: incorporation of machine parts into the bodily ego, as in the case of the line men (where the subject *has* the machine-phallus); and through bodily ego armoring, as in the case of the lieutenant—he *is* the machine-phallus. Neither identification process could take place, however, if they were not pleasurable; incorporation is pleasurable in that it allows the subject to claim the immensity of the machine's accomplishments as his own while being affirmed (for his integration) via the family wage; while in *becoming* (or masquerading as) the machine, the lieutenant-subject experiences directly the pleasure of paternal affirmation and, with it, a job. Through his antics, then, Chaplin clarifies the economic baseness of machine-centric desires and the unwitting and materially differentiated homosocial pleasures to be had by those violating *and* those being violated (Nast 2002).

Deindustrialization and Paternal Abandonment: New Beginnings

> Everything to know about me
> Is written on this page
> The number you can reach me
> My social and my age
> Yes I served in the army
> It's where I learned to shoot
> Eighteen months in the desert
> Pourin' sand out of my boots
> No I've never been convicted of a crime
> I could start this job at any time
>
> ...
>
> I got a strong back
> Steel toes
> I'm handy with a wrench
> There's nothing I can't drive
> Nothing I can't fix
> I work sun-up to sun-down
> Ain't too proud to sweep the floors
> Bank has started calling
> And the wolves are at my door
> Three dollars and change at the pump
> Cost of livin's high and goin' up.
> (Excerpt from Ronnie Dunn's country and western song, "Cost of Living")

Industrial wages in the US began stagnating in 1973, industrial growth rates dramatically declining over the next two decades. Despite a brief recovery in the 1990s, industrial growth since 2000 has scarcely been higher than what it was in the 1930s. Throughout the postwar industrial heartland of North America, Western Europe, and Japan, similar forms of wage stagnation and slowed industrial growth took hold, varying in detail and severity from one case to the next, but rarely departing greatly from the US pattern. Real wage decline was accompanied by the emergence of dual-income-earning households, hollowing out any notion of male exceptionalism. Other bastions of the white working class largely disappeared: industrial unions were busted and, along with them, presumptions that (white) men naturally required a superior (family) wage. At the same time, colorized labor streams were let in, legally or through other means, to carry out the most arduous labor at reduced rates. Capital investments in industry shifted largely (if not entirely) to formerly colonized and subordinated agrarian nations that had long been racially denigrated and (accordingly) deprived of the machine. Here, families were characteristically large in size, their increasing displacement from traditional lands producing plentiful and cheap reserves of labor for neo-industrial endeavors.

Given the machine's embeddedness in the phallic life of whiteness and the (first industrial) nation, de-industrialization was bound to have widespread, devastating, and variously scaled effects. Most importantly, it left white working class men libidinally stranded, their machinic prostheses unmoored from their material foundations even though psychical identifications continued. Many white working class subjects, in their attempts to explain work stoppages, turned hysterically to finger those outside the libidinized industrial economy of whiteness, refusing to countenance paternal abandonment as a reason "why." De-industrialization consequently came to be accompanied by xenophobia and an accelerated formation of white supremacist nationalist groups. Variously colonized and colorized persons became special targets of white working class hysteria and hate: Algerians in France; Kurds in Germany; Senegalese in Italy; Mexicans in the US, to name a few. The negation of colorized others speaks not only to previous rounds of neo/colonization upon which white industrialization and identification first depended and later proceeded, but to a refusal by the working class to identify de-industrialization as a process of willful capital/ist withdrawal; as a process of willful paternalistic divestment and abandonment; and, even more radically, as a process whereby the colorized and feminized now have access to the formerly coveted machine. To think such thoughts requires confronting the political economic utility and artifice of all kinds of difference in the economic life of the machine and, hence, slow and painful processes of dis-identification with the machine and the forging of new identifications through difference's pain and struggle.

The defensiveness of some has manifested itself in such acute expressions of hate that even in limited doses the compensatory actions of a few have been devastating for many. Corporate interests have capitalized on worker hysteria, re-upping disenfranchised white bodies through a variety of military-industrial complexes. Through the latter, myriads of disenfranchised groups have been re-filialized into soldiers for, and defenders of, vested private and public interests. The same desire to be desired has been taken up by the working poor, rewarded not with a family wage, but with incarnations as "heroes" best qualified to protect. Instead of identifying the paternal as that which abandons its sons, then, a new paternal has emerged that commands and rewards filial protection of assets, whether this be through recruitments of the poor into military and police establishments, private contracting companies, paramilitary groups, or private and public security firms. In the process, arms have become the new machine by which whiteness can feel itself refreshed, even if the process is wrought (as it always has been) with contradictions; large numbers of the colorized poor in relatively wealthy nations joining military and police establishments, just as the neocolonialized poor have taken up arms (for different, but related reasons) in the context of so-called failed or unstable states.

Arms have become a new kind of international currency, insinuated into popular aesthetics and forms of entertainment, including video games, films, and TV series as well as toys, paintball venues, extreme sports, and camouflage clothing. The bodily ego of many has concomitantly been recast, men's biceps now identified as "guns" rather than steel. The manifestations of what Cowen and Siciliano (2011) have called "surplus masculinity" are complex, articulated otherwise across lines of difference.

The economic might of internationalized racial supremacies has meant that industry proper has been re-signified, becoming a mark of national and human debility rather than strength. Just as in the industrial past where colonial nations were rendered racially inferior by the machine's lack, today, it is the machine's *presence* that racially marks bodies and nations as inferior. Associated with sweatshops, forced labor, nonunionized labor, and export processing zones, the machine has been de-linked from white racial and national pride. The industrial paternal has simultaneously been recuperated as an affirming agent of transformation. New lines of identification today proceed through consumption-oriented lines of investments—finance, retail, restaurants, and so on—that require concerted militarization and securitization to proceed. Racialized finance-capital elites are those best positioned to capitalize on the cheapest goods made in the cheapest places by the racialized poor.

From the perspective of racial supremacy, the machine has become a punitive masculinist device levied by racial hegemons operating transnationally across class lines. The monumental efficiencies of today's machinery and the heightened racialization and transnationalization of class relations offer little with which subalterns can identify and affirm. The machine, it appears, has taken on almost eugenic proportions, helping to separate out the pure from the racially abject and dirty, a compensatory gesture that helps to keep the good father intact.

Acknowledgements

I am grateful to Jo Alyson Parker for alerting me to the Mrs Dalloway passage and for discussing with me ideas about the libidinized sadistic qualities of clock time. Additional thanks go to Rachael Dimit, research assistant extraordinaire, and to Norma Moruzzi and Dacia Harrold for their careful reads. A longer version of this article is forthcoming in *Psychoanalytic Inquiry*.

References

Adas, M. 1989. *Machines as the Measure of Men: Science, Technology, and Ideologies of Western Dominance.* Ithaca, NY: Cornell University Press.

Barrett, M. and McIntosh, M. 1980. The "family wage": some problems for socialists and feminists. *Capital and Class*, 4, 51–72.

Bartoletti, S.C. 1996. *Growing up in Coal Country.* New York: Houghton Mifflin.

Berg, M. 1991. Women's work and the industrial revolution. *Refresh: Recent Findings of Research in Social & Economic History*, 12(Spring), 1–4.

Boydston, J. 1990. *Home and Work: Housework, Wages and the Ideology of Labor in the Early Republic.* Oxford: Oxford University Press

Chaplin, Charlie. 1936. *Modern Times.* Directed and produced by Charlie Chaplin.

Connell, R.W. 1995. *Masculinities.* Cambridge: Polity Press.

Coontz, S. 1993. Review of home and work by Jeanne Boydston. *International Review of Social History*, 38(2), 247–52.

Cowen, D. and Siciliano, A. 2011. Surplus masculinities and security. *Antipode*, 43(5), 1516–41.

Du Bois, W.E.B. 1965. *Black Reconstruction in America: An Essay Toward a History of the Part Which Black Folk Played in the Attempt to Reconstruct Democracy in America, 1860–1880.* New York: The Free Press.

Ettinger, B.L. 2007. From proto-ethical compassion to responsibility: besideness and the three primal mother-phantasies of not-enoughness, devouring, and abandonment. *Athena: Philosophical Studies*, 2, 11–145. Available at: www.ceeol.com [accessed: 23 April 2014].

Foster, H. 1997. Prosthetic Gods. *Modernism/Modernity*, 4(2), 5–38.

Freedman, R. 1994. *Kids at Work: Lewis Hine and the Crusade against Child Labor.* New York: Houghton Mifflin.

Freud, S. 1961 [1931]. Female sexuality. *The Standard Edition of the Works of Sigmund Freud* XXI. London: Hogarth, 225–43.

Huyssen, A. 1981–82. The vamp and the machine: technology and sexuality in Fritz Lang's *Metropolis*. *New German Critique* No. 24/25, Special Double Issue on New German Cinema, 221–37.

Keaton, Buster. 1926. *The General*. Directed by Buster Keaton. USA: United Artists.

Kornweibel Jr., Th. 2010. *Railroads in the African American Experience: A Photographic Journey*. Baltimore: Johns Hopkins University.

Lacan, J. 1994 [1956–57]. *Le Seminaire de Jacques Lacan. Livre IX. La relation d'objet*. Ed. Jacques-Alain Miller. Paris: Seuil.

Lacan, J. 2002 [1958]. The signification of the phallus. *Écrits: The First Complete Edition in English*, translated by Bruce Fink. New York: W.W. Norton & Company.

Lang, Fritz. 1927. *Metropolis*. Directed by Fritz Lang. Germany: Universum Film.

Licht, W. 1983. *Working for the Railroad: The Organization of Work in the Nineteenth Century*. Princeton: Princeton University Press.

MacKenzie, S. and Rose, D. 1983. Industrial change, the domestic economy, and home life. *Redundant Spaces in Cities and Regions*, edited by J. Anderson, S. Duncan and R. Hudson. London: Academic Press, 155–200.

Marx, K. 1915. *Capital: A Critique of Political Economy, Volume 1*, edited by Fredrich Engels. Chicago: Charles H. Kerr & Company.

Nast, H.J. 2002. Queer patriarchies, queer racisms, international. *Antipode*, 34(5), 939–74.

Nelson, S.R. 2006. *Steel Drivin' Man: John Henry, the Untold Story*. Oxford: Oxford University Press.

O'Brien, P. 1993. Metal and meat—the human in the age of non-biological reproduction. *Circa*, 65, 22–7.

Szasz, T.S. 1958. Men and machines. *The British Journal for the Philosophy of Science*, 8(32), 310–17.

Tati, Jacques. 1958. *Mon Oncle*. Directed and produced by Jacque Tati.

Thomas III, W.G. 2011. *The Iron Way: Railroads, the Civil War, and the Making of Modern America*. New Haven: Yale University Press.

Thompson, E.P. 1967. Time, work-discipline, and industrial capitalism. *Past and Present*, 38, 56–97.

Welter, B. 1966. The cult of true womanhood, 1820–1860. *American Quarterly*, 18, 151–74.

Wigley, M. 1992. Untitled: the housing of gender, in *Sexuality and Space*, edited by Beatrix Colomina. Princeton, NJ: Princeton Architectural Press, 327–89.

Woolf, V. 2005 [1925]. *Mrs. Dalloway*. Orlando: Harcourt Books.
Zelizer, V. 1985. *Pricing the Priceless Child*. New York: Basic Books.

Chapter 16

A Small Narrow Space:
Postcolonial Territorialization
and the Libidinal Economy

Maureen Sioh

Gunboats are no longer necessary ... it is really much cheaper ... to use [financial] pressure in order to achieve the effect of colonisation.

Mahathir Mohamad

[T]he unconscious is a large hall and consciousness is a small narrow space.

Sigmund Freud

This chapter explores the motivations behind the foreign direct investment (FDI) decisions in the last decade of an East Asian Government Linked Corporation (GLC), the largest company in the world of its kind in terms of agricultural specialization, as it has expanded operations into Asia and Africa. The African plantations had been abandoned by a subsidiary of the GLC because of labor unrest and subsequent financial losses. If the motivation is always profit, why did the GLC take over the African venture? The conventional explanation by business commentators and political economists for investment decisions is profit. What other motive could there be?

To write about the economy is to broach the battleground between our desires and their distorted twin, anxiety. Chalmers Johnson (1982: 25) recognized these stakes as the driving force behind economic growth when he described it as "arising from a desire to assume full human status and compelling others to treat it as an equal." Thus, the tensions between costs and rewards are high; as Johnson implies, to succeed is to assume the pleasures of full human status, whereas to fail is to confirm one's darkest anxieties of selfhood. Astutely, Johnson extended insights on anxiety usually confined to the domain of the individual psyche and interpersonal relationships to nation-states and international relations. Using the psychoanalytical framework of the libidinal economy as a set of affect-driven decisions, I examine how anxiety, the insatiable lack in the libidinal drive, is acted out in the global economy. I rework concepts of the traumatic moment, anxiety, and the defense mechanisms of fetishism and cathexis to analyze the GLC's hyper-reproduction of capital as territorial displacements of the libidinal economy. Thus, libidinal economies invest political economic decisions with the savage competition beyond the endpoint of pure material accumulation. Specifically, I argue that FDI for emerging economies in East Asia became a defensive strategy to counter their anxieties of financial predation as a proxy territorialization strategy by western actors during the Asian Financial Crisis of 1997–98. While inward FDI has long been used to upgrade a country's international position, the Asian financial crisis changed *how* FDI was used to strengthen competiveness in the affected countries (Goldstein and Pavanond 2008: 419). During the financial crisis, anxieties of imperialism were triggered by the predatory actions of western private and public sector actors (Sioh 2010). Using one GLC as an illustration, I argue that in the aftermath of the crisis, the home country, as with many East Asian countries, embarked on a two-fold strategy to carve out financial space to buffer itself from the predatory tactics of western countries. The defensive response depended on a preemptive strategy to carve out financial territory as sovereignty buffers through accumulating financial reserves and OFDI. I am arguing that one of the most far-reaching financial strategies of our time can best be understood as a defensive mechanism that is affect-driven by historical legacies reaccentuated through the contemporary competition of hyper-capitalism.

East Asian emerging economies, many of which are also post-colonial, have become significant actors in globalization processes accounting for 50 percent of the inward FDI but also 27 percent of outward FDI, henceforth referred to as OFDI (UNCTAD 2012), while their GLCs are some of the biggest multinationals in terms of capitalization—4 out of the top 10 in the world in 2012 (http://www.gfmag.com/tools/global-database/economic-data/11935-largest-companies.html). These GLCs are spearheading the economic *and* geopolitical strategies of emerging economies as they participate as active shapers of globalization through their investments. In the process, they are also reconceptualizing what territory means to the nation-state in the era of globalization. The corollary, not surprisingly, is that their global rise has been accompanied by friction which Goldstein (2009: xviii–8) describes as triggering off a new *Great Game*, the term used to describe the nineteenth-century imperial competition for territory.

Explaining Investment Motivations

So far, I have been trying to unpack the emotional stakes that anchor economic decisions. These, in globalization, are underwritten by a value system derived from implicit political, cultural and racial hierarchies that have evolved historically and continue to build on the anxieties of the consequences of being on the losing end of global competitions. While there is no consensus explaining the motivations of emerging economy OFDI trends, the most popular international business model is the eclectic paradigm, which even its proponents agree is an ad hoc assembly of factors based on minimizing transaction costs (Sauvant 2008; Ramamurti 2010). Studies on multinationals from emerging economies have focused mainly on the private sector (Sauvant 2008; Ramamurti 2010) and even those focusing on GLCs have assessed success solely from the criterion of profit maximization (Ghesquiere 2007; Buckley et al. 2008; Fleury and Fleury 2010; Williamson and Zheng 2010). However, if we accept that GLC policies are determined by the "rules of the game" (Ghesquiere 2007; Buckley et al. 2008; Goldstein 2009) that implicitly include cultural and political considerations, then we need a better understanding of what constitutes those rules.

North (http://www.nobelprize.org/nobel_prizes/economics/laureates/1993/north-lecture.html), whose views I summarize below, coined the expression "rules of the game" which retained traditional economic assumptions of scarcity and hence competition, but concentrated on how cultural values inform economic aspirations and are acquired collectively and intergenerationally. Institutions, in North's conception, are humanly devised constraints that structure human interaction and can be formal as in laws and constitutions, or informal such as norms and conventions. He said, "Our theory must include ... the processes that generated the actor's subjective representation of the decision problem, his or her frame." And, "History demonstrates that ideas, ideologies, myths, dogmas and prejudices matter." But what are the rules in a libidinal economy? This study begins with the premise that the rules of the new Great Game involve a complex dynamic between emerging economies and their more established competition that are framed by perceptions of threats to their sovereignty and, thus, survival. Virtual economic space has become the synecdoche for territorial control, yet the libidinal stakes inherent mean that the rules of global capitalist engagement can only be glimpsed through disavowals and displaced associations.

Neo-Imperialism aka the GOD Imperative

David Harvey (1984, 2005, 2011) has articulated over the long span of his career that imperialism and now globalization, the contemporary stand-in term for capital's geographical expansion, is the logical result of a crisis of over-accumulation which would otherwise lower profit margins. In this argument, capital in its search for surplus value invests in real estate transforming ground rent into fictitious capital through speculative profit. The geographical expansion of capital is often referred to as the "grow or die" or GOD imperative (Schweickart 2009; Kallis 2011). Referring to the speculative nature of the profit, Benjamin Kunkel (2011: 12) refers to it as "capitalism's geography of anxious anticipation." While territorial forms of social organization and place-making have existed throughout history, they have been transformed by capital accumulation and circulation to create new maps of political power (Sassen 2006; Harvey 2011). Harvey (2011: 205) defines territorial logic as political, diplomatic, economic and military strategies deployed by the state in its own interest. By this definition, I argue that GLCs are territorial in their activity. If command over space is a form of social power exercised by a group, conversely, preempting control over space is to deny social power. It follows that perceptions of security and threat can be invoked to mobilize collective action (Castells 1992). We need to understand how these perceptions articulate with the "anxious anticipation" to underwrite hyper-capitalism's new Great Game.

Psychoanalytical Approaches

For Sigmund Freud (1965: 84) ideology and material conditions could never entirely explain social behavior as "'Mankind' never lives entirely in the present." If the unconscious is that part of our mental life that operates out of sight to influence our actions powerfully then any theory of motivation must describe and explain the framework through which we know the world. And this framework may persist, even as its existence is disavowed when faced with other evidence, because it was formed in such emotionally or physically threatening conditions (Kahn 2002: 8–9). Freud (1966: 340) used trauma such as war and physical accidents as models of the threats that produce anxiety. The term anxiety, derived from *angst*, a compound of *angustiae* and *enge* which in the original German and Latin words mean "narrow place" and "straits," has a two-fold origin—as a direct consequence of the traumatic moment and as a signal anticipating the moment repeating itself (Freud 1965: 118, 1966: 493, note 9). Freud distinguished between realistic anxiety, which is "intelligible" as a signal to expect injury from an external threat, and neurotic anxiety which is "free floating" and attaches itself to any possibility that threatens the loss of love (Freud 1965: 103, 110, 116). Cathexis, the resultant defensive mechanism against anxiety, is an unconscious process by which libidinal energy is displaced onto certain practices and objects (Freud 1965: 104, 1966: 515). Without implying too literally a commensurable relationship, Freud's (1962b: 62–4) German term for cathexis, "*besetzung*" has a territorial connotation meaning to occupy or fill a space. This study, recall, is about the motivation for postcolonial extra-territorialization.

I suggest that the process through which an individual fears loss of love can find its group correlate in the fear of humiliation and loss of social power of which the (once-)colonized is a good example. Moreover, Freud's distinction between real and neurotic anxiety is less likely to hold the lower down the economic food chain individuals or countries are positioned as the threat to survival becomes very real. According to Jean Francois Lyotard (Cooper and Murphy 1999: 231) every economic exchange has an incommensurability not captured in political economy. This incommensurability is most apparent in counter-intuitive decisions that can best be understood as a set of affect-driven decisions, in other words a libidinal economy. But as I noted at the start, libidinal economies invest political economic decisions with a savage competition beyond the endpoint of material accumulation. Within the framework of a libidinal economy, we can ask, *after* Johnston (2004: 263), how an emerging economy constructs the meaning about its participation in the international political economy. But first, two methodological points need to be raised. Can we extend influences beyond the family to the larger social realm? And do groups and individuals respond in the same manner given similar affective triggers? To answer no in one or both cases assumes that an essential difference exists between intra-subjective and intersubjective dynamics (Johnston 2004: 259–60). And Freud himself (1959, 1962a, 1965: 84–5) extended the psyche to groups including nations.

Foregrounding psychoanalysis in political economy, particularly in a racialized context, Frantz Fanon (1967) argued that colonial anxieties were anchored in the socio-economic realities of powerlessness and its attendant humiliations experienced by the colonized. Fanon's contribution to postcolonial analysis lies in understanding the psychopolitics that connects subjectivity under oppression to political pathologies (Hook 2004). Fanon (1967: 134) poignantly describes the experience of living within a dominant culture as "meaning that was already there, pre-existing, waiting for me." The alienation from indigenous value systems that tracks itself to colonialism is one of the norms of a valorized Western modernity which has become internalized by postcolonial subjects. That these are also subjects of contemporary economic globalization mean that they continue to live according to the rules of the game that have been devised elsewhere (Sioh 2010).

For Lacan, desire is not a biological drive but a seeking of recognition from the Other (Lacan 2002: 181). Humiliation is the experience of the Other's negative evaluation of oneself, not necessarily the gaze we actually encounter, but how we *think* we appear to the Other (Adamson and Clark 1999: 8–9) This is especially true of the idealized Other. Anxiety manifests itself in the form of both what is feared *and* what is desired. The abjected (humiliated) self simultaneously desires and internalizes the characteristics of the powerful Other (Fanon 1967: 18, 43–7, 111, 161–5). Thus, the postcolonial subject experiences anxiety about future humiliation as a legacy of collective past humiliations and reconstructs this abjected self-image each time it imagines itself incorporating the values of western, capitalist modernity such as those of the international financial system. Simultaneously, the subject seeks to disassociate and disavow the abjected part whether it be racial identity or association with the state. For the purposes of this chapter, a logical extension of this insight is that the abjected subject cathects to certain financial practices as a defense against the anxiety of potential humiliation.

Teresa Brennan's work links spatial constriction, aggression and anxiety to create a framework of a libidinal economy that explains modern political economy, particularly imperialism. For Brennan (1993: 11–2) the defining trait of powerlessness lies in immobility or constraint in space. In a libidinal economy, anxiety of powerlessness is resolved through the cathexis that breaks the constraint, which in my argument results in territorial expansion through OFDI. When history and political economy interact with the collective psyche in many emerging economies, I am arguing, after Fanon and Brennan, that the traumatic moment lies in the colonial encounter when capitalism induces scarcity in the local population by appropriating agricultural land. But the powerless impotence in the face of this externally induced scarcity results in more than just an immediate material lack; it results in anxiety whenever the memory is invoked in the future. Yet, in Brennan's (1993: 41–9, 80–81) schema, neo-imperialist fantasies of expansion can never banish anxiety because they generate anxieties of retaliation leading to further aggression. For the rest of my chapter, I will illustrate how one GLC cathects to investment such as OFDI, directed to the accumulation of different fetishes, as its conception of defending national sovereignty evolves from controlling more land (physical territory) to controlling non-land based forms of territory, that is, virtual economic space.

The Narrow Space of the Postcolonial Nation

The EGLC in question is an East Asian publicly traded, multinational conglomerate with a workforce of over 100,000 employees established by the British in 1910 before being nationalized in 1981. Its directors tend to be ex-politicians or senior civil servants and its majority shareholder is a government trust agency; this point is significant in light of the subsequent disavowals of government association in the interviews I conducted. Its investments range across energy, utilities, property and healthcare in 20 countries although its core revenue generator remains agricultural. In the early 2000s the national government realigned its globalization strategy to exploit its strengths in the agricultural sector. Its landbank currently stands at over 800,000 hectares and is the largest in the world as it prepares to expand another 300,000 hectares.

Iconography

Regional business culture recognizes that the myths and beliefs of a GLC frame its decision-making. In 2012, to celebrate national Independence Day, the GLC released a commercial that encapsulates within a minute its perception of its role in national mythology. Beginning with the symbolism of a seedling being planted by an older white male and ending with a seedling being planted by a small Asian girl, the commercial sends the message that the agent of national history has changed; moreover, by the switch in gender, that the nation is progressive and inclusive. This message is reinforced by the accents of the narrators seemingly transitioning from older western male to younger Asian male then to an Asian female, although the diction of the speakers implies that class background remains constant. The commercial then lists the traumatic moments in national history claiming that the GLC has stood shoulder-to-shoulder with the nation before summarizing its role in the nation's patrimony by reducing foreign ownership (re-territorialization) and globalizing its business operations (extra-territorialization). Before analyzing the GLC's expansionary policies from a psychoanalytic perspective, I briefly want to summarize the practical material justification. Countries that emerged out of the Asian financial crisis in better shape than their neighbors exploited the firesale of assets, including plantations, elsewhere. Additionally, the high price of commodities in 2007–08 encouraged the government to pursue an aggressive expansionary policy. Unfortunately, many East Asian countries perceive Africa as the last "available" land mass.

In the following pages, unless a source is attributed, all information was obtained through personal interviews. The primary criterion for the interviewees was that they had to have had a senior role in the GLC's major investment decisions. In keeping with the narrative structure that the interviewees used which, incidentally, coincides with the libidinal economy framework, I begin with a description and analysis of the GLC's expansionary practices (cathexis) with particular attention to the counterintuitive decisions, then the justifications that reference anxiety ([dis]associations and disavowals), through which I link to the traumatic moment of colonialism.

Cathexis

Internal Territorialization

Government takeover of the GLC, then a private company, began in 1976 as part of the larger strategy to nationalize commodity companies. While the strategy made sense from an economic perspective—commodities were the country's main income generator—the strategy went beyond economic. In business deals, the intuition is to bargain to get the best price possible to ensure the highest profit. While it makes sense for the sellers to boast of getting the maximum price, buyers rarely advertise getting the worst of the deal. Yet participants on *both* sides of the negotiation agreed that the government paid above market value. But the symbolism inherent in the repatriation of control of the companies that were the most visible agents of colonialism had a priceless significance more important than even the national oil company and current top revenue earner because of the "land dimension." Interviewees told me that their brief was a "conscious decision to nationalize the company" and eventually to refocus growth through investment in Asia rather than Europe even if European investments were seen as safer choices at the time in terms of guaranteed profit.

We see a turn towards investment rather than outright commodity production in the 1970s and 1980s, in the 1990s as the proportion of the GLC's activities switched, supposedly to reflect government instructions that it become more activist in investment, leading the GLC to take on the management of troubled banks and environmentally controversial projects that had symbolic value. In the late 1990s, influential businessmen advised the Prime Minister to merge the plantation companies as part of a strategy "to create a global presence" for the nation. The idea stalled owing to the Asian financial crisis but was revived in 2005. The GLC was chosen to head the merger bypassing other GLCs with more experience because the latter's corporate culture had "stayed very British." While the primary concern driving decision-making remains national control as a defense against neo-imperial predation, the cathexis switches from a focus on land within national borders to controlling credit availability. In each case described above, the decision can be viewed as counterintuitive from a profit maximization motive.

Extra-territorialization

If the GLC was nationalized to control key resources from 1980s onwards, the reconceptualization of what was considered a national resource, that is, no longer a place-specific tangible object but social power in the control of its agents, meant that GLCs were slated to spearhead investment in high risk areas that were seen as politically necessary even if financially risky. Interviewees revealed a keen susceptibility among the national elites to the notion that to be a viable sovereignty required a global presence as early as the 1980s, long before mainstream development studies caught up with the economic rise of East Asia. Similarly, as in the case of internal territorialization, the orders to embrace risky ventures such as investment in Oman and Qatar and Central Asia meant counter-intuitively abandoning lucrative activities domestically. Interviewees emphasized that the GLC's African ventures, as in their other extra-territorial ventures, should be contextualized within a larger geopolitical strategy of south–south cooperation which began in the early 2000s, plausibly accounting for why investment in African countries continues despite losses. To apply Cooper's and Murphy's (1999) insights, the GLC's actions, unaccountable from a profit motive, indicate the presence instead of a libidinal investment. Recall that if anxiety is defined as a narrow space and cathexis is at root about occupation (Freud 1966: 340, 1962b: 62–4) and Brennan (1993: 11–12) links constraint and anxiety to aggressive expansion, we can read the GLC's extra-territorial ventures as attempts to create a defensive buffer beyond the constraints of national borders. The GOD imperative in action can be seen literally as escaping the narrow space through occupation of other spaces.

Anxious Anticipation

The above described extra-territorial investments can be adduced partly to a reasonably justifiable anxiety born of economic over-reliance on a scarce resource—oil. Currently, 40 percent of the country's GDP is thought to be funded by oil revenues and the time-frame of 30 years of oil income has thrown the government back to relying once again on the plantation sector. More intriguingly, the country's extra-territorial strategy after the Asian financial crisis may have originated in the Gunboat Diplomacy Ver. 2.0 seen during the Crisis. The Malaysian Prime Minister Mahathir, observing the IMF enforced sale of national assets in the affected Asian countries that evoked the powerlessness and anxiety described by Fanon (1967), reflected widespread Asian anxiety when he remarked "Gunboats are no longer necessary ... it is really much cheaper ... to use [economic] pressure in order to achieve the effect of colonisation" (Lim et al. 1998: 97). Traditionally, to use gunboats is to besiege a place and constrain its peoples within that place; in a globalized economy, constraint is achieved through financial tactics. But if financial practices are the modern version of besieging a country, then financial practices can be a way of breaking the siege and pre-empting future sieges. Moreover, recall Brennan's (1993: 41–9, 80–81) point that each expansionary act feeds into a cycle of further expansion. In the aftermath of the crisis, OFDI became a priority for just about every rising East Asian economy. Tracking the anxieties of resource scarcity to that of neo-imperial humiliation, the conviction among my interviewees was that their role was to "protect national assets."

I would argue that the GLC's policy shifts, as the agent of national economic and geopolitical strategy, takes place in this context in which OFDI becomes the cathected practice that creates virtual economic buffer space rather than fixing on land as a defensive fetish against the anxieties of neo-imperial victimization. The country's Prime Minister stressed that landbanks would take up only 10 percent of investments in the future. This can be tied to the attempt to escape the dilemma posed by tying up capital in fixed assets such as real estate which is prone to depreciation. In contrast, the strategy of non-fixed assets in the form of OFDI as pre-emptive counter-territorialization of economic buffer space allows the break up and reassembling of symbolic territory in more stable financial markets. It is notable that the majority of the emerging economy OFDI is headed towards the global north, since in this case, profits and protecting national sovereignty or championing its profile coincide. According to my own calculations derived from the most recently reported complete central bank figures in 2010, East Asian countries held reserves amounting to 1/3 of the US debt or $4 trillion; since then, China alone has raised that figure by over a trillion dollars.

Rules of the Game: "[T]he meaning that was there ... waiting for me"

One of my conundrums in this study was whether it was possible to trace a common root to the anxiety that permeated the interviews. If we accept a psychoanalytic explanation for the investment decisions in this study, the common root must lie in a traumatic moment even if anxiety is associated with a variety of triggers (Freud 1965: 103, 110, 116–18). Instead, given the emotional stakes in a libidinal economy, the anxieties voiced traced back to associations the speakers wanted to make or disavow, thereby implying internalization of a default value system rather than referencing a specific moment. My task was to identify common themes that underwrote those values which could be linked to each other and to an historical moment in which they originated.

When I began this study, I referred to the GLC as a state-owned enterprise. While I expected to be challenged on this definition, I was surprised at the insistence of all my interviewees on contesting the term quite vehemently, finally agreeing on the term government-linked corporation. Moreover, all the interviewees, while accepting that the GLC was a government vehicle, were keen to insist that at least until the 1990s, in a number of cases pushing the date to the 2000s, government policy influence was minimal. Yet, as I have stated earlier, there is no dispute that the directors and members of the board of both the GLC and its majority shareholders were politicians or civil servants strongly identified with the state. The common theme was an anxiety about being associated with the state to the point that disavowal or even degrees of disassociation mattered. Certainly, even in many western countries, notably the United States, we have become used to the public discourse denigrating associations with the public sector as signifying inferior performance standards. In the case of this GLC, one interviewee described it as not possessing a "culture of excellence" claiming that "they were not used to working hard" and had "a 9 to 5 mentality." Two interviewees described it as having a "public sector mentality" where employees and employer alike began with "high expectations and high performance" but eventually dropped down to the "institutional level."

In a culture that eschews psychoanalytical explanations at the personal level, psychoanalytical vocabulary gleams through most of the interviews when assessing GLC economic performance. One interviewee began by saying ironically, "[I]f the country could only get its act together, it was frightening to think how much it could achieve. As it is, it wasn't doing too badly." Regardless of the opening preamble, the conversation would then move on to racial identity anxiety that was linked to a "psychology of crisis" that framed economic decision-making. A basic assumption in all the speakers but one was an association between race and competence. Fanon (1967: 134) might have recognized the assumption as the meaning already there awaiting us. One interviewee claimed that if financial losses became severe, the GLC would appoint the most competent candidates before pointing out the racial background of various competent decision-makers. I use race rather than ethnicity in keeping with the term used by the interviewees. Interestingly, all the speakers distinguished between the different nationalities of the GLCs that saw losses during the financial crisis. While their *own* losses were attributed to incompetence, other national losses were attributed to global events beyond their management's control. We see Fanon's (1967: 18, 43–7, 111, 161–5) psychopolitics at work in the acceptance of a racialized hierarchy of competence in the abjected subject that has internalized and situates itself within a value system that is a legacy of the colonialism.

Contradictorily, even when criticizing a public sector mentality interviewees were convinced that the state had a significant role in education, environment and infrastructure (health was not mentioned) even as the speakers sought to distance themselves from appearing to be directed by it. One interviewee who described himself as a Thatcherite, went on to list all the irreplaceable roles played by the state, emphatically stating that inequality hurts everyone in the end. The central theme that emerged from the interviews was the need to protect national assets in a global world. It bears remembering that all my interviewees are extremely successful in the global economy and have little personal anxiety about their economic standing. But contradicting western business models that claim nationality and culture have little bearing on competitiveness, they acutely recognize the realities of differential cultural power in making the rules of the global market. Perhaps the capacity to ignore cultural and geopolitical power in slanting outcomes in the global economy is simply a privilege of those born on the winning side for the last 250 years. Finally, while the theme of anxiety and not measuring up to global capitalism's predatory standards came up again and again, no one extolled the pleasures of capitalist success. The few positive comments all had to do with the success of infrastructure provision be it transportation or telecommunications, especially the internet. The delights of the temples to consumption that lay all around us during the interviews did not merit any positive comment on achievement, and two interviewees went so far as to decry the vulgarity of the symbols of capitalist achievement.

The Insatiability of the Great Game

If the greatest anxiety for these emerging economies is the helplessness in the face of neo-imperialism manifested as financial practices, then the counter-strategy is to pre-empt the financial siege by embarking on an extra-territorialization strategy themselves and creating economic buffer space through OFDI. Using one GLC's investment strategies for illustrative purposes, I have argued that we cannot understand political economy, in this case OFDI decisions, without understanding the affects rooted in history that drive these decisions, an explanatory framework I have termed the libidinal economy. The GLC's policy transformations and subsequent economic activities are rooted in an evolving national identity bequeathed by colonialism and struggle to compete in the global market. These actions have inaugurated a new Great Game resulting in more participants. Interestingly, the tension between the anxiety and pleasures of capitalist competition and success that I expected to find were not borne out in the interviews in this study where anxiety was predominant. It seems that the Great Game is insatiable and every expansion brooks a new round of aggression in the increasingly savage competitions of hyper-capitalism. If striving for economic growth is to strive for full human status as Johnson (1981: 25) noted, then participants will yield no quarter.

Acknowledgements

I am grateful for the support extended by DePaul University and the Department of Geography. My thanks also to Lee Yoke Har for her help and encouragement.

References

Adamson, J. and Clark, H. 1999. Introduction: shame, affect, writing, in *Scenes of Shame: Psychoanalysis, Shame and Writing*, edited by J. Adamson and H. Clark. Albany: SUNY Press, 1–34.

Brennan, T. 1993. *History After Lacan*. London and New York: Routledge.

Buckley, P., Clegg, J., Cross, A., Voss, H., Rhodes, M. and Zheng, P. 2008. Explaining China's outward FDI: an institutional perspective, in *The Rise of Transnational Corporations from Emerging Markets: Threat or Opportunity?* edited by K.P. Sauvant. Cheltenham: Edward Elgar, 107–57.

Castells, M. 1992. Four Asian tigers with a dragon head: a comparative analysis of the state, economy and society, in *States and Development in the Asia Pacific Rim*, edited by R. Appelbaum and J. Henderson. Newbury Park: Sage Publications, 33–70.

Cooper, B. and Murphy, M. 1999. "Libidinal economics": Lyotard and accounting for the unaccountable, in *The New Economic Critcism: Studies at the intersection of Literature and Economics*, edited by M. Woodmansee and M. Osteen. London and New York: Routledge, 229–41.

Fanon, F. 1967. *Black Skin, White Masks*, translated by C.L. Markmann. New York: Grove Press.

Fleury, A. and Fleury, M.T.L. 2010. Brazilian multinationals: surfing the waves of internationalization, in *Emerging Multinationals from Emerging Markets*, edited by R. Ramamurti and J. Singh. Cambridge, UK and New York: Cambridge University Press, 200–243.

Freud, S. 1959. *Group Psychology and the Analysis of the Ego*, translated by the Institute of Psycho-Analysis and A. Richards. New York and London: W.W. Norton and Company, Inc.

Freud, S. 1962a. *Civilization and Its Discontents*, translated by J. Strachey. New York and London: W.W. Norton and Company, Inc.

Freud, S. 1962b (1894). *The Standard Edition of the Complete Psychological Works of Sigmund Freud*, edited and translated by J. Strachey, Vol. 3. London: Hogarth Press.

Freud, S. 1965 (1933). *New Introductory Lectures on Psycho-Analysis*, translated by J. Strachey. The Standard Edition. New York: W.W. Norton.

Freud, S. 1966 (1920). *Introductory Lectures on Psycho-Analysis*, translated by James Strachey. The Standard Edition. New York: W.W. Norton.

Ghesquire, H. 2007. *Singapore's Success: Engineering Economic Growth*. Singapore: Thompson Learning.

Goldstein, A. 2009. *Multinational Companies from Emerging Economies: Composition, Conceptualization and Direction in the Global Economy.* Basingstoke: Palgrave.

Goldstein, A. and Pavanond, P. 2008. Singapore Inc. goes shopping abroad: profit and pitfalls. *Journal of Contemporary Asia*, 38(3), 417–38.

Harvey, D. 1984. *Limits to Capital.* London: Verso.

Harvey, D. 2005. *A Brief History of Neoliberalism.* Oxford: Oxford University Press.

Harvey, D. 2011. *The Enigma of Capital.* Oxford: Oxford University Press.

Hook, D. 2004. Frantz Fanon, Steve Biko, "psychopolitics," in critical psychology, in *Critical Psychology*, edited by D. Hook. Landsdowne: UCT Press, 85–114.

Kahn, M. 2002. *Basic Freud: Psychoanalytic Thought for the 21st Century.* New York: Basic Books.

Kallis, G. 2011. In defence of growth, in *Ecological Economics*, 70(5), 873–80.

Kunkel, B. 2011. How much is too much? in *London Review of Books*, 3 February, 9–14.

Johnson, C. 1982. *MITI and the Japanese Miracle: The Growth of Industry Policy 1925–1975.* Stanford: Stanford University Press.

Johnston, A. 2004. The cynic's fetish; Slavoj Žižek and the dynamics of belief. *Psychoanalysis, Culture and Society*, 9(3), 259–83.

Lacan, J. 2002. *Écrits: A Selection*, translated by B. Fink, H. Fink and R. Grigg. New York: W.W. Norton & Co.

Lim, K.W., Ho, R. and Yee, M.F. 1998. *Hidden Agenda.* Kuala Lumpur: Limkokwing Integrated Sdn Bhd.

Ramamurti, R. 2010. Why study emerging-market multinationals?, in *Emerging Multinationals from Emerging Markets*, edited by R. Ramamurti and J. Singh. Cambridge, UK and New York: Cambridge University Press, 3–22.

Sassen, S. 2006. *Territory, Authority, Rights: From Medieval to Global Assemblages.* Princeton: Princeton University Press.

Sauvant, K.P. 2008. The rise of TNCs from emerging markets: the issues, in *The Rise of Transnational Corporations from Emerging Markets: Threat or Opportunity?*, edited by K.P. Sauvant. Cheltenham: Edward Elgar, 3–14.

Saw, S.H. and Low, L. 2009. *Sovereign Wealth Funds.* Singapore: Saw Centre for Financial Studies.

Schweickart, D. 2009. Is sustainable capitalism an oxymoron? *Perspectives on Global Development and Technology*, 8(2–3), 559–80.

Sioh, M. 2010. The hollow within: anxiety and performing postcolonial financial policies. *Third World Quarterly*, 31(4), 581–98.

UNCTAD. 2012. *World Investment Report 2012*. Available at: http://www.unctad-docs.org/files/UNCTAD-WIR2012-Chapter-I-en.pdf [accessed: 23 April 2014].

Williamson, P. and Zheng, M. 2010. Chinese multinationals: emerging through new global gateways, in *Emerging Multinationals from Emerging Markets*, edited by R. Ramamurti and J. Singh. Cambridge, UK and New York: Cambridge University Press, 81–109.

Chapter 17

The Uncanny in the Beauty Salon

Elizabeth R. Straughan

Relating to the Skin

In this chapter I consider the experience of receiving facial treatment in the context of the beauty salon where, as Kafka describes, 'the process of growing old and becoming dirty and wrinkled ... [as] matter of negligence and fault' (in Benthian 2002: 111), is being fought. That is, the contemporary beauty industry has taken the ephemeral nature of youthful skin into account and developed what it contends to be, a means of slowing down the ageing process with the use of cosmeceuticals. Considered to straddle the divide between drug and cosmetic, these are anti-ageing skin care products such as microdermabrasion kits, chemical peels, and serums, products that have disease fighting, or healing properties (Mukul et al. 2011). Resonating with the science of 'regenerative medicine', which claims to recharge cells, such products offer a space for 'create[ing] a new set of social relations ...' (Hogle 2003: 62) and in so doing signals that '[l]ike Space, like Place, skin is never just one thing, nor does it make just one geography' (Pile 2010: 38).

It is to the relations and power dynamics that play out in the process of encountering such products in the form of facial treatment that this chapter attends, through an analysis of this experience, which accounts for the sense of touch as a sense capable of generating 'qualities of feeling' in line with the uncanny (Freud 2003). While geographers have produced psychoanalytic considerations of urban spaces and dynamics of power and politics at work within such sites (Pile 1996; Hook 2005), in this chapter I attend to the contact between the bodies of client and beautician within the beauty salon using the psychoanalytic frame of the uncanny as an analytical guide, in order to draw out different (although related) components of vulnerability and politics.

Acknowledgment of the role the sense of touch played in the emergence of the ego, formed part of Freud's initial approach to psychotherapy. This was, however, a short-lived psychotherapeutic foray for Freud and some of his colleagues, as it was felt this sense proved a hindrance to scientific objectivity as 'the dangers of touch within the intimacy of intense transferential relationships' (Eiden 1998), were perceived to evolve into 'a downward spiral [of] full sexual engagement' (Fosshage 2000: 178). Recourse to touch in Freud's clinical practice then, was relegated to its acknowledgment within a client's fantasy world and its role within the Oedipal System (Eiden 1998). Instead Freud argued that the body is '[s]een like any other object' (Freud 1961 [1927]: 25) an observation which directed his sensory focus upon 'visibility', namely of the phallus or lack thereof.

This focus was however, met with critique by feminist theorists who took issue with the representation associated with Freud's focus on the secondary process of this system and its emphasis on the symbolic realm, the phallus. Julia Kristeva for example, found cause for concern with this system's exclusion of the mother and with it the maternal. The maternal was for Kristeva (1982) a means to consider the temporality of materiality, as opposed to its supposed stasis implied by the symbolic, a temporality highlighted in her work on the *abject* which, considered the movement of corporeal fluids from inside the body to outside, a movement which Gambaudo points out, is suggestive of, 'the subject's biology: its origin (the maternal) or its death (waste, decay)' (2007: 121). For Kristeva, then, 'the abject is the equivalent of death' (Kristeva 1982: 26). In her recourse to the maternal and with it the body's materiality, Kristeva notes the inadequacy of a visual focus, highlighting that, '[t]he deepest depths of horror can't be seen, though perhaps they may be heard' (Kristeva in Sjöholm 2005: 101). As such, what Kristeva's abject establishes in critique of Freud phallocentrism, is the centrality of the body's materiality and with it, the corporeal capacity for sensation and transgression beyond both the visual and the living.

Taking stock of this critique, which brings the body's materiality to the fore, I deploy Freud's uncanny as a means of analysing the experience of receiving facial treatment through an acknowledgment of the role the sense of touch plays in this context. In order to relay the uncanny effects of facial treatment, I want to take seriously Royle's assertion that '[i]t is impossible to think about the uncanny without this involving a sense of what is autobiographical, self-centred [and] based in one's own experience' (2003: 16). In order to unpack the uncanny moments woven through this particular facial treatment, this chapter is framed through the narration of a particular cosmeceutical encounter that I experienced in a Washington DC beauty salon, located near to the Association of American Geographers 2010's conference venue. Focusing on the uncanny 'qualities of feeling' mobilised not only by the experience of being touched on the 'passive' surface of my face, but also the emotional responses of the psyche or self to such contact, I draw on Lucé Irigaray (1993) and her concept of 'porosity', by which she refers to the skin's capacity for vulnerability, and the manner in which, entities such as the beauty salon take advantage of the body's continual 'a-morphe' or 'gestations'.

An Autoethnographic Facial

Lured into the Washington DC salon by a half price deal, the facial treatment started like any other I had received in my home country, the UK. I filled out a consultation form in the waiting room amongst the salon hairdressers and their clients before my cosmetologist (or beautician) introduced himself and escorted me upstairs to a treatment room before leaving me to get comfortable. A short while later he returned, dimmed the lights, turned on some relaxing music, put a cap over my hair, sat on a stool by my head and started to gently steam my face. This facial, then, commenced with an array of similarities between its feel and content, in comparison to those facials I had received previously, in London. That is, within this facial as with others, the environment and experience was designed to generate an engineered affective atmosphere (Anderson 2009) through the use of dimmed lights and relaxing music, as well as through the performance of actions, pressures and movements deployed at first, to steam my face (Straughan 2012).

It was not until he started applying the cleanser, smoothing it gently over the skin on my face, that an unfamiliar aspect of this particular treatment started to emerge. Unlike all my previous, UK based facials, the cosmetologist in Washington DC wore plastic gloves. Recollecting an interview held with a beautician in my hometown of Aberystwyth, Wales, I remembered the emphasis that had been placed on the importance of 'feeling' the problems of a client's skin and in so doing questioned the import of those gloves (Straughan 2012). In keeping with Paterson (2007) and Sedgwick's (2003) assertion that touch is part of a sensory collective, it was not so much the feel of the gloves that drew my attention so much as their material qualities, for they rustled and crinkled in contact with my skin as the cleanser was applied. This difference in kind did not cause any anxiety as such, but it does speak to the uncanny, which for Jentche emerges when the familiar becomes unfamiliar causing intellectual uncertainty, a point that Freud takes up. Despite his doubts on the role of intellectual uncertainty for instilling a sense of the uncanny, links between the familiar and unfamiliar signal the crux of Freud's thinking on this concept, that is, the role of recurrence: the compulsion to repeat. As such, Freud was concerned with what had been known, or repressed, secreted away only to reappear as something that 'became alienated to the mind precisely through repression' (Hook 2005: 5).

Following Freud (2003[1919]), Hook (2005) thus suggests the uncanny has to do with a precognitive-gap, whilst Freud himself heralds the import of the unconscious as the key to uncanny qualities of feeling. There is a two-fold explanation for such a gap. On the one hand, the uncanny is bound to a repression of the unconscious that harks back to 'primitive' stages of man and for example, a belief in 'the old, animalistic conception of the universe, which was characterised by the idea that the world was peopled with the spirits of human beings' (Freud 1919: 12). Freud termed this 'narcissistic overestimation of subjective mental processes' the 'omnipotence of thoughts' (Freud 1919: 12), a term that encompassed magical thinking and 'events which question our concept of reality' (Hook 2005: 699). His second explanation however, was concerned with the re-appearance of 'largely forgotten and inaccessible infantile material derived from *repressed realms of the unconscious*' (Hook 2005: 698). Freud was careful to point out that this repression did not involve a 'removal of *belief* in an object's reality (Freud 1919: 17), rather Freud was 'concerned [with] an actual repression of some definite material and a return of this repressed material' (Freud 1919: 17). These two poles of animism and repression are, Hook notes, 'intermingled at the level of experience' (2005: 698) and as such, the uncanny is not only a disjuncture between the body and the soul, but also a disjuncture between the body and history, for the uncanny is a relationship between past and present or, with regards to the case study presented here, between past and present facial treatment.

At this point of the facial however, the gloves proved to be an impediment to a sense of relaxation rather than an uncanny moment, as the plastic rustled in contact with the skin near to my ear. The cosmetologist continued, applying a cleansing cream that he rubbed around my face. A tap was turned on in the sink to the cosmetologist's right, he picked up a towel and soaked it in warm water before lifting it, wringing out the excess, and draping it over my face. Starting at my forehead he folded it down and around my cheeks, padding it as he went. While the warmth of the towel was relaxing in and of itself, this padding acted almost as a gentle massage. A minute or so later the pressure deployed through the towel changed as the dabs turned to wiping movements that felt somewhat harsher, though not unpleasant. The gloves were forgotten.

Such moments draw out the 'psychoanalytic claim that all subjectivity arises initially from the body as a kind of surface of emergence', which Hook states, is to understand that the ego is, 'initially and necessarily bodily in origin' (Hook 2005). However, I want to consider the 'touching' occurring here which, instils my distracted and then relaxed response to the encounter of textures and temperatures as well as the sounds they create, as indicative of an inter-subjectivity encounter. I take my lead here from Irigaray's concept of porosity where she argues that touch has a temporality, it situates the skin as a threshold, opening the body out to possible futures and in so doing highlights the 'state of imperfection, the unfinished condition of every living being' (Irigaray 1993: 192). As Freud and Hook's comments on the role of the familiar and unfamiliar suggest Irigaray's philosophy is of import here, for the uncanny is not simply a disjuncture of the body, but of time as well and is thus bound up with questions of life and death. Questions that suggest our own mortality, to which Freud (2003) acknowledges our unconscious is unreceptive. It is the body's somewhat vulnerable capacity, its 'continual gestation' and openness to change (Irigaray 1993), its temporality, that the beauty industry harnesses in the implementation of skin care through the use of treatments and products. It is to the role that these play within the facial that I now turn.

Uncanny Products

After my skin was cleansed and dried the cosmetologist turned to its exfoliation through the use of an enzyme mask, a product that acts upon the materiality of the epidermis. Using what felt like a thick paintbrush as the method of application he slowly coated my face, starting at my chin, and moving up toward my forehead whilst carefully sweeping around my closed eyes. As the mask was applied I felt a tingling encompass my face and was told this arose from dead cells breaking down as the peel acted on them, signalling the 'active' capacity of this product as it disintegrated my dead skin cells.

The disintegration of skin draws attention to the continual gestation of the body and is for Goethe, an elemental process embraced by a variety of living entities whether 'the bark of trees, the skin of insects, the hair and feather of animals, even the epidermis of man [and woman], [these] are coverings forever being shed, cast off, given over to non-life' (cited in Benthien 2002: 85). Straddling the boundary between the living and the dead, the skin's exfoliation by active products exacerbates not so much a 'casting off' of skin, as a peeling away of the epidermis with a chemical solution that simultaneously smooths the skin and stimulates the dermis beneath to grow. Peeling skin is, for Connor, associated with its de-classification, for, 'the skin itself is no longer a skin once

it is detached. By being peeled away from the body, it has ceased to be itself'
(Connor 2004: 29). Instead, for Connor, it becomes *another body* and thus
signals, in part, the 'immaterial, ideal, ecstatic, [of] a skin that walks itself'
(Connor 2004: 29) such that products, which highlight a physical fragmentation
of the skin, problematize its singularity as a 'whole' organ coating the body.

The tingling sensation instilled by the enzyme mask, itself a chemical peel,
was symptomatic of an uncanny effect for this activity served to render the dead
cells on my face as, at once both of my body, but also separate from it. That
is my dead skin cells held a dual identity, both an embodied absence, but also
a disembodied presence still registered as mine through the tingling sensation,
the very sensation that questioned their status as dead. These are for Hook
(2005) the two poles of Freud's uncanny, which he understands is underwritten
with 'anxieties concerning variants of *embodied absence* on the one hand, and
disembodied presence on the other' (Hook 2005: 697). Freud provides some
examples of such uncanny absence and presence in the form of '[d]ismembered
limbs, a severed head, a hand cut off at the wrist, feet which dance by themselves'
(1919: 14). For Hook, this premise signals the uncanny as an 'ontological anxiety',
for the 'status of the object' is confounded by its possible and simultaneous
'*status as human*' (Hook 2005: 697). Specifically, we find here an anxiety about
the soul and its absence or presence within a body. Such ontological anxiety is
not only, Freud notes, tied to questions of animation and inanimation in objects
or subjects, it is also inherent within the motif of the double.

For Freud, the double invariably suggests the person who 'looks exactly alike'.
As a concept of the uncanny then, the double emerges as a mode of relationality
wherein identities merge, leading to uncertainty as to who or what the 'true' self
is. This is, according to Freud, a 'creation tied to a primitive phase in our mental
development' where, during evolution of the self, 'the ego had not yet clearly
marked itself off against the world outside and from others' (2003: 143). As
Schwartz highlights however, Freud was not the only psychoanalyst to ponder
over the phenomenon of the double, Jung too 'considered that primitive twin
known as the shadow' (Jung in Schwartz 1996: 83). Yet, for Jung, the 'primitive
twin' emerged not so much from a porosity of boundaries between infant and
world, as from a duality of the self. The double, he explained is an 'encounter
with the dark half of personality' (Jung in Schwartz 1996: 83), such that it
emerged when, Jung states, 'I experience the other in myself and the other-than-
myself' (Jung 1996).

The animation and subsequent disintegration of dead skin cells by chemical
peels resonates with the double, for an uncanny quality of feeling emerges here

as a result of the body's openness to change, for in the process of gestation skin is shed to become that which is 'other-than-myself'. In the context of the Washington DC facial however, this uncanny quality was premised upon feeling the 'other-than-myself' as a tingling sensation. There is a similarity of sensuous encounter here between the uncanny quality of feeling that this facial product produced and the affective register of uncanny effects suggested by Pile, which he notes, make hairs stand up on the back of your neck (2011). Here however, I suggest that embodied sensation of this facial product is an uncanny effect in and of itself, tied to the skin's materiality.

Crisis of the Proper

While the facial to this point worked through various uncanny qualities associated with the tangibility of materials and embodied feeling, it was not until the cosmetologist manoeuvred a magnifying glass suspended on a tripod, over my face to increase the visibility of my skin, that an uncanny quality of feeling emerged from the contact between the hands of the cosmetologist and the skin on my face. As a means of increasing the visibility of the skin, the tripod was not an unusual piece of equipment to encounter in the treatment room. However, whilst it had in the past led to chastisement of my skin's texture and condition and with it a suggested lack of care, in the Washington treatment room I was greeted with an unfamiliar sensation, a cacophony of pinches that meandered over and around my nose.

I found myself suddenly glad of the towel that had been placed over my eyes to protect them from the bright light that had also been positioned over my face, hiding my eyes and hopefully my sense of shock. For Tomkins (in Demos 1995; Sedgwick and Frank 1995), the skin on the face is that which holds the greatest importance in producing the feel of affect. But this is not simply an alignment of facial expression with affect, rather the skin on the face is considered by Tomkins to be affect in motion. As the pinches came again and again my body froze as, pinch by pinch, the cosmetologist's hands moved around my nose. For Freud repetition is certainly an aspect of the uncanny, but this was not a 'repetition of the same' that arises from a mobile search that leads back, again and again, to the same place, such as in the experience of being lost in the woods, an example used in Freud's (2003) conceptualisation of uncanny repetition. In the salon my body was static, frozen with shock to the treatment bed.

But there was more to this uncanny moment. It was as if nothing else existed for the cosmetologist but my magnified nose. Did he approach it as disembodied, separate from its 'owner'? Something that Freud might term 'highly uncanny'. This was certainly how it felt in the uncanny silence that characterised this process, a mode of the uncanny that Freud considered an element in the production of 'infantile anxiety, something that most of us never wholly overcome' (2003: 159). There was no prior warning, no 'right I am just going to clean out your pores', no 'are you comfortable with me doing this?' Lying on the treatment table I thought back to all my interviews with beauticians and my previous facial treatments and the comments made by these research participants on the importance of making clients feel at ease. Here however, instead of a friendly comment to make me feel calm, to inform or warn me of this 'technique', there was silence. And in this silence I digested the situation and reconsidered the purpose of those plastic gloves.

The central role that this silence played in my increasing sense of anxiety was tied to my personal experience of receiving facials, a history important to consider as '[o]n what occasions anxiety appears – that is to say, in the face of what objects and in what situations – will of course depend to a large extent on the state of a person's knowledge and on his [or her] sense of power *vis-à-vis* the external world' (Freud 1991: 442). A few more facials down the line, I learnt from a beautician back in the UK that this process of pinching at pores is called 'extraction' and while the US cosmetologist wore plastic gloves his UK counterpart used tissues to remove what I was told was 'a build up of product'. These protective layers signal another uncanny element in the experience of extraction, for the use of those gloves resonated with Wilton's assertion that 'bodies themselves are, a source of anxiety since it is upon the surface of the body that the social-cultural meanings of infection, contagion, illness and death are inscribed' (1998: 181).

Touch, contact between bodies, is central to Irigaray's concept of porosity, which hinges on the reciprocity of this sense; the openness of one body to another through touch. She presents a motif of '[t]he hands joined, palms together, fingers stretched, [which] constitute a very particular touching' (1993: 135), one that Grosz explains as a 'relation of symmetry between the two hands' (1994: 105). A symmetry that acknowledges the non-hierarchal character of touch; the ability of both bodies involved in a touch to feel. Irigaray describes the encounter of touching as follows, she states '[t]he internal and external horizons of my skin interpenetrating with yours wears away their edges, their limits, their solidarity. Creating another space – outside my framework. An opening of openness' (1993: 59). Touch then, presents the skin as a porous boundary between, though not separating, self and world. A skin whose '[p]orosity [enables] the ability of strange substances [material and immaterial] to cross the subject's own boundaries and in doing so change the very contours of identity' (Fullagar 2001: 179). In the facial treatment room the cosmetologist's gloves served as a register of this porous quality, as 'a recognition of the significance of boundaries in relation to the sense of vulnerability' (Fullagar 2001: 180).

In the treatment room then, the gloves served to signal my skin as different and 'other', but also similar or familiar to the cosmetologist's, for we both have a permeable skin. This I suggest produces a sense of anxiety, for the use of plastic gloves highlights not only my vulnerability to the cosmetologist's actions, but also his vulnerability to the touch of my skin and its oily excretions. Such reciprocity is a means to acknowledge 'the spectre of our mutual vulnerability and mortality as in tactile contact, the gestation of our bodies is highlighted' (Wilton 1998: 181). Indeed, as Fullagar goes on to suggest, '[t]ouch generates an ethical moment in which the flesh and mortality of the self and other is felt' (2001: 180). Uncanny qualities of feeling established through touch, then, accentuate the role of the uncanny as not simply a disjuncture of the body, but of time as well, enrolling both as facets bound up with questions of life and death.

In this, what was for me a deeply affective moment, we might say there was an 'uncanny crisis of the proper: ... a disturbance of personal or private property' (Royle 2003: 340) as the 'build up of product' was pinched from interior to exterior. Such a passage signals the material crux of Irigaray's concept, one that considers the movement of mucus from inside to outside the body which, for Irigaray are 'mucous membranes [that] evade my mastery' (1993: 170). Demonstrating a material dynamic to Irigaray's understanding of porosity, such a passage is uncanny as it puts us 'at odds with ourselves' generating a 'sense of strangeness given to dissolving all assurances about the identity of the self' (Royle 2003: 6). Indeed the skin as the interface between self and world, is at once both public in its external frontage and, through both its material connectivity to the body via tissue, nerves and flesh, as well as the porosity of its pores with their ability to secrete oily substances, the skin is also positioned as a private space. The cosmetologist's actions then, sat at the nexus of this dualistic reading of skin as he acted to affect the internal and somewhat private spaces of my nose.

In this 'crisis of the proper' several things ran through my head culminating not in an uncanny fright, but a feeling of dread (Freud 2003). For while I lay there wondering what to do and celebrated a feeling of calm at the thought of the facial's imminent conclusion, I considered the environment into which I would return post-treatment with a bright red nose: the annual

Association of American Geographers conference. The comparative calm left me and my body tensed once more, as a sense of dread for the thought of exiting the treatment room came over me. Indeed as Gelder and Jacobs note, the uncanny acknowledges the possibility of being both 'being in place and out of place simultaneously', (1998: 46) a positionality that would be highlighted with my delegate bag and unsuitably dishevelled presentation.

Conclusion

Within this chapter I have used an autoethnographic approach to unpack the experience of receiving facial treatment in the context of the beauty salon, to consider a series of uncanny effects that evolved through the various qualities of the sense of touch. In conclusion however, it is pertinent to remember that while '[i]t may be that the uncanny is a feeling that happens only to oneself, within oneself, [it is however] never one's own: its meaning or significance may have to do, most of all, with what is not oneself, with others, with the world "itself"' (Royle 2003: 2). The uncanny then, provides a set of co-ordinates through which to acknowledge the relationality at work in the facial treatment room, not only between bodies, but also materials such as the technology of the chemical peel and its potential to have an effect upon the skin. As such Freud's concept resonates with Irigaray's notion of porosity (1993) wherein we can consider the skin, here the skin of the face, as a threshold between client and cosmetologist which, Shildrich (2001) suggests, exposes and makes the self vulnerable to the exterior world and bodies.

The anxiety that arose for me in the treatment room emerged from tactile encounters at my body's threshold, my skin, inter-connections that highlight the significance of that which is not oneself in the establishment of an uncanny feeling. As Royle explains, the uncanny 'has to do with the strangeness of framing and borders, an experience of liminality that disturbs any straightforward sense of what is inside and what is outside' (Royle 2003: 2). This is a liminality, a connectivity sensed through touch which, I suggest establishes a certain 'doubling'. Indeed for Freud the doubling of subjects is uncanny if 'a person may identify himself (or herself) with another and so become unsure of his true self; or he may substitute the other's self for his own' (2003: 142). In the inter-connectivity between myself and the cosmetologist, the uncanny emerged not as a replacement of identity or a substitution but as a co-emergence with the textures, pressures and movements proffered in facial treatment.

As such the uncanny is more than an affective or emotive 'quality of feeling', it is also one connected to materiality and its capacity to mobilise sensation, such as the particular qualities of the sense of touch through which, the 'self may thus be duplicated, divided and interchanged' (Freud 2003: 142).

References

Anderson, B. 2009. Affective atmospheres. *Emotion, Space and Society*, 2(2), 77–81.

Benthian, C. 2002. *Skin: On the Cultural Border Between Self and the World*. New York: Columbia University Press.

Connor, S. 2004. *The Book of Skin*. London: Reaktion.

Demos, E.V. 1995. *Exploring Affect: The Selected Writings of Silvian Tomkins*. Cambridge: Cambridge University Press.

Eiden, B. 1998. The use of touch in psychotherapy. *Self and Society* [Online]. Available at: http://www.integrazioneposturale.it/varieftp/eiden.pdf [accessed: 9 December 2011].

Gelder, K. and Jacobs, J. 1998. *Uncanny Australia: Sacredness and Identity in a Postcolonial Nation*. Melbourne: Melbourne University Press.

Hogle, L. 2003. Life/warranty: rechargeable cells. *Remaking Life and Death: Toward an Anthropology of the Biosciences*, edited by S. Franklin and M. Lock. Santa Fe: School of American Research Press, 61–96.

Hook, D. 2005. Monumental space and the uncanny. *Geoforum*, 36(6), 688–704.

Fosshage, J. 2000. The meanings of touch in psychoanalysis: a time for reassessment. *Psychoanalytic Dialogues*, 9(6), 721–4.

Freud, S. 2003 [1919]. *The Uncanny*, translated by D. Mclintock. London: Penguin.

Freud, S. 1991. *Introductory Lectures on Psychoanalysis*. London: Penguin.

Freud, S. 1961 [1927]. *The Ego and the Id*. London: The International Psychoanalytical Press.

Freud, S. 1919. *The Uncanny* [Online]. Available at: http://web.mit.edu/allanmc/www/freud1.pdf [accessed: 29 September 2012].

Fullagar, S. 2001. Encountering otherness: embodied affect in Alphonso Lingis' travel writing. *Tourist Studies*, 1, 171–83.

Gambaudo, S. 2007. *Kristeva, Psychoanalysis and Culture: Subjectivity in Crisis*. Aldershot: Ashgate.

Grosz, E. 1994. *Volatile Bodies: Toward a Corporeal Feminism*. Bloomington: Indiana University Press.

Irigaray, L. 1993. *An Ethics of Sexual Difference*, translated by C. Burke and G.C. Gill. London: Cornell University Press.

Kristeva, J. 1982. *The Powers of Horror*. New York: Columbia University Press.

Mukul, S., Surabhi, K. and Atul, N. 2011. Cosmeceuticals for the skin: an overview. *Asian Journal of Pharmaceutical and Clinical Research* [Online], 4(2). Available at: http://www.ajpcr.com/Vol4Issue2/260.pdf [accessed: 19 September 2011].

Paterson, M. 2007. *The Senses of Touch: Haptics, Affects and Technologies*. Oxford: Berg.

Pile, S. 2011. Intensities of feeling: cloverfield, the uncanny, and the always near collapse of the city, in *The New Blackwell Companion to the City: Blackwell Companions to Geography*, edited by G. Bridge and S. Watson. Chichester: Wiley-Blackwell, 288–303.

Pile, S. 2010. Skin race and space: the clash of bodily schemas in Frantz Fanon's *Black Skins, White Masks* and Nella Larson's *Passing*. *Cultural Geographies*, 18(1), 25–41.

Pile, S. 1996. *The Body and the City: Psychoanalysis, Subjectivity and Space*. London: Routledge.

Royle, N. 2003. *The Uncanny*. Manchester: Manchester University Press.

Schwartz, H. 1996. *The Culture of the Copy: Striking Likenesses, Unreasonable Facsimiles*. New York: Zone Books.

Sedgwick, E.K. 2003. *Touching Feeling: Affect, Pedagogy, Performativity*. London: Duke University Press.

Sedgwick, E.K. and Frank, A. 1995. *Shame in the Cybernetic Fold: Reading Silvan Tomkins*. Chicago: The University of Chicago Press.

Straughan, E.R. 2012. Facing touch in the beauty salon: corporeal anxiety, in *Touching Space, Placing Touch*, edited by M. Paterson and M. Dodge. Aldershot: Ashgate.

Sjöholm, C. 2005. *Kristeva and the Political*. Oxon: Routledge.

Wilton, R. 1998. The constitution of difference: space and psyche in landscapes of exclusion. *Geoforum*, 29(2), 173–85.

Chapter 18

What Does it Mean for Young Women to get Drunk? A Kleinian Perspective on Young Women's Relationship with Alcohol

Melissa Stepney

On a cold December night in 2008, I was returning from a night out. For the most part it had been like any other ordinary night; Reading is a large town in the South East of the UK with a bustling night-time economy comprising several hundred well-known bars and nightclubs like Revolutions and JD Wetherspoons, where the usual heady ingredients of dancing, crowds, music, chatter, encounters, fights and drunkenness regularly occur. I had spent the night in the police station 'observing' all this from the setting of a CCTV room. This research, which was a qualitative study on young women's relationship(s) with alcohol in the UK and the Netherlands, felt timely: young women appear to be at the centre of a number of anxieties and concerns about drinking, drunkenness and debauchery on city centre streets at the weekend. Indeed, the persistent and dogged media coverage of 'young women' as a troublesome group is both commonplace and relentless, particularly in the UK (Day et al. 2004; Measham and Østergaard 2009; Jayne et al. 2011). At the police station, I had entered into familiar conversations: do British women drink too much? How much is too much? Do European women (and men) have 'better', or more sophisticated, ways of drinking? Should bars be open all night? And so on.

Alcohol consumption and its associated consequences have come to signify a number of highly charged social, political and economic debates. Alcohol (policy) discourse frequently draws on ideas around anti-social behaviour, on 'fixing' our night-time streets; on 'fixing' British women, on the merits of greater (or lesser) taxation; the effects of minimum pricing, and changes to the licensing laws. These debates continue apace and are largely reflected in the literature from medical studies, anthropology, criminology and sociology to more recent interventions by geographers (see Jayne et al. 2011 for a comprehensive review). Yet despite this, alcohol discourse seems stuck in a logical, pragmatic and *conscious* narrative. During the last five years of researching this subject, I have felt uneasy with these stories which appear to be anchored in an episode of *Booze Britain* (a UK television series which proclaims to chart the 'highs and lows of UK binge drinking culture'). Here, the endless rote commentary cites the need to 'crack down' on the 'drink problem'. The drive towards 'sensible drinking' appears to promote a neutral, in-between 'space' – which is difficult to refute because it relies on a language of 'common sense'. Yet it seeks to rationalise behaviour by eliminating ambiguity – that very ambiguity we need to understand It sometimes seems too obvious to ask questions about who drunkenness lets you be (perhaps someone else or more yourself? Or perhaps a bit of both?). Yet, current political imperatives and pressures to come up with answers, solutions and measurable outcomes are inherent parts of a wider neoliberal response to uncertainty. Appealing to individuals' conscious, rational and logical decision making about drinking does not seem to solve the problem of why our A&E departments are full on Friday nights due to drunken mishaps and accidents, despite people knowing full well the risks. Might there be something else to say about drinking?

As my research journey progressed from that typical December night in 2008, I have been drawn to the ways in which psychoanalytic theory might offer something else in understanding the complexities and ambiguities of intoxication. As a distinct sub-discipline since around the turn of the twenty-first century, psychoanalytic geographers have begun to explore how people's feelings, emotions, fears, impulses, desires, and internal and external conflicts influence their relationship with others (Pile 1996; Kingsbury 2003; Sibley 2003; Bondi 2007; Thomas 2011). By offering a number of comprehensive (albeit contested) theories and conceptual frameworks for understanding people's everyday lives, struggles and contradictions, psychoanalysis illuminates the workings of the unconscious (Frosh 2002). Following Thomas (2007: 543) it is important for research to loosen '[...] its grip on the logical world' and consider 'the seemingly illogical, the unspeakable, the deniable, and the invisible connections between social action and psychic life'. If we begin to acknowledge the unconscious then our knowledge about the world and of thoughts is not transparent and straightforward (Lemaigre 2005). My particular use of psychoanalytic theory is therefore a deliberate move away from the logical, fixated narratives circulating around current alcohol discourse. Rather, I seek to understand how particular investments in drunkenness might suggest that policy messages on 'sensible drinking' are largely ineffective.

In exploring young women's experiences of drinking I use psychoanalytic insights, specifically those of Melanie Klein, to tease out the contradictions and ambivalences in both the young women's own narratives about their drinking behaviour and the wider discourse on women's drinking in public spaces. I consider Klein's theories to provide an illuminating account of the ways in which the self can be understood in relational terms (primarily in relation to other 'objects' in the world, namely people and things), and how conflict and splitting in the individual's mind relate dialectically to the negotiation and ordering of social space.

A Psychoanalytic Approach: The Work of Melanie Klein

Melanie Klein (1882–1960) was an Austrian born psychoanalyst who had a profound impact on both British and international psychoanalytic circles (Bronstein 2001). Her theoretical contributions and work were based on many of Freud's ideas yet also went further by challenging some of his theories (Whitford 1992; Segal 2004). Klein was interested in the internal world of the child, in particular the role of anxiety, early defence mechanisms and internalised objects. In following Freud's theory of the death drive, Klein saw there to be a fundamental conflict between the life and death drives, love and hate which are the deepest source of ambivalences (ibid.). Klein believed that the ego, through fear, repudiates the death drive that Freud talked about – and that this arouses intolerable feelings of love and hate in the infant. These feelings then get directed towards the child and her internal and external objects (Stein 1991).

Klein developed this as a theory of what she called 'positions'. These are modes of psychic functioning which alternate throughout our lives (Bronstein 2001). These positions refer to the child's experience of objects with the accompanying conflict and anxieties between impulses and defences that the ego sets up against them (ibid.). In her work with children, Klein became convinced of the importance of aggression; the infant's phantasy of projecting and expelling intolerable feelings onto the first other – the mother's body – is where hate and love are confused and in such conflict, the projected content always threatens to have its revenge (Britzman 2003, 2010). Individuals try to manipulate these conflicts unconsciously through splitting, projecting, introjecting and idealising parts of themselves which correspond to two basic emotional positions: the paranoid-schizoid (P-S) (splitting of the ego and the object into extreme feelings of good and bad) and the depressive position (tolerating the feelings) –

the latter of which is seen as a more balanced, integrated position which eliminates the persecutory, threatening feelings (Stein 1991).

Klein believed that the paranoid-schizoid and depressive position are descriptions of mental structures which can be found in both adults and children. More specifically, the depressive position refers to the child's more pronounced sense of separateness in understanding that feelings of love and hate are actually directed at the same person. There is constant fluctuation between persecutory anxiety and depressive anxiety related to emotions of love and hate, where the infant is inundated by its fantasies of aggression against the body of the mother coupled with senses of guilt and wanting to make reparation (Kahane 1992). Klein's 'positions' thus refer to a 'state of organisation of the ego – the nature of the internal object relations and the nature of the anxiety and the characteristic defences' (Klein 1935 cited in Temperley 2001: 47). Klein suggested that the oscillation between these positions continues throughout life (Temperley 2001). These fluctuations are the movement between periods of emotional integration (depressive position) and disintegration and fragmentation (paranoid-schizoid position) (Steiner 1988). Other psychoanalysts like Wilfred Bion (1963 cited in Steiner 1988) have suggested that these two positions are dynamic in relation to each other in a life-long cycle of development.

Klein's paranoid-schizoid position helps us to understand the schizoid and contradictory narratives surrounding women and alcohol: from the anxious mix of titillation and scorn directed at women's drunkenness in the media, to the 'split' stories that young women in my study told. Here, splitting is central to the negotiation of our own (drinking and gendered) identities. The ambivalence towards women's use of alcohol (both in policy and behaviour) culminates in processes of splitting between notions of 'good', 'sensible' drinking and 'bad' drinking behaviour. The paranoid-schizoid position is dominated by the mechanism of 'splitting' as a defence to protect and preserve the 'good' object by splitting off its 'bad' aspects. Here I use splitting in the psychoanalytic sense – a splitting in the ego and the object – as well as in the cultural sense where the many dualisms paradigmatic in Western thinking since Descartes are of critical relevance to social theory (Dimen 2002). Political and social discourses about 'good' and 'bad' drinking behaviour, particularly directed at women, may be understood as a deep ambivalence about women's lives in public space, a splitting and disintegration in the struggle for integration related to that which Klein (1946) describes in her paranoid-schizoid position. In this, there is evidence of contradictory tensions and oscillations that relate to gender identity and performance of 'good' and 'bad' ways of doing gender.

In the next section I demonstrate through the young women's narratives how occupying this ambivalent space perversely sets up the stage for a polarisation in drinking (and gender) behaviour: that drunkenness both suspends such contradictions by easing such tensions. In other words, drawing on Benjamin (1988), drunkenness as a form of drinking polarity might allow a breakdown in tension for the psyche (Benjamin 1988).

Empirical Research into Stages of Drunkenness and the Desire for an 'Ideal'

In my research, semi-structured interviews were conducted with a sample (N=46) of young female university students in Reading (UK) and Groningen (the Netherlands). Elsewhere I discuss the differences in empirical data from the two cohorts and the wider implications for femininity and gender identity (Stepney 2010). Participants in both countries talked about a number of stages of drunkenness and a desirable stage of drunkenness that they wanted to reach. In the interviews, I asked students in both localities to describe how they felt when they were most recently drunk, what motivated them to drink and also how they knew they were drunk. I left the definition and interpretation of 'drunk' to the participant as I felt this opened up new possibilities for understanding conceptions of drunkenness (rather than contracting discussion with set definitions or government guidelines) and also because, as the interviews progressed, it became clear that many participants were unsure of the exact amount they drank on a night out. What seemed important here was this was a starting point for a more in-depth conversation about embodied feelings and interpretations of these experiences.

Participants in both localities sought an 'ideal' drinking identity: as such there was a desire to be drunk enough (which entailed not too sober, but not too drunk). Getting 'tipsy' was seen as the 'ideal' level of drunkenness, which included both control and some loss of control. British participant Kim and Dutch participant Marijke describe these different stages of drunkenness:

> You've got like sort of just feeling it a little bit. And then you've got like the merry stage and then you've got the pleasantly drunk sort of thing, where you've got a little bit more confidence and then you can go too far and you're in the 'dodgy stages' you know that if you have one more then that's it, you're probably going to be not really knowing what you're doing and wake up with blank pauses in your

memory the next day [...] unless that's what you want [laughs]! (Kim, 21-year-old British student).

[...] my favourite stage is the second, just when you've begun [...] that's the best bit, when you can feel it working in a bit [...] a bit warm, a bit happy, almost as if you're feeling a bit loved up like [...] but not really of course (Marijke, 19-year-old Dutch student).

Kim highlights the precarious nature of drunkenness with her one more then that's it – however, paradoxically, she talks about this sometimes being desirable ('unless that's what you want!') – thus drunkenness is both dangerous ('dodgy') and desirable ('more confidence; a bit warm, a bit happy'). It also has an ideal ('my favourite stage'). Psychoanalytically we might suppose that there is an accompanying anxiety that the 'good' aspects of drinking ('feeling a bit loved up' as Marijke comments) are always in jeopardy or in danger of becoming too much, or not enough (feeling too sober).

Many participants cited the positive effects of drinking (although throughout the research process the British students were also highly aware of the social implications and judgements of this). When I asked what alcohol provided to participants, a number talked about a suspension from social conventions and how it, as a tool, provided them with the ability to transgress social boundaries. British student Amy told me that alcohol makes 'someone a different person when they're drunk'. When I asked if that applied to her as well, she agreed that she could understand why people do get drunk as it helps with confidence and 'letting go'. British student Abby told me that drinking allowed you to be more yourself as it lets 'your personality comes out a lot stronger' and like many participants, it made her 'feel more fun'. For Dutch student Maaike she felt that alcohol allowed her to express desires and feelings that normally she would not ('you can say stuff you wouldn't otherwise'). Therefore alcohol seemed to provide a legitimate tool for expressing openness that was not possible when sober during the day. Some participants talked about interacting with someone they were attracted to when out and how the fear of 'feeling too sober' in the moment was awkward. Here Maaike sums this up when she met a guy in a nightclub:

It's a feeling that you both build up [...] you both know, but you both don't talk about it [that you like each other] directly [...] And if you haven't drunk alcohol then you'd be scared of making a fool of yourself. It's a really different feeling with that.

A too sober feeling! At that moment, you just feel great – you feel good no matter what. If he blew you off, or he wasn't that interested, then you still find it funny, it's still OK even if that is the case. [...] it gives you self-confidence I think. You let go of your inhibitions and you feel just better, at a more secure height.

Here, a particular (un)conscious transference ('a feeling that you both build up') is being facilitated and enhanced through alcohol. Alcohol provides a security ('a secure height') against the possibility of loss in case the other person rejected or 'blew you off'. Thus alcohol facilitates a connection, an intimacy or closeness whilst providing a simultaneous distance in the event of disappointment. The appeal of alcohol therefore might be that it can allow an (un)conscious expression of vulnerability whilst forming a barrier or defence should this vulnerability lead to pain or disappointment. In this way it encourages a feeling of social harmony and cohesiveness even if this might mask anxiety.

Maaike also indicates the ways in which alcohol links to intimacy. Drinking alcohol creates feelings of closeness and intimacy in people (even if we might argue intimacy is annihilated through drunkenness itself or that drunkenness provides a pseudo intimacy). In this way alcohol challenges conceptions or idealisations of intimacy because it works in a dialectic way, oscillating between distance and proximity. Either way, Maaike indicates the fragility of such intimacy: the possibility of, and conflict between making connection(s) and disconnecting altogether.

Thus, so far I have explored how, in Kleinian terms, participants talked about the 'good' aspects of drinking alcohol. At the same time these stories were 'split' as there was an ever-present corresponding awareness and anxiety about the possibility of it going awry or 'bad'. As such, notions of good and bad drunkenness had social reprisals. Feeling too sober was not fun enough or induced questioning (many participants suggested they needed a reason for not drinking – see below), whilst being too drunk presented the possibility of shame and embarrassment. In sum, there were co-present and competing desires to integrate a number of these aspects and occupy a space of 'in-between'. It is this intersubjective space in which these young women negotiated their contradictory identities of wanting to be a bit out of control (coded 'fun') whilst remaining still in control (coded 'ladylike'). This of course sets up an ambivalent space:

There is a fine line between it [drinking] being a lot of fun and a total disaster (Eloise, 18-year-old British student).

Drunkenness therefore is inherently spatial: being drunk is OK, but for these young women, there is an edge, a boundary, a limit that they are (un)consciously always aware of. This was particularly feminised:

> I [...] think [...] after a certain amount of drinks people are liable to do anything especially girls and women and stuff [...] I really do [...] I genuinely believe that [...] You've got to be so careful with it cos I think [...] women are particularly more vulnerable.

Here British participant Vivian remarks that women are 'liable to do anything' when drunk and she indicates a vulnerability – thus there are, as explored earlier – both conflictual desires to show vulnerability (and approachability) alongside a very real anxiety and fear of becoming vulnerable. For the British students this was a very prominent theme: there was a strong sense of self-monitoring. Controlling the self in public space uses a particular feminism – one that is deployed and disguised in a language of choice, empowerment and freedom (McRobbie 2009). Arguably, such social controls have become a key mechanism for the production of sexual difference through normalisation (ibid.). In other words it is expected that young women ought to take steps to mitigate drink spiking and ought to be alert to the messages they convey when drinking, and so on.

Psychoanalytically, society reinforces the ideal and omnipotent figures of the paranoid-schizoid position (alcohol as good/bad) onto young women by directing feelings of guilt, responsibility and concern wholly towards the self (Temperley 2001). Therefore when drinking, the idea is not simply that young women must behave in more controlled ways, rather they must embody being both in control and out of control ('a lot of fun' but not 'a total disaster'), thus setting up a number of conflicts (the ego is both the source of antagonism and reprimand in the task of 'self-awareness'). This is seen crucially as navigating a fine line or a precarious path. The idea of an 'ideal' female drinking identity has great resonance with Klein's oscillatory splits between phantasies of good and bad object relations, and the subsequent desire for integration of these. As Klein (1946: 7) writes, 'two interrelated processes take place: the omnipotent conjuring up of the ideal object and situation, and the equally omnipotent annihilation of the bad persecutory object and the painful situation'. As such, the 'ideal' level of drunkenness masks a defence – a splitting up – of and against the bad aspects of the object. British student Anna tells me:

> I'm quite a good drunk really [...] I've always been the kind of like 'the responsible one' [laughs] [...] I get drunk but I don't get as drunk as like a lot of my friends do.

Whilst being both responsible and drunk might seem a contradiction in terms, Anna positions herself as able to navigate this by being both in control and drunk. Here there is an attempt to integrate both the good and bad aspects of drunkenness in which the ambivalence is tolerated (Temperley 2001). This position is also relational as she compares her drunkenness to that of her friends, with her own position being relatively more responsible. Anna's conception of 'good drunk' also has sexual signification, as being good also fits in with particular conceptions of femininity (being in control, and being 'good'). Much of the desire for particular stages of drunkenness centred on finding and staying in the 'ideal' stage of drunkenness. Thus, recourse to simple explanations of drinking as just about losing control, miss a much more complex set of relationships between losing and retaining the right amount of control, that tells us about young women's desire to transgress yet also comply with specific gendered norms and femininities.

The landscape of drunkenness therefore is a representation of ambivalence – competing desires and anxieties about control and loss of control which have broader implications relating to women's role in society in trying to find an 'ideal' space. One comment from the *girlsdrinkdiaries.com* website stands out here (this was an online discussion forum set up as part of the research which allowed women between the ages of 18–30 to share their experiences and opinions about drinking and alcohol):

> Long gone are the days of social repression where women were forced indoors to drink tea. Now women work as hard and want to socialise as hard as boys. And let's face it, trying to find a partner, hold down a job that pays enough so you can look good and afford decent clothes and shoes is damn hard work. No wonder girls want to 'let off steam' at the weekend. I find the notion of 'lady-like' quite repressive actually. I think women are fed up of being dictated to along the lines of Victorian attitudes. We're meant to be feminist and independent but at the same time submissive and 'good'. There is a lot of pressure to 'have it all' (Tinkerbell, girlsdrinkdiaries.com participant).

Tinkerbell expresses here the contradictions and pressures in 'hav[ing] it all'. The desire to have all the benefits that men enjoy ('women work as hard and want to socialise as hard as boys') whilst also retaining a place within heteronormative society by 'find[ing] a partner, hold[ing] down a job' and actively participating in consumer culture are difficult. Tinkerbell's historical comparison (the Victorian attitude of being lady like as repressive) is an expression of how 'modern' women desire to be free of social repression yet in being a subject (independent) must also embrace notions of being object ('submissive and "good"'). As Dimen (2002) suggests the development of femininity is a compromise between the two, which creates a contradiction or conflict. Indeed psychoanalytic theory, specifically object relations theory, suggests that social structures become internalised in processes 'mediated by fantasy and conflict' (Chodorow 1978: 50, cited in Heenan 1998: 99). As oscillating between the two positions Klein refers to is not easy, we can understand Tinkerbell's desires to let off steam (and by this we might infer going to get drunk) as a way of dealing with this (see also Stepney 2014).

Setting the Stage for a 'Drinking Polarity'

So far I have suggested that occupying the (psychical and physical) spaces of 'good drunk' is precarious; for many participants there was an anxiety around the possibility of being too drunk or not drunk enough – both of which have social reprisals. I would like to suggest that this sets up the stage for a 'drinking polarity'. How so? Crudely put, if having to take into consideration all these expectations and social mores consciously and unconsciously, then a tension arises between two (sometimes) opposing aspects which cannot be integrated (Benjamin 1988).

If drunkenness is one polarity in drinking behaviour, what is the other? A small number of the participants in this research completely abstained from drinking alcohol altogether and this could indicate an emerging trend in drinking behaviour that has been noted by others (see Nairn et al. 2006). For those who talked about drinking no alcohol or very little on a night out, their reasons were varied: health issues, religious reasons and/or a bad experience or trauma associated with drinking that now made them worried about their drinking habits. What is critical here is that a reason needed to be given. For those students who abstained, even for one night, their drinking was demarcated (by themselves) as 'very different' from their friends although they were keen to emphasise to me that their friends understood and respected their decision not to drink. Participants often remarked that having a reason or a form of explanation was one way of vocalising their alternative drinking identity.

Vivian told me that she often chose to be the designated driver in her group because this meant that she would definitely not drink at all. When I asked about nights when she was not a designated driver she told me:

> If I start drinking then I don't tend to […] stop […] until I've gone back home […] so I know that if I don't start then that […] then I won't carry on drinking […] yeah so that's kind of the best way. If I'm out and I wanna have a good night […] and I'll have one drink then ill carry on and carry on and carry on […] thinking oh well I might as well make the most of it. If I sort of don't start then I won't have anything at all.

What seemed apparent was that, for several participants, occupying the conflictual demands within a space of losing some control and retaining some control sometimes gave way to a polarity – drunkenness or complete abstinence. Therefore for participants like Vivian, she preferred either to drink (with the possibility of drunkenness) or not drink at all. This would seem a 'logical' response to the complexities and ambivalences of occupying a space in-between.

Drawing on Benjamin (1988) and Klein (1946) I want to suggest that the stage is set for polarization and splitting in drinking behaviour, in part driven by the notion of drinking 'ideals' and the spatial ambiguity of inbetweenness. Much of this reflects the contradictory conceptions about femininity and locating a 'correct' female identity in public spaces at night. Drunkenness appears to provide a tool for navigating some of these contradictions of this in-between space for young women. This is inherently gendered as young women are subject to cultural critique in occupying either position (being too 'fun' or not 'fun enough'). Alcohol serves as a temporary 'break' or anaesthetic from such ambivalent gendered identities – and has, in the process, become a marker of (self) control and transformed into a language of choice (Power 2009).

Using Melanie Klein's paranoid schizoid position of both 'good' and 'bad' here might actually serve to reinforce such dichotomies. However, relationships with alcohol are split and ambivalent, (re)made by dialectics, negotiations and conceptions centred on good/bad drunkenness. These binary framings persist precisely because subjectivity is contradictory, contested and fractured. Tinkerbell (earlier) refers to a pressure for young women to have it all – a state which is hard to achieve. The requirements for young women to fulfil this are, as she indicates, incredibly difficult, and so letting off steam, getting drunk and losing control reinstates a particular polarity. Klein's positions might consequently be read not as static but dynamic (oscillatory) positions on a continuum that demonstrate how movements between integration and disintegration are central to the structures of emotional life (Roth 2001). In following Bondi and Davidson (2003) the idea of moving 'beyond' dualistic ideas or indeed, beyond difference, might be problematic. As Sibley (2001: 247) suggests, psychoanalytic propositions of 'splitting' take seriously how the self is mediated, constituted and negotiated through boundary-making processes of self/other. Thus, acknowledgement and strategic acceptance of such paradoxes and contradictions around binaries might be necessary in 'doing', thinking, theorising and writing about alcohol and drunkenness (Bondi and Davidson 2003).

Conclusion

This chapter has sought to introduce the uncertainties and ambivalences that are reflected in young women's narratives about drinking. Through a psychoanalytic lens, I have explored how there are desires to reach a particular stage of drunkenness, yet this is accompanied by considerable anxiety of being too drunk or not drunk enough. Perversely, taking a polarity in drinking behaviour might be explained as one way to navigate the ambiguities and contradictions of occupying a space of in-between. Current alcohol discourse needs to move beyond conscious, rational understandings and take into account the complexity of attachments and investments in both losing control and remaining in control which are inextricably tied to the performance of 'correct' gender identities. It is the act of getting drunk, going beyond what might be considered 'sensible', that signals the (un)conscious collapse of tension which ambiguity creates.

Whilst I concur with Jayne et al. (2010) who suggest that there is a stark contrast between popular and political representations of drinking and the realities of experiences of alcohol across social groups, there is still a need to fully explore how drunkenness signals an expression of contradiction, vulnerability and ambivalence. To echo Spivak (2004) understanding what message the act of getting drunk contains, allows the debate (and its ambiguities) to continue. By not asking about the contradictions of drinking, we are in danger of rationalising the stage even further, perhaps leading to starker drinking polarities. This in itself is an impasse that resists identifying potentially uncomfortable social and cultural processes in society that are reflected in drinking beyond the 'sensible'.

References

Benjamin, J. 1988. *The Bonds of Love. Psychoanalysis, Feminism and the Problem of Domination*. New York: Pantheon.

Bondi, L. and Davidson, J. 2003. Troubling the place of gender, in *Handbook of Cultural Geography*, edited by K. Anderson, M. Domosh, S. Pile and N. Thrift. London: Sage, 325–43.

Bondi, L. 2007. Psychoanalytic theory. [Online papers archived by the Institute of Geography, School of Geosciences, University of Edinburgh. GEO-035]. Available at: http://www.era.lib.ed.ac.uk/bitstream/1842/1894/1/lbondi006.pdf [accessed: 8 August 2010].

Britzman, D.P. 2003. *After-Education: Anna Freud, Melanie Klein and Psychoanalytic Histories of Learning*. Albany: State University of New York Press.

Britzman, D.P. 2010. Reading Sigmund Freud's group psychology today. Keynote Lecture. Open University Centre for Citizenship, Identities and Governance, Milton Keynes, 13 April 2010.

Bronstein, C. 2001. Introduction, in *Kleinian Theory: A Contemporary Perspective*, edited by C. Bronstein. London: Whurr Publishers, xv–1.

Chodorow, N.J. 1978. *The Reproduction of Mothering: Psychoanalysis and the Sociology of Gender*. Berkeley: University of California Press.

Day, K., Gough, B. and McFadden, M. 2004. Warning! Alcohol can seriously damage your feminine health. *Feminist Media Studies*, 4(2), 165–83.

Dimen, M. 2002. Deconstructing difference: gender, splitting and transitional space, in *Gender in Psychoanalytic Space*, edited by M. Dimen and V. Goldner. New York: Other Press, 41–62.

Frosh, S. 2002. *Key Concepts in Psychoanalysis*. London: British Library.

Heenan, M.C. 1998. Feminist object relations theory and therapy, in *Feminism & Psychotherapy: Reflections on Contemporary Theories and Practices*, edited by I.B. Seu and M.C. Heenan. London: Sage, 96–114.

Jayne, M., Valentine, G. and Holloway, S.L. 2010. Emotional, embodied and affective geographies of alcohol, drinking and drunkenness. *Transactions of the Institute of British Geographers*, 35(4), 540–54.

Jayne, M., Valentine, G. and Holloway, S. 2011. *Alcohol, Drinking, Drunkenness: (Dis)Orderly Spaces*. Farnham: Ashgate.

Kahane, C. 1992. Object relations theory, in *Feminism and Psychoanalysis: A Critical Dictionary*, edited by E. Wright. Oxford: Blackwell, 284–90.

Kingsbury, P. 2003. Psychoanalysis, a gay spatial science? *Social & Cultural Geography*, 4(3), 347–67.

Klein, M. 1935. A contribution to the psychogenesis of manic-depressive states, in *Love, Guilt and Reparation and Other Works 1921–1945: The Writings of Melanie Klein*, Volume I. London: Hogarth Press (1975), 236–89.

Klein, M. 1946. Notes on some schizoid mechanisms. *International Journal of Psychoanalysis*, 27, 99–110.

Klein, M. 1959. Our adult world and its roots in infancy. *Envy and Gratitude and Other Works: 1946–1963*. London: Virago, 247–63.

Lemaigre, B. 2005. Philosophy and psychoanalysis. *International Dictionary of Psychoanalysis*. [Online]. Available at: http://www.encyclopedia.com/doc/1G2-3435301080.html [accessed: 2 January 2010].

Mann, C. and Stewart, F. 2000. *Internet Communication and Qualitative Research: A Handbook for Researching Online*. London: Sage.

McRobbie, A. 2009. *The Aftermath of Feminism: Gender, Culture and Social Change*. London: Sage.

Measham, F. and Østergaard, J. 2009. The public face of binge drinking: British and Danish young women, recent trends in alcohol consumption and the European binge drinking debate. *Probation Journal*, 56(4), 415–34.

Nairn, K., Higgins, J., Thompson, B., Anderson, M. and Fu, N. 2006. 'It's Just Like the Teenage Stereotype, You Go Out and Drink Stuff': Hearing from Young People who Don't Drink. *Journal of Youth Studies*, 9(3), 287–304.

Paccagnella, L. 1997. Getting the seats of your pants dirty: strategies for ethnographic research on virtual communities. *Journal of Computer-Mediated Communication*, 3. [Online]. Available at: http://www.ascusc.org/jcmc/vol3/issue1/paccagnella.html [accessed: 15 August 2008].

Pile, S. 1996. *The Body and the City: Psychoanalysis, Space and Subjectivity*. London/New York: Routledge.

Power, N. 2009. *One-Dimensional Woman*. Hants: O books.

Rich, A. 1986. *Blood, Bread, and Poetry: Selected Prose, 1979–1985*. London: Virago Press.

Roth, P. 2001. The paranoid-schizoid position, in *Kleinian Theory: A Contemporary Perspective*, edited by C. Bronstein. London: Whurr Publishers, 32–46.

Segal, J. 2004. *Melanie Klein*. 2nd Edition. London: Sage.

Sibley, D. 2001. The binary city. *Urban Studies*, 38(2), 239–50.

Sibley, D. 2003. Geography and psychoanalysis: tensions and possibilities. *Social & Cultural Geography*, 4(3), 391–9.

Spivak, G.C. 2004. Terror: a speech after 9–11. *Boundary 2*, 31(2), 81–111.

Stein, R. 1991. *Psychoanalytic Theories of Affect*. London: Karnac.

Steiner, J. 1988. The interplay between pathological organizations and the paranoid-schizoid and depressive positions, in *Melanie Klein Today Developments in Theory and Practice*, Volume 1: Mainly Theory, edited by E. Bott Spillius. London: Routledge, 324–55.

Stepney, M. 2010. *Women, Alcohol and the Night Time Economy: Psychoanalytical Spatial Practices and Narratives of Drinking Amongst Young Female Students from the UK and the Netherlands*. PhD thesis. University of Reading.

Stepney, M. 2014. The rise and fall of 'Girlsdrinkdiaries.com': dilemmas and opportunities when creating online forums to investigate health behaviour. *Health and Place*, 27(1), 51–8.

Temperley, J. 2001. The depressive position, in *Kleinian Theory: A Contemporary Perspective*, edited by C. Bronstein. London: Whurr Publishers, 47–62.

Thomas, M.E. 2007. The implications of psychoanalysis for qualitative methodology: the case of interviews and narrative data analysis. *The Professional Geographer*, 59(4), 539–48.

Thomas, M.E. 2011. *Multicultural Girlhood: Racism, Sexuality, and the Conflicted Spaces of American Education*. Pennsylvania: Temple University Press.

Whitford, M. 1992. Klein, Melanie, in *Feminism and Psychoanalysis: A Critical Dictionary*, edited by E. Wright. Oxford: Blackwell, 191–3.

Chapter 19

Gender, Sexuality, and Race in the Lacanian Mirror: Urinary Segregation and the Bodily Ego

Sheila L. Cavanagh

A train arrives at a station. A little boy and a little girl, brother and sister, are seated across from each other in a compartment next to the outside window that provides a view of the station platform buildings going by as the train comes to a stop. "Look," says the brother, "we're at Ladies!" "Imbecile!" replies his sister, "Don't you see we're at Gentlemen."

Jacques Lacan (2006: 417)

This chapter argues that what Freud called the bodily ego is projected into public space and I use the example of bathrooms to show how normative projections are gendered and sexualized as white. I offer notes toward a psychoanalytic of gendered and racialized space particular to modern, western architectural design and immortalized in the above cited parable by Jacques Lacan about "urinary segregation." If, as Steve Pile (1996) contends, in his discussion of the body, city, space, and subjectivity, there is a means by which bodily egos are projected into public space, then it is crucially important to understand how this projection mirrors normative able-bodied coordinates and does not reflect, avow, or incorporate those who fall out of normative gender, sexual, and racialized alignment.

The Bodily Ego

The bodily ego is a psychoanalytic term designating the fantasmatic process through which individuals learn to map, embody, give shape, and consistency to a material body. For Freud, the bodily ego is a mental projective of a surface. He wrote that the ego "is first and foremost, a bodily ego; it is not merely a surface entity, but is itself the projection of a surface" (Freud 1961 [1923]: 27). The body corporeal does not define or delimit the bodily ego. Didier Anzieu explains that the "[s]elf does not necessarily coincide with the psychical apparatus; in many patients, part of the body and/or the psyche are experienced as foreign" (1989: 19). The bodily ego is, as Patricia Elliot (2001) argues, shaped by libidinally invested fantasies, identifications, significations of loss, desire, and sensory capacities.

Bodily egos are sensorial, as Freud tells us and shaped by visual, acoustic, tactile, and olfactory envelopes (Anzieu 1989); sensory systems through which we cultivate a seal (or what Didier Anzieu refers to as a skin ego) or bodily boundary. Kaja Silverman tells us that there is a "nonvisual mapping of the body's form" (1996: 16) in space which should, ideally, collaborate an internalized visual mirage of the body. People strive toward a "smooth integration of the visual imago with the proprioceptive or sensational ego" (Silverman 1996: 17) so that they can arrive at what Lacan terms méconnaissance: the misrecognition foundational to identity that produces an internally felt bodily coherence. A lack of integration, by contrast, produces a felt lack of corporeal integrity.

There is an important visual component to the bodily ego that takes shape during the mirror stage. According to Lacan, there is an externalizing element to the mirror stage because the image is outside the contours of the body. The subject, therefore, identifies with the image that is not the self proper but a reflection. "Lacan suggests that the subject's corporeal reflection constitutes the limit or boundary within which identification may occur" (Silverman 1996: 11). The image enables the subject to project boundaries onto a previously undifferentiated infantile body space. Lacan describes the psychically invested contours of the body as "an identification with a form conceived of as a limit, or a sack: a sack of skin" (Lacan quoted in Silverman 1996: 11).

Queer and transgender scholars have been using the psychoanalytic concept of the bodily ego to theorize gender and transsexuality respectively. The "lesbian phallus" is, of course, Judith Butler's (1993) key example of an internalized bodily part that doesn't correspond to a visual anatomy, though somatized through what we might call a transmasculine, butch and/or lesbian identification. Similarly, in an important article about the bodily ego and transsexuality, Gayle Salamon explains: "the body can and does exceed the confines of its own skin ... both body and psyche are characterized by their lability rather than their ability to contain" (2004: 108). Knowing where the body ends, and another body begins is integral to human subjectivity, even when the body-envelope is best characterized by a libidinally cathected fantasy (as opposed to an actual material cut or corporeal limit). The gender embodiments had by those who are transgender and cisgendered (non-transgender) should not be characterized by an absolute difference in the way the visual imago and sensational ego are psychically negotiated, but rather by a difference in the degree to which each are felt to be compatible.

Gender, Sexuality and Race in the Lacanian Mirror

In recent years, trans activists and gender theorists have been contesting the gendered architectures of exclusion produced by the dimorphic toilet doors (Cavanagh 2010; Halberstam 1997; Browne 2004; Rasmussen 2009;), but less work has been done on how the gender signifiers operate in conjunction with a racial symbolic that functions (not alongside but) beyond and in excess of the supposed two dimensionality of the door frames. In *Desiring Whiteness*, Kalpana Seshadri-Crooks contends that "racial difference must be distinguished from, but read in relation to, sexual difference" (2000: 7) and that the subject of race is subjected to a fantasy of wholeness—promised by Whiteness as a master signifier of race—made real by the inability of the sexual symbolic to write woman. In other words, Whiteness is a master signifier that operates in and through the impossibility of writing sexual difference. "The signifier Whiteness tries to fill the constitutive lack of the sexed subject. It promises a totality, an overcoming of difference itself. For the subject of race, Whiteness represents complete mastery, self-sufficiency, and the *jouissance* of Oneness" (Seshadri-Crooks 2000: 7). Whiteness, thus, signifies being and those racialized as "not-white" are violently confronted with what Seshadri-Crooks calls, a lack of lack in the face of the manifest so-called "evidence" of race (hair, skin and bone). The racially symbolic impacts upon the bodily ego as a "regime of visibility. Certain marks of the body then become privileged and anxious sites of meaning" (Seshadri-Crooks 2000: 36). The "desire" of the racialized subject (who is uniquely subject to the signifier of Whiteness) is to "symbolize totally" in a regime of visibility that is (a) dependent upon the indeterminability of the sexed subject, and (b) trying to make up for the break-down of sex(ed substance) by promising wholeness (complete subjectification) (Seshadri-Crooks 2000: 21) in a racialized economy that doesn't promise full subject status to all persons.

The bodily imago of the Lacanian mirror stage is made possible by the signifier that, as Seshadri-Crooks contends, operates in a sexual symbolic mediated by the master signifier of Whiteness. The bodily ego, dependent upon a regime of visibility and spectacular imagery, is thus reliant upon a symbolic gender binary that is heteronormative and racialized as white though nonexistent. Toilets spatialize dominant body politics and, as I will argue in what follows, produce abject or unlivable—Lacan might say nonsignifying—zones of geographical exclusion as they also libidinize external coordinates beyond or, rather, in excess of the spaces authenticated by gender signs. Bathroom designs mirror and enable us to externalize libidinally cathected body parts. The spatialization of the gendered bodily ego in the grammatical designs of the public toilet is readily apparent. There is an internal logic or grammar to what Silverman calls the idealized body projected into space. This bi-gendered logic is most evident when lavatory designs defy normative bodily ego coordinates as in, for example, the female urinal in the Whiskey Café in Montreal, Canada (Figure 19.1).

Figure 19.1 L'urinette, the urinal for women, at the Whiskey Café in Montreal, Canada

Source: Photo © Sian James / Toilets of the World.

Silverman also notices the "refusal on the part of the normative subject to form an imaginary alignment with images which remain manifestly detached from his or her sensational body, and his or her stubborn clinging to those images which can be most easily incorporated" (1996: 24). People tend to aggressively assimilate the corporeal coordinates of the other or refuse the difference of the other in callous disregard and disassociation. Both are equally violent in their erasure and negation of difference. We need a "displacement of the hegemonic symbolic of (heterosexist) sexual difference and the critical release of alternative schemas for constituting sites of erotogenic pleasure" (Butler 1993: 91).

I contend that this Symbolic is operative in the toilet and that we negotiate the internal grammar of the toilet at the level of the bodily ego. "The structures of a building are unconsciously imitated and comprehended through the skeletal system unknowingly ... [and] Every building or space has its characteristic sound of intimacy or monumentality, rejection or invitation, hospitality or hostility" (Pallasma 1994: 36–7). In his seminal article on space, the psyche, and landscapes of exclusion, R.D. Wilton similarly notes that changes in the "morphology of social space may be experienced at the level of the bodily ego" (1998: 176). In other words, the bodily ego is spatialized. Architectural theorists have also suggested there is a relationship between bodily or sensory rhythms and modern spatial designs.

> So, one might rightly suggest that bodily rhythm is affected by change of perspective line, parallax vision, the hue of color on walls, the feel of the building material, and the play of shadow and light at different times of day, in a way that is similar to the impact of melody, thematic alteration, tonality, and the "color" of instrumentation in music (Rush 2009: 100–101).

While there are sensorial mirrors other than visual bearing on bodily ego functioning, in this chapter, I will focus on the primary function of vision in the negotiation of psychically invested bodily coordinates and upon the constitutive capacities of the signifier as theorized by Lacan in his discussion of urinary segregation.

Jacques Lacan coined the term "urinary segregation" in his now famous essay titled "The Agency of the Letter and in the Unconscious, or Reason since Freud." He challenges the linguistic theories of Ferdinand de Saussure by insisting that there is no "signified-in-waiting" (Lacan 2006 [1901]: 72) behind any one signifier. The signifier, for Lacan, does not gesture to but, rather, constitutes the signified (however slippery and imprecise the latter may be). "Ladies" and "Gentlemen" are linguistic signifiers as opposed to essential biomaterial entities. The gendered signs writ large on the front doors enacts a split or cut that engenders dimorphic subject positions.

> To these children, Gentlemen and Ladies will henceforth be two homelands toward which each of their souls will take flight on divergent wings, and regarding which it will be all the more impossible for them to reach an agreement since, being in fact the same homeland, neither can give ground regarding the one's unsurpassed excellence without detracting from the other's glory (Lacan 2006 [1901]: 417).

Lacan's parable is meant to show how one signifier (Gentlemen, for example) is always dependent upon another signifier (Ladies, for example) and that the signifier is unwed to any given signification. In fact, two identical doors are indicated by different signifiers and each child imagines they have arrived at a different destination. Lacan further contends that the signifier "enters the signified—namely, in a form which, since it is not immaterial, raises the question of its place in reality" (Lacan 2006 [1901]: 417). The signifier's "constitutive encroachments" (Lacan 2006 [1901]: 418) on the signified cause the latter to perpetually slide under yet another signifier. Virginia Blum (1998) explains, in relation to the Lacanian doors, that the children arrive at gender (the signifiers "Ladies" and "Gentlemen"), not sexed anatomy. "The anatomical, then, appears to be an effect of spatial significations whereby the selection of the door tells you what you *have* (or lack, as the case may be)" (Blum 1998: 264). But the joke is on those of us who believe in the foundational (material) status of the signified. We find shit (behind closed doors) where an essential body part (in this case, genitalia) was supposed to be.

In her discussion of the Lacanian doors and the agency of the (black) letter, Maia Boswell (1999) contends that "blackness" is metonymically linked to "excrement," in Lacan's text, and that shit signifies "excess" or that which is beyond signification or significance. Hence the mysterious tree in the Lacanian diagram that exists outside (or, rather, as an unspecified space in relation to) the binary gender division of doors.

> Lacan links the signifier, the material trace ... to (human) waste ... [the] waste product, is thus bound to the "letter," to the material trace that cannot be reassimilated by the semantic or symbolic order. Visually at the center of the

picture is excrement, blackness, a void, the silence of the mark itself (Boswell 1999: 128).

Shit is in, and yet appears outside, the body: it is extimate. Similarly the racialized other of the American South occupies a urinary space outside the signifying chain (no colored door in the Lacanian parable) but, also, paradoxically within it. The tree occupies a spatial position beyond the identical doors but is also meant to denote the material signified we seek but never find. The tree also signifies the natural world along with the animals, the non-human. The unmarked third door—along with the references to the subject being a "slave of discourse," to the "negress," and to the woman "ready for the auction block" in the essay—harkens back to the institution of the racially segregated toilet which, as Boswell convincingly argues, functions as an absent presence integral to the functioning of the sexual symbolic. Elizabeth Abel further notes that Lacan's analytic of sexuation underscores the predominance of racial difference in his use of the term "urinary *segregation*" ("les lois de la segregation urinaire") (Abel 1999: 438), a term that entered into the French lexicon in the 1950s. She also contends that the colored "signs on bathroom doors ... constitute a racial symbolic that stabilized itself by appropriating, and thereby inadvertently destabilizing, the structure of sexual difference" (1999: 442).

In essence, there is an excess in the signifying chain. Lacan tells us that every chain has other signifying chains suspended vertically. The original chain signifies more than it intends and thus produces waste (shit) or, more to the point, abject and inhuman spaces. Racialized positions may appear outside the binary produced by the signifying chain but, as Boswell writes, "the black figure in some ways occupies a privileged position, a position outside—like materiality or the letter itself—or constitutively 'beyond' the margins of the official system or meaning" (1999: 123–4). Blackness is other to, or outside, the gender binary (enabled by signifiers) and as such interrupts the fantasy of interiority promised (and consequently deferred by) the signifier. Racialized others, Boswell, concludes are, in Lacan's parable, identified with the "materiality of the signification" (1999: 129) and as such a vanishing point beyond the urinary signifying chain. Lacan thus troubles the two-dimensional gendered geographies of the bathroom doors through deferral and absence. Others (racialized subjects, for example) are conspicuously present (though non-significant) in the spaces failing to materialize. Those spaces "beyond" the dimorphic doors (like the one signified by a picture of a tree) are a function of desire as they are also in excess of the significations proper.

Homoerotic desire is also in excess of the heterosexuality presumed by the architectural designs separating "men" from "women." French philosopher Michel Foucault (1979) further elaborates upon the panic about gay male sex in his discussion of the institution of the short cubicle door (to survey, monitor, and police illicit touching) built into French boys' schools. The heteronormativity of toilet designs (separating "men" and "women") curiously invite a homoerotic ("same" sex space) the rooms only seem to mid against. Let's take the example of Marcel Duchamp's controversial art installation, titled *Fountain* (an actual urinal) to illustrate the interfacing significations of normative gender archetypes (masculine and feminine) and sexual (heterosexual and homosexual) binaries along with the "excess" (or non-signifiability) of an unofficial (or substratum) signifying chain. The mass produced, white porcelain urinal manufactured in 1917 that Duchamp dubbed as "Ready Made" art, "make works of art that are not works of art" (Mundy 2008: 24), is now hailed as one of the most significant contributions to modern art (Franklin 2000: 26). It was, however, rejected from the open exhibition of the Society of Independent Artists in 1917, New York City, because it was said to be immoral and vulgar (although it was unofficially "shown" in the exhibition behind a partition whereby its presence was hidden from view by Man Ray, one of the board members of the exhibition banning the submission). Contemporary art historians contend that this "quintessentially masculine object is feminine in gender and, thus, yet another heterosexual rendering of the white female body" (Franklin 2000: 26). Others suggest that the *Fountain* (urinal) resembles a uterus along with the lines of a feminine form. Amelia Jones writes that the installation is "a urinal shaped like a womb, ready to embrace the 'piss' ejaculate of every male passerby" (quoted in Franklin 2000: 26).

Paradoxically, the *Fountain* is read as both grotesque and sublime, as a receptacle for male piss and as a Madonna or Buddha with clean, white porcelain curves. In his fascinating discussion of the *Fountain* and queer art history, Paul B. Franklin (2000) contextualizes the now infamous urinal in New Yorker and Parisian debates about *pissoirs* and the rise of gay male public sex in urban spaces. He theorizes the "queer coupling of the penis and the anus" (Franklin 2000: 35), the homosociality of the (almost) all male art "exhibition" (which ironically rejected Duchamp's submission), the opportunities "comfort stations" offered men to transverse the "entrenched cultural divisions of sexuality, race, ethnicity, class and geography" (Franklin 2000: 29) in metropolitan city space, along with the way the *Fountain* signifies masculine homoerotic anxieties, encounters with lack (symbolized by the vulnerable, open anus in the presence of other men) and the mirrorrical return of that vulnerability in the form of a (self)image.

Studies of public toilet designs institutionalized in Canada and the US also note how images of genitals are built into receptacles. It is not a well-kept secret that the urinal resembles an enlarged vagina and that the enclosed oval toilet bowl resembles an anus (Kira 1966). The former is public and visible whereas the latter is hidden by stall partitioning and a closable door. Receptacle shapes and designs, along with their positioning in lavatory space, don't, in the Lacanian sense, mirror human anatomy but, rather, constitute anatomical difference. There are, of course, significant cultural and class specific variations to the way these receptacles are used—depending upon the context and location—but the generic design in North America is meant to accentuate the difference between feminine and masculine urinary positions (while other axis of difference including disability, for example, are, like the colored washrooms of the southern states, positioned "yonder," outside, or in excess of the binary). The oval pedestal enclosed by stall partitions functions to quarantine the feminine, while the masculine is displayed before the urinal in full frontal (open) view. Female genitalia are rendered invisible (nothing to see) as they are also visual emblems of castration. Male genitalia are hyper visible but not to be subject to optical scrutiny, prohibitions on looking while at the urinal are but one example. The urinal, as a larger or more publicly visible receptacle, amplifies and exaggerates the presence of masculine genitals while the glass mirror (more prominently displayed and less likely to be broken in the women's room) aligns feminine people with the visual, deceptive appearances that hide or, rather, amplify and imagined genital or phallic lack. Those in excess of the white, heteronormative, able-bodied, masculine signifying chain proper to the geo-political landscape of the toilet—namely those who are transgender or gender variant, physically disabled, racialized as "other," and so on—are either relegated to un-marked zones (the bathrooms out yonder, by the tree) or forced to navigate an intermediary space between official signs.

What remains to be understood is how modern gendered lines in a space saturated by whiteness—most toilets are painted or lacquered white—are libidinized by the way we project our bodily egos into space. Space mirrors as it also assembles the body in an artificial field of whiteness. We project our own libidinal coordinates into a sanitized space as we also rely upon it to secure, however provisionally, gendered bodily coordinates. The built environment is sometimes felt to be a bodily prosthetic, an extension of the subject in space. This is well evidenced in the spatialization of a racially and class specific body-politic. The gendering of the modern, porcelain, toilet oval as white is also significant. The English water closet played an important role in the disciplining of non-Western bodies living under colonial rule and in what Anne McClintock (1995) calls commodity racism. The legacy of the racial imagery of Pears soap advertisements in the late nineteenth century is a case in point. The whiteness of the modern lavatory reveals a special contempt for those racialized as non-white (or unclean), including those who are underhoused and underemployed (and thus non-consumers), along with the feminine as an ill-formed or incomplete subject. "At the level of the symbolic, the feminine is said to be on the side of the abject, the irrational, the unformed, the horizontal, the liquid, like bodies of water that take the form of their vessel; just as the masculine is said to be on the side of the subject, the rational, the normative, the distinct, the vertical, the categorical, the specific" (Morgan 2002: 172). But, again, race complicates the signifying equation and spatial axis. Black men are often gendered feminine (and thus emasculated) while black women are often gendered masculine and seen to be unfeminine in racist discourses positing both outside (or, rather, beyond) the binary. The toilet designated for persons with disabilities is also (conspicuously) lacking a gender sign. A third dimension (or void median)—Homi Bhabha (1994) would call this a third space—in excess of the gendered doors is metonymically linked to "darkness," to "dirt," in short, to the scatological.

Purity and Abjection in the Toilet

Perhaps Judith Butler said it best in her discussion of gender, identity and abjection when she wrote that there is a "mode by which Others become shit" (1990: 134) in object relations. Butler contends that the normative subject boundaries between interiority and exteriority are "confounded by those excremental passages in which the inner effectively becomes outer, and this excreting function becomes, as it were, the model by which other forms of identity-differentiation are accomplished" (1990: 133–4). She later notes that abjection "designates a degraded or cast out status within which the terms of sociability" (1993: 243, footnote 2). In other words, social abjection denotes a process through which people constituted as different (or as Other), are literally banished to "zones of inhabitability" (Butler 1993: 243, footnote 2), or used as objects of projective identification.

Hygienic interest in clear gender demarcations intersect with a late modern contempt for dirt which Mary Douglas (1966) defines as "matter out of place." Along with this contempt for dirt comes the use of hard, refractive materials, synthetics, and enameled tiles that reveal "matter [or fluids] out of place." The architecture and design of the toilet is meant to ensure subject integrity in a space coded as dirty and abject. In his discussion of the modern bathtub, William Braham (1997) notices that rules of hygiene are not just about health and safety, but about visual integrity; one must be able to see the body unencumbered by dirt. "The appearance of the modern bathroom surface—smooth, white, shiny, sanitized—offers sufficient guarantee of protection from disease" (Braham 1997: 217). But the glow and appeal of the oval toilet bowl receptacle, urinal or sink basis in illusory, offering only an imaginary defense against subject entanglement (or exposure to others). Smooth, white porcelain tubs, toilet-bowls and urinals are desirable because they mirror a neutral tertiary space where the body will be presumably unexposed to the mess and spillage of others. The rim of the toilet-bowl must appear to be clean. This is not because people worry about disease and infection (although we do), but because people are anxious about whiteness (denoting purity) and gendered subject integrity. We must see our own image in the receptacle—it should be that clean and reflective. The mirage should cultivate the illusion of absolute subject integrity, purity, and separation from abject remains.

> Bathroom finishes must resist the accelerated tendency of matter to change state under the influence of water ... the glazed surface of the tub and of the tiled walls in the standardized room fixtures is unchanging, or nearly so, requiring little of the regenerative maintenance demanded by other materials (Braham 1997: 219).

The object constancy of bathroom fixtures is designed to quell anxieties about ego-boundaries and their instability. By appealing to an obsessive fantasy of extermination and removal (no part objects or floaters in the toilet bowl) the lavatory caters to a modern narcissistic and white puritanical wish to be unencumbered by the difference of the other, her (and sometimes his) shit and residue.

It must be remembered that because the "rules of cleanliness were previously the province of religious doctrine" (Braham 1997: 217), and such inscriptions relied upon whiteness as a trope and emblem of purity, there is, in the present day manifestation of the hygienic superego, a compulsion to exterminate (by over-sanitization) that which is not white (coded as dirty or abject) reminiscent of the older, Christian practice, of ablution.

> Holy water doesn't run; its job is to resist loss, whether by drain, sin, or evaporation. Anointing and baptism originate in practices related to strengthening life, to the human seed (which chrism imitates), to fecundity and virility, also to extending the life of the soul past death. Bathing and oiling the body imply not just surface cleanliness, but replenishment through penetration of the body's depths. Life is liquid. Religious ablution is meant to pierce the skin on its way to the soul ... twentieth century soul-saving requires twentieth-century plumbing (Lahiji and Friedman 1997: 36–7).

The hygienic superego with its appeal to medical and science, epidemiology, and disease control now supersedes religious teachings and pastoral ethics proper. The hygienic superego is rationalized (and inculcated) by science in the secular age. But, like Christianity, the hygienic superego is beholden to the dialectics of purity and impurity; good and bad, self and other, which are fantastic and illusory.

Modern architectural design has taken the quest for purity in design too inhuman ends. Pallasma contends that contemporary designs not only mid-against "sensual curiosity" (1994: 29) but that they blunt and deaden the senses. "Contemporary images of architecture appear sterile and lifeless ..." (Pallasma 1994: 32). By "casting space as neutral, architecture is able to avoid the specificity of difference that is the very structure of sexuality, insofar as sexuality is paradigmatically about the specificity of, identity through, and competition between gender differences" (Ingraham 1992: 262). Luce Irigaray (1985) argues that there is a focus on what she calls an unsexed and universalist law of objective reasoning, homogeneity, and the associated masculinist fantasy of sexual sameness (negation of the feminine) in modern architectural design. The sexed subject is not only negated by modern design but actively incorporated into a unisex or (allegedly) gender neutral and racialized space of non-difference. There is nothing like a maze of stalls, metallic walls, glass mirrors, and urinals to confuse gender identity and to alienate subjects "out of (signifying) place." The architecture invites auditory and visual confusion as it also enforces what are, for many, arbitrary and illusory mappings of the body in space. Even vision—the so-called "distance" sense (more apt to enable subject differentiation and discernment consistent with the ethic of modern industrial design)—is overpowered by white florescent lights.

Conclusion

Gender is a matter of positioning in space and this positioning is moored by sight lines obscuring a racial signifying chain. Modern lines secure subject coordinates. The vertical body is erect and discernable; masculine and autonomous. The horizontal body is feminine (relational, unstable, leaky, ill-defined, or abject). But racial difference (along with other subject based differences, sexuality and disability, for example) is mapped along a third axis: a dimension obscured by right angles and modern architectural sight lines: "The vertical of the right angle dominates not only the tradition of architecture but also the ethics of modernity" (Lahiji and Friedman 1997: 46). The horizontal must be overcome by the plumb-line. But the horizontal (feminine space) is not unlike the third (unmappable) space. Both are, albeit in different ways, extimate. Lacan defines extimacy as paradoxically "inside" and "outside," as "me" and "not me," and as part and parcel of an intersubjective structure. The liminal, ill-defined (or unplumable space) of modernity is symbolically coded as vile, indeterminate, and abject.

In her discussion of hysteria, Elisabeth Bronfen writes that the construction of femininity authorized by the Oedipal story not only translates femininity into an enigma but is symptomatic of how the "masculine subject projects the recognition of mortality and falliability" on to the feminine subject (1998: 17). Projective identification (a defensive process first recognized by Melanie Klein in 1946) involves the "phantasy that it is possible to split off a part of one's personality and put it into another person" (Salzberger-Wittenberg 1970: 138). But the subject forgets what has been jettisoned by the self and fails to recognize the other apart from the projected material which becomes extimate. The subject is outside or ex-centric and the unconscious, structured like a language (with innumerable vertical chains that intersect at multiple points) is intersubjective. Bronfen contends that the "phallic narrative represses this traumatic knowledge by deflecting all the values connected with the paradigm of mortality onto the sexually different feminine body, finding its oblique articulation there" (1998: 17). But it is not only the feminine body, but various bodies, outside the official signifying chain, that are repositories for not only phallocentric but also white, heterosexual, and able-bodied projectiles. If bodily egos are negotiated in a space infused with gendered and racialized grammatical significations—there to be seen and not seen—we must redesign the sites so that they don't mirror a white aesthetic and sanitized ideal of purity beholden to investments in unisex sameness and a petrified narcissistic ideal of subject stasis. The rooms must write the differences of the chains failing to signify so that others, constituted as "not me" (or inhuman), are faced in the mirror.

References

Abel, E. 1999. Bathroom doors and drinking fountains: Jim Crow's racial symbolic. *Critical Inquiry*, 25(3), 435–81.

Anzieu, D. 1989. *The Skin Ego*, translated by C. Turner. New Haven and London: Yale University Press.

Bhabha, H.K. 1994. *The Location of Culture*. London and New York: Routledge.

Blum, V. 1998. Ladies and gentlemen: train rides and other Oedipal stories, in *Places Through the Body*, edited by H. Nast and S. Pile. London and New York: Routledge, 263–80.

Boswell, M. 1999. "Ladies," "gentlemen," and "colored": "the agency of (Lacan's black) letter" in the outhouse. *Cultural Critique*, 41(Winter), 108–38.

Braham, W.W. 1997. Sigfried Giedion and the fascination of the tub, in *Plumbing: Sounding Modern Architecture*, edited by N. Lahiji and D.S. Friedman. New York: Princeton Architectural Press, 201–24.

Bronfen, E. 1998. *The Knotted Subject: Hysteria and Its Discontents*. Princeton, NJ: Princeton University Press.

Browne, K. 2004. Genderism and the bathroom problem: (re)materializing sexed sites, (re)creating sexed bodies. *Gender, Place and Culture*, 11(3), 331–46.

Butler, J. 1993. *Bodies That Matter: On the Discursive Limits of "Sex."* New York: Routledge.

Butler, J. 1990. *Gender Trouble: Feminism and the Subversion of Identity*. New York: Routledge.

Cavanagh, S.L. 2010. *Queering Bathrooms: Gender, Sexuality and the Hygienic Imagination*. Toronto: University of Toronto Press.

Douglas, M. 1966. *Purity and Danger: An Analysis of the Concepts of Pollution and Taboo*. Boston: Ark Paperbacks.

Elliot, P. 2001. A psychoanalytic reading of transsexual embodiment. *Studies in Gender and Sexuality*, 2(4), 295–325.

Foucault, M. 1979. *Discipline and Punish: The Birth of the Prison*. New York: Vintage.

Franklin, P.B. 2000. Object choice: Marcel Duchamp's Fountain and the art of queer art history. *Oxford Art Journal*, 23(1), 23–50.

Freud, S. 1961 [1923]. The ego and the id, in *The Standard Edition of the Complete Works of Sigmund Freud*, vol. 8, edited and translated by J. Strachey. London: Vintage Press.

Halberstam, J. 1997. Bathrooms, butches, and the aesthetics of female masculinity, in *Rrose is a Rrose is a Rrose: Gender Performance in Photography*, edited by J. Blessing. New York: Guggenheim Museum, 179–89.

Ingraham, C. 1992. Initial properties: architecture and the space of the line, in *Sexuality and Space*, edited by B. Colomina. New York: Princeton University Press, 255–71.

Irigaray, L. 1985. *This Sex Which Is Not One*, translated by C. Porter. Ithaca, NY: Cornell University Press.

Kira, A. 1966. *The Bathroom: Criteria for Design*. New York: Center for Housing and Environmental Studies, Cornell University.

Lacan, J. 2006 [1901]. The instance of the letter in the unconscious, or reason since Freud, in *Écrits*, by J. Lacan, translated by B. Fink. New York and London: W.W. Norton and Company, 412–41.

Lahiji, N. and Friedman, D.S. 1997. At the sink: architecture in abjection, in *Plumbing: Sounding Modern Architecture*, edited by N. Lahiji and D.S. Friedman. New York: Princeton Architectural Press, 35–61.

McClintock, A. 1995. *Imperial Leather: Race, Gender and Sexuality in the Colonial Conquest*. New York: Routledge.

Morgan, M. 2002. The plumbing of modern life. *Postcolonial Studies*, 5(2), 171–95.

Mundy, J. (ed.) 2008. *Duchamp, Man Ray, Picabia*. New York: Tate Publishing.

Pallasma, J. 1994. An architecture of the seven senses, in *Questions of Perception: Phenomenology of Architecture*, edited by S. Hall, J. Pallasma and A.P. Gómez. Tokyo: atu Publishing, 27–38.

Pile, S. 1996. *The Body and the City: Psychoanalysis, Space and Subjectivity*. New York: Routledge.

Rasmussen, M.L. 2009. Beyond gender identity. *Gender and Education*, 21(4), 431–47.

Rush, F. 2009. *On Architecture: Thinking in Action*. New York: Routledge.

Salamon, G. 2004. The bodily ego and the contested domain of the material. *Differences: A Journal of Feminist Cultural Studies*, 15(3), 95–122.

Salzberger-Wittenberg, I. 1970. *Psycho-Analytic Insight and Relationships: A Kleinian Approach*. New York: Routledge and Kegan Paul.

Seshadri-Crooks, K. 2000. *Desiring Whiteness: A Lacanian Analysis of Race*. New York: Routledge.

Silverman, K. 1996. *The Threshold of the Visible World*. New York and London: Routledge.

Wallon, H. 1934. *Les Origines du Caractère Chez l'Enfant: Les Préludes du Sentiment de Personnalité*. Paris: Boivin et Cie.

Wilton, R.D. 1998. The constitution of difference: space and psyche in landscapes of exclusion. *Geoform*, 29(2), 173–85.

Index

Page numbers in *italics* refer to figures.